AAUSC Issues in Language Program Direction 2010

Critical and Intercultural Theory and Language Pedagogy

Glenn S. Levine

Alison Phipps

Editors

HEINLE
CENGAGE Learning·

Australia • Brazil • Japan • Korea • Mexico • Singapore • Spain • United Kingdom • United States

HEINLE
CENGAGE Learning™

AAUSC Issues in Language Program Direction 2010: Critical and Intercultural Theory and Language Pedagogy
Glenn S. Levine
Alison Phipps
Editors

Publisher: Beth Kramer

Editorial Assistant: Laura Kramer

Senior Marketing Manager: Ben Rivera

Marketing Coordinator: Janine Enos

Marketing Communications Manager: Glenn McGibbon

Project Management: PreMediaGlobal

Print Buyer: Amy Rogers

Senior Rights Acquisitions Specialist/Text: Katie Huha

Rights Acquisitions Specialist/Image: Jennifer Mayer Dare

Cover Designer: PreMediaGlobal

Compositor: PreMediaGlobal

For product information and technology assistance, contact us at
Cengage Learning Customer & Sales Support, 1-800-354-9706
For permission to use material from this text or product, submit all requests online at
cengage.com/permissions
Further permissions questions can be emailed to
permissionrequest@cengage.com

Library of Congress Control Number: 2010937494

ISBN-13: 978-0-495-80007-1

ISBN-10: 0-495-80007-4

Heinle
20 Channel Center Street
Boston, MA 02210
USA

Cengage Learning is a leading provider of customized learning solutions with office locations around the globe, including Singapore, the United Kingdom, Australia, Mexico, Brazil and Japan. Locate your local office at **international.cengage.com/region**

Cengage Learning products are represented in Canada by Nelson Education, Ltd.

For your course and learning solutions, visit **www.cengage.com**

Purchase any of our products at your local college store or at our preferred online store **www.cengagebrain.com**

Contents

Acknowledgments

Heraclitus's well-known aphorism that no one ever steps in the same river twice rings especially true for the work of an edited volume such as this one. Like a river, the flow of creating the volume was in flux from the moment of the initial concept to the last phase of editing. The people stepping into the river—all of those who contributed to the volume—also changed, we suspect, hopefully through their lively interactions with us and with each other. And we changed, for the better. We are so grateful to the twenty contributors for the privilege of being part of this wonderful process and for its result in the 2010 AAUSC volume on critical and intercultural theory and language pedagogy. Their hard work, engaging discussions, insightful analyses, professionalism, and superb dedication to the project have been immensely rewarding to both of us.

We thank the editorial board of the AAUSC for their approval and support of the volume and series editor Carl Blyth for his infectious excitement for the project and for his prompt and spot-on comments and recommendations throughout. We also thank Beth Kramer at Heinle Cengage Learning for making the whole process go so smoothly.

We are grateful to the University of Glasgow, Faculty of Education, for supporting Alison's time and travel needed to coedit the volume.

At the University of California, Irvine (UCI), we thank all the departments and programs that generously supported the 2009 symposium, at which many of the contributors presented drafts of their papers.

For his outstanding editorial assistance, we offer our heartfelt thanks to UCI PhD student Kurt Buhanan; he showed an intuitive sense of structure and style and a true gift for editing.

Finally, we are truly grateful to Ursula Levine for being so supportive and encouraging over the past two years and to Rima Andmariam and Robert Swinfen for patiently allowing the house in Glasgow to be taken over by the book project for those last intense days of work.

AAUSC Editorial Board 2010

Annual Volumes of *Issues in Language Program Direction*

1996: *Patterns and Policies: The Changing Demographics of Foreign Language Instruction*
Editor: Judith E. Liskin-Gasparro

1995: *Redefining the Boundaries of Language Study*
Editor: Claire Kramsch

1994: *Faces in a Crowd: The Individual Learner in Multisection Courses*
Editor: Carol A. Klee

1993: *The Dynamics of Language Program Direction*
Editor: David P. Benseler

1992: *Development and Supervision of Teaching Assistants in Foreign Languages*
Editor: Joel C. Walz

1991: *Assessing Foreign Language Proficiency of Undergraduates*
Editor: Richard V. Teschner

1990: *Challenges in the 1990s for College Foreign Language Programs*
Editor: Sally Sieloff Magnan

Chapter 1

What Is Language Pedagogy For?

Alison Phipps, University of Glasgow

Glenn S. Levine, University of California, Irvine

Abstract

In this chapter, the authors take a critical look at two main issues: the relationship of theory to language pedagogy and the place of language pedagogy relative to "the state of the world." This examination is used to set the tone and introduce the chapters of this volume, showing how language pedagogy, far from being "atheoretical," is in fact deeply infused with theory; it is always theory-driven practice. The contributions of the volume bring the paradigms of language teaching and learning—and the paradigm shifts that have been under way for some time—into focus, linking them concretely with pedagogical practice. It argues that "theory" is not a reified object but rather is embodied in our teaching and learning practices, often in ways that are unassumed and even unrecognized. A step back to think and reflect on our practice and to consider patterns that are emergent in language pedagogy gives us an exciting glimpse of change and new directions, of new embodiments of thinking about teaching in practice. The authors suggest that language pedagogy needs emergent and critical conceptual tools to move beyond a heavily skills-based approach and take an active part in addressing the dire needs of a changed world, a globalized community in which conflicts are or should be worked out by people at every level of society. Deep knowledge of languages—or translingual and transcultural competence as formulated by the Modern Language Association (MLA) Ad Hoc Committee Report (MLA, 2007)—is a crucial component of this change. To this end, picking up where the ACTFL *Standards* (National Standards in Foreign Language Education Project, 2006) left off, the authors frame the contributions to the volume in terms of five "new Cs": context, complexity, capacity, compassion, and conflict:

> We can never be "after theory" in the sense that there can be no reflective life without it. We can simply run out of particular styles of thinking as our situation changes. (Eagleton, 2003, p. 221)

Language Pedagogy: What's It All For?

Let's be honest about this: this book began on the back of a napkin and over a beer with Beethoven in the background. It also began as a pair of complaints. The first was that language pedagogy is atheoretical, and the second, rather more broadly, was about the state of the world. Let's take them head-on.

Language Pedagogy Is Atheoretical

Language teaching remains, despite the cultural turn of 1990s, distinct from the larger work and the mission of the humanities, where languages are usually taught. In fact, language pedagogy has construed itself as a functional skills acquisitional mode of being where the aim is simply to get good at speaking, writing, reading, and listening and to get students the grades that say that they have become good at this.

For their part, language instructors and language program directors have become incredibly good at helping students get good at speaking, writing, reading, and listening. A whole host of methods, approaches, techniques, practices, and technologies has grown up over the decades since the functional and communicative turns that have enabled many students to finish their language courses with another language inside of themselves that they can indeed speak, write, read, and listen to.

The State of the World

The world is in a bit of a mess, as are our human attempts to make things better. The anthropologist Mary Douglas (2002) makes the stunning claim that "the whole of the universe is harnessed to men's [sic] attempts to force one another into good citizenship" (p. 4). In a social and historical moment that places virtue predominantly in the acquisition of goods and skills, then, the energies of the universe are harnessed in the service of functional skills production. And so it has been. Energy is not harnessed toward the creation of beauty or the transformation of conflict, to the understanding of subtle contingency or the fostering of compassion.

The State of the Language Pedagogy World

Skills—language skills for our purposes—are what will save the day and make for a good life; this appears to be the popular "theory" about language pedagogy. With good grades in their language skills (and with good grades generally), students will get jobs, contribute to the economy, and make money, and all will be well. What is said in conversation, what is read or written during work or leisure time, is not as important as the fact that the skills exist for it to be said, heard, read, or written, to varying levels of competency.

When money makes the world go around, when society enjoys stability and security, such luxuries are affordable. Jobs and skills, jobs and skills. Language skills.

These statements may come across as compressed, but they are not intended to be simply dismissive of current practices; rather, our intention is to communicate the conviction that there is a deeper ethical basis for language pedagogy, one that teachers in the classroom know and feel daily but that often is not reflected systemically in the larger discourses about teaching and learning. We acknowledge that language teachers, in enacting their ethical practices, are often brought into conflict with established paradigms, one of which we believe to be the economic paradigm (but there are others). This dilemma of orientation is the product of theoretical analysis. The analysis is that of the theories that underpin the present global order: free trade, goods, and services make for good citizenship, so the labor force and citizenry need to possess the wherewithal to enable this to continue. It's a product of positivism and modernist rationalism. What you put in is what you get out. The more resources we commit to solving a problem or deficit, the more easily we will solve the problem and make up the deficit. In short, language pedagogy characterized in this way, somewhat simplistically for the sake of brevity, is a *theory-driven practice*. The theory is now so ingrained, so deeply inculcated, that it does not feel like a theory any longer. Theory has to feel clumsy and difficult, we imagine. As such, the ideological energy that underpins the common practice of language pedagogy has been assumed to have lost its bearings, as Arens, Kramsch, and van Lier attest to in this volume.

How has this happened? Paradigms change, towers fall; ideologies are challenged, and new presidents are elected; what makes for good citizenship is not what used to make for good citizenship. Or, as Yurchak (2006) shows us in his book about the collapse of the Soviet Union, *Everything Was Forever until It Was No More* (Yurchak, 2006), we don't tend to notice the extent of paradigmatic change until a transition is well and truly under way or is accelerating perceptibly.

The obvious way to tackle the complaints we had on our napkin is with arguments for theory as the thing that solves the deficit problems—to argue for the benefit of "theory" for practitioners in solving their deficit problems, be they language teachers and practitioners or state-of-the-world practitioners. This seemed obvious. Somewhat arrogantly—or with some irony, we thought—if these people had only read Foucault, postcolonial theory, Bourdieu, Kristeva, and so forth, then we wouldn't be in this mess. However, to do this would be to fall into the same plug-and-play, functional-solutions model as we have just critiqued. It would be to propose theory as a new technical fix to a supposed theory deficit in language pedagogy. But we have just argued that far from being a deficit, the present state of theory in language education is one of an *excess*—an excess of positivist, functional rational modernist theory. And such an argument presupposed, also somewhat arrogantly, that somehow those who are versed in theory have answers for practitioners and that practitioners don't know what they are doing. And so we go around and around a perennial circle of complaint that classroom practitioners bring to theorists, which is one of countering the questioning of their legitimacy with a counterquestioning of the legitimacy of theory. Stalemate.

From its inception and throughout its development, this has been the refrain, back and forth, in the dialogue between ourselves as editors ("what are we going to offer to the language program directors?") and between contributors in a two-day symposium at the University of California, Irvine, to the instructions from ourselves to contributors and editors, to the discussions around the framing of the volume once the final chapters had been reviewed, revised, and received. In other words, in our own thinking we too have framed the questions around the "theory debate" and the deficit, the problem of the atheoretical nature of language teaching, as we have seen it in our complaint. The dominant ways of seeing the world are very pervasive, especially the theoretical ones. And yet the invitation to pause, to think about how we think about the language classroom, in a time of transition, opens a space for old ideas and new ones to meet and converse in the pages of this volume. Each of the chapters here represents not so much a *plaidoyer* for theory in the classroom or even "something practical for the language teacher"; rather, they offer a redescription of the present reality of the language classroom and some ways of thinking about the way things now appear to be; reflections, we might say, on the state of the language pedagogy world. As such, they are reflections on the paradigms in transition and offer a new set of descriptors of dispositions for "languagers," which are the seeds of theorizing the ways in which this world is changing. In our view, these chapters also serve to demystify a range of theoretical models and thinking about theory as a distant, esoteric object and bring it up close for language program directors and language teachers. What is often discussed as a perceived "theory–practice gap" becomes instead a newly framed understanding of language pedagogy, of all kinds, as embodiments of assumed theories about the world and the way it is. What becomes clear through this collection is that there is no gap at all: theory is practice is theory.

Raymond Williams referred to this kind of reflective activity, this kind of transition, these seeds in language, literature, and art, as a "structure of feeling": "For structures of feeling can be defined as social experiences in solution, as distinct from other social semantic formations which have been precipitated and are more evidently and more immediately available" (Williams, 1977, p. 143). The social experiences in transition, or "in solution," as Williams would have it, are those of the former things that are presently crumbling and revealing the extent to which they can neither make us safe nor make us happy. Skills and competences, goods, and trade as the basis for theory-driven practice have failed us in both regards. From this very realistic and practical understanding of the limits to our past and ongoing functional practices come tentative tryouts, partial glimpses of alternatives, signs of confidence in different ways of being and doing language pedagogy. The astute, often subtle descriptions and analysis of these social experiences from language classrooms are what offer us alternative theories and enable us to "structure feeling," to show what is distinct from the way things were and the ways we thought would be forever but that are now, it seems, no more. Put another way, theoretical and paradigmatic change occurs first in myriad everyday practices and personal reflections manifested in practice; in essence, paradigm shifts are *emergent*, to use a term from complexity theory, not storm-the-barricades revolutions.

To link this notion to language teaching and the chapters of this volume, it is usually teachers, with their intimate knowledge of their learners and the changes they intuit in their classrooms and through their students' work, who start to notice and adapt to the changes. Every contributor in this volume is now or has been a language teacher—and a passionately committed one at that. We see evidence of their teaching and feel their hard-won understandings of the transitions between the pages of this volume and in the diversity of voices that come together here. In fact, these are some of the most committed of language practitioners who happen also to be gifted in thinking about and describing the new realities of the worlds they are finding emerging in the classrooms of this time of transition. From out of the old certainties we find a tone, hesitant in places, full of excited conviction at discovery in others but determined to describe in fresh words something of the way the world may be becoming.

Transition and change of any kind is a tricky business. Anthropologists theorize movement from one structured state into a new set of social structures, as a "liminal" phase, an antistructure, where the old certainties are dismantled and new ones have not yet solidified. The transitions described in this volume are not comfortable. They point to serious dangers to the humanities, to our self-understandings, to the economic and social ways in which we have organized ourselves, and they show that language pedagogy is embedded and implicated in different ways in the competing alternatives of the future as we try, again, with the philosophers of old, to work out what it is that might make us safe and happy and what languages and their learning and living have to do with this. Because, of course, languages are relational; they show us that other worlds are possible and offer a redescription of reality with their own cadence and poetry, principles, patterns, and possibilities for living.

So out of these chapters emerge loose sets of principles for, at the very least, curricular design and, at best, concrete steps for classroom practice, even though this involves an interpretive reduction of theory that itself might at times fly in the face of the original theory. Pedagogy and curriculum are of necessity reductive, so that they can be conveyed to others in a package for implementation. It's part of the quandary of the "theory–practice gap" that bedevils the teaching profession overall. At what point does a paradigm shift, including the constructivist, sociocultural, and ecological one that the chapters in this volume largely represent, become dilettantish dogma, unreflected and unquestioned, so that, as we said in the opening, it becomes so deeply ingrained and inculcated that it does not feel like theory any longer? It is our hope that the probing, provocative message of many of the chapters—and indeed the set as a whole—will mark a milestone toward a paradigm that remains not just critical but *self-critical* as well so that the paradigm shifts cease to be pendulum swings based on pronouncements that earlier we just had it all wrong, toward recursive, emergent layers of new insights, at all times keeping the well-being and benefit for our students at the center of our attention.

In sum, what these chapters index is initial evidence of a different theoretical project/language that is growing out of the intense relational experience of different kinds of language classrooms, language students, and expectations of good citizenship. They are all relational chapters in that they are reflecting on dimensions in the experience of being language teachers and program directors that jar with the heavily theoretical activities (assumed practices) that dominate the skills-based language teaching and on the changing nature of educational materials, the body social, and the students themselves.

Why "Critical and Intercultural"?

From the outset, we knew that including "critical and intercultural" in the title was going out on a limb. We might have simply called the volume "Theory and Language Pedagogy" and been done with it. For this book is not placed squarely in the areas of inquiry generally subsumed under critical theory, such as postcolonial theory, feminist theory, psychoanalytic theory, Marxist theory, and so forth. While the works of Derrida, Bourdieu, Kristeva, Butler, Freire, and others are cited and discussed in several of these chapters and many of the analyses and assertions in them are rooted in the philosophical traditions in which these critics also operate, the volume is not just about how works in critical theory or philosophy can inform language pedagogy. Rather, we understand "critical" in broader terms, in the ways it is used by poststructuralist scholars themselves, and similarly to the way Pennycook (2001) or van Lier (2004) approach criticality. Leo van Lier (2004) writes that "critical language education should be neither proselytizing nor indoctrinating, because then it basically ceases to be critical, it just becomes dogma, and dogma controls thought and action, and that is not being critical" (p. 189). For van Lier, a critical approach is "an explicit and overt rational, moral and ethical stance to the treatment, interpretation and documentation of a particular state of affairs" (p. 191). For addressing our two initial complaints about language pedagogy and the state of the world—and how we see the language classroom as a site to address both of these—*critical* theory is a means for language program directors, teachers, and students to unpack, examine, and transform assumptions that have become so ingrained in curricular, language-program-direction, and teaching practices that they are considered second nature. This is the critical dimension of theory, as theory without the "critical" is simply a means of understanding or explaining a given phenomenon. Our aim is to emphasize with a critical dimension the stakes of theorizing about language pedagogy.

The term "intercultural" is used broadly and widely not only in applied linguistics and language pedagogy but also in the world of business, government, and even the military. But unlike critical theory, there isn't really a field of "intercultural theory" that one can turn to. There are numerous theorists who examine the scope and depth of the intercultural; in language pedagogy, the most notable are Claire Kramsch (1993, 1998, 2002, 2006, and this volume) and Mike Byram (1997, 2008; see also Byram, Nichols, & Stephens, 2001). Some colleagues who heard the planned title of the volume asked, "Why not translingual and transcultural?" following the MLA Report? The best answer is that while there is no clearly identifiable field of intercultural theory, translingual/transcultural competence as a construct does not purport to be theory at all. This is the reason that Kramsch's contribution to this volume aims to draw connections to that term and theory and/or to lay the theoretical foundation for its usefulness to language pedagogy. For her part, Kramsch distinguished between intercultural competence and translingual/transcultural competence with the dimension of discourse and with the placement of the learner *operating between cultures*. For Byram (1997, 2008) and for many of the contributors to this volume, envisioning the intercultural is a fundamentally theoretical undertaking, one that goes well beyond the nuts-and-bolts creation of curriculum and teaching practices. It is about seeing the learner in her or his own "third place," to use Kramsch' s (1993) pedagogical notion. This is not just between cultures but rather is indicative of a culture all its own, a learner's culture. And there is a good deal of theory that delves into that world, most notably sociocultural theory; ecological approaches to language, learning, and communication; and critical pedagogy.

To varying degrees, *all* the contributions to this volume thematize and explore both the critical and the intercultural as we have just framed these terms. What is more, all the essays in this volume are deeply personal; these are not simply intellectual exercises to help get you, the reader, thinking in new ways about language teaching and learning, though they hopefully will also achieve this. The analyses and assertions derive from the authors' own experiences as teachers, teacher trainers, and learners and from their most passionately felt convictions about teaching and learning as well as about the transformative power of learning and teaching overall and, of course, the state of the world.

In this regard, these contributions are not merely astute analyses of the central issues of language teaching and learning but rather also a testimony of *why* and *how* what language teachers and program directors do matters to students and their education and to our colleagues in the academy.

The MLA Report

Serendipitously, the concerns and complaints that we sought to address with this volume, about the problem of theory in language pedagogy and the state of the world, coincided with the publication and scholarly discussion of the 2007 MLA Ad Hoc Committee Report, titled "Foreign Languages and Higher Education: New Structures for a Changed World." The report identified several key problems of (especially) U.S. foreign language departments and language programs and offered a set of specific proposals to address those problems (MLA, 2007). This document has served many of the contributors to the volume as a foundation on which to build their analyses or as an anchor to prevent their explorations of theory and language pedagogy from drifting off into the stratosphere. The problems detailed in the MLA Report all center around the division between skills-based language teaching and literature "content" teaching, between the lower- and upper-division curricula of many language/literature departments, between nontenured lecturers and tenure-track and tenured faculty, and, fundamentally, between language specialists and humanities researchers. In other words, there are deep-seated structural and institutional obstacles that often undermine the very missions and objectives we set for ourselves as language departments and schools of humanities.

With the aim of forcing our collective focus toward the goals of teaching and learning, the MLA Ad Hoc Committee that drafted the report proposed that we move toward

> a broader and more coherent curriculum in which language, culture, and literature are taught as a continuous whole, supported by alliances with other departments and expressed through interdisciplinary courses, will reinvigorate language departments as valuable academic units central to the humanities and the missions of institutions of higher learning. (MLA, 2007, p. 3)

The primary proposal the committee offers is thus to frame the objective of language teaching toward "translingual and transcultural competence." As will be cited several times in this volume, this is defined as

> the ability to operate between languages. Students are educated to function as informed and capable interlocutors with educated native speakers in the target language. They are also trained to reflect on the world and themselves through the lens of another language and culture. They learn to comprehend speakers of the target language as members of foreign societies and to grasp themselves as Americans—that is, as members of a society that is foreign to others. They also learn to relate to fellow members of their own society who speak languages other than English. (MLA, 2007, p. 4)

Students learn not just functional language abilities (though they also learn these) but also "critical language awareness, interpretation and translation, historical and political consciousness, social sensibility, and aesthetic perception" (MLA, 2007, p. 4). A very tall order, to be sure. The means the report proposes to help students achieve translingual and transcultural competence are built around the transformation of degree programs, in which the two-tiered system of skills first and then content is done away with, along with reforms to who teaches what and who has a say over what is taught and how. Part of this transformation is also a reorientation of basic language teaching and integrating language learning in meaningful ways with work in other departments and fields, in essence, to enhance the institutional imperative to study languages other than English in degree programs.

For our purposes in this volume, the report on the one hand holds important theoretical implications and on the other mandates a somewhat unified theoretical framework to ground it. In this vein, several of the contributors have opted to more or less explicitly orient their papers toward the MLA Report as a way of linking theory and practice. This has proven quite fruitful, showing that the report is successful thus far as a means of getting many language professionals—and indeed whole departments—pulling in a common direction toward reform. That being said, the present volume should serve not simply as a response to the MLA Report but rather as a path for language teachers and language program directors toward a theoretical foundation and the conceptual tools with which to implement the report's recommendations.

Five New Cs

In chapter 14 of this volume, Katherine Arens links the "theory projects" of recent generations to both the MLA Report and the "five Cs" of the ACTFL *Standards* (National Standards in Foreign Language Education Project, 2006). As is generally known, these are communication, cultures, comparisons, connections, and communities. Arens argues that they are useful not only for theorizing language practice but also for framing research in the humanities, in particular in literature and culture studies. For the purposes of our introduction to this volume, rather than offer a laundry-list synopsis of the chapters to come, we offer five additional Cs, ones that relate to and help structure our own "theory project" in this volume, and mention which chapters overlap with each of these. They are context, complexity, capacity, compassion, and conflict.

Context

An ecological approach to language teaching and learning does not view context as just a factor to be considered when analyzing how teaching or learning happens or should happen. Rather, what happens in the classroom responds to aspects of the context, and the context is also created out of teaching, learning, and language use. In Goffman's terms, context is not just a separable "frame" surrounding a system that is needed to describe its behavior (Goffman, 1974, cited in Larsen-Freeman & Cameron, 2008, p. 35); the context shapes what happens in the classroom and is shaped by it. What this means for language pedagogy and theory is that the learners, teachers, and program directors; the physical space in which learning happens; and the materials used for learning, such as books, Internet resources, reference grammars, and so forth—all are part of context and must be considered in designing curriculum and teaching students. In addition, the historical arc of the teaching taking place, including the institutional norms and their history, is also a part of the context of teaching and learning. In this volume, several pieces address aspects of context. Kramsch and van Lier deal most explicitly with the complexities of teaching and learning contexts. Train considers in depth the historical trajectories of language pedagogies, showing us ways to regard how contemporary teaching practices derive from centuries of multifaceted practices. Parker also traces and critiques the historical progression of classical language teaching against the backdrop of the MLA Report. Lu and Corbett delve into a particular context, that of intercultural language learning for medical professionals. Likewise, Coleman and colleagues unpack the contexts of distance learning. Arnett and Jernigan show us how grammar teaching, through the model of Cognitive Grammar, can be enriched by principled consideration of many aspects of context often ignored when considering grammar curriculum. Urlaub offers a way to explore pedagogical, literary, and filmic contexts through hermeneutics.

An ecological and sociocultural perspective of language and language learning asserts that everything is about context, that everything in a given context is contingent on everything else in that context. It also makes explicit the contingencies that shape languages—the contingencies of the body, of the languages already embodied, and of context—which suggest that—and this is a signal to our shifting paradigm—we cannot have it all, that there are limits, and that is true as much of money and resources as it is of languages. Contingency suggests a certain pragmatism that will accept that contexts will suggest which languages may most usefully—or even justly—be taught in a given place or time and also how this may be done with greatest expediency and attention to conflicting pulls and directions. Put another way, context doesn't just mean we look at *everything* when examining a system such as teachers and learners in the classroom; contingency shows us—and validates—which aspects of context are most salient to solving the problems at hand. Thus, the contributions of Coleman and colleagues, Dasli, Lu and Corbett, Arnett and Jernigan, Parker, Elola and Oskoz, Gramling and Warner, and Urlaub all elegantly parse out dimensions of context based on the contingencies identified among aspects of the pedagogical problems to be solved. Their analyses can serve the reader as a sort of how-to of identifying contingencies in their own contexts of practice, of engaging in a "thick description" of their own theory-driven practices.

Complexity

That language and language learning are complex is not a new idea. This complexity confronts teachers every day in the classroom. In recent years, several scholars have sketched out what this means for language and language learning, in particular the ways that language and learners learning language are complex systems and how this notion relates to pedagogical choices (Larsen-Freeman & Cameron, 2008; van Lier, 2002, 2004). In a nutshell, an ecological or complexity approach sees all aspects of language—its use, structures, and the ways these change and, of course, its development in individuals and groups—as complex, dynamic systems. Complex systems are comprised of agents, elements, and processes, each of which can be a complex system unto itself. In order to understand any one part of the system, one must consider not only all the other parts of the system but also the parts in relation to each other. This is also context as described above, which is not extraneous to the system but is part of the system itself. With regard to language pedagogy, a complexity approach means viewing the entire system in which learners learn a new language, which includes the curriculum and all its components, as a social ecosystem. In this volume, complexity is thematized explicitly in several chapters. For example, van Lier offers a useful framework for regarding language learning in different time scales and regards through an ecological lens notions of awareness, agency, and autonomy. Gramling and Warner's innovative notion of contact pragmatics flows from a view of literary discourse "as a dynamic site of intersection between language and culture." Kramsch frames translingual and transcultural competence in part in terms of an ecological, that is, a complex and dynamic, approach to teaching and learning. Train delves into lived complexity in the classroom. Though not explicitly grounded in complexity or complexity theory, the contributions of Brenner, Arnett and Jernigan, Elola and Oskoz, and Train accord seamlessly with the idea that the language classroom is a complex, dynamic system, as does the paradigmatic thinking of van Lier and Kramsch and the ethnographic orientation of Dasli.

Capacity

It is one thing to be competent; it is another thing entirely to have the creative capacity, which is developed and enabled, to *language*, to work with others—be they teachers or other social actors—in such a way as to enable a new language to grow, both within and outside the classroom's own enabling context. For contributors in this volume, this creative, collaborative capacity overlays competency as a disposition for action. It is important that a person tries to overcome conflict, consider critically, reflect on context and contingency, and perhaps one day do this very well, as part of a lifelong endeavor. However, it is not about how well someone can do something but rather about continuously creating conditions in which the capacity to language is nurtured, out of which full competency may one day be achieved.

Capacities, abilities, competences, and literacies: these are all terms that have been used to conceptualize and describe what foreign language students should know and be able to do. We all agree that we need to envision the goals of what we do, and we treat these as synonyms. But the nuances of meaning become important when decisions about educational resources and practices are at stake. The MLA Report is all about the development of translingual and transcultural competence, as things students should be able to know and do. The five Cs of the ACTFL *Standards* (National Standards in Foreign Language Education Project, 2006) also make up a set of competences for learning and using language.

Byram (1997) offers his "five *savoirs*" to frame the intended outcomes of foreign language learning and use. And the Council of Europe, following the dimensions outlined by Michael Byram together with Genevieve Zarate (see Byram, Zarate, & Neuner, 1997), has sought to bring these forward as the frame for language teaching and learning in intercultural context across the European Union and supported by many different European pedagogical research projects. All these are useful documents that provide us with many ways of approaching curriculum design, language program direction, and classroom teaching. Byrnes (2006) offers "capacities" as a further elaboration. Byrnes notes that "competence" and "performance" had long ago become "theoretically burdened and needlessly dichotomous," and even "communicative competence is essentially restricted to mostly oral and mostly transactional performance" (p. 4). She also notes that the "capacities" clearly can include "literacies," whereas competences alone may not. The term "capacities," synonymous as it may be with "abilities," allows us to move past competence in a dichotomous relationship with performance, or an overemphasis on oral communication to the exclusion of literary and other modes of communication.

　　Yet beyond the theoretical and terminological distancing from older debates, how is "capacity" really different from competence? We suggest that it is the disposition for action, not just about how well someone can do something but with competences subsumed beneath it. It is the *capacity for creativity and collaboration*, which is above all what foreign language education should expect of learners. This notion is a thread in several of the chapters in this volume. Brenner argues for ways critical pedagogy can help language learners move beyond their own frames of reference and cultural norms. Kramsch offers a model for framing the MLA Report's translingual and transcultural competence as a means for learners to "trans-late" between cultures and languages in creative and empowering ways. In concrete ways, Elola and Oskoz, Arnett and Jernigan, Coleman and colleagues, Train, and Gramling and Warner and, through their hermeneutic approaches, Parker and Urlaub show us ways to convey creative and collaborative capacities into classroom action for learning and language use in the "real world."

Compassion

Language learning is compassionate. In the chapters by Brenner, van Lier, Lu and Corbett, and Train, we find the dimension of compassion coming to the fore. In answer to an implicit question—what is language pedagogy for?—we find these authors showing us that it is for compassion. Again, compassion in language pedagogy is contextual. For Lu and Corbett, it is in the context of health care and of learning to offer empathy to those suffering physical pain in intercultural contexts. For Brenner and for Train, we also find language learning explicated in contexts of pain and as a compassionate activity: for those suffering the pain of inequality and for those experiencing legacies of colonialisms. Dimensions of affect and support, dimensions of accompaniment and critical friendship, require languages to body forth compassionate modes of being, individually and, critically, in intercultural social contexts. Much of this learning fuses the long lessons we have learned from both Marx, in the social domain, and from Freud, in the therapeutic context. It shows that the social bond is not given but made in language, in its often most basic form. To meet and greet someone who is traveling, tired, suffering, or just thirsty, in their language, in whatever the context—from hospital to tourist bar— embodies language in compassion. Language learning under this paradigm is not for functional transaction but for compassionate transaction.

Conflict

Related in a somewhat ironic link-up to compassion is the notion of conflict. Freirian critical pedagogy, as well as the interpretations of it by American scholars, such as Graff (1996), Reagan and Osborn (2002), and Giroux (1992, 2001), brings the whole project of emancipatory education together with grassroots community programs to encourage transformation. Such programs also include language ped- agogy and the careful work of enabling intercultural communication in areas of deprivation, conflict, and rapidly changing language diversity. This literature has been both transformational and, at times since its inception, tamed. The use of such transformational methods in leadership programs and in management stud- ies to support the status quo of present hegemonic structures is a reminder of the dangers of co-option. Language of change and transformation can move in many directions, some of which are highly conflictual and oppressive and a long way from being emancipatory. As always, there is a need for the contextual historical under- standing of the conditions that produce Freire's work and that of other emanci- pator educators, such as bell hooks, and to the necessity of political action and conflict transformation. Docile bodies, as Foucault (1991) called them, or banking knowledge, in Freire's (1970, 1998) terms, produce the amiable and anodyne and translate into classroom-sized examples that never get beyond the classroom to challenge the structures that keep the outdating functionalisms in place.

There are two basic dimensions to keep in mind in thinking about pedagogy and the classroom as a site of social conflict. Brenner, Arens, and Dasli, all in their own distinctive ways, show that Graff's maxim that we should "teach the conflicts" (Graff, 1992, 1996) and Agar's (1994) insistence on the value of critical incidents or "rich points" are crucial sites of learning, that is, if, following Brenner and Dasli, they are taught through a critical and intercultural lens.

Conflict can occur anywhere where language is in play: domestically, intergenerationally, in diverse linguistic communities, ecologically, economically, and politically. Each of these contexts, in a translingual world, requires language pedagogies that can rise to the challenges of conflict transformation because conflict transformation occurs in languages and is sensitive to language as potentially inflaming or transforming the injustice that leads to conflict. The past three decades have seen research and understanding of conflict transformation and peace building develop out of contexts of considerable violence and suffering. This literature has not touched the world of language pedagogy to any great degree, except perhaps in the context of the British Council Peacekeeping English Project (available at http://www.britishcouncil.org/learning-elt-pep.htm), where language, particularly the English language, was understood to be crucial for the peacekeeping activities of the armed forces around the world.

Throughout the contributions to this volume, we see thinking on language pedagogies and examples of practice that arise from tackling profound conflicts: conflicts of ecology (van Lier), conflicts of understanding (Urlaub), of colonial and imperial histories made manifest in language classrooms (Train), in the political challenges of enabling new programs to come into existence (Parker), and in struggles to evidence change brought about by technological revolution and to ensure access for all (Coleman et al. and Elola and Oskoz). So, far from language pedagogy being a technicist add-on enabling diplomacy or military phraseologies, we find the critical and intercultural theorized from the different conflicts that occur at interfaces with cultures, languages, curriculum designers, humanities policymakers, and technological innovators. Without the conflicts and their considered integration into a conflict-transformational framework for language pedagogy, the strong peace-building potential of languages for everyday and for extraordinary life circumstances is not laid down.

Conclusion

They are not small challenges, those outlined in this volume, those beginning on the back of a napkin, those that had us initially moaning about theory and practice and the state of the world and then engaging with a rich array of descriptions of alternative understandings of how language pedagogy can step up and be fit for its twenty-first-century purposes: purpose-driven language pedagogy where the purposes are creative and collaborative, critical and yet contingent, striving for compassion, conflict transformation, and capacity shaping for unknown complexities and ecological diversity. We believe that the chapters of this volume are practical and necessary for the purposes of language pedagogy. More than anything, though—and something we find implicit through this volume—we believe that the purposes here require considerable courage and imagination. Change is never easy and only sometimes welcome. Many stand to lose as established and ingrained ways of doing language pedagogy are challenged and critiqued and as alternatives are offered. It is never an easy thing to watch what one has been very good at and what has offered privilege and success giving way to something not yet fully tested, not really fully theorized or understood. The chapters in this volume offer us way markers, showing us both how and why we might move into a different theory as practice.

References

Agar, M. (1994). *Language shock: Understanding the culture of conversation.* New York: William Morrow.

Byram, M. (1997). *Teaching and assessing intercultural communicative competence.* Clevedon: Multilingual Matters.

Byram, M. (2008). *From foreign language education to education for intercultural citizenship: Essays and reflections.* Clevedon: Multilingual Matters.

Byram, M., Nichols, A., and Stephens, D. (2001). *Developing intercultural competence in practice.* Clevedon: Multilingual Matters.

Byram, M., Zarate, G., & Neuner, G. (1997). *Sociocultural competence in language learning and teaching.* Strasbourg: Council of Europe Publishing.

Byrnes, H. (2006). Locating the advanced learner in theory, research, and educational practice: An introduction. In H. Byrnes, H. Weger-Guntharp, & K. A. Sprang (Eds.), *Educating for advanced foreign language capacities: Constructs, curriculum, instruction, assessment* (pp. 1–14). Washington, DC: Georgetown University Press.

Douglas, M. (2002). *Purity and danger: An analysis of the concepts of pollution and taboo.* London: Routledge. (Original work published 1966)

Eagleton, T. (2003). *After theory.* New York: Basic Books.

Foucault, M. (1991). *Discipline and punish: The birth of the prison* (A. Sheridan, Trans.). London: Penguin.

Freire, P. (1970). *Pedagogy of the oppressed* (M. Bergman Ramos, Trans.). London: Penguin.

Freire, P. (1998). *Pedagogy of freedom: Ethics, democracy and civic courage* (P. Clarke, Trans.). Lanham, MD: Rowman & Littlefield.

Giroux, H. (1992). *Border crossings: Cultural workers and the politics of education.* London: Routledge.

Giroux, H. (2001). *Theory and resistance in education.* Westport, CT: Bergin and Garvey.

Goffman, E. (1974). *Frame analysis.* London: Harper and Row.

Graff, G. (1992). *Beyond the culture wars: How teaching the conflicts can revitalize American education.* New York: Norton.

Graff, G. (1996). Advocacy in the classroom—or in the curriculum? A response. In P. M. Spacks, (Ed.) *Advocacy in the classroom: Problems and possibilities* (pp. 425–431). New York: St. Martin's Press.

Kramsch, C. (1993). *Context and culture in language teaching.* Oxford: Oxford University Press.

Kramsch, C. (1998). The privilege of the intercultural speaker. In M. Byram & M. Fleming (Eds.), *Foreign language learning in intercultural perspective* (pp. 16–31). Cambridge: Cambridge University Press.

Kramsch, C. (2002). Introduction: "How Can We Tell the Dancer From the Dance?" In C. Kramsch (Ed.), *Language acquisition and language socialization: Ecological perspectives* (pp. 1–30). New York: Continuum.

Kramsch, C. (2006). From communicative competence to symbolic competence. *Modern Language Journal, 90*(2), 249–252.

Larsen-Freeman, D., & Cameron, L. (2008). *Complex systems and applied linguistics.* Oxford: Oxford University Press.

Modern Language Association. (2007). Foreign languages and higher education: New structures for a changed world. Retrieved from http://www.mla.org/flreport

National Standards in Foreign Language Education Project. (2006). *Standards for foreign language learning in the 21st century: Including Arabic, Chinese, classical languages, French, German, Italian, Japanese, Portuguese, Russian, and Spanish.* Yonkers, NY: Author.

Pennycook, A. (2001). *Critical applied linguistics: A critical introduction.* Mahwah, NJ: Lawrence Erlbaum Associates.

Reagan, T. G., & Osborn, T. A. (2002). *The foreign language educator in society: Toward a critical pedagogy.* Mahwah, NJ: Lawrence Erlbaum Associates.

van Lier, L. (2002). An ecological-semiotic perspective on language and linguistics. In C. Kramsch (Ed.), *Language acquisition and language socialization: Ecological perspectives* (pp. 140–164). New York: Continuum.

van Lier, L. (2004). *The ecology and semiotics of language learning: A sociocultural perspective.* Boston: Kluwer.

Williams, R. (1977). *Marxism and literature.* Oxford: Oxford University Press.

Yurchak, A. (2006). *Everything was forever until it was no more: The last Soviet generation.* Princeton, NJ: Princeton University Press.

Chapter 2
Theorizing Translingual/Transcultural Competence

Claire Kramsch, University of California, Berkeley

Abstract

"Translingual and transcultural competence" has been proposed by the 2007 Report of the Modern Language Association (MLA) Ad Hoc Committee on Foreign Languages as the desired goal of foreign language majors at U.S. colleges and universities (MLA, 2007). How can such a competence be conceptualized? This chapter uses as a point of departure an international research project on multilingualism/multiculturalism in which native speakers of French and native speakers of English grappled with each other's categorizations of events and their underlying ideologies for an ultimate publication in French. The challenges of cultural translation encountered in the course of this project serve as a basis to reflect on the three challenges posed by the MLA Report: (1) the need to "operate between languages," (2) mediation and translation, and (3) the relationship of language and culture in discourse. After proposing a definition of translingual/transcultural competence, the chapter draws on various theories in applied linguistics and critical cultural studies to stake out an ecological theory of translingual/transcultural competence that includes language and cultural relativity, the social construction and emergence of meaning, the dynamics of intertextuality, and the fundamentally symbolic nature of transcultural competence. The chapter ends with a concrete example of classroom discourse in an upper-intermediate German course and examines to what extent each of the ecological tenets mentioned above were or could have been activated.

Introduction

For four years, between 2003 and 2007, I had the opportunity to coordinate with two French colleagues, one Geneviève Zarate from the *Institut des Langues Orientales* in Paris, the other Danielle Lévy from the University of Macerata in Italy, an international research team on plurilingualism and pluriculturalism in the teaching of foreign languages. The team comprised some 90 researchers from 68 academic institutions in 20 different countries in Europe, Africa, North America, and Australia. The working language was French, but half the researchers were nonnative speakers of French, and if they were native speakers, like myself, they worked within an Anglo-Saxon field of research and published mostly in English. On the surface, the joint construction of knowledge by members of the team went along smoothly, and it developed into an edited volume published in French by the *Editions des Archives Contemporaines* in Paris (Zarate, Lévy, & Kramsch, 2008).

But beneath the surface, many linguistic and cultural tensions remained unresolved (Kramsch, 2009a). As we were discussing, for example, the role of attitudes and beliefs in the development of cross-cultural competence, the anglophones were still unclear what the French meant by *représentation sociale,* a term from social psychology used to denote the social schemata that social actors carry in their heads and with which they make sense of social reality. As we discussed the construction of identities within multilingual speech communities, the English speakers could not understand why the term *communautarisme* had such negative connotations for the French.[1] French speakers, in turn, could not understand what the English speakers meant by "individual agency" or "cultural hybridity," two terms that come from an Anglo-Saxon liberal ideology of individualism and ethnic diversity that the French contrast with *citoyenneté* and *pluralité*.[2] We became painfully aware of the boundaries between disciplines, national ideologies, and political traditions.

Both the French and the English speakers made claims about the universal validity of their views, but the francophones meant something different with *universel* than the anglophones with "universal."[3] The francophones' view of education as the formation of the good republican citizen working for the common good clashed with the anglophones' view of education as the training of the employable individuals on the job market and the pursuit of individual happiness. But there were also differing conceptions of the relation between morality and politics. For the French, the "good" republican citizen is not a moral concept—and certainly not a religious one—but a political one; the "common good" has to do with the civic observance of the laws, not with the imperatives of any particular religious moral conduct. This means not that the laws are amoral but that politicians and educators avowedly measure the efficacy of social action not according to moral but according to civic criteria.[4] While many of the francophone participants were not French and many of the anglophone team members were not Americans, the two languages seemed to convey concepts and values that were historically grounded in the respective ideologies of the French and the American nation-states. Despite the fact that everyone spoke French, we constantly bumped against the larger ideologies of a republican versus a liberal brand of democracy and the differing role of the state in various educational systems.

Our discussions led us to realize that it was not the meaning of words that had to be negotiated, nor was it cultural facts, but rather the very categories of our thoughts, the very metaphors by which each of us lived had to be explained or, rather, translated. But attempting to translate from French into English and vice versa only compounded the problem. We would have needed a third common language on which we could see eye to eye. Within the interdisciplinary field of applied linguistics, we had no common disciplinary language: some of us came from education, others from applied linguistics or literary studies, and others from anthropology or sociology. And because each of these fields is differently cut up and conceptualized in francophone and anglophone research, the challenge was not finding the right answers but rather finding the right questions to ask.[5]

In the introduction to our book, we capture this conundrum as follows: "Linguistic and cultural pluralism is more than the mere coexistence of various languages. It is primarily about the transcultural circulation of values across borders, the negotiation of identities, the inversions, even inventions of meaning, often concealed by a common illusion of effective communication" (Zarate et al., 2008, p. 15; my translation). I want to use this statement to reflect on what kind of foreign language education is needed if we want to teach foreign languages for linguistic and cultural pluralism rather than just for communicative competence in one foreign language. I first reflect on three challenges posed by the 2007 MLA Report to the way we teach foreign languages in this country: (1) "translingual and transcultural competence" and the need to "operate between languages," (2) mediation and translation, and (3) the relationship of language and culture in discourse. After proposing a definition of translingual/transcultural competence, I discuss how this notion can be theorized, that is, captured by various theories in applied linguistics and a critical cultural studies theory of culture. I consider in the end some implications for the practice of teaching and learning foreign languages in higher education.

The Three Challenges Posed by the MLA Report

The experience of managing an international research team across multiple languages and educational cultures contributed to shaping my views as I served during the same time period on the MLA Ad Hoc Committee on Foreign Languages and helped to write the 2007 MLA Report. In particular, it influenced my participation in the committee's discussions of the notion of communication across cultures advocated in this report. There were many terms to choose from to characterize the new orientation the committee wanted to advocate. While it was clear to us that foreign language education in the United States needed to accord a greater place to cross-cultural understanding in the teaching and learning of foreign languages, the notion of "intercultural competence," advocated by intercultural communication experts like Bennett, Bennett, and Allen (2003) and Byram (1997), seemed to lack a discourse dimension that we felt was essential for language teachers.[6] The notion of "global competence" seemed too politically focused on U.S. economic competitiveness and military superiority. The phrase we settled for, "translingual and transcultural competence," has been the object of a controversy that I discuss briefly below.

Operating between Languages

One of the most cited passages of the MLA Report has been the one regarding the goal of the foreign language major:

> The language major should be structured to produce a specific outcome: educated speakers who have deep translingual and transcultural competence. The idea of translingual and transcultural competence places value on the multilingual ability to operate between languages. (MLA, 2007, pp. 3–4)

This phrasing was conceived as a radical departure from the traditional goals of foreign language education that have been the approximation to a monolingual native speaker norm as represented by the standard national grammar, vocabulary, and pronunciation of a radio broadcaster in Paris, Rome, or Berlin. Here the goal was, instead, to train educated multilingual speakers who do not strive to become like monolingual speakers but rather who can draw profit from shuttling from one to the other of their languages. This shuttling was conceived not as an encouragement to code switch with abandon or to use a hybrid pidgin but as an incentive to capitalize on the surplus of meaning that multilingualism can bring about. Of course, language teachers must continue to teach the structures of one symbolic system and ensure that their students master those structures, but the committee wanted to go beyond structure. It saw language teachers as teachers of meaning—social, cultural, historical, and aesthetic meanings (Kramsch, 2008), meanings that become contaminated, infiltrated by other meanings when in contact with other languages.

The formulations "translingual and transcultural competence" and "the ability to operate between languages" were proposed by Mary Louise Pratt, the chair of the committee and a comparatist herself, and they were enthusiastically endorsed by the committee. These words have to be understood within Mary Pratt's postcolonial work and, in particular, her 2002 article "The Traffic in Meaning: Translation, Contagion, Infiltration," in which she reflects on the idea of "cultural translation" in the case of the Spanish colonization of Peru. She shows how excruciating the transposition of one semiotic code into the other can be when the two languages represent incompatible worldviews, incommensurable political and economic interests, and unequal relations of power. The ability to operate between languages is not an exercise in playful polyglottism or inconsequential code switching. It is the much more risky circulation of values across historical and ideological time scales, the negotiation of nonnegotiable identities and beliefs.

Mediation and Translation

The MLA Report goes on to state that students "are also trained to reflect on the world and themselves through the lens of another language and culture" (MLA, 2007, p. 4). This phrase could be understood to mean that one national language can be mapped onto one national culture, which is clearly not the case. As Chad Wellmon (2008) pointedly remarked in his response to the report, such a statement requires that foreign language departments reinvent the notion of culture in cultural studies not only from literary studies to anthropology but also away from homogeneous national narratives and toward culture as historicity and subjectivity. In our world of cross-national migrations and global communications, culture has become something that people carry in their heads in the form of deterritorialized *lieux de mémoire*, myths, personal and textual memories, advertisements, and literary quotes and metaphors. Such *lieux de mémoire* are now very much commercialized, commodified; like Hollywood movies, they create a cultural reality that requires sophisticated linguistic and political interpretation. Reflecting on the world and oneself means reflecting on the way that our and the Other's realities mutually construct each other through symbolic systems like language, texts, films, and the Internet.

The MLA Report's recommendations have raised fears of undue stereotyping. It recommends that language students "learn to comprehend speakers of the target language as members of foreign societies and to grasp themselves as Americans, that is, as members of a society that is foreign to others" (MLA, 2007, p. 4). But in California, some students call themselves Korean or Chinese even though they are, in fact, Americans; they associate Americans with White European Americans and are keen on retaining their cultural identity over their national membership. The term *society* has become for many an idealized cognitive model taught in schools and replayed in political speeches but with little relation to reality. This doesn't mean that there is no such thing as American society that is different from German society, but students don't talk about "their membership in American society"; rather, they talk about belonging to a "community" or building "communities." The phrase *nationale Gemeinschaft* (national community) would make a German cringe because of its national socialist connotations, but so would the word *communautarisme* for a French speaker because of the civic ideals embodied in the French Republic (see endnote 1). The development of translingual and transcultural competence requires us to critically examine the very categories by which we compare ourselves to others.

The Relation of Language and Culture in Discourse

The MLA Report finally underscores the importance of infusing not only language classes with cultural content but also content classes with an awareness of language in discourse:

> This kind of foreign language education systematically reflects on the differences in meaning, mentality, and worldview as expressed in American English and in the target language. (MLA, 2007, p. 4)

Such a statement has been correctly understood as advocating a return to close reading and interpretation. Nicoletta Pireddu (2008) calls for paying attention at all levels to the intra- and interlingual differences in styles and discourses. Her essay echoes similar statements made in Europe by the educational research team that I mentioned in the beginning and that calls for the transcultural circulation of values across borders. But how to translate one's values into someone else's vocabulary? One important aspect that has been overlooked in this passage of the MLA Report is the crucial link it makes between language practice on the one hand and explicit reflection on the practice on the other, a link that should lead to "transcultural understanding":

> In the course of acquiring functional language abilities, students are taught critical language awareness, interpretation and transla- tion, historical and political consciousness, social sensibility, and aesthetic perception. (MLA, 2007, p. 4)

The MLA Report understands language as much more than just the acquisition of forms in the lower division taught by graduate students or lecturers, to be filled with meaning in the upper division courses taught by literature professors. It is, from beginning to end, about the traffic in meaning through reflection, trans- lation, and an awareness of the power of language in discourse. By holding up a foreign linguistic mirror to our students' familiar world, we are helping them defamiliarize this world and problematize communication across borders. We are not reinforcing their sense of linguistic or cultural universality; rather, we are engaging them in the vital necessity of translation, without recourse to the com- mon language of shared economic interests and shared political beliefs but with the hope that what language has divided, language can also bring back together. In the following section, I explore the theoretical underpinnings of the notion "translingual and transcultural competence."

Relevant Theories of Language and Theories of Culture

Doubts have been raised as to why we need to move foreign language education in the direction of translingualism when it is difficult enough to make our students communicatively competent in one language. The problems with my research team described above should make it clear that accurate, fluent, and efficient exchange of information is not sufficient to ensure successful communication among people from different cultures. To understand why, we need to consider different ways of describing the relation of language and culture. In the following, I describe two ways of conceptualizing the ability to "operate between languages": ecological perspectives in applied linguistics and cultural translation in critical cultural studies. The use of an unfamiliar vocabulary to talk about familiar things can open up new ways of reflecting on what we do as language teachers and language program directors.

Applied Linguistics

If, as the MLA Report advocates, we want to educate "multilingual speakers who can operate between languages," we need a theory that views language not merely as a closed linguistic system with a logic of its own but as an ecosystem in which language learning and language use are seen as "a relational human activity, co-constructed between people and their various languages, contingent upon their position in space and history, and a site of struggle for the control of social power and cultural memory" (Kramsch, 2002, p. 5).

This way of talking about language and language learning has been captured by three related theories of language that I call "ecological." In ecolinguistics (Fill & Mühläusler, 2001; Kramsch & Steffensen, 2008), language is understood as a symbolic system that both structures and is structured by the social reality that we call "culture." In conversations with others and through written, spoken, and virtual texts, we produce, reproduce, subvert, and vie for meanings through which we frame events according to the discourses we have been socialized in, and others we have acquired along the way. Complexity theory, usually applied to complex dynamic systems like the weather or the market, has been applied by Larsen-Freeman and Cameron (2008) to language learning; it has helped explain how the words we hear or utter can reproduce prior discourses and operate, so to speak, on different time scales. Ethnographic theories of language as communicative practice (Hanks, 1996; Ochs, 2002) reinforce the notion that communicative competence is not so much a matter of exchanging objective information in a task-based or performance-based environment as a matter of indexing various subjective values and evoking historical memories through one's stylistic choices.

According to these theories, foreign language learners would no longer be seen as owners of a first language trying to appropriate for themselves a second-language code in which to express the ideas, feelings, and memories they have in their first language. Such a way of viewing language is part of the conduit metaphor fallacy decried by Michael Reddy (1993)—as if ideas, preexisting their formulation in words, could be packaged, transmitted, and thus communicated without being affected by the very conduit used for their expression and transmission. Instead, ecological theories of language learning would see the world constructed in French as different from the world constructed in English. In this perspective, multilingualism is not just the mastery of different labeling systems; rather, it is the ability to give different meanings to events depending on the language used. This meaning-making activity operates in various ways.

1. Language relativity. The ecological theories mentioned above conceive of language as one of many symbolic systems that construct the meaning we give to objects, people, and events. The verb "construct" is important here because all too often language teachers take culture and cultural meanings to be separate from language. By now, the language relativity hypothesis needs no disclaimers to remind us that social reality as we know it is precisely the meaning that a speech community has given over time to events as seen from its historical perspective. For example, by constantly referring to "individual agency," the American researchers on our team were constructing a multilingual world in which speakers had "choices" and "chose" to use one or the other language where the French would see not agency and choice but rather the expectations of interlocutors or the demands of an institution.

2. Cultural relativity. The meaning of one cultural phenomenon cannot be understood separately from the meanings ascribed to other phenomena because we think in categories or prototypes (idealized cognitive models) that carry with them a whole semiotic context. For example, we cannot understand the value of French *diversité* if we don't know that the rather right-wing current French President Nicolas Sarkozy borrowed the term from American public discourse and therefore that it has, for French educators, who tend to be left-wing oriented, a negative connotation. These educators oppose to the American term "diversity"—a term, they say, that conceals economic interests and capitalistic values—the notion of *pluralité*, a political term that purports to retain a respect for multiple values.

3. Meaning is constructed, not given. The meanings of social phenomena are not only conventional/social, shared by members of a speech community, real or imagined. They are also subjective/individual, realized through stylistic and pragmatic choices, choices of code (when to use English, when to use another language), forms of address, intonation, and other contextualization cues that inflect our perception of ourselves and others (Kramsch, 2009b). For example, one Australian member of our research team, when translating her entry into English for an English version of the *Précis*, stumbled on the problem of how to translate *plurilinguisme* and *pluriculturalisme*. She e-mailed the group: should she retain "plurilingualism/pluriculturalism" or make it into "multilingualism/multi-culturalism"? A French team member responded by laying out the difficulties:

Trois logiques s'affrontent:

-celle des usage en anglais qui utilisent majoritairement le préfixe "multi," là où le français utilise plus facilement "pluri"

-celle du politique qui en France, voit dans le "multi" (-linguisme, culturalisme) le signe du recul des valeurs laïques, calqué sur un modèle anglo-saxon et antirépublicain français.

-celle du Conseil de l'Europe qui distingue le "pluri" = logique des individus du 'multi" = logique des sociétés.

[We are confronted with three kinds of logic: 1) differences in usage: English speakers prefer the prefix "multi," French speakers prefer "pluri"; 2) political differences: some in France see in "multi" (lingualism, culturalism), borrowed from an Anglo-Saxon model that is also an antirepublican French model, a retreat from the traditional republican values in education; 3) Common European Framework of Reference that distinguishes between "pluri" applied to individuals and "multi" applied to societies (my translation)].

This short exchange illustrates the way the participants tried to construct a space of negotiation between nonnegotiable polarities through a combination of text, footnotes, scare quotes, parentheses, choice of code, translations, and the like.

4. Dynamics of intertextuality. In ecological theories of language, meanings are not really fixed by grammars or dictionaries; rather, they change according to the dynamics of talk in interaction, especially when meanings in one language are infiltrated by the hidden meanings of other languages in the consciousness of multilingual speakers. For example, one of the reasons why the anglophone educators might have had such difficulty understanding the notion of *représentation sociale* is because the French term combines thought (*representation*) and action (*sociale*), whereas the anglophone researchers tended to see language as a psycholinguistic phenomenon distinct from social and political action. The dynamics of our discussions were strongly affected by this. Anglophone educational linguists preferred to talk of "schemata," "attitudes," or "beliefs"—psychological concepts with which they felt more comfortable than sociological notions like *acteur social* or *représentation sociale*. In the English version, the English word "representation" bears traces of the French, which might create misunderstanding.

5. Emergent meanings. An ecological perspective on language learning posits that meanings emerge in the contact zone between the expectations of listeners and the anticipations of speakers. They are constructed on various time scales that irrupt in the present in what the postmodern sociolinguist Jan Blommaert (2005) calls "layered simultaneity." Memories of other communicative practices may make the current ones strange or outright incomprehensible, as was the case on that international research team. Moreover, meanings on the microlevel of face-to-face interactions are but fractals of larger (ideological or philosophical) meanings. For example, the rejection of the word *communauté* by French educators is a fractal of the larger historical rejection, by the founders of the French nation-state, of communities based on family, lineage, class, or religion in favor of a unified republican society based on national values like secularism and patriotism.

6. Symbolic competence. Finally, an ecologically oriented theory of language puts into question speaker intentionality as the ultimate criterion of truth. The expression of meanings can have unintended consequences; words can mean more than they were intended to mean. Within the modernist conception of

language learning represented by communicative language teaching, it was theorized that norms of interpretation needed to be expressed, interpreted, and negotiated like all the other dimensions of communication (Breen & Candlin, 1980). However, in late modern times, such a negotiation has become more complex. Inquiring about a speaker's intentions can run the risk of being interpreted as facetiousness, ill will, or undue suspicion about the speaker's motives. What foreign language learners need to develop is an ability to recognize the discourses behind the words, what could have been said but was not, or could have been said differently (Kramsch 2006a, 2009b; Kramsch & Whiteside, 2008). I discuss some of these implications at the end of this chapter. But first we have to examine how ecological theories in applied linguistics converge with critical cultural studies theory of the postmodern kind to which I now turn.

Critical Cultural Studies

The notion of translingual and transcultural competence as seen from the perspective of critical cultural studies represents a challenge to the complacency of what is generally called "multiculturalism" or "diversity." One of the key concepts in this regard is the notion of *translation*, which the MLA Report advocates teaching explicitly in foreign language education. It is interesting in that respect to compare Mary Louise Pratt's and Judith Butler's views on translation with regard to what Pratt (2002) aptly called the transcultural "traffic in meaning" (see also Kramsch 2006a, 2006b).

As mentioned earlier, the notion of transcultural competence grew out of Pratt's postcolonial study of the attempts at "cultural translation" between the Andean Indians and the Spanish colonizers in the seventeenth and eighteenth centuries. In her 2002 article, she describes the ambiguous efforts in 1781 by the Spanish judge Jose Antonio de Areche in Lima to translate for the Spanish crown the Indian practices that were slated to be destroyed. Pratt comes to the conclusion that whatever his intent, the translator had had to come to grips with the entanglements of incompatible meanings. Quoting Clifford Geertz, Pratt (2002) writes, "The path to apprehending the cultural imagination of another people runs not *behind* the interfering glosses that connect us to it, but *through* them" (p. 30), and she adds, "In talking about cross-cultural meaning making, it's essential to attend to fractures and entanglements, their makeup, asymmetries, ethics, histories, interdependencies, distributions of power and accountability" (p. 33).

However, because the translation paradigm sustains differences, Pratt does not think it can take into consideration the infiltration and contagion of each side by the other that occur in the course of these translations and the new subjectivities and interfaces that eventually come out of entanglements over time. Ultimately, she feels that translation might not be an adequate basis for a theory of transcultural meaning making, especially not in the case of multilingual speakers. She writes,

> The multilingual person is not someone who translates constantly from one language or cultural system into another, though translation is something multilingual subjects are able to do if needed. To be multilingual is above all to live in more than one language, to be one for whom translation is unnecessary. The image for

> multilingualism is not translation, perhaps, but *desdoblamiento,* a
> multiplying of the self. (Pratt, 2002, p. 35)

In her book *Just Being Difficult,* Judith Butler (2003) takes a rather different position. She argues that translation, as the process of making oneself understandable
to others, is our unavoidable predicament. Whether we want it or not, we are always translating ourselves to ourselves and to others. Moreover, it is an illusion to
believe that translation will solve our transcultural communication problems on
the basis of some commonsensical human language that deep down we all share.
This, she argues, is an imperialistic or colonialist view. Because language constructs our social reality and because we always find ourselves in one language
or another, there is no common place from which we could mediate the crossing
between languages. "Even the core terms, the ones we cannot do without, such as
universality and *justice* and *equality,* the ones we believe are essential to politics,
do not have a simple or already established meaning" (Butler, 2003, p. 205).

The two views on translation presented here are not incompatible as a theory
of transcultural competence. As the ability to "operate between languages,"
Pratt's view of translation focuses on the personal engagement that such an
activity requires and how that engagement itself can bring about understanding, if only an understanding of the limits of translation. If Pratt's metaphor
of *desdoblamiento* captures the spatial dimension of the multilingual speaker's
subject position, Butler's points to the equally risky task of getting a hold on
its temporal dimension. Multilingual speakers have to translate themselves to
others without knowing what the future holds or how their translation will be
received. In both cases, multilingualism is a gamble: it can bring new insights
and enhance the meaning of one's life, but it can also bring more insecurity and
unpredictability into the system.

Implications for the Study of Foreign Languages at the College Level

The view of language as proposed by applied linguistics and by critical cultural
studies prompts us to revisit the notion of "culture" in foreign language
education—no longer culture as pragmatic behaviors, social customs, and
historical facts but culture as symbolic codes and discourses, symbolic *lieux
de mémoire,* habits of the mind and habits of the heart, national historical
values and debates around those values, educational philosophies, and language
ideologies (Kramsch, 2007). The ability to read and interpret spoken and written
discourse, identify the symbolic value of words and metaphors, grasp their social
and historical significance, contrast them with metaphors in one's own language,
and reframe one's interpretation of events has been called "symbolic competence"
(Kramsch, 2006, 2009b). An example might illustrate the pedagogical challenge
that such a view presents to the foreign language teacher.

The bombing of Dresden, Germany, on February 13, 1945, was the topic
of discussion in an intensive German language course taught in Germany for

American students preparing to study at a German university. The teacher was a highly experienced Goethe Institute instructor, and the students were college students who had reached an intermediate level of oral and written proficiency. The following is reconstituted from my field notes. The reading for the day was an autobiographical account of the destruction of Dresden, written for children by the well-known German author Erich Kästner (Schmidt & Schmidt, 2007) in my English translation. Worksheets provided the necessary background information:

> Yes, Dresden was a beautiful city. You can hardly believe how beautiful it was. But you must believe me! Today, none of you, however rich your father might be, can take the train and go there to see if I am right. For the city of Dresden doesn't exist any more. Except for a few remains, it has disappeared from the surface of the earth. The Second World War in a single night and through a small flip of the hand wiped it out. Its incomparable beauty had been built over centuries. A few hours were sufficient to magically make it disappear from the surface of the earth. That happened on the 13th of February, 1945. Eight hundred airplanes dropped explosives and fire bombs. What remained was a desert. With a few giant ruins that looked like stranded oceanliners. (Erich Kästner, *When I was a little boy*, 1957)

The following questions figured below the text:

1. Which information does Kästner give his young readers regarding the bombing of Dresden?
2. What linguistic features did you notice in this text?
3. How do you feel about the way Kästner described the bombing of Dresden in February 1945?
4. Can you imagine that there might be good, i.e., legitimate, reasons in times of war for destroying a whole city and killing its inhabitants?
5. Do you know of cases throughout history where such reasons were given?

After having a student read the text aloud, the teacher led the discussion, drawing on questions 1 to 3 above:

T. what do you associate with the name Dresden?

Ss. bombing ... Caspar David Friedrich ... protest movements ... (plays a recording of text by Erich Kästner himself)

T. how do you feel about the way the story is told?

S1. no causes given!

S2. Kästner didn't say who did it nor why

T. why didn't he?

(long silence)

S2. because the Germans tend to feel guilty

S3. bombing Dresden was the only way to get Germany to its knees

T.   to *force* Germany to its knees. *In die Knie zwingen* (writes on board)

S4. German texts always favor passives, where no one bears responsibility whereas English prefers the active voice=

T.   =but the text doesn't have a single passive!

S5. the text has a performative effect—is that the correct word? It hides the truth

T.   is the story appropriate for children? What information do they get?

S1. I wouldn't tell the story like that to children nowadays. I would give them the historical truth

After class, I interviewed some of the students:

R.   Why didn't you ask the teacher what he felt about the bombing of Dresden and the way Kästner tells the story?

S1. The language classroom is not really the place to learn about values, history and culture.

S2. Cultural articles are used to pique our interest, but we don't have the vocabulary to talk about political topics.

S3. Some German instructors want to raise our consciousness about us being Americans. It's debilitating.

S4. The language teachers are great. They are facilitators, catalysts, they are not professors. They understand the science of language. They know we need to talk to each other, so they remain back seat riders.

I also interviewed the instructor:

R.   Why didn't you tell your students how you understand the way Kästner tells the story?

T.   I am very aware of the discrepancy in linguistic abilities between them and me. I will only engage in such a discussion with people on equal linguistic footing. Moreover, one of the principles of the Goethe Institute teacher training is that the teacher should not speak more than 10% of classroom time.

R.   So how would *you* explain why Kästner didn't name those who dropped the bombs?

T.   In 1957, Kästner was a pacifist and the most vocal opponent of the rearmament of Germany. He didn't want to raise children who would put all the blame on the Allies, as had been done by the Nazis at the time. He didn't want children to grow up "like them." In this text, Kästner is by no means politically neutral [*unparteiisch*].

This class seemed to have missed an opportunity to tie the teaching of language and the teaching of culture in more meaningful ways. How could the class be reoriented to foster in students not just a communicative but also a symbolic competence that would enable them to "operate between languages and cultures" and to see themselves as others see them? The challenges, based on the data above, seem to be as follows:

1. The students seemed to believe that learning a language is totally distinct from learning about the culture and the history of speakers of that language.

2. The students seemed to have internalized the hierarchy between professors who teach content and language teachers who teach linguistic forms.

3. The teacher has been trained to be a mere facilitator of student talk.

4. He had been trained to bring nonnative speakers up to the linguistic level of native speakers, not to understand the values and cultural schemata embedded in both the students' first language and their second language.

5. Students and teacher didn't necessarily know or understand each other's cultural frames, historical mentalities, and values.

6. The communicative approach used here focused on grammatical and lexical accuracy, oral fluency, and pragmatic appropriateness but not on the exploration of foreign worldviews and understanding of history.

7. It considered communication as the transmission and exchange of information, not as the negotiation of norms of interpretation.

In the concrete case at hand, reorienting classroom discourse would mean addressing the following questions proposed by the theories reviewed in this chapter:

1. How is language relativity activated here? Language activity is to be understood not as a labeling process but as a process of categorization. Words and phrases are conceptual metaphors with their image schemas, their connotations and entailments. For example, *Dresden* is not just a name on a map but an icon of cultural sophistication, and the bombing of Dresden is an issue of hefty current debate as to the meaning of war and its moral justification. *In die Knie zwingen* is not just a lexical phrase but a conceptual metaphor for humiliation, shame, and dishonor. Language teachers are responsible for teaching language—but language as categories of the mind and discourse structures, not just linguistic forms.

2. How does the cultural phenomenon of the bombing of Dresden implicate other cultural phenomena through patterns of repetition in texts or intra-intertextualities in the representation of events (Blommaert, 2005; Fairclough, 2003)? The repetition of metaphors such as *disappear from the surface of the earth, wiped out, a desert,* and *stranded ocean liners* indexes not only physical disappearance but an erasure from memory and the shipwreck of the dreams associated with ocean liners. Their repetition enacts a crescendo in the feeling of loss and humiliation that the narrator tries to convey to his young readers.

3. How are meanings constructed and negotiated through ongoing discourse? This is done by engaging the learners in exploring the differences between their own construction of events and Kästner's way of telling the story. The teacher can ask

the students to choose a perspective (a mother, a grandmother, an American pilot in World War II, an American soldier in Iraq) and write their own "children's story" on the bombing of Dresden based on the ample historical information given on the worksheets. The teacher can also engage in writing his or her own "children's story." The class can then compare the various stories or "translations" of the Kästner story into the vocabularies of the other narrators in the class. This should be conceived of not as an exercise in creative writing or to improve the students' writing but as a way of comparing narrators' constructions of the historical event and of questioning the larger discourses they draw on. My experience has shown that by focusing not on whether the bombing of Dresden was "justified" but on the subjective emotions and ambivalent feelings it elicits to this day, students are able to recognize some of the ambivalent feelings they might have toward their own family, community, or country and identify with Kästner on the basis of their common subjectivity.

4. How does meaning emerge from this comparison? By sharing with the class his or her own experiences, readings, and reflections on the event, the teacher can bring culture down to a personal subjective level and make the meaning of the event meaningful to the students. However, this would require that he or she temporarily step out of his or her mandate to remain in the background and "let the students talk." It should be stressed that regardless of the methodology, the teacher is as much a participant in a language class as any of the students, with her or his own experiences and viewpoints.

5. How are speakers' intentions not the only makers of meaning? Asking the German teacher and the American students to construct together the meaning of the bombing of Dresden, even if only in its narrative representation, is confronting them with the task of dealing with the various discourses on the event that have been produced by various scholars and journalists since then (e.g., Hage, 2003; Kempowski, 2001; Mulisch, 2003; Taylor, 2004), particularly on the occasion of the sixtieth anniversary of the event and again recently (e.g., Packer, 2010). The sensitive nature of these discourses, both in the United States and in Germany, shows that the development of transcultural and translingual competence requires an emotionally safe environment. In this case, objective communicative truth and authenticity are best replaced by the subjective apprehension and acceptance of ambivalences and tragic dilemmas. For today's American adolescents, most of whom have never experienced war except in video games and Hollywood movies and for whom fighting a war overseas is a "job" that needs to "get done" by professionals and that has little to do with their daily lives (Scott, 2010), transcultural competence would mean being able to withhold judgment about "good guys" and "bad guys" and to empathize with a German resident of Dresden who, like Kästner and many Germans today, is a convinced pacifist. It would mean accepting the fact that one can at the same time love one's homeland and be proud of its cultural achievements and hate the evil that one's nation has inflicted on others.

Such a reorientation would foster the goals advocated by the MLA Report: "critical language awareness, interpretation and translation, historical and political consciousness, social sensibility, and aesthetic perception." It would bring to the fore the "fractures and entanglements" in the writing of history and the role of affective memory in the acquisition of foreign vocabularies. Most of all, it would reorient the teaching of communicative competence from the exchange of objective, authentic information toward the development of a symbolic competence focused on the representation and interpretation of subjective, truthful meanings.[7]

Conclusion

The two theories I have discussed here—ecological/complexity theory and translation theory—underscore the limits of intentionality in the expression of meaning and the irreducible boundaries in the pursuit of cross-cultural understanding. What the notion of translingual and transcultural competence offers the language student is not the prospect of crossing wide-open spaces into exotic foreign territory. Rather, it reveals an eye-opening horizon of entanglements, ruptures, illusions, and disillusions associated with language itself. Translingual competence is not the simple juxtaposition of two equally valid dictionary meanings, nor is transcultural competence the bland coexistence of multiple cultures under the happy banner of diversity. Rather, both represent an awareness of the symbolic value of language and a willingness and ability to engage in the difficult task of cultural translation.

By making the multilingual subject and not the near-native speaker or the 1+ speaker on the ACTFL scale the goal of foreign language education at the college level, the MLA Report is in effect redefining the very way we conceive of language, language learning, and language use. It offers an ecological and a postmodern view of the language learner that is better in tune with our ambivalent times and with the conflicted feelings our students are experiencing right now. Language teachers, who have themselves experienced these conflicts and the sometimes incompatible worldviews expressed in languages other than their own, are in the best position to help young people deal with similar conflicts at this crucial stage in their personal development.

Notes

1. *Communautarisme* is decried as being antithetical to the republican ideal of free, equal individual citizens. Touraine (1997), for example, sees in the domination of the market (*la domination des marchés*) and the power of communities (*les pouvoirs communautaires*) a threat to the autonomy of the individual.

2. *Citoyenneté* is not just a bureaucratic label that you acquire when you become a citizen of a nation-state. It is an act of allegiance to the republican ideal of *liberté, égalité, fraternité*, to the separation of church and state, to the rights and obligations of a parliamentary democracy and the concomitant responsibility of the state to work for the common good.

3. The French notion of *universalité* is steeped in the eighteenth-century values of human reason, human dignity, and tolerance of difference—values that are deemed universal because all humans are rational beings who can be convinced to work for the common good. The Anglo-Saxon notion of universality is also traceable to the eighteenth century but is imbued with utilitarian values: all humans are entitled to pursue their economic well-being or happiness (Scollon & Scollon, 2001). The French notion is more compatible with a catholic

mentality that puts culture before economics. The Anglo-Saxon notion is more compatible with a protestant mentality that gives priority to economics.

4. These deep cross-cultural misunderstandings arose again recently in reaction to the news that at the joint session of Congress on September 9, 2009, South Carolina representative Joe Wilson shouted at President Obama, "You lie!" in front of the whole assembly. My French colleagues felt that such an outburst was "childish" (personal communication). In the American press, some called such a remark "racist" (Dowd, 2009), and others called it "populist" (Brooks, 2009). But what Obama and his critics have in common is a deep American conviction that politics and morality go hand in hand. "Telling the truth" or "telling a lie" might seem to Europeans to be an affair between children and their parents, not between politicians and their constituencies.

5. Ultimately, however, the need for translation was overshadowed by the imperatives of the French publishing industry that, like its English counterparts, requires that any scientific book published in France be 90 percent in French. Like English language publishers, French publishers assume that readers will recognize and accept the ideas indexed by the French words the same way French scholars would.

6. Since then, European educators have been keen on incorporating a discourse dimension in their study of intercultural competence (see Hu & Byram, 2009). In the past five years, the term "intercultural competence" has gained in prominence in U.S foreign language education (e.g., Schulz & Tschirner, 2008).

7. I wish to thank Nikolaus Euba and the participants at the DAAD seminar at the University of California, Berkeley, in October 2009 and the AATG workshop at the Goethe Institute, San Francisco, in February 2010 for their wise insights regarding how to teach such a unit.

References

Bennett, J., Bennett, M., & Allen, W. (2003). Developing intercultural competence in the language classroom. In D. Lange & M. Paige (Eds.), *Culture as the core: Perspectives in second language education* (pp. 237–270). Greenwich, CT: Information Age Publishing.

Blommaert, J. (2005). *Discourse.* Cambridge: Cambridge University Press.

Breen, M., & Candlin, C. (1980). The essentials of a communicative curriculum in language teaching. *Applied Linguistics, 1*(2), 89–111.

Brooks, D. (2009, September 18). No, it's not about race. *New York Times*, p. A27.

Butler, J. (2003). *Just being difficult.* Stanford, CA: Stanford University Press.

Byram, M. (1997). *Teaching and assessing intercultural communicative competence.* Clevedon, UK: Multilingual Matters.

Dowd, M. (2009, September 13). Boy, oh, boy! *New York Times*, Week in Review, p. 17.

Fairclough, N. (2003). *Analysing discourse.* London: Routledge.

Fill, A., & Mühlhäusler, P. (Eds.). (2001). *The ecolinguistics reader: Language, ecology and environment.* London: Continuum.

Hage, V. (2003). *Zeugen der Zerstörung: Die Literaten und der Luftkrieg, Essay und Gespräche.* Frankfurt am Main: Fischer.

Hanks, W. (1996). *Language and communicative practices.* Boulder, CO: Westview Press.

Hu, A., & Byram, M. (Eds.). (2009). *Intercultural competence and foreign language learning. Models, empiricism, assessment.* Tübingen: Gunter Narr.

Kempowski, W. (2001). *Der rote Hahn: Dresden im Februar 1945.* Munich: Btb.

Kramsch, C. (2002). Introduction. How can we tell the dancer from the dance? In C. Kramsch (Ed.), *Language acquisition and language socialization: Ecological perspectives* (pp. 1–30). London: Continuum.

Kramsch, C. (2006a). From communicative competence to symbolic competence. *Modern Language Journal, 90*(2), 249–251.

Kramsch, C. (2006b). The traffic in meaning. An answer to Mary Louise Pratt. And responses by Azirah Hashim and Alastair Pennycook. *Asian Pacific Journal of Education, 26*(1), 97–116.

Kramsch, C. (2007). In search of the intercultural. *Journal of Sociolinguistics, 6*(2), 275–285.

Kramsch, C. (2008). Ecological perspectives on foreign language education. *Language Teaching, 11*(3), 389–408.

Kramsch, C. (2009a). La circulation transfrontalière des valeurs dans un projet de recherche international. *Le Francais dans le Monde, 46*, 66–75.

Kramsch, C. (2009b). *The multilingual subject.* Oxford: Oxford University Press.

Kramsch, C., & Steffensen, S. V. (2008). Ecological perspectives on second language acquisition and language socialization. In N. Hornberger (Ed.), *Encyclopedia of language and education: Vol. 8. Language and socialization* (2nd ed., pp. 17–28). Heidelberg: Springer-Verlag.

Kramsch, C., & Whiteside, A. (2008). Language ecology in multilingual settings: Towards a theory of symbolic competence. *Applied Linguistics, 29*(4), 645–671.

Larsen-Freeman, D., & Cameron, L. (2008). *Complexity theory and language learning.* Oxford: Oxford University Press.

Modern Language Association. (2007). Foreign languages and higher education: New structures for a changed world. Retrieved from http://www.mla.org/flreport

Mulisch, H. (2003). *Das steinerne Brautbett* (G. Seferens, Trans.). Frankfurt am Main: Suhrkamp Verlag.

Ochs, E. (2002). On becoming a speaker of culture. In C. Kramsch (Ed.), *Language acquisition and language socialization: Ecological perspectives* (pp. 99–120). London: Continuum.

Packer, G. (2010, February 1). Letter from Dresden: Embers. *The New Yorker*, 32–39.

Pireddu, N. (2008). Literature? *C'est un monde*: The foreign language curriculum in the wake of the MLA Report. *Profession 2008*, 219–228.

Pratt, M. L. (2002). The traffic in meaning: Translation, contagion, infiltration. *Profession 2002*, 25–36.

Reddy, M. (1993). The conduit metaphor. A case of frame conflict in our language about language. In A. Ortony (Ed.), *Metaphor and thought* (2nd ed., pp. 164–201). Cambridge: Cambridge University Press.

Schmidt, S., & Schmidt, K. (2007). *Erinnerungsorte: Deutsche Geschichte im DaF-Unterricht.* Berlin: Cornelsen.

Schulz, R., & Tschirner, E. (Eds.). (2008). *Communicating across borders: Developing intercultural competence in German as a foreign language.* Munich: iudicium.

Scollon, R., & Scollon, S. (2001). *Intercultural communication: A discourse approach* (2nd ed.). Oxford: Blackwell.

Scott, A. O. (2010, February 7). Apolitics and the war film: A fit for these times. *New York Times*, Week in Review, p. 1.

Taylor, F. (2004). *Dresden: Tuesday February 13, 1945.* London: Bloomsbury.

Touraine, A. (1997). *Pourrons-nous vivre ensemble? Egaux et différents.* Paris: Fayard.

Wellmon, M. C. (2008). Languages, cultural studies, and the futures of foreign language education. *Modern Language Journal, 92*(2), 292–295.

Zarate, G., Lévy, D., & Kramsch, C. (Eds.). (2008). *Précis du plurilinguisme et du pluriculturalisme.* Paris: Edition des Archives Contemporaines.

Chapter 3

Classrooms and "Real" Worlds: Boundaries, Roadblocks, and Connections

Leo van Lier, Monterey Institute of International Studies

Abstract

In this chapter, I examine the language classroom and its relations to the rest of the world. I take an ecological approach; that is, I focus on the relationships among the various places and situations that members of language classrooms find themselves in and how these relationships are affected by a variety of constraining and enabling factors. In particular, I look at three sets of issues, two of them (named boundaries and roadblocks) constraining and the third (named connections) enabling. The chapter discusses ways in which the various issues raised have been and can be researched and reviews key theories and approaches, including the tension between micro- and macroperspectives and emic and etic perspectives. Questions addressed include the following: How do classrooms turn out the way that they do, and in what ways are they shaped by society or by their inhabitants? What are the factors that promote or limit connections between social ecosystems such as the family, the peer group, and the social/institutional ecosystem of the classroom? The sketch provided here is a very partial one, but in the last part of the chapter, some suggestions are offered that can make the classroom into a learning space that may forge connections between learning and the rest of the students' lives.

Introduction

My purpose in this chapter is to take an ecological approach to the study of what happens in classrooms and why. In past research on this topic, I have focused primarily on the microlevel interactions of the participants, and I believe that this is still a very necessary and crucial line of investigation. It involves taking the ethnomethodological notion of "indifference" to prior theories and external contextual models seriously (as described by Garfinkel, 1967; see also van Lier, 1988) and thus takes a strongly emic, as opposed to etic, stance. The consequence of such a stance is that any analytical argument must come from the data themselves, not from any other source of information extraneous to the data, whether it be the researcher's own purposes, beliefs, and convictions or presumed characteristics of institutional or sociopolitical forces and constraints. This can be so basic as to refuse, in a transcript, to distinguish a priori between a teacher and a student. The argument is that, if a particular person consistently or even just from time to time behaves in a "teacher-like" fashion (of course, sometimes students do this, and sometimes teachers do *not* do this) or is overtly addressed as "Teacher" or "Miss" or "Sir," then this participant is construed as "doing teaching," regardless of his or her employment status, certification, salary, or whatever. A complication to this austere approach is that "teacher-like" and "doing teaching" need to be evidenced directly in the data. For example, an analyst's opinion that "Mary was behaving like a teacher" is not good enough because it draws on a preexisting notion of what it is like to behave like a teacher. So the only way to draw a conclusion would be if an interlocutor said something like, "Look, don't lecture at me," but even that comment presupposes that we all know that "doing teaching" involves lecturing at people. In this and similar ways, conversation analysis sets out to cut through assumptions, presuppositions, preconceived ideas, received wisdom, unexamined claims, and so on.

Normally, we know perfectly well in an instructional setting who the teacher is (i.e., we do not need to ask for his or her credentials or most recent paycheck). It tends to be clear from the age, the positioning, and the language use, among other indicators. But what are these indicators (more precisely, what makes an observable entity into an indicator?), and, most important, what kinds of language use can be incontrovertibly designated as being "teacherese" or "teacher-like" language?

On the other side of the coin, however, there is no doubt that the sorts of things that happen in classrooms and the kinds of talk that occur do not come out of the blue but that they are influenced by many factors in the wider environment of the school, the family, local and global policies, people's beliefs about what "good education" should "look like," and so on. These are macrolevel issues, and one of the perduring problems in social science research has long been the micro–macro split. Ethnomethodologists resolve this split by the deliberate indifference mentioned above, whereas many researchers build contextual models of various kinds. Others attempt to integrate micro and macro concerns (e.g., Kramsch & Whiteside, 2008; Rampton, 1995; Wortham, 2006). But let's begin now by looking at the classroom as an entity in the real world.

In ecological terms, the classroom can be seen as a niche. In nature, niches are parts of ecosystems that are particularly suited for particular organisms. There are two aspects to a niche: it has in and of itself properties that suit the organism and that provide affordances, but in addition, it is to a greater or lesser degree constructed by the organism, to make it even more suitable (enhancing existing affordances and creating new ones).

A niche offers important advantages to the organism: safety, shelter, rearing of offspring, proximity of food, and so on. It also introduces constraints: limitations on movement, flight, or foraging; the need to defend the niche to would-be intruders; and a disincentive to explore other (and possibly better) niches.

Going back to the classroom as ecological niche, the first thing to note is that it is preconstructed to a large degree. It is designed for its perceived and intended purpose. Students walk in for the first time and encounter walls, desks, and a certain arrangement of artifacts, barren or cluttered. These things are givens in the same way that a certain cave is a given for a bear or an empty snail shell is an affordance for a growing hermit crab.

But very few places are accepted exactly for what they are, and teachers and learners, similar to organisms in nature, adapt, reconstruct, and change in various ways the place that is the niche candidate (or niche designate) and turn it into a proper niche for themselves, one that fits them and one that they fit into.

In this way, in each classroom, the teacher, and the learners reshape the classroom that they were assigned to into *their* classroom. The amount of wiggle room (and incentive) they have to do that, in literal and figurative terms, is one of the topics of this chapter.

The other topic is the extent to which the classroom niche is a second-language-oriented safe haven, retreat, or temporary cage and to what extent it is a place from which to do two things: (1) venture forth and hunt for language stuff and (2) bring back language stuff to share, savor, and digest. The venturing forth and bringing back can be seen literally, virtually, or symbolically. That is, one can perfectly well stay in a seat and venture forth into imagined worlds and come back to share them with neighbors. Or one can stay in the seat and enter virtual social worlds, thus transforming the notion of niche into something completely new and not bounded by physical space.

There are three aspects of classroom as niche that I want to explore. First are the *boundaries* between the classroom and the rest of the participants' worlds. These boundaries can be more or less permeable and porous. Second are the *roadblocks*, or the things that can go wrong when moving in and out of classrooms. Third are the *pedagogical connections* that teachers and learners can make between their classroom and their worlds. These three topics can be explored from the vantage point of several different spatiotemporal scales.

In addition to taking a conversation analysis perspective, research can be carried out using various models of contextual (or situated) inquiry: cultural-historical activity theory (Engeström, 1987), systems theory/practice (Checkland, 1981), and nested ecosystems (Bronfenbrenner, 1979), among others. Each one provides a set of different lenses and foci and a loosely bundled set of practices. I am assuming that a conversation analysis approach can be combined with (or juxtaposed with) one or other contextual model, provided that it is an open model rather than a closed one (see particularly the perceptive remarks on this point by Checkland, 1981).

Boundaries

There are three boundaries that I want to explore:

Boundary 1: Inert knowledge (Whitehead, 1929)

   Knowledge that "counts" in the classroom but is irrelevant elsewhere

Boundary 2: Classification and Framing (Bernstein, 2000)

   The control and power that underlie pedagogical discourse

Boundary 3: Pedagogical discourse (Bernstein, 2000)

   Instructional discourse

   Regulative discourse

I discuss these boundaries in turn in the following subsections.

Boundary 1: The Manufacture of a Classroom Genre

Long ago, Alfred North Whitehead (1929) warned against the "inert knowledge problem," that is, knowledge that is important inside classrooms and educational institutions, crucial on tests, and decisive on grade sheets and diplomas but virtually useless (irrelevant or unusable) in real-world activities and tasks. Students know this, or at least sense this every day, as they cross the border between their family, work or dorm life, and the classroom life. They may accept it as an inevitable aspect of educational reality, or they may rebel against it. Either way, "border skirmishes" are likely to be a part of their struggles for multicompetence.

It is quite common for "school" language to sound bizarre in out-of-school contexts. I remember my German teacher in middle school explaining the difference between *Geschäft* and *Laden* to us, as two names for different kinds of shops. I had just spent a summer in Germany with relatives and raised my hand, saying that, actually, we kids bought our candy and snacks at the *"Bude."* This was not appreciated. Soon thereafter, a second linguistic clash occurred: the teacher explained that a lollipop was called a *"Luksussaugebonbonmitholzhandangriff,"* or, literally, a "luxury sucking candy with wooden handle." A lovely word—and one that beautifully illustrates the compounding power of the German language. However, I knew from experience that people in Germany did not say that because I had had direct experience with lollipops in Germany; in fact, I had bought them several times (at the *Bude*). I probably should have known better by then, but I raised my hand again and said that, actually, we called it a *"Dauerlutscher"* (a "lasting sucker"). Once again, this was rejected as some sort of vulgar aberration. I got the message, and from then on I toed the line and used only classroom-friendly and test-compatible language, far from real life but close to the grade.

Not to belabor the point, but let me add one more example from a teacher training context. The reader can surely add many more once I'm done. As an English language teacher in training, I remember a session on vocabulary in context. The professor was explaining that the word "square" can have different meanings, for example, a space in a city for hanging out (Leicester Square or a town square in general; it could of course be round—expressions of merriment appreciated), or it can mean a specific mathematical shape. I raised my hand and opined that there was another meaning: "old-fashioned" or "boring," as in the Elvis Presley song: "You're so square, baby I don't care." The professor's response was that this example did not count because it was clearly slang (i.e., not legitimate language).

Such anecdotes may seem small and insignificant, but they can have a profound influence on the learner's perception of the authenticity of the classroom in relation to the real world of second-language use. Three responses are possible: first, you can reject the classroom version of the second language and immerse yourself in the real-life version (in effect, drop out); second, you can shut out the real-world language and just concentrate on the exam language (Lantolf & Genung, 2002); or, third, you can play the game and use one language without and another one within the educational sphere. Unfortunately, I am afraid that many students get caught in a confusion of all three of these elements. Language gets separated into (1) that which is validated in school but largely useless outside and

(2) interesting stuff that you hear outside the classroom but that is not considered legitimate inside the classroom. In the end, a student might well ask, which language is "really real"? Why does language get stopped at the classroom–life frontier, both on the way in and on the way out?

Boundary 2: Classification and Framing

This second boundary relates to Bernstein's (2000) theory of educational sociology. It consists of two parameters. The first, classification, is about control—control of what counts as legitimate knowledge in particular domains of subject matter and what counts as illegitimate trespassing *across* different domains. The second, framing, or power, refers to the types of language use, argumentation, and logic that are permissible within a particular classified domain, that is, the sorts of language that will be counted as relevant and legitimate *within* a domain.

These two parameters are very tightly interpenetrated, but they refer to two distinct discursive and institutional forces: the force to separate areas of educational endeavor and human knowledge into different autonomous fields (that are walled off from criticism by other fields) and the force, within a field, to produce discourses that enhance and perpetuate the field's separate and legitimate identity.

Bernstein's (2000) analysis is very dense and incisive and by the same token not easy to grasp. Yet it captures the sense of a seemingly inevitable habitus (Bourdieu & Passeron, 1977) and institutional reproduction machinery that we experience when we spend some time in a school (or, indeed, any organization) and become socialized into its practices and register.

First, classification sets up the boundaries between one field and another, and, next, framing establishes the ways of communicating within a particular field that has achieved or aspires to achieve "field" status. In second-language acquistion, for example, cognitively and socioculturally oriented researchers regularly dispute the boundaries of the relevance, evidence, and importance of their perspective in the field and assign quite different meanings to such commonly used terms as "negotiation," "interaction," "acquisition," and "use" (Block, 2003; Firth & Wagner, 1997, 2007; Gass, 1998).

Boundary 3: Pedagogical Discourse

The third boundary derives from the previous two. It relates to the sorts of language use that are pedagogically preferred or mandated. Often these sorts of language use are in the classroom because they will also be on the test. Or perhaps they are on the test because they have always been in the classroom (an interesting rip-current dynamic of washback and washforward; see below). As a result, certain linguistic exhibits are legitimate because they are within the testing discourse. Other uses of language are out of bounds because they are not part of the approved testing arena.

The centripetal force of the testing apparatus reduces and narrows down the sorts of things that are worth saying (or writing or listening to) in the classroom. A common result is that language variation is not or only sporadically addressed since only the "standard variety" is assessed. Whether this "standard" or, indeed, the notion of "native-like," which is often held up as an ideal goal, is definable, realistic, or desirable is left unexamined.

A commonly used term in the testing literature is "washback." Popular phrases related to this are "work for washback" and "bias for best" (Swain, 1985). This means that the types of tests used have a tendency to work their way back into what is taught. If the test is one that measures rote memorization, a circumscribed set of approved patterns, accents, or phrases, then the incentive to talk about interesting topics in class is probably dampened.

Paradoxically, there is also a possibly even more insidious force in the teaching–testing dynamic, one that operates on a slower time scale and that is for that very reason less visible and more treacherous. This force, which I call "washforward," goes in the opposite direction, from pedagogical practices to assessment procedures. This force says that deep-seated pedagogical structures may eventually whittle away at innovative tests so that the latter little by little fall in line with ingrained pedagogical practices that resist change. An example of washforward is the demise of narrative assessments at the secondary or tertiary level. Over time, such qualitative (nonnumerical) assessments have tended to be interpreted and recast unofficially into letter grades so that a certain turn of phrase in a narrative paragraph would signal ("stand for") a clear B, C minus, and so on.

A second example are oral proficiency interviews, which are intended to be holistically graded. It is often the case that in practice, decisions are over time made on the basis of certain criterial features, such as the use of preterit versus imperfect tense in Spanish or the accurate use of the *ba* or *le* construction in Chinese. In other words, in spite of proclaimed holistic and functional grading, formal criteria take the upper hand and determine band crossings, thus turning the oral proficiency interview at least partly into a discrete point grammar test.

Roadblocks

In this section, I discuss three kinds of phenomena that can constrain learning in classrooms. I call these phenomena *roadblocks*: first, the roadblock of gaps and clashes between school and neighborhood; second, the roadblock of incompatible (or oppositional) discourses; and, third, the roadblock of conflicting identities.

Roadblock 1: Gaps and Clashes

We have all walked into classrooms, and we know (or recall) that we enter into a place that has its own ambience, rules, rituals, sense of humor, practices, and participation structures. It is an ecological niche, designed for education. In earlier times, on wintry days, children left their coats, muddy boots, or wooden shoes outside and went into a room with rows of desks, a black coal-burning stove in the back, and a blackboard and teacher's desk in front. What else were children expected to leave outside the classroom besides their winter clothes? Perhaps the things that worried them: family problems; things they had learned from uncles, aunts, and other people; fears and hopes; and so on? Perhaps they had a rare teacher who managed to connect the classroom to the students' lives as a whole or perhaps one who focused only on drills, book knowledge, and facts legitimized by the curriculum. Today, students bring their laptops, cell phones, iPods, and other paraphernalia because their world incorporates a virtual one, transportable and unbounded by time and space. The gaps and clashes may be of a different nature, or perhaps, underneath all the electronic paraphernalia, they remain essentially the same. Perhaps the present-day rare teacher knows a way to channel the new social media into productive pedagogical directions.

Many of us, using our own experiences, can undoubtedly come up with various examples of gaps and clashes between school and life. Let me just give a couple of well-known vignettes from two films, *El Norte*, and *Entre les Murs*:

> In *El Norte*, two young Mayan refugees from Guatemala, Enrique and Rosa (brother and sister), are taking English-as-a-second-language (ESL) classes in the Los Angeles area. In the film, real-life demands, such as learning how to operate a sophisticated washing machine, working in a restaurant kitchen, "migra" raids, separation, and illness, are juxtaposed with ESL lessons in which the teacher conducts "conversational" drills about the often-foggy weather in Los Angeles and other bland topics.

> In *Entre les Murs*, a class of multicultural students in France is given the task by their well-meaning teacher of writing an essay about their feelings and reflections about their daily pursuits. Students protest the validity of the assignment, saying that it is only a task, not something that is really interesting to anybody, least of all the teacher. When the teacher protests that he *is* interested, one girl says, "Well, you just say that because you're a teacher. It's not really true."

Classroom lessons are not therapy sessions, I think we can all agree, yet one might wish for some connection between the school and the rest of the student's life. The school, for those who are earmarked for failure, by virtue of background or lack of opportunity, becomes an alien authoritarian institution, one that has nothing to offer to the unsuccessful student. How many students dread to set foot on the school campus every morning and for the sake of survival set up defense mechanisms? David Little (1991, p. 39) has argued that there is a barrier between education and "the rest of living" and that this barrier must be broken down.

Roadblock 2: Incompatible Discourses and the (Im)Possibility of Dialogue

It was Bourdieu (1994) who said that in classrooms "attempts to establish a dialogue between [teachers and students] quickly degenerate into fiction or farce" (p. 11). Freire argues that all education is premised on communication but then, somewhat paradoxically, claims that true communication is only possible among equals. Where does that leave the school, the teacher, and the student?

Paul Willis (1977), in his classic ethnographic study of working-class lads in a British school, speaks of an oppositional culture that involves what he calls *differentiation*, a reinterpretation of the school's discourses of goals, standards, legitimated behaviors, and definitions, in terms of a countercultural positioning. Similar processes are recounted in Eckert's (1989) *Jocks and Burnouts* and Rampton's (1995) *Crossing*.

Roadblock 3: Identity Conflicts

In Willis's (1977) study, students are divided into "ear'oles" and "the lads," and this appears similar to the distinction in Eckert's study between "jocks" and "burnouts"—or students who play the educational game and those who do not. To a certain extent, of course, identifications that emerge in school settings mirror those that exist outside school. The divisions between Latinos and Anglos are not created in school, but somehow the school, even if it professes to "leave no child behind," somehow cannot resist the processes of classification and self-identification that are evident on nearly every campus. And in every school cafeteria, let alone in Advanced Placement, core, and other courses, these processes become institutionalized even though the institution officially rejects them. Some of the ways in which these creations of identities arise are described in detail in the work of Wortham (2006), who tracks their emergence over time in classrooms. There are processes of "selving" and "othering" (Riggins, 1997) that identify and separate students into groups.

Connections

Above I have sketched two sets of phenomena, *boundaries* and *roadblocks*, which constitute potential hindrances to a high-quality education for all learners. In particular, the phenomena described would appear to affect certain populations more than others. The populations most affected would be those that have low cultural and linguistic (we might add educational) capital (Bourdieu, 1994) to begin with, and these lacks of capital will usually combine to result in low educational capital. This low educational capital can be further exacerbated by a societal and institutional culture of low expectations for the groups or individuals in question.

In this section, I point to an ecological approach to education aimed at counteracting the negative effect of boundaries and roadblocks that instead looks for opportunities and success where all too often failure seems to be the norm. Such an ecological approach rests on an integrated focus on *awareness*, *authenticity*, and *agency*, a "triad of As" that I first proposed well over a decade ago (van Lier, 1996) but have now further developed in ecological directions.

Awareness

The basis all learning is perception, and perception is both the result and the origin of action (see the second A, agency, below). Larsen-Freeman (2003) notes that learning grammar is largely a matter of "learning how to see." Various studies, from case studies by Schmidt (1983) and Schmidt and Frota (1986) to experimental research (Tomlin & Villa, 1994), have shown that learners have to notice things in the input data in order to be able to process them and incorporate them into their interlanguage. But there is more to perception than focusing one's attention. In order to truly see (and hear, feel, and so on), one has to move around. An immobile perceiver is severely limited in terms of the diversity of what he or she can perceive. Linguistic environments require "rummaging around," picking up, nudging, fiddling, trying out, and so on, like the way you go around the marketplace. And yes, they also require bargaining about the value of particular items.

Agency

Agency has been provisionally defined by the anthropologist Ahearn (2001, p. 111) as the "socioculturally mediated ability to act." In an ecological perspective, agency can be more simply defined initially as *movement* (Bohm, 1998; van Lier, 2008). Movement can be self-initiated and other-initiated, yet in both cases it remains agentive. It can be accidental or deliberate, forced or free, but it is still agency in both cases. Perversely, though, in the case of humans (perhaps also higher mammals), absence of movement can also be agentive: where movement would be expected, given certain preconditions, an agent can refuse to move, and that is also agency. It's moving against the stream, as it were, a movement of *"nicht mitmachen* (not going along)." There is thus an agency of movement and an agency of nonmovement. The latter seems contradictory to my opening statement, but if we recast it as *resistance*, then it becomes understandable as an agentive act. Agency thus comprises both movement and resistance to movement. Things are further complicated by the fact that movement or resistance can be either physically or cognitively/emotionally realized, which means that agency is not always observable.

Authenticity

Authenticity is defined in many different ways, but usually it incorporates such notions as "produced for native speakers by native speakers" or "not designed for teaching or learning purposes." I argued in my 1996 book that this is an untenable definition, citing in support arguments made by Breen (1985) and Widdowson (1990). I am now even more convinced than in 1996 that the two purported characteristics mentioned above are red herrings in the authentic/inauthentic debate. Just like beauty is supposed to be in the eye of the beholder, authenticity is in the eye (and ear and so on) of the learners and their teachers. It is no more and no less than a process of authentication. Other words that basically mean the same thing are "buy-in," "engagement," "attunement," and "intersubjectivity."

Voice

What does it mean to have voice? According to Eco (2000), voice comes to the infant in the womb and is the primary source of identification. It is original Firstness (Peirce 1992, 1998), the beginning of all semiosis (or meaning making) to come. Interestingly, a long time after these relevant remarks by Eco and Peirce, child language development researchers such as Patricia Kuhl, Janet Werker, Ann Meltzoff, and others at the University of British Columbia (e.g., Byers-Heinlein, Burns, & Werker, 2010) have established that babies can have multilingual perceptual abilities before birth. We are not necessarily born monolingual, so educationally perhaps we do not have to be cured from that condition; rather, we can work toward preventing the prevailing sociopolitical doxa from neutering us into monolingualism.

Voice is thus experienced at first quite viscerally. Later on, however, children strive to develop their own voice, and they work quite hard at it, usually being quite well rewarded socially for expressing a budding voice (unless, perhaps, they get too "uppity"). The same is true for second-language learners, who have to be encouraged to develop a voice in a second-language and to be applauded for attempts to do so regardless of their initial linguistic infelicities. It is, after all, possible to develop a multilingual identity only if you have a voice to express it in, and this voice requires to be listened to for the meanings that it attempts to express.

The notions of awareness, authenticity, agency, and voice suggest a powerful agenda for education, one that can be effective in counteracting the detrimental effects of the various forces I have highlighted under the headings of boundaries and roadblocks.

Conclusion

In this chapter, I have attempted to take an ecological look at classrooms and their place in the wider world, focusing in particular on some of the things that can happen when students and teachers move in and out of classrooms, day in and day out, from home to school and back again. I have attempted to point out some of the boundaries (almost like border crossings) that need to be navigated and the roadblocks that may stand in the way of smooth traffic and harmonious connections. There appear to be rather formidable obstacles that militate against a happy integration of school and society (except, perhaps, for some fortunate groups who appear to possess a large amount of educational capital and who will fare well regardless of the shortcomings of any particular pedagogy or curriculum).

In the "Connections" section, I suggested that there are specific approaches and mind-sets that can provide a counterbalance to the boundaries and roadblocks that many individuals and groups experience in their educational endeavors. Such approaches naturally focus on the quality of educational experience rather than on the quantities of numbers produced by test scores. The solution is really quite simple in terms of commonsense ideas, but it has eluded successful realization, despite centuries of sincere and often brilliant efforts, because of the boundaries and roadblocks that societies have been unable to erase.

References

Ahearn, L. M. (2001). Language and agency. *Annual Review of Anthropology, 30*, 109–137.

Bernstein, B. (2000). *Pedagogy, symbolic control and identity: Theory, research, critique*. Lanham, MD: Rowman & Littlefield.

Block, D. (2003). *The social turn in second language acquisition*. Edinburgh: Edinburgh University Press.

Bohm, D. (1998). *On creativity*. London: Routledge.

Bourdieu, P., & Passeron, J-C. (1977). *Reproduction in education, society and culture*. London: Sage.

Bourdieu, P. (1994). *Language and symbolic power*. Oxford: Polity Press.

Breen, M. (1985). Authenticity in the language classroom. *Applied Linguistics, 6*(1), 60–70.

Bronfenbrenner, U. (1979). *The ecology of human development*. Cambridge, MA: Harvard University Press.

Byers-Heinlein, K., Burns, T. C., & Werker, J. F. (2010). The roots of bilingualism in newborns. *Psychological Science, 21*(3), 343–348.

Checkland, P. (1981). *Systems thinking, systems practice*. New York: Wiley.

Eckert, P. (1989). *Jocks and burnouts: Social categories and identity in the high school*. New York: Teachers College Press.

Eco, U. (2000). *Kant and the platypus: Essays on language and cognition*. New York: Harcourt Brace.

Engeström, Y. (1987). *Learning by expanding: An activity-theoretical approach to developmental research.* Helsinki: Orienta-Konsultit.

Firth, A., & Wagner, J. (1997). On discourse, communication, and (some) fundamental concepts in SLA research. *Modern Language Journal, 81*(3), 285–300.

Firth, A., & Wagner, J. (2007). Second/foreign language learning as a social accomplishment: Elaborations on a "reconceptualized" SLA. *Modern Language Journal, 91*(5), 800–819.

Garfinkel, H. (1967). *Studies in ethnomethodology.* Englewood Cliffs, NJ: Prentice Hall.

Gass, S. (1998). Apples and oranges: Or, why apples are not orange and don't need to be. A response to Firth & Wagner. *Modern Language Journal, 82*(1), 83–90.

Kramsch, C., & Whiteside, A. (2008). Language ecology in multilingual settings: Toward a theory of symbolic competence. *Applied Linguistics, 29*(4), 645–671.

Lantolf, J., & Genung, P. (2002). "I'd rather switch than fight": An activity theoretic study of power, success and failure in a foreign language classroom. In C. Kramsch, (Ed.), *Language acquisition and language socialization: Ecological perspectives* (pp. 175–196). London: Continuum Press.

Larsen-Freeman, D. (2003). *Teaching language: From grammar to grammaring.* Boston: Heinle.

Little, D. (1991). *Learner autonomy: Definitions, issues and problems.* Dublin: Authentik.

Peirce, C. S. (1992). *Selected philosophical writings* (Vol. 1) (Nathan Houser and Christian Kloesel, Eds.). Bloomington: Indiana University Press.

Peirce, C. S. (1998). *Selected philosophical writings* (Vol. 2) (The Peirce Edition Project, Ed.). Bloomington: Indiana University Press.

Rampton, B. (1995). *Crossing: Language and ethnicity among adolescents.* London: Longman.

Riggins, S. H. (1997). The rhetoric of othering. In S. H. Riggins (Ed.), *The language and politics of exclusion: Others in discourse* (pp. 10–30). Thousand Oaks, CA: Sage.

Schmidt, R. (1983). Interaction, acculturation, and acquisition of communicative competence. In N. Wolfson & E. Judd (Eds.), *Sociolinguistics and second language acquisition* (pp. 137–74). Rowley, MA: Newbury House.

Schmidt, R., & Frota, S. (1986). Developing basic conversational ability in a second language: A case study of an adult learner of Portuguese. In R. Day (Ed.), *"Talking to learn": Conversation in second language acquisition* (pp. 237–326). Rowley, MA: Newbury House.

Swain, M. (1985). Large-scale communicative language testing: A case study. In Y. P. Lee, A. C. Y. Y. Fok, R. Lord, & G. Low (Eds.), *New directions in language testing* (pp. 35–46). Oxford: Pergamon.

Tomlin, R. S., & Villa, V. (1994). Attention in cognitive science and SLA. *Studies in Second Language Acquisition, 16*(4), 183–203.

van Lier, L. (1988). *The classroom and the language learner: Ethnography and second-language classroom research.* London: Longman.

van Lier, L. (1996). *Interaction in the language curriculum: Awareness, autonomy and authenticity.* London: Longman.

van Lier, L. (2008). Agency in the classroom. In J. P. Lantolf & M. E. Poehner (Eds.), *Sociocultural theory and the teaching of second languages* (pp. 163–186). London: Equinox.

Whitehead, A. N. (1929). *The aims of education.* New York: Free Press.

Widdowson, H. (1990). *Aspects of language teaching.* Oxford: Oxford University Press.

Willis, P. (1977). *Learning to labor: How working class kids get working class jobs.* New York: Columbia University Press.

Wortham, S. (2006). *Learning identity: The joint emergence of social identification and academic learning.* Cambridge: Cambridge University Press.

Chapter 4

Understanding Comprehension: Hermeneutics, Literature, and Culture in Collegiate Foreign Language Education

Per Urlaub, University of Texas at Austin

Abstract

In this chapter, I propose a connection between hermeneutics and foreign language education. This connection generates insights into the process of literary reading in the second language, guides curriculum development, supports the articulation of educational goals, and provides a pedagogical framework for the effective use of cultural materials in the language classroom. Language program directors face many challenges in the context of the implementation of contemporary undergraduate curricula. To achieve effective curricular modifications, language program directors have to engage an entire department, often composed of literary scholars, linguists, and applied linguists. However, this multidisciplinary structure results often in a cacophony of methodological approaches and jargons. A framework to conceive and articulate culture-centered undergraduate curricula that relies not entirely on applied linguistics may therefore contribute the collaborative process of reforming a language program. The chapter introduces insights from both applied linguistics and hermeneutics and shows that fundamental concepts from both fields are congruent. These insights challenge intuitive assumptions of literary reading in the second language, provide the vocabulary to articulate educational goals in an integrated undergraduate curriculum, and reject the traditional two-tier curriculum. Further, I argue that hermeneutics can be of practical value to implement literature and cultural artifacts in the advanced language classroom. I illustrate this claim and demonstrate how hermeneutic theory can guide the didactization of foreign films in relation to their Hollywood remakes.

Introduction

Teaching undergraduate students to read and understand literary narrative in the target language will remain a major objective of collegiate foreign language education. In this chapter, I propose a connection between two separate fields of scholarship, namely, hermeneutics and applied linguistics. This connection generates insights into the process of literary reading in the second language, guides curriculum development and the articulation of educational goals, and provides a pedagogical framework for the effective use of cultural materials in the language classroom. Language program directors will benefit from this perspective because this connection not only supports the refinement of literacy-oriented learning environments but also generates a concrete template to integrate literary narrative and other media, such as film, into contemporary foreign language classrooms that are geared toward the development of transcultural literacy.

The first section of the chapter focuses on tasks and challenges that language program directors face in the context of the implementation of contemporary undergraduate curricula. In order to achieve effective curricular modifications, language program directors have to engage an entire department in a collaborative process. Since a modern languages department is typically composed of literary scholars, linguists, and applied linguists, a variety of methodological approaches and disciplinary jargons coexist that are used to reflect on literature and culture and their roles in second-language instruction. Consequently, interdisciplinary frameworks are required to conceive and articulate culture-centered undergraduate curricula. Besides tracking changing realities in foreign language curricula over the past 15 years, this section also provides an overview of the growing body research on the role of literary reading in collegiate second-language education.

The second section of the chapter introduces insights from both applied linguistics and hermeneutics. First, I argue that, in the past, the profession relied mostly on intuition to approach literature in the second language, which was reflected in a sequenced curriculum that separated language instruction and cultural content. Second, I show that fundamental concepts from applied linguistics and hermeneutics are compatible, that they challenge intuitive assumptions of literary reading in the second language, and that they can provide the vocabulary to articulate educational goals in an integrated undergraduate curriculum. In addition, I demonstrate how hermeneutic theory can frame the didactization of cultural materials in a foreign language classroom that is geared toward transcultural learning. To do so, I consciously outline an example that describes the implementation of film remakes in the second-language classroom. This case demonstrates that a pedagogical framework based on hermeneutics is relevant for the implementation of cultural materials from a variety of art forms and is not limited to literary narrative in the second-language classroom.

The Language Program Director, the Literary Text, and Culture

Language program directors are reformists. They are constantly rethinking learning environments in response to a growing body of research on learning and teaching, the recommendations of professional organizations, the explicit policies and unstated cultures that regulate individual institutional settings, and the day-to-day experiences of their teaching staff. In addition, language program directors have to communicate the rationale for new or modified curricular elements to a variety of stakeholders within and outside the language program director's foreign language department. Over the past 15 years, many colleagues have questioned the sequential structure of the conventional collegiate foreign language curriculum that strictly segregates the lower-division language classroom from upper-division literature/cultural studies learning environments. The basic research that initiated this development toward an integrated curriculum was published in the first half of the 1990s. Three monographs introduced a more nuanced understanding of cultural literacy to the profession and stimulated an avalanche of culture-centered, literacy-oriented second-language research (Bernhardt, 1991; Kramsch, 1993; Swaffer, Arens, & Byrnes, 1991). The theoretical insights appeared in time to provide theoretically informed responses to an increasingly dramatic enrollment situation in collegiate foreign language education. Studies in the contexts of new curricular paradigms supported the notion of learning environments that integrate language and culture on all levels of instruction (see Bernhardt & Berman, 1999; Byrnes & Kord, 2002; Swaffar & Arens, 2005). This development towards an integrated curriculum achieved a recent climax with the publication of the 2007 Modern Language Association (MLA) Ad Hoc Committee Report (MLA, 2007), which endorses a curriculum that fosters transcultural and translingual development and that is committed to both linguistic and cultural development on all stages of the undergraduate curriculum.

These developments have expanded the efficacy of the language program director far beyond administrative tasks regarding the beginning language learning environments (see Katz & Watzinger-Tharp, 2005; Levine, Melin, Crane, Chavez, & Lovik, 2008). In a more distant past, many of the language program director's ideas and decisions had an immediate effect only on the beginning language sequence. Departmental colleagues, who teach primarily literary and cultural studies, were only indirectly affected by the language program director's activities. Today, most departments have embarked on a restructuring of their undergraduate curriculum and need to rely heavily on the pedagogical expertise of the language program director to redesign the program on all levels. Curricular initiatives spearheaded by literature experts and language program directors in tandem represent important templates for reforms and highlight the impact of language program directors (see Bernhardt & Berman, 1999; Byrnes & Kord, 2002). These expanded responsibilities have created exciting opportunities for many language program directors, whose tasks have become more diverse, intellectually engaging, and politically complex.

Simultaneously, instructors with a research emphasis in literary and cultural studies have become more committed to the language classroom. Institutional changes at many departments in response to declining upper-division enrollments have moved tenured and tenure-track faculty closer to the lower-division language classroom. Many colleagues embraced this opportunity as they rediscovered the intellectual stimulation that the observation and reflection of learning and teaching processes offer. Their sophisticated understanding for literature and culture as well as their expertise as teachers resulted in highly effective didactizations of aesthetic artifacts from the target culture for language learners at all levels. In addition to these structural changes within departments of foreign languages, intellectual concepts that provide a link between critical thought and the classroom have emerged since the 1980s. Inspired by reader-response theory, developed by Iser (1978, 1980) and Jauss (1982), many literary scholars have recalibrated their theoretical focus from the text to the reading process, the perception of culture, and its reception in their classrooms. For example, Fish (1982), Scholes (1985), and Graff (1987) theorize extensively the role of literature in the profession and in instruction, and although they do not explicitly address the situation of the second-language reader in relation to the literary text, these scholars have profoundly affected how literature instructors and applied linguists frame second-language reading theoretically and in the classroom (see Carlisle, 2000; Davis, 1989, 1992; Hirvela, 1996; Swaffar, 1988).

It is a familiar debate for readers of these pages that many foreign language departments have not only fragmented curricula but also divisions between members who are involved primarily with literature and cultural studies and colleagues whose research and teaching are concerned with second-language studies (see, e.g., Barnett, 1991; Berman, 1994; Kern, 2002; Maxim, 2006). When describing this division, Kern (2002, p. 21) characterizes the divide as an "epistemological-linguistic-cognitive-methodological" split within the profession, but he also suggests that an interdisciplinary focus on literacy has the potential to reconcile the language–literature split. Although many of the points that have been raised during these debates are still a bitter reality, it is also important to stress that substantial progress has been made both in integrating language and literature personnel and in conceiving approaches to integrate language and culture in the classroom.

The shifting departmental ecologies of the 1990s have generated a growing body of research articles and best-practices publications that explore the dynamics of the literature and culture in foreign language education. Although a vast majority of second-language reading researchers investigate nonliterary reading processes (Bernhardt, 2001; Marshall, 2000), Carter's (2007) and Paran's (2008) review articles present an impressive research database on literary texts in foreign language education. They operate mainly from the perspective of English as a second language and as a foreign language, but they also include relevant articles that focus on literary reading in target languages other than English. Both authors register a dramatic increase in research output in recent years, even though their review articles are incomplete, as they miss the contributions of literary scholars, as Melin (2010) observes. Whereas some research contributions are entirely theoretical and others documentations of best practices, those that are highly regarded by Paran (2008) combine theory and practice. The following account represents seminal contributions and demonstrates the breadth of the research output and the connections between theory and practice: Bernhardt (1990) generates insights on the effect of cultural background knowledge on literary reading in the second language, but the article also helps instructors to teach German short stories of the postwar era to American students of a post-Wall generation. Chun and Plass (1996) measure empirically the acquisition of vocabulary knowledge in a multimedia setting, but at the same time their article introduces and evaluates a digital learning environment for the acquisition of literary reading skills. Mittman (1999) discusses emerging curricular contexts and theorizes the text-selection process in order to design effective integrated curricula. Fecteau (1999) compares first- and second-language reading comprehension and inference skills of adult learners and shows how many aspects of literary reading can be compared to comprehension processes of nonliterary texts. A number of more recent articles continue this trend and contribute simultaneously to the theoretical knowledge base and pedagogical practice. Langston (2006) analyzes the particular role that popular culture can assume to teach critical theories of affect, feminism, and cultural difference and offers at the same time a didactization of Benjamin Lebert's (1999) text *Crazy*.

Maxim (2006) demonstrates that popular romance novels can help adult learners to develop effective text-processing strategies for literary narrative in the second language, and he proposes a five-stage process to implement this text type into first-year learning instruction. Melin (2010) delivers 10 arguments for teaching poetry to language learners, and each of the rationales represents an instructional principles for poetry in the second-language literature classroom.

However, fundamental principles regarding the development of reading skills for literary texts in the second language have remained largely unaddressed. To this day, most of the research on literature in the second-language classroom tends to focus more on the text than on the reading/learning process, an observation that has been made already in reference to the research activities and language pedagogies of the 1980s and early 1990s (Bernhardt, 1995). This gap has decelerated the design of assessment procedures, didactical principles, and teaching methods that are geared toward the actual cognitive and affective development of the emerging reader of literature in the second language. The profession has yet to develop a coherent, intellectually rigorous, and pedagogically meaningful model of the development of cultural literacy in the second language that integrates perspectives from both applied linguistics and critical theory. This chapter provides only a modest step toward such a model by demonstrating the compatibility and pedagogical relevance of a fusion of approaches from applied linguistics and hermeneutics in order to effectively integrate literature and culture in the second-language classroom.

Understanding Comprehension

In the past, the design of collegiate foreign language curricula has relied heavily on unstated intuition, disciplinary traditions, and responses to the failures caused by overreliance on intuition and tradition. Bruner (1996) argues that many teachers rely on folk pedagogy that is composed of "wired-in human tendencies and some deeply ingrained beliefs" (p. 46). The two-tiered structure of the undergraduate curriculum has rested on an intuitively appealing but factually inaccurate view that the development of linguistic skills and the development of interpretative skills are two relatively independent processes. The traditional two-tiered curriculum design suggests this idea: as a first step, the readers acquired linguistic skills in a communicative language classroom; as a second step, the readers used these skills to interact with aesthetic artifacts from the target culture in the target language. However, insights from both applied linguistics and hermeneutics challenge the two-tiered curriculum and provide an interdisciplinary template for curriculum design and teaching methodology for language instruction that targets the development of transcultural literacy.

Cognitive psychologists generally define comprehension as the ability to relate incoming information to existing knowledge structures. According to Kintsch (1998), text comprehension "occurs when and if the elements that enter into the process achieve a stable state in which the majority of elements are meaningfully related to one another and other elements that do not fit into the pattern of the majority are suppressed" (p. 4). An important contributor to comprehension, or the formation of the text's mental representation, is the reader's ability to connect the input to prior knowledge structures; readers can more easily process texts that deal with a familiar topic as compared to texts that feature an unfamiliar topic. Therefore, the activation of background knowledge is widely regarded as an important objective of the prereading activity. Further, comprehension is a mental process that should be defined by "the product of this process: the mental representation of the text and actions based on this construction" (p. 4). For Kintsch, the processes of linguistic comprehension and interpretation are inseparable. He regards the ability of text interpretation as an integral part of the comprehension process. This view challenges the notion of linguistic preparedness for upper-level instruction that is at the foundation of the two-tiered curriculum.

Schema theory helps one understand the effect of background knowledge on reading comprehension. Schema theory is a learning theory that views organized knowledge as an elaborate network of abstract mental structures. These structures represent one's understanding of the world (Anderson, 1984). Schemata are highly connected modules that, in their multiplicity, constitute the human mind. If a reader recognizes a familiar pattern, a module is activated. Schemata are also important factors in second-language reading comprehension. Steffenson, Joag-Dev, and Anderson (1979) demonstrate that schemata are frequently constructed on the basis of experiences made in the reader's primary cultural context and that, depending on the level of incompatibility between these schemata and the second-language text, these knowledge structures will complicate the cross-cultural reading process.

None of the theories of comprehension in cognitive psychology suggest that second-language reading consists of two relatively independent processes and thus legitimize a two-tiered curriculum. In fact, quite the contrary is true: the notion of parallel processing has been a guiding principle for cognitive scientists constructing models of language processing since the late 1970s (see Stillings et al., 1987), and this principle has had a significant impact on reading models. For example, Stanovich (1980) proposed an interactive-compensatory model for first-language reading, where multiple knowledge sources contributed simultaneously to the comprehension process. A reader may compensate weak awareness for contextual cues by superior vocabulary knowledge or vice versa. The idea of parallel processing has also inspired second-language reading models. Bernhardt's (2005) model of second-language reading development suggests that first-language reading ability and second-language linguistic competence are interactive-compensatory knowledge sources.

In addition to the insights from cognitive psychology and reading comprehension research, hermeneutics can contribute significantly to the debate on literature and culture in the second-language classroom. Hermeneutics is a central philosophical strand in intellectual history and is usually defined as the study of interpretation. Hermeneutic theories describe the conditions of understanding. Traditional hermeneutics refers to methods of accessing the truth behind textual sources, and theologians, legal scholars, and historians have developed norms for systematic reading and understanding for centuries before Friedrich Schleiermacher (1768–1834) explored the nature of understanding to all genres of textual expression, including literary texts. During the late nineteenth century and the twentieth century, Wilhelm Dilthey (1833–1911) and Martin Heidegger (1889–1976) broadened the scope of hermeneutics even further by relating interpretation to the widest range of linguistic and nonlinguistic discourse systems. Although Hans-Georg Gadamer (1900–2002) was a student of Heidegger and relied to a large degree on his teacher, his notion of hermeneutics as a theory of knowledge represents, in some way, a deradicalization of the existentialist strand of hermeneutics. Among other questions, Gadamer elaborated on a problem that was already identified by traditional hermeneutics: the distance between the text and the reader (Ferraris, 1996). Schleiermacher and, in particular, Gadamer offer multiple possibilities for bridging second-language reading research with literary theory in order to conceptualize effective approaches to culture-centered second-language teaching.

Schleiermacher's work demonstrates how closely hermeneutics is related to second-language studies. In *Hermeneutics and Criticism*, published posthumously in 1838 based on lectures held between 1807 and 1810, Schleiermacher (1998) explicitly brings the reading of texts in a foreign language into the scope of his inquiry. When Schleiermacher defines hermeneutics here as the art of understanding, he clarifies that his theory is not limited to the understanding of "difficult passages in foreign languages" (p. 5). Further, he adds that his ideas on hermeneutics are also valid in situations "when the language has not yet died out" (p. 4). Schleiermacher initially considers hermeneutics as a reflection on understanding a text in a language unfamiliar to the reader. He then uses the second-language reading situation as a basic paradigm that is familiar to his contemporaries and translates this familiar paradigm from the second-language reading situation to the first-language situation. For Schleiermacher, the gap between the reader and the text was never merely the historical distance, but it always included a linguistic gap between contemporary languages and the linguistic code of the source text.

In spite of the fact that Schleiermacher acknowledges the linguistic dimension of the hermeneutic challenge, however, his value as a proto-reading researcher is limited. He sees the reader as a passive recipient of ideas and any distance between text and reader as a disadvantage. His idealized reader is fully immersed in the writer's original thoughts, and the further removed the actual reader is linguistically, historically, and culturally from the writer's original thought processes, the more fragmentary the process of understanding. Schleiermacher has a negative understanding of hermeneutical distance and does not recognize the productive aspect of the distance between reader and text in the reading process in a second language.

Gadamer has a more positive understanding of hermeneutical distance than Schleiermacher, and he presents a more detailed concept of the organization of the reader's background knowledge. In *Truth and Method*, Gadamer (1989) outlines the comprehension process with the concepts of prejudice and fore-projection. These preexisting knowledge structures that the reader brings to the text resemble Anderson's (1984) description of schemata in cognitive psychology. Gadamer argues that the concept of prejudice received its negative connotations only during the Enlightenment. He tries to liberate the concept from these negative connotations by showing that any act of understanding depends on the reader's preexisting background knowledge structures. Text comprehension is only possible for a reader who performs, what Gadamer calls, a fore-projection, and integrates preexisting background knowledge into the reading process. The reader "projects a meaning for the text as a whole as soon as some initial meaning emerges in the text. Again, the initial meaning emerges only because he is reading the text with particular expectations in regard to a certain meaning" (Gadamer, 1989, p. 269). Gadamer's hermeneutics resembles very much the basic paradigm proposed by cognitive psychologist Kintsch (1998), who suggests that comprehension is a result of connecting preexisting knowledge structures to incoming information.

Gadamer considers the distance between text and reader as a potentially positive factor. He is critical of Schleiermacher's ideal of reading as being immersed in the author's original thought patterns. Instead, Gadamer's ideal is an active reader and a text that share common contextual knowledge. Gadamer's argument is based on the idea that the meaning of the text is richer than the author's communicative intention. Comprehension and understanding are not merely receptive but also productive behaviors and depend on the reader's active contribution, so therefore "understanding is not merely a reproductive but always a productive activity as well" (Gadamer, 1989, p. 296). According to Gadamer, the active contribution of the creative reader can be stimulated through a larger hermeneutical distance between text and reader. This distance helps a reader to become more actively and critically engaged. Temporal distance between text and reader is a positive factor, and is not something that must be overcome. This was, rather, the naïve assumption of historicism, namely that we must transpose ourselves into the spirit of the age, think with its ideas and its thoughts, not with our own, and thus advance toward historical objectivity. In fact, the important thing is to recognize temporal distance as a positive and productive condition enabling understanding. (p. 297)

Gadamer's argument about the positive contribution of the temporal distance between text and reader can be translated into the second-language context. If temporal distance represents a positive contribution toward understanding a text, then the same argument can be made for the linguistic distance between reader and text, and reading a literary text in the second language must have a similar effect on a linguistically proficient and culturally aware recipient. And if the reader interacts with a literary text in the second language, the linguistic difference between text and reader serves as a constant reminder that the reader is interacting with a text that is shaped by a potentially fundamentally different cultural context. Russian formalist Viktor Shklovsky's (1990) essay *Art as Device* from 1917 supports this argument since he regards that linguistic foreignness of a literary text provides a stylistic quality that deautomatizes the reading process and sensitizes the reader better for aesthetic qualities of literary discourse. For the linguistically proficient nonnative reader, the text's linguistic extraneousness is a marker of the complex transcultural encounter between the reader and the text.

Gadamer's thoughts about the positive contributions of hermeneutical distance provide further theoretical contexts for Kramsch's (1997) theory of the nonnative speaker's privileged position. Literary reading in the second language represents a unique cognitive challenge compared to any other intellectual activity in the humanities, but a nonnative reader with high linguistic proficiency and a high degree of cultural awareness is able to interact with second-language literature on the most sophisticated levels. Therefore, the overarching major goal of collegiate foreign language education should be to shape linguistically proficient nonnative readers, who are aware and sensitive to the cultural dynamics between themselves and the texts and discourse systems with which they interact. This learner requires a learning environment that integrates linguistic and cultural components throughout the four years of the undergraduate curriculum and one that explicitly fosters the ability to critically interact with products and practices that are not familiar to the learner from his or her native culture. This learning environment must acknowledge the advantage of the linguistic and cultural distance that only seemingly prevent learners from developing informed and nuanced opinions of the target culture's discourse systems. Granting this level of interpretative authority to language learners does not only resonate strongly with the theoretical contribution of reader-response theorists (Iser, 1978, 1980; Jauss 1982); this pedagogical principle also anchors the report of the MLA Report, which encourages departments to rethink their traditional emphasis on the reproduction of native speakers and to invest more energies in their students' translingual and transcultural education.

The task of making effective use of literary and aesthetic artifacts from the target culture in order to generate learning environments that foster transcultural literacy remains a challenge for instructors in foreign language departments. However, a further concept of Gadamer's hermeneutics provides guidance here. In the following, I describe Gadamer's idea of the *fusion of horizons* and argue that it relates to Homi Bhabha's concept of the *third space* (Bhabha, 1994; see also Rutherford, 1990), which had a significant influence on the language classroom's shift from a cross-cultural focus toward transcultural learning. Gadamer's concept provides a powerful template for the implementation of narrative in the second-language classroom, and I will demonstrate this by showing how film remakes can create a learning environment that provides learners with opportunities for the fusion of horizons and thus fosters the development of transcultural competence.

Culler (2000) states that interpretation "depends upon what theorists have called the reader's 'horizon of expectations'" (p. 63). The metaphor of the horizon as an interpretative framework roughly resembles the concept of schema in cognitive psychology (Anderson, 1984; Kintsch, 1998), and it is also important for the analyses of the reception process performed by reader-response theorists (see Iser, 1978, 1980; Jauss, 1982). Gadamer's hermeneutic theory utilizes the metaphor of the horizon, but he criticizes Schleiermacher's (1998) and Nietzsche's (1997) previous notion that recipients need to transpose themselves into a variety of closed horizons in order to understand texts that originate from a variety of cultural and historic contexts. Instead, Gadamer (1989) proposes a fusion of horizons and states that there "is no more isolated horizon of the present in itself than there are historical horizons which have to be acquired. Rather, understanding is always the fusion of these horizons supposedly existing by themselves" (p. 305). Gadamer's theory implies the reader's creation of an interpretative framework that is composed of the reader's previous background knowledge and the information provided with and within the incoming text.

Applying Gadamer's theory of the fusion of horizons to second-language education provides guidance on how to use aesthetic materials in order to push classroom discourse from cross-cultural comparisons toward transcultural reflections, and it resonates with Bhabha's (1994) concept of the *third space*, which originates in postcolonial theory and theorizes notions of hybridity and translation of cultures in contact. Like Gadamer's theory, the third space rejects the notion of cultures as monolithic closed systems, fundamentally questions duality as a structural principle for cross-cultural analysis, and suggests that contact situations stimulate subject and discourse to create an alternative interpretative framework. Unlike Gadamer's theory, Bhabha's concept has significantly inspired foreign language education (Byram, 1997; Kramsch, 1996; Swaffer & Arens, 2005). Instead of comparing and contrasting native culture with the target culture, Kramsch (1996) suggests "that language teachers [should] focus less on seemingly fixed, stable cultural entities and identities on both sides of national borders, and more on the shifting and emerging third place of the language learners themselves" (p. 8).

The following example illustrates the fusion of horizons in the second-language classroom and shows how the use of film can provide the learner with the opportunity to fuse horizons in order to increase transcultural literacy. The remake of successful international productions for the domestic market has been a staple among Hollywood film studios since the 1930s. Remakes use the foreign text as a starting point for the development of a new product. The resulting film can represent a radical visual and narrative departure from the source text, such as the science-fiction thriller *Twelve Monkeys* (Gilliam, 1995), based on the French short *La Jetée* (Marker, 1962), which consists entirely of still images, or the remake may be aesthetically similar to the original, such as *No Reservations* (Hicks, 2007), based on the German film *Bella Martha* (Nettelbeck, 2001). In any case, filmic productions are shaped by social and aesthetic norms and values of their origin, and European cinematic productions are mostly designed to attract the audiences of relatively closed national film markets.

Although *Bella Martha/No Reservations* is on the surface "a factory-sealed romantic comedy," the narrative's driving force is its "enlightened attitude towards parenthood and work" (Seitz, 2007). Using this observation by an American reviewer of the remake as a point of departure, an obvious instructional strategy would be to confront learners with sequences of the original and the remake and prompt the class to identify differences and similarities between the two texts, in particular those that represent social norms and values regarding children, career, and courtship in the two cultures (V. VanderHeijden, personal communication, January 22, 2010). In this learning environment, however, the learner would simply compare and contrast elements from two distinct products from two cultures and regard these elements as symptoms of two isolated cultural systems. This cross-cultural analysis would result in perceiving the two cultures as two monolithic systems, possibly reinforcing old or generating new national stereotypes and universal claims about German and American culture. This approach is deficient because it encourages learners to see artworks from the target culture as a product of closed systems: their identities as learners and their background knowledge as contributors to the interpretation remain unacknowledged. The learner's cultural horizon will not fuse with the artwork's horizon.

A more effective approach to teach culture must give learners the opportunity to fuse the horizon of the artwork with that of their own cultural identity and background knowledge. Learners must be able to create a third space that fuses elements from the artwork's cultural contexts and their own cultural identity. Therefore, instead of comparing and contrasting two closed system, learners should use only one version of the narrative as a point of departure and collaboratively construct possible configurations of the parallel text. For example, learners can view a short sequence of an American remake in class and then use small-group discussions, synapses, storyboarding techniques, or—if time, resources, and skills permit—camcorders to envision a cinematographic version of that scene that, in their view, could originate from the target culture. Certainly, this scenario can be reversed, and students will linguistically and culturally translate a scene from a European production into an American remake. In any case, this approach allows the learner to creatively construct interpretative authority. They are encouraged to integrate their identity as language learners into the process of understanding discourses of the target culture. The third space materializes in the students' intellectual and creative production, which integrates their cultural knowledge and linguistic skills of the target language and culture with their identity as language learners. These kinds of activities contribute to transcultural awareness as they result in the fusion of horizons.

Conclusion

The ideas I propose in this chapter regarding the teaching of literature and culture in the second language rely on an integration of insights developed in the fields of applied linguistics, in particular comprehension research and hermeneutics. This view helps language program directors in the following ways:

1. Theorizing the foreign language curriculum through hermeneutics questions the notion of linguistic preparedness as a basic condition for interpretative reading, and thus rejects the architecture of the two-tiered curriculum. The language program director can use ideas and terminology from the field of hermeneutics to conceptualize and communicate the merits of a fully integrated language/culture curriculum. Using hermeneutics in tandem with applied linguistics as a conceptual framework is particularly useful in a curriculum development process where colleagues from a variety of subfields collaborate. Supplementing the repertoire of a language program director with a conceptual framework that transcends the realm of applied linguistics will help him or her to craft an effective argument for a contemporary curriculum and be a strong advocate for this learning environment within and beyond the department.

2. Hermeneutics and comprehension research acknowledge the interpretative authority of the language learner. This provides a powerful argument for the language program director to challenge his or her department to adopt more learner-centered teaching practices. In contrast to most language instructors, there tends to be more resistance among literature instructors to develop and use innovative learning formats. Since the fully integrated language/culture curriculum will no longer have "pure" language versus literature instructors, the entire faculty needs

to rethink their teaching, and some colleagues might benefit from theorizing their instruction through hermeneutics.

3. Hermeneutics can also be applied to foreign language pedagogy in order to help conceptualize and articulate educational outcomes of individual foreign language programs. This will be of great benefit to a language program director who wants to engage an entire department in a collaborative effort to reform an undergraduate program. A redefinition of educational objectives is the initial step of any fundamental curricular reform, and conceiving and articulating new goals entirely through the discourse of language acquisition theory may not only create dissonances in a department but also result in a set of educational goals that remain biased against the development of critical literacy skills and cultural awareness.

4. Applying Gadamer's concept of the fusion of horizons to second-language acquisition provides a surprisingly practical template for the effective implementation of literary and visual narrative in the second-language classroom. The present chapter exemplifies this with its brief discussion of implementing foreign films and their American remakes into an advanced undergraduate classroom. Gadamer's fusion of horizons relates directly to transcultural approaches to foreign language education. Therefore, hermeneutics can assume a very practical role in responding to the challenges laid out in the 2007 MLA Report by aiding in the development of pedagogical approaches and practices that reinvigorate the curriculum on all levels by emphasizing transcultural literacy.

In addition to these practical concerns for the language program director, an application of hermeneutics to foreign language education contributes significantly to the theory–practice debate: a contemporary curriculum in collegiate foreign language education not only will have to provide the learner with linguistic training and "a critical appreciation of the accomplishments and failings of the other culture" (Bernhardt & Berman, 1999, p. 30) but ultimately must challenge students to develop an awareness of culture that transcends the all-too-common binary of *us* versus *them*. Integrating hermeneutics with foreign language education provides an opportunity to articulate this goal and a template for instructional models. Hermeneutics is therefore at the same time a practical addition to the language program director's toolbox and a theoretical framework to fundamentally rethink and redesign a variety of ingrained structures in collegiate foreign language education.

References

Anderson, R. C. (1984). Role of the reader's schema in comprehension, learning, and memory. In R. C. Anderson, J. Osborn, & R. J. Tierney (Eds.), *Learning to read in American schools: Basal readers and texts* (pp. 243–257). Hillsdale, NJ: Lawrence Erlbaum Associates.

Barnett, M. A. (1991). Language and literature: False dichotomies, real allies. *ADFL Bulletin, 22*(3), 7–11.

Berman, R. A. (1994). Global thinking, local teaching: Departments, curricula, and culture. *ADFL Bulletin, 26*(1), 7–11.

Bernhardt, E. B. (1990). A model of L2 text reconstruction: The recall of literary text by learners of German. In A. Labarka & L. Bailey (Eds.), *Issues in L2: Theory as practice/practice as theory* (pp. 21–43). Norwood, NJ: Ablex.

Bernhardt, E. B. (1991). *Reading development in a second language: Theoretical, empirical, and classroom perspectives.* Norwood, NJ: Ablex.

Bernhardt, E. B. (1995). Teaching literature or teaching students? *ADFL Bulletin,* 26(2), 5–6.

Bernhardt, E. B. (2001). Research into the teaching of literature in a second language: What it says and how to communicate it to graduate students. In H. Tucker & V. Scott (Eds.), *SLA and the literature classroom: Fostering dialogues* (pp. 189–204). Boston: Heinle.

Bernhardt, E. B. (2005). Progress and procrastination in second language reading. *Annual Review of Applied Linguistics, 25,* 133–150.

Bernhardt, E. B., & Berman, R. A. (1999). From German 1 to German studies 001: A chronicle of curricular reform. *Die Unterrichtspraxis/Teaching German, 32*(1), 22–31.

Bhabha, H. (1994). *The location of culture.* London: Routledge.

Bruner, J. (1996). *The culture of education.* Cambridge, MA: Harvard University Press.

Byram, M. (1997). *Teaching and assessing intercultural communicative competence.* Clevedon: Multilingual Matters.

Byrnes, H., & Kord S. (2002). Developing literacy and literacy competence: Challenges for foreign language departments. In H. Tucker & V. Scott (Eds.), *SLA and the literature classroom: Fostering dialogues* (pp. 31–69). Boston: Heinle.

Carlisle, A. (2000). Reading logs: An application of reader-response theory in EFL. *ELT Journal, 54*(1), 12–19.

Carter, R. (2007). Literature and language teaching 1986–2006: a review. *International Journal of Applied Linguistics, 17*(1), 3–13.

Chun, D. M., & Plass, J. L. (1996). Research on text comprehension with multimedia. *Language Learning and Technology, 1*(1), 60–81.

Culler, J. (2000). *Literary theory: A very short introduction.* Oxford: Oxford University Press.

Davis, J. N. (1989). The act of reading in the foreign language: Pedagogical implications of Iser's reader-response theory. *Modern Language Journal, 73*(4), 420–428.

Davis, J. N. (1992). Reading literature in the foreign language: The comprehension/response connection. *French Review, 65*(3), 359–370.

Fecteau, M. L. (1999). First- and second-language reading comprehension of literary texts. *Modern Language Journal, 83*(4), 475–493.

Ferraris, M. (1996). *History of hermeneutics.* Atlantic Highlands, NJ: Humanities Press International.

Fish, S. (1982). *Is there a text in this class? The authority of interpretive communities.* Cambridge, MA: Harvard University Press.

Gadamer, H.-G. (1989). *Truth and method* (J. Weinsheimer & D. G. Marshall, Trans.). New York: Crossroad. (Original work published 1960)

Gilliam, T. (Director). (1995). *Twelve monkeys* [Motion picture]. United States: Universal Pictures.

Graff, G. (1987). *Professing literature: An institutional history.* Chicago: University of Chicago Press.

Hicks, S. (Director). (2007). *No reservations* [Motion picture]. United States: Warner Bros. Pictures.

Hirvela, A. (1996). Reader-response theory and ELT. *ELT Journal, 50,* 127–134.

Iser, W. (1978). *The implied reader: Patterns of communication in prose fiction from Bunyan to Beckett.* Baltimore: Johns Hopkins University Press.

Iser, W. (1980). *The act of reading: A theory of aesthetic response.* Baltimore: Johns Hopkins University Press.

Jauss, H. R. (1982). *Toward an aesthetic of reception* (T. Bahti, Trans.). Minneapolis: University of Minnesota Press.

Katz, S., & Watzinger-Tharp, J. (2005). Toward an understanding of the role of applied linguistics in foreign language departments. *Modern Language Journal, 89*(4), 489–502.

Kern, R. (2002). Reconciling the language-literature split through literacy. *ADFL Bulletin, 33*(3), 20–24.

Kintsch, W. (1998). *Comprehension—A paradigm for cognition.* Cambridge: Cambridge University Press.

Kramsch, C. (1993). *Context and culture in language teaching*. Oxford: Oxford University Press.

Kramsch, C. (1996). The cultural component of language teaching. *Zeitschrift für interkulturellen Fremdsprachenunterricht, 1*(2), 1–13. Retrieved from http://zif.spz.tu-darmstadt.de

Kramsch, C. (1997). The privilege of the nonnative speaker. *PMLA, 112*(3), 359–369.

Langston, R. (2006). Feels like teen spirit: Teaching cultural difference through the body, affect, and gender. *Women in German Yearbook, 22*, 94–118.

Lebert. B. (1999). *Crazy: Roman*. Cologne: Kiepenheuer & Witsch.

Levine G. S., Melin, C., Crane, C., Chavez, M., & Lovik, T. A. (2008). The language program director in curricular and departmental reform: A response to the MLA ad hoc report. *Profession 2008*, 240–254.

Marker, C. (Director). (1962). *La jetée* [Motion picture]. France: Argos Films.

Marshall, J. (2000). Research on response to literature. In M. L. Kamil, P. B. Mosenthal, P. D. Pearson, & R. Barr (Eds.), *Handbook of reading research* (Vol. 3, pp. 381–402). Mahwah, NJ: Lawrence Erlbaum Associates.

Maxim, H. H. (2006). Integrating textual thinking into the introductory college-level foreign language classroom. *Modern Language Journal, 90*(1), 19–32.

Melin, C. (2010). Between the lines: When culture, language and poetry meet in the classroom. *Language Teaching, 43*(3), 349–365.

Mittman, E. (1999). In search of a coherent curriculum: Integrating the third-year foreign language classroom. *Foreign Language Annals, 32*(4), 480–493.

Modern Language Association. (2007). Foreign languages and higher education: New structures for a changed world. Retrieved from http://www.mla.org/flreport

Nettelbeck, S. (Director). (2001). *Bella Martha* [Motion picture]. Germany: Bavaria Film.

Nietzsche, F. (1997). *Untimely meditations* (D. Breazeale, Trans.). Cambridge: Cambridge University Press.

Paran, A. (2008). The role of literature in instructed foreign language learning and teaching: An evidence-based survey. *Language Teaching, 41*(4), 465–496.

Rutherford, J. (1990). The third space. Interview with Homi Bhabha. In J. Rutherford (Ed.), *Identity: Community, culture, difference* (pp. 207–221). London: Lawrence and Wishart.

Scholes, R. (1985). *Textual power: Literary theory and the teaching of English*. New Haven, CT: Yale University Press.

Schleiermacher, F. D. E. (1998). *Hermeneutics and criticism and other writings* (A. Bowie, Trans.). Cambridge: Cambridge University Press. (Original work published 1838)

Shklovsky, V. (1990). *Theory of prose* (B. Sher, Trans.). Naperville, IL: Dalkey.

Seitz, M. Z. (2007, July 27). If you can't stand the analysis of work and parenthood, get out of the kitchen. *New York Times*. Retrieved from http://www.nytimes.com

Stanovich, K. E. (1980). Toward an interactive-compensatory model of individual differences in the development of reading fluency. *Reading Research Quarterly, 16*(1), 32–71.

Steffensen, M., Joag-Dev, C., & Anderson, R. (1979). A cross-cultural perspective on reading comprehension. *Reading Research Quarterly, 15*(1), 10–29.

Stillings, N. A., Feinstein, M., Garfield, J. L., Rissland, E. L., Rosenbaum, D. A., Weisler, S. E., et al. (1987). *Cognitive science: An introduction*. Cambridge, MA: MIT Press.

Swaffar, J. (1988). Readers, texts and second languages: The interactive processes. *Modern Language Journal, 72*(2), 123–149.

Swaffar, J., & Arens, K. (2005). *Remapping the foreign language curriculum: A multi-literacies approach*. New York: Modern Language Association.

Swaffar, J., Arens, K., & Byrnes, H. (1991). *Reading for meaning: An integrated approach to language learning*. Englewood Cliffs, NJ: Prentice Hall.

Chapter 5
Toward a Contact Pragmatics of Literature: Habitus, Text, and the Advanced Second-Language Classroom

David Gramling, University of Arizona

Chantelle Warner, University of Arizona

Abstract

Drawing on field/practice theory and pragmatic stylistics, this chapter proposes a new aggregate model for upper-level second-language literature teaching called "contact pragmatics." While fostering a native-like reading context, teachers can simultaneously encourage students to recognize literature as a form of social practice articulating to various, loosely concentric fields of interpretation: from the native "ratified" reader to the "unintended" second-language reader position. Contact pragmatics shifts pedagogical focus to the interstices, overlaps, misalignments, and disjunctions between these concentric fields, acknowledging that at their center lies a linguistic utterance designed to operate within certain fields of opposition and exchange. Contact pragmatics thus expands the scope of pedagogical inquiry from the historical, national, and cultural resonance of a given text to its social embeddedness in a shifting landscape of linguistic markets. The chapter offers concrete, classroom-based examples of the pedagogical dilemmas and experiences that gave rise to this concept as well as suggestions for how to incorporate it in curricular design.

Introduction

We begin with a story of split expectations, or—as social theorist Pierre Bourdieu might call them—"misaligned habituses." The homework for the day was to read the short text "Familie in Kürze" (Family in Brief) by Elisabeth Alexander. Because of its relatively simple vocabulary and sentence structures, this particular literary vignette often appears in second- and third-year German language textbooks. The version displayed in the second-year German text *Mitlesen, Mitteilen*, in use in the course at hand, prefaces Alexander's domestic portrait with a short biography of the author:

> Elisabeth Alexander was born in 1932 in Linz/Rheinland and lives in Heidelberg. She attended a Catholic girls school but married before completing her secondary education. She later earned her *Abitur* the hard way by attending an *Abendgymnasium*. Her career as a writer began with the publication of poems in 1963. Since 1970, she has been a freelance writer and journalist. In this story as well as in her many other short stories and two novels, she depicts the role of a wife and mother in a male-dominated bourgeois society. "Familie in Kürze" (Family in Brief) is taken from her collection

Damengeschichten (Stories of Ladies), first published in 1983. She has also written a collection of *Herrengeschichten* (Stories of Men; 1990). (Alexander, 2008, pp. 26–27)

This introduction positions the spotlighted literary text for a certain didactic function in a third-semester course, a content-based language class covering post-World War II German history and culture. That week, the class was beginning a chapter on Germany in the 1970s and 1980s that included a section on feminism and women's movements. The references made here to Alexander's bourgeois childhood and young marriage link her biography to an interpretation of "Familie in Kürze" (Family in Brief) that the textbook authors expect to solicit—namely, that this text depicts "the role of wife and mother in a male-dominated society." For the instructor, a female graduate student, terms like "male-dominated" and "bourgeois," coupled with the date of publication, 1983—arguably the peak of the German women's movements— could signal nothing if not a deliberately critical view of gendered divisions of labor in modern German society. While the story is told tersely and soberly by a third-person narrator, the extensive details about this housewife and mother's cooking and clean- ing, as well as the lack of information about her feelings and thoughts, could—from the instructor's point of view—not possibly be interpreted as an euphoric tableau of women's social subjectivity. Moreover, this was an understanding that she expected her students would easily share, and her lesson plan was designed to direct students toward the linguistic means by which this critique was being waged and then to begin to tie in some historical information in preparation for the following day's lesson. She was then appropriately caught off guard when two of her eight students, both female, had come to a completely different interpretation. "I would rather be the woman in this story, because she takes good care of her family and feels happy and fulfilled," wrote one of the female students.

There was clearly nothing wrong—inferentially or analytically—with the student's response to this first of the textbook's suggested discussion questions: "Would you rather be the woman or the man in this story?" After all, the question directly asks for a personal preference, and yet, in light of the second question— "The style of the author is such that she narrates without commentary. Does she also narrate without any criticism? Why?"—it also seems to be guiding students to reiterate the same socially critical reading that the instructor had assumed, a reading that would perhaps come as second nature for the story's intended German audience. Yet nothing explicit within the text addresses the happiness or unhappiness of the female figure. Whether her life leaves her feeling fulfilled remains unthematized. What we do know is that she "cooks well. She cleans well. She can also bake well." The vocabulary and grammatical structures were clear to the student, giving the text a "consistent interpretation" (Carrell, 1984). Can it possibly be said, then, that the students had misread the text?

To pose the question differently, what constitutes an appropriate reading of such a text by our advanced second-language students? Numerous studies have demonstrated the vital role that background knowledge and interpretive schemas play in analytical reading (Altmayer, 2002; Bernhardt, 1991; Carrell, 1984; Swaffer, Arens, & Byrnes, 1991). It could be argued that the students lacked the cultural knowledge and experience that had guided the instructor and textbook authors to treat Alexander's vignette as a critique and that the contextualization provided was simply not sufficient to attune the students to the cultural climate of Germany in the 1980s. However, citing *contextualization* as a supporting pedagogical framework only raises more—and more precarious—questions about our use of the literary text in an advanced second-language classroom. What is the advantage of teaching literary works at the intermediate and advanced levels of language study if not to expose students to exactly this kind of cultural information in a more embedded format, while also introducing them to longer and more complex stretches of text?[1] This leaves instructors in a methodological double bind. Either the cultural information must be supplied by the instructor and/or the textbook, thus railroading a specific, sanctified, "native" interpretation of the literary text, risking cultural reification, and preempting students' readings of the text, *or* lessons focus on the students' personal readings that emanate from their experiences as nonnative language learners. In the latter case, one risks neglecting the fact that other readers, including—and perhaps most importantly—the intended audience of the text, might be operating under other schemas of interpretation that are themselves socially inculcated and thus as analytically consequential as the cultural content that the text was meant to provide.[2] Most textbooks' historicist treatments of literature include a mixture of both of these approaches, and yet neither really gets students to any deeper understanding of literary discourse as a dynamic site of intersection between language and culture, nor do they promote the development of literacy in the sense of the ability "to reflect critically on communication in all the forms it takes" (Kern, 2002, p. 23).

Contextualizing the Language/Literature Curriculum Today

Of course, this contemporary classroom scenario of text and context resides within a peculiar institutional context of its own. As language instructors, program coordinators, and university professors, we find ourselves in an era characterized by at least three complex trends: (1) the diplomatic, one-language/one-culture model of cross-cultural study is losing its heuristic credibility (see Block & Cameron, 2002; Kramsch, Howell, Warner, & Wellmon, 2007); (2) administrative and enrollment concerns have led to a fragmentation of curricular priorities among both students and teachers (the perennial vicissitudes and alternating primacy among culture, literature, or language) (see Katz, 2001; Maxim, 2006; Modern Language Association [MLA], 2007); and (3) a revolution in the *very nature* of the second language as a language-in-use, as hypertext communication technologies make daily innovations in the living language accessible to advanced students in a formidable variety of forms (see Thorne & Reinhardt, 2008). No matter how vigorously we may prize the unique permanency of the literary utterance for intellectual and pedagogical reasons, technology has decentered the literary text in advanced foreign language learning. The stable literary text now holds a minority position in relation to the reservoir of linguistic practices our students will tend to encounter every time they enter multilingual, multimedial cybertraffic.

For these reasons among others, this chapter foregrounds examples of a contact-pragmatics approach—a concept we hybridize from contact linguistics and literary pragmatics—an approach that shifts the focus of analysis from the "text itself" to the gaps and overlaps among the ways disparate native and nonnative readerly communities may tend to "comprehend" that text in variously appropriate ways. Rather than providing a native-like reading context, teachers can encourage students to recognize literature as a form of social practice articulating to various, loosely concentric fields of interpretation: from the native "ratified" reader to the unintended second-language reader. Contact pragmatics shifts pedagogical focus to the interstices, overlaps, misalignments, and disjunctions between these concentric fields, acknowledging that at their center lies a linguistic utterance designed to operate within certain primary domains of opposition and exchange.

With his analysis of the practice called "la perruque" (the wig), Michel de Certeau (1984) afforded critical value to the dynamics of what might be called the "appropriate misuse" of authoritative materials:

> La perruque is the worker's own work disguised as work for his employer. It differs from pilfering in that nothing of material value is stolen. It differs from absenteeism in that the worker is officially on the job. La perruque may be as simple a matter as a secretary's writing a love letter on "company time" or as complex as a cabinetmaker's "borrowing" a lathe to make a piece of furniture for his living room. Under different names in different countries this phenomenon is becoming more and more general, even if managers penalize it or "turn a blind eye" on it in order not to know about it. (p. 25)

What is it, then, that second-language learners "borrow on company time"— emotionally and semiotically, intentionally or unintentionally—from target-language texts and course materials designed to nurture them toward the orderly labors of native-like comprehension? Are these furtive borrowings, in the final analysis, learning practices or resistance practices? In either case, are we to "turn a blind eye" to the symbolic domains in which these reappropriative practices take place, as de Certeau suggests French factory managers do, or would we do well to welcome them into the realm of classroom analysis, perhaps under the intellectual auspices of "translingual competence"? (MLA, 2007).

We claim that contact pragmatics can augment existing literature-intensive advanced foreign language curricula, through a shift in scope, one that can be realized without a grand methodological overhaul. The subject of our consideration is not the individual classroom teacher or learner per se but rather—in Pierre Bourdieu's words—"the social and intellectual unconscious embedded in [his or her] analytic tools and operations" (Bourdieu & Wacquant, 1999, p. 36). Our wager is that advanced language teaching can complicate the myth of a unitary Germanness or Frenchness while making students aware of how culturally inculcated schemes of perception do structure how we speak, write, understand, interpret, and respond to language. We suggest a series of concepts—from practice theory, language ecology, pragmatics, and stylistics—that may be put to use in intermediate and advanced language teaching with the goal of setting some new stakes for the intersection of language, culture, and literature.

It is something of a misfortune for literary scholars working in stylistics and pragmatics that "fallacy" has been so mortally affixed to authorial "intention" in literary studies. The curse of *intentional fallacy* often means a forcible disarticulation of authoriality from text, of text from context, of utterance from field of possible utterances.[3] The proscription on so-called authorial readings still holds sway over literature curricula, and one's demonstrated willingness to bracket out an author's intended meaning has served as nothing less than a rite of passage for literary enthusiasts who wish to become literary researchers. A by-product of this doctrine is that it impedes discussion of the practical (stylistic) choices that authors make in relation to the field of possible utterances on which that text stakes its meaningfulness in a given society, that is, of how differential relations are manifested linguistically. (Said another way, the author moratorium throws the baby of sociostylistic relationality out with the bathwater of biographical reading.)

Meanwhile, though the vice of "intentional fallacy" still haunts most literature-oriented classrooms, teachers of literature tend to be much less forthright in insisting that students resist what might be called a "national fallacy," that is, the tendency to preferentially locate a text within the singular temporal and geographical construct of a given national literary history—such as "*Vormärz*," "post-Wall literature," or "the German women's movements"—and also to resist the broader assumption that a given literary utterance is primarily of interest in discourses of "Germanness" or the "German cultural tradition." Even in curricula that are conceptualized as cultural studies or viewed through the lens of New Historicism, the second-language text is most often made to perform, artificially and/or preemptively, on a stage of national identity construction. In fact, many of the texts that we, as foreign language teachers, assign—not to mention many that we might assign if it weren't for this bias—are relatively *disinterested* in the national as a rhetorical or cultural category. Often—and despite the titles of our courses—their stakes lie in arenas that are at best tangential and in many cases fundamentally oblique to national coherence. Though allowing such texts to mean in "anational" or nationally indifferent ways may at first seem to destabilize our curricular paradigms, doing so will help students reflect on and expand the palette of contexts in which readers might situate a given text.

In order to describe the social universes in which social practices—including those that are predominantly linguistic or literary-textual in nature—live out their symbolic life from conception to reception, Bourdieu introduced the concept of *field*. Field, according to Bourdieu's practice theory, is a system of relative values within which a given act accrues social capital—be it implicitly or explicitly—in relation to the actions and possible actions of other players on that field (Bourdieu, 1991). Field, like context—and such related notions as "cultural moment" or "historical background"—helps to explain the social universe in which a particular work or linguistic utterance becomes possible, comprehensible, and then compulsory—in situ and in posterity. Field as a concept, however, differs from context in a few notable ways. Unlike how "context" is often operationalized in sociocultural theory, fields have durable histories that extend beyond the immediate situation of the utterance. Field is, however, not reducible to a historical background, neither in the sense of a grand national narrative nor in the material and economic conditions of a singular temporal and geographical space. Furthermore, because of the rigorous syntactical regularity of human languages, linguistic practices have a logic all their own that cannot be explained with recourse to the level of cultural discourse. For this reason, Bourdieu (1993, p. 181) cautions against what he calls the "short-circuit effect," the attempt to partner works of art directly to social or historical structures. Differential linguistic repertoires, including style and genre, are the basis for the relational value of a given literary utterance, but they are not immediately derivable from cultural history.

Turning again to the classroom anecdote with which we began, we can reexamine the problem of context, which was arguably to blame for the diverging interpretations among the instructor and her two students. Through the course materials and the thematic unit within which this text was read, the students had been presented with a historical context for the vignette, namely, the German women's movements of the 1970s and 1980s. They had been given some biographical context in the form of the introductory paragraph cited earlier. The historical background and biographical information were intended to direct the students' attention toward the historically situated thematic unit within which the vignette had been featured, but Alexander's text does not explicitly thematize women's problems. On the contrary, the critique is waged not through what is emphasized but through that which is left unsaid. This is pointed out in one of discussions questions included in *Mitlesen, Mitteilen* that asked students to consider what we as readers *don't* learn about the woman through the text and what significance this might have (Morewedge, 2008). In order to see how "Familie in Kürze" functions as social criticism, what the students seemed to be missing was an awareness of the sociostylistic context, for example, the textual practice of using life stories as socially critical exempla—a practice that was peaking in the midst of the German social movements of the mid-1970s. Treating the story primarily as a conveyor of themes, the textbook led students to focus on the "what," the informational value of a stretch of discourse, but their unfamiliarity with stylistic and generic contexts left them unable to critically apprehend the "how." As a lens through which we locate and organize texts and the social work that they perform, the concept of *field* reminds us that historical epochs, national discourses, and the biographical situations make up only one sphere of a given work's "context."

Reading Relationally

Theorists from Norbert Elias to M. A. K. Halliday to George Lakoff have stressed how our "ordinary language" privileges metaphors that close the door on certain lines of thought. For Elias, the problem is that our languages privilege substances and states rather than relations and processes, thereby making it difficult for us to perceive linguistic utterances as socially situated practices rather than as ideal forms or inherent structures. If this is true in our "ordinary languages," the problem is only compounded when one is struggling to figure out what "ordinary language" might be in a second-language context. Caught up in the earnest work of sorting out new grammars, new vocabularies, and new frameworks of meaning making, our students tend therefore to approach the language as structural sets and rules rather than as moves and tactics within a dynamic field of social play. Without pedagogical encouragement, they are therefore *far less likely* to pursue a relational stance toward speaking in that second language than, perhaps, in their home languages. Generic schemas, in the sense of typified ways of producing and receiving texts, are vastly less accessible to foreign language readers regardless of their surface-level proficiency.[4] Generic markers also point to the fields in which a given utterance participates and to which positions it will conventionally be assigned. This is one of the reasons behind the much-cited fact that foreign language learners often have trouble understanding the more global and social meanings of a text, even as they clearly understand individual words and sentences (see Carrell, 1988; Kaplan, 1966; Long, 1989; Nostrand, 1989).

For instance, Byram and Kramsch (2008) describe the difficulties inherent in teaching texts that presume interpretive schemas very different from those familiar to the students, through the example of a fourth-semester German class at the University of California, Berkeley. The students in the course were asked to read a series of literary texts from or about East Germany. The authors note that although students were making use of the structures and vocabulary they had learned while reading literary works about adolescence in East Germany, their understanding of the concepts and ideas in the texts was circumscribed by their own personal experiences. Byram, the instructor of the course in question, notes in an excerpt from the teaching logbook that she kept at that time,

> Most of my students were too young to remember a time when socialism was a viable worldview, and class discussions showed that their interpretations and evaluations of texts by East German authors were colored by their post-Communist American viewpoint. Even more distressing, they seemed unable to recognize that their perspective was influenced by their historical and ideological circumstances. (Byram & Kramsch, (2008, p. 28)

In other words, the students were accessing "American" schemas in order to understand "German" texts. Byram goes on to observe that, for this reason, the students in the course immediately dismissed texts narrated from a "socialist" perspective as propaganda while understanding similar texts told from a more familiar "Western" point of view as informative. The pedagogical problem that Byram and Kramsch highlight here is similar to the one introduced earlier with Alexander's "Familie in Kürze." Rather than treating the texts relationally as products and processes of complex social exchange, the students were evaluating only the information presented, and they were doing so through the only interpretive frameworks that they knew. But how could they be helped to understand that categorizing discourse into "propaganda" versus "information" was a positional practice and that the same text might be read very differently by someone who had been raised and educated in different cultural and ideological circumstances?

Bourdieu's concept of the habitus can help us to understand the difficulties that we, as language teachers and learners, face when confronted with new schemas and new fields/worlds of representation. The sociological concept of habitus, as used by theorists such as Norbert Elias and Marcel Maus, refers to those aspects of culture that are anchored in the everyday habits of individuals or groups. Bourdieu later defined habitus, notoriously, as "systems of durable, transposable dispositions, structured structures predisposed to act as structuring structures" (Bourdieu, 1977, p. 72). In short, the habitus encompasses the many schemas with which a person might be socially inculcated as well as a sense of who can use them, in what fields of practice they appear, and what values and meanings they will typically garner. Because it operates through our predisposed habits, tastes, and beliefs in relation to the fields within which we do our linguistic practices, the habitus serves a preemptively normalizing function. Though habitus does not mechanically determine the positions taken by social actors, such as our students, we nonetheless come to anticipate—through its "structuring structures"—certain types of social action from certain actors in certain fields. This is even the case when the "social actors" we encounter are our very own selves in the midst of practice, as we assess (often subconsciously) what actions are feasible and favorable. The habitus accounts for the fact that our thought structures are tied to social and material conditions of everyday practices (see also Lantolf & Thorne, 2006); the cognitive is thus always already cultural. By virtue of the habitus, individuals are inclined to seek certain pursuits, avow certain tastes, and interpret in certain ways (Bourdieu, 1991). In the vocabulary of language ecology, the habitus works to determine what "affordances," what opportunities for acting we (human actors) perceive as possible or appropriate. A given reader's or speaker's habitus, as it articulates to the fields germane to that person's social position, drives two important processes: *euphemistic censorship*, the sanctioning of certain ways of acting, speaking, and interpreting, typically without any external directive or coercion; and *misrecognition*, the symbolic manifestation of social power in ways that make it appear to be a force of some other kind—something rooted in atemporal or natural truth, value, or necessity (Bourdieu, 1991). In our estimation, it was this second operation of *misrecognition* that led the students in Byram and Kramsch's account simply to accept the familiar perspective as information while dismissing another perspective as propaganda. Misrecognition can in turn lead to censorship in that it becomes an interpretive disposition shared by individuals who participate in the same field(s). This is perhaps one of the most powerful lessons at the higher levels of foreign language study: recognizing that one's angle on the world (or a text) is not commonsensical or truthful. Advanced language learners are not just incrementally honing their proficiency; they are accessing and inhabiting new frameworks of conceptualization as well.

Yet, thanks to the "durability" of habitus, social actors such as our students spontaneously reproduce long-held ways of "styling" in the world—unintentionally, contrary to their acquired second-language proficiency, and without considering these behaviors on the level of discourse. For centuries, explicit grammar instruction has served as an artificial booster for teaching adult learners certain types of linguistic forms by highlighting structural norms and recurring paradigms that are socially incommensurable with those learners' habitus. Similarly, a differential stylistics grounded in practice theory could help learners to become cognizant of the ways in which discursive effects are generally linked with particular, authorized and legitimated forms. In order to make students aware of how unfamiliar schemas operate and how they are signaled through symbolic means—such as schema headers, linguistic deixis, and point of view—our task as language teachers is to make apparent that which is typically misrecognized, or "read over."

The key is therefore not to generate advanced language learners who speak, think, or react in a certain way but rather to promote active recognition of the field-contingent restraints on legitimate and authorized language in a given genre of speech or text—in other words, to invest in a habitus-based understanding of how people read, how they "precognize" the position they are to take up in the *social* game of reading. Meanwhile, they become aware of the fact that there are other players taking positions, simultaneously, in their midst: other students, teachers, reviewers, authors, native and nonnative speakers, social entities, and communities. This kind of relationality is the proper purview of twenty-first-century language curricula and a pedagogy that *teaches* through an idiom of traffic, translation, positionality, and relationality. In the realm of foreign language learning, this network of position-takings is doubly rich with what contact pragmatics (i.e., a convergence of at least two universes of expectation) can bring to bear on a particular text and its relation to intended and nonintended readers. To return to a question posed at the beginning of this chapter, the assessment of reading comprehension is not reducible to whether students have correctly or incorrectly understood a text. Instructors and students together must also consider the ways in which the legitimacy of different interpretations is regulated, how linguistic styles and genres are connected to these processes, and what new meanings their emerging transcultural positions as second-language learners might tend to privilege.

Contact Pragmatics and Differential Stylistics

In developing a working definition of contact pragmatics, we consider the following aspects: (1) the universe of discursive precognitions that "native" (i.e., intended) readers may have of a certain text; (2) the oblique, ill-fitted, and unsanctioned presumptions that nonnative, second-language readers of such an utterance may tend to have; (3) the generic, stylistic, and formal properties of the text where the precognitions mentioned in items 1 and 2 may overlap; and (4) the constellation of differences (or, in Bourdieu's terms, the distribution of symbolic capital) that obtain when the first three aspects are analyzed in tandem and with equal weight. Contact pragmatics would assume that neither the native nor the nonnative interpretive presuppositions are more analytically "correct" than the other and that much can be learned about the legitimacy conditions of a given field by playing on these using "the wrong rules," as some of the students reading Alexander's text did.

In the illustrations of contact pragmatics that follow, we hope to demonstrate how texts can index a socially situated exchange by stylistic means—one not only between a solitary, abstract implied author and a solitary, abstract implied reader but also between the following:

- Two or more social entities (persons, groups, imagined communities) obliged by institutional orthodoxy or societal directive to address and listen to one another on certain topics of interest and not others;
- Two or more social entities who monitor each other's expectations and responses to the textual artifact in question, often through paratexts and posttexts;
- Two or more social entities who use intratextual means to preempt, or "precognize," the responses of others;
- Two or more social entities with obliquely overlapping linguistic repertoires, where these overlaps are an explicit or implicit concern of the text;
- Two or more social entities with heavily documented and often ritualized modes of perceiving, addressing, imposing on, offending, hailing, or describing one another;
- More than two social entities, one of which is implicitly or explicitly an unconsecrated bystander to the symbolic exchange taking place between two others. (Often, this oblique position is where our second-language students find themselves located.)

From this point of view, texts are occasions not only for aesthetic appreciation, but, in the words of Irving Goffman (1964), also for "mutual monitoring possibilities" among actors as they position themselves within a social landscape. Our pedagogical purview thus extends to the contacts and conflicts that have ensured the text its exchangeability in situ. The question remains, can one teach toward such a pragmatic critique by using primarily intratextual means?

To provide or not to provide context is, however, a dilemma that arises in almost any given advanced second-language teaching method. Granting primary emphasis to national-historical context can cause students to feel unsteady about the legitimacy of their own interpretations, leading even those individuals who enjoy reading to proclaim that they dislike "the study of literature." This became clear in a recent seminar taught by Chantelle Warner at the University of Arizona that had the ambitious goal of relating more than nine centuries of German cultural history to a group consisting of both advanced undergraduates and first-year master's students. One of the longer works read during the semester, Johann Wolfgang von Goethe's *Die Leiden des jungen Werther* (The Sorrows of Young Werther), elicited some of the strongest reactions from the class participants. In the reaction journals, which they kept as part of the course work, several students decried Werther's "whininess" and an allegedly pervasive "melodrama" in the work. Their encounter with Goethe's epistolary novel had been complemented by readings and in-class discussions of the historical background, including the literary historical context of *Storm and Stress*, to which the work belonged, and they were more than capable of relating these facts to aspects of the work; however, what was leaving them cold was the fact that their responses of disdain, repulsion, and in some cases even empathy or amusement so often had no place in upper-division language and literature courses (see Krueger, 2001). They were, to borrow the words of Sally Magnan (2004, p. 97), not being ratified as "participant users" of Goethe's text. Moreover, they had not gained any further understanding of literary language as anything more than a conveyor of historical discourses, something bereft of social power, sociolinguistic intimacy, and pragmatic force.

What was initially missing from the lessons was a pedagogy that could enable students to analyze their own affective and stylistic reactions to the text as something intellectually relevant, something that they could channel into a better understanding of the pragmatic horizon of the work in Goethe's time. The first step was to recognize that the evaluative adjectives with which students peppered their journal entries—whiny, annoying, and melodramatic—were responding to identifiable stylistic effects of language in the text and not to overall, extralinguistic mood or aura. The sentence breaks, exclamations, and parenthetical interjections that "characterize" Werther are discrete features of the language, as is the overwhelmingly subjectivist perspective that obtains in its epistolary form. Using these textual features as a starting point, students could be encouraged to explore phenomena of "contact" from various angles. The following are sample activities:

- Consider what descriptive words Goethe's contemporaries might have used to describe the effects of the same textual features that had led students to perceive Werther as whiny. The students can be given examples from contemporary reception (e.g., from Reclam's corresponding *Erläuterungen und Dokumente*) and cull their answers from these documents. Examples: "empfindungsvoll" (sentimental), "allzuweiches Herz und feuerige Phantasie" (an all-too-tender heart and fiery fantasy), "Schwärmerey" (excessive sentimentality), "überspannt" (high-strung), "entsprungene Desperation" (emanating desperation), "dieses gefährliche Extrem des sentimentalischen Charakters" (this dangerous extreme of the sentimental character). Based on this list of descriptive terms, students can ascertain to what degree Goethe's eighteenth-century readers were evaluating the same textual features negatively or positively and compare them with the reception by the class. In the case of *Werther* reception, students may notice that many of Goethe's contemporaries also viewed Werther's outbursts of emotion with derision or alarm. The analysis of these varied pragmatic effects also allows students to explore the dynamic and often contested fields of practice within which the work played out as opposed to seeing the text as merely a point within a static line of literary history.
- Are there genres or fields of practice in contemporary U.S. society in which comparable textual features might be found? If so, what are the typical effects of these stylistic devices? In considering stylistics in this way, students are able to see that the various meanings that linguistic features bear are themselves social and conventional. Students might, for example, note that many of the same stylistic devices can also be found in Twitter and texting genres, with their frequent use of exclamatory expressions and ellipses. This leaves them to contemplate whether the sense of melodrama that they perceived is also linked to other textual

and extratextual features of the work, such as the *foreignness* of the eighteenth-century German or the topic at hand: Werther's love for the figure Lotte.

- Are there genres or practices today that you would describe using the terms that some of Goethe's contemporaries applied to his work? For example, what texts do you perceive as "empfindungsvoll" (sentimental)? Discuss the differences between the textual features of these phenomena and of Goethe's *Werther*. Are there notable differences between the fields of practice within which they participate? Like the previous set of questions, the aim of this line of inquiry is to turn students' attention to points of convergence and divergence between the pragmatic effects of a given text in two distinct times and places—in other words, in two fields of practice.

Such activities not only create new intellectual inroads by which students can access the larger historical context, which was the stated objective of this survey course, but also recast the works as *socially* situated acts of symbolic exchange in which the students may not be the most ratified of interlocutors but are nevertheless legitimate participants.

Another face of contact pragmatics emerges when we consider the works of the contemporary Berlin-based author Emine Sevgi Özdamar, whose texts regularly destabilize the pragmatic horizons that demarcate a field such as "multicultural literature" or "new German literature." Acutely aware of the position of cultural contact that her texts inhabit between multiple pragmatic universes, Özdamar routinely exploits the uneven distribution of symbolic capital between "native" and "nonnative" reading practices by including utterances and backchannel references that would bear symbolic capital among some readerships and not others. Whereas the previous example suggests how twenty-first century students can become "participant users" of Goethe's late eighteenth-century novel, Özdamar's texts dramatize the social dynamics by which legitimate "participation" in a textual event is afforded and intratextually rescinded, often in the course of one turn of phrase.

As we suggested in the introduction earlier, twentieth-century literary-theoretical legacies provide ample support for both historicist (whether New or old) and text-immanent (i.e., New Critical or New Formalist) approaches to analytical reading in classroom settings. Under these two spheres of influence, the text is either a freestanding aesthetic artifact or a bearer of historicity and an actor on history. (In the main, teachers of upper-level literature and culture courses tend to allow texts to be, in some way, both aesthetic and historical.) What is less than present on this binary spectrum, however, is the possibility that a given text may be social and perhaps primarily so: that its gamut of investments and intensions may be part of a situated exchange—or an extended stretch of talk—between persons, communities, and institutions. While this notion of text as embedded social act comes as no surprise to researchers in linguistic anthropology, education, or discourse analysis, the social nature of textual artifacts remains itinerant, if not homeless, in literary studies—despite inroads from reader-response and reception theories of the 1980s. While historicist approaches continue to locate textual meaning through webs of intertextuality, they neglect the fact that Bakhtinian dialogism, from which Julia Kristeva later developed this concept, referred not merely to an infinite matrix of literary citation but also to the social call-and-response in which the work engages (Bakhtin, 1994; Goffman, 1964).

Taking Özdamar's 1988 *Karagöz in Alamania* as an example, a text can thus be apprehended not as a stand-alone literary artifact but as an opening "response bid" in a cycle of bidding about "multiculturalism" in post-Wall Germany that would last 20 years. Its appreciability as an aesthetic artifact notwithstanding, this text is quintessentially "excitable" speech, in Judith Butler's (1997) sense of language with consequences, but it is also excited and exciting speech—at the level of the word, the sentence, and the work as a whole: excited because it is the refined rebuttal to a sustained institutional campaign throughout the 1980s to confer native-informant value on a certain narrative regime related to multiculturalism and Turkish migration in West Germany and exciting because it is structured and stylized in such a way as to hail various social personae among its readers as interlocutors, thereby questioning not only the position of "minority author" but also the field of "multicultural literature."

To further our conceptual exploration of contact pragmatics in second-language classrooms, the following analysis of *Karagöz* will try to push beyond the tropes that tend to garnish multiculturalist literary analysis—particularly those of "playing with the reader's expectations," "undermining stereotypes," and "destabilizing norms." While these are indeed time-honored rhetorical operations, the tropes themselves are not specific enough to account for the rich contact-pragmatic aura of this text. Özdamar's *Karagöz in Alamania* is designed to oscillate between accommodation and opacity, between consolation and disintegration; its routine overtures to the reader intend not only to ensure transparency for German readers but also to simultaneously undermine native-speaker privilege. Its bilingual title, for instance, *Karagöz in Alamania/Schwarzauge in Deutschland* (Black Eye in Germany) obscures as much as it clarifies about the story's translingual bearing. To translate the Turkish "karagöz" into the German "Schwarzauge" (Black Eye) does very little to inform the addressee about the word's meaning; *karagöz* is an Anatolian tradition of satirical shadow puppetry. Still, the gesture of translation itself transfers interpretive responsibility away from Turkish-speaking readers and onto German speakers. Meanwhile, the translation of Alamania into "Deutschland" (Germany), in turn, indexes a discrepancy between oral and written cultures; the standard Turkish for "Germany" is the three-syllable "Almanya" rather than the potentially four- or five-syllable "Alamania" used here (Özdamar, 1998). What appears to have been the writer's polite accommodation of the non-Turkish-speaking reader is also simultaneously an imposition and subterfuge. A disorienting, stereoscopic function of utterance is thus in force even in the text's title.

While an advanced second-language classroom discussion about this text might typically prompt students to identify lexical clusters such as its first line, "Es war einmal ein Dorf" (Once upon a time there was a village), in order to orient students toward genre-specific conventions, a contact-pragmatics approach helps students understand not "what" the text is but rather "where it stands" in a field of social negotiations. Questions for students might include the following: Why is a bilingual (i.e., subtitled) title such a strange symbolic gift for a writer to confer on his or her readers? What social circumstances tend to be inscribed in such an exchange? Students may take this occasion to describe their beliefs about translation and translatability as such: Is a translation a replacement for an original language? Is a translation usually between two languages only? Does translating guarantee both equivalence of meaning and equity of access? Does it increase understanding or rather perpetuate cultural alienation? Given appropriate time to prepare, students can narrate stories about situations in which they have experienced translation as a kind of violation, when translational acts have exacerbated understanding or consensus as much as it facilitated them.

As they read the first few pages of the text, students may be asked whether they notice ways in which translation—as a mode of social exchange—continues to structure the narrative. The narrator frequently interprets for the characters whose utterances she animates, using such on-record gestures of disambiguation as "Er meinte damit, dass . . ." (With that he meant that . . .) Perhaps students will also notice the writer's oddly bald-faced metadiscursive explanation about the conversation underway between the two protagonists: "Die beiden sprachen über dieses Geschäft nicht direkt, sondern in Sprichwörtern" (Neither character said anything about this business directly; rather, they spoke in sayings). Like the text's intended domestic audience, advanced second-language students might register frustration about how this sentence preemptively flouts Grice's (1975) pragmatic maxim of quantity—a contribution ought to be as informative and only as informative as is required for the current purposes of the exchange. Shouldn't the textual evidence itself—the words the characters exchange with one another on the page—suffice to indicate to readers whether their talk is direct or indirect, whether it is explicit or parabolic? Why, then, the quizzical rhetorical surplus and ostentatious interventionism on the part of the narrator? Students might then consider a situation in which one of their friends or relatives—perhaps even someone who speaks the second language they are learning—overexplained a practice or phenomenon of apparent mutual interest. What social roles does such an occasion distribute and/or reinscribe? How does it feel to be told how to understand something when one has already labored to produce a perfectly sufficient homegrown explanation? What might compel someone to translate others' actions in this way? Does the overexplainer do so out of habit, malice, institutional prescription, or merely misplaced good faith? In what ways does a reader feel imposed on by a narrator, and how is this affective realm particularly relevant in teaching to translingual competence? Such questions, which foreground the social and emotional physics of translingual behavior, can stimulate language students' intellectual inquiry into the vast palette of symbolic actions that constitute "language" in use.

Another early feature of Özdamar's story indicates the playfulness that can result from textual "contact" between two or more linguistic habituses. Take, for instance, the progressive constitution of new social positions that occurs over the text's first pages, as the narrator attempts to naturalize one of the figures into an emergent, artificial lexicon between writer and reader. At first, each character is named loosely according to his or her actions: the one who stole apples, the one who possesses a tree. Gradually, as the narrative establishes a space for precedent and mutual orientation among writer and intended addressee, the everyday, descriptive noun phrases "the possessor of the apple tree" are replaced by the bureaucratically tinged neologism apple-tree-possessor (Özdamar, 1998). From a contact-pragmatic point of view, we can understand this progressive series of reified equivalences as an ironized recasting of German immigration discourse—that is, the institutional invention of civic identities for non–European Union immigrants through legal categories like *Gastarbeiter* (guest worker), *Kontingenzflüchtling* (contingency refugee), *Heimatvertriebene* (person driven out of his or her homeland and those expelled from parts of Germany annexed by Poland or Russia), *Aufenthaltsbefugnis* (residence warrant), *and ausländische Mitbürger* (foreign fellow citizen), all of which bear the durable power to regulate nonnative activity on German soil. Through the inconspicuous dubbing of an *"Appletreepossessor,"* the narrator dramatizes a process of euphemistic implantation by social-pragmatic means: how an inchoate, unprecedented phenomenon becomes a recognizable term through cooperative talk and discursive exchange. Pragmatic "contact" is signaled here also through the narrative's incremental, tactical appropriation of a linguistic feature of German that does not exist as such in Turkish (or in English), namely, a fondness for compound words.

An aspect of contact is simultaneously afoot as the classroom-based second-language student, the intended domestic-native reader, and the Turkish-German multilingual author symbolically converge on the dubious linguistic legitimacy of "appletreeposessor"—in implicit opposition to, say, "guest worker." By learning through such examples that the appropriateness conditions for a given language item develop not through a central native authority but rather through contact and conflict between various speech communities, students can develop a nuanced understanding of the politics of generativity in a second-language context and the pragmatic schemas that underlie it.

Implications

We have sought to highlight how literary texts are, with few exceptions, the artifacts of infinitely many subtle calibrations and recalibrations of appropriate social exchange as they are experienced and encoded in a given field of practice. The pragmatic transactions we have traced need not detract, however, from more traditional literary-aesthetic inquiries in the classroom. Though classroom discussions of such questions of readerly habitus may appear at first glance to do little to inform students about themes of contemporary German-Turkish affairs or the Storm and Stress period of the eighteenth century, they provide a broader metacritical occasion as students come to terms with the affective construction of nativeness and the implicit assumptions about who has a right to respond to literary texts and in what ways.[5] A contact-pragmatics approach to the teaching of texts in the foreign language classroom forces us to complicate what we accept as reading comprehension.

Students at the advanced level of language learning—and to some degree already in the earlier levels—can be reasonably expected to reflect on a few facts that should embolden, not short-circuit, a sense of purpose in their chosen field of study:

1. The metaphors of "mastery" and "acquisition," which construe language as stable, substantial, and finite, often run counter to the spirit of critical language studies, which places emphasis on positionality and relationality.

2. Language studies, considered broadly, *should* become more difficult and ambiguous in scope as one progresses to the advanced levels in a second language. Students who graduate from a communicative language program and stream into an upper-level class often assume that the only thing that has become more difficult and decentering for them is the sheer amount and complexity of the language on the pages they are assigned to read. In fact, something much more formidable is taking place. They are stepping into a field of symbolic exchanges that extends far beyond the denotative and connotative reaches of any discrete text.[6] They are becoming participant users whose legitimacy within the second language will be brokered through social dynamics rather than through accuracy or proficiency alone.

3. Intercultural understanding is not the only goal. Success in advanced language studies often simply means being able to *mark* the epistemic blind spots in a given translingual situation, not necessarily in being able to overcome that limitation—to enact the intercultural virtue known as "bridging the gap." Advanced language proficiency is arguably about being able to see those gaps even when they are not to be expeditiously overcome. Yet the diplomatic thrust of many textbooks often overlooks this fact either by adopting a rhetoric of bicultural relations, which assumes an equally invested, imagined native interlocutor on the other end, or by privileging universal conceits—rather than local takes—on topics such as gender, the environment, or multiculturalism.

In developing advanced language curricula, we instructors and program directors can also unambivalently embrace two realities: a number of students insist that they want to study language and culture but not literature. Meanwhile, we continue to attract a fair number of students who are drawn to the language exactly because they are interested in literature.[7] By seeing literature as situated social practice, we are able to speak to both. Language students today from both factions are prepared, by the globalizing tendencies of their era, to engage in a more reflexive mode of language analysis, one no longer wedded to the ideal of learning about a single national culture. They are ready to explore the varied and complex ways in which texts participate in multiple social worlds and to reflect on the stakes these texts maintain in the ever-emerging multilingual subjectivities of their readers. Engaging soberly and playfully with such questions can lead students toward a renewable curiosity about what it means to take up a lifelong position as a second-language (or third- or fourth-language) speaker and reader.

Notes

1. See, for example, the discussion of literature in the teaching of English as a foreign language in Hall (2005).

2. Compare with Schultz (2002). See also Bretz (1990), wherein she argues that students in classrooms where interpretation is driven by the instructor or the textbook may learn a lot about those particular texts but learn very little about practices of reading and interpretation.

3. The term "intentional fallacy" was coined by literary critics William Wimsatt and Monroe Beardsley in their essay of the same name, which was published in 1946 in *Sewanee Review* (Vol. 54). It was revised and republished in Wimsatt's 1954 book *The Verbal Icon: Studies in the Meaning of Poetry* (University Press of Kentucky: Lexington), pp. 3–18.

4. Compare with the Georgetown Multiple Literacies Project, which in practice emphasizes primarily linguistic features of genres, such as narrative structural markers of temporality, syntactic phrasing, and lexicogrammatical features (see Curriculum Project, n.d.).

5. Recent interdisciplinary conversations on world literature and literary comparatism have also been turning toward the social pragmatics of literary dissemination across languages as crucial topics for literary criticism, ones that can no longer relegated to translation studies or the sociology of literature (Apter, 2006; Casanova, 1999; Moretti, 2005).

6. Carroli (2008), Katz (2001), and Scott (2001) demonstrate how working with literature can help language students explore the multiple layers of meaning in a given text.

7. Interestingly, Paran (2008) notes that students continue to find the reading of literature an enjoyable part of foreign language learning as long as they are exposed to a healthy balance of learner-centered and text-centered approaches.

References

Alexander, E. (2008). Familie in Kürze. In R. T. Morewedge (Ed.), *Mitlesen, Mitteilen: Literarische Texte zum Lesen, Sprechen, Schreiben und Hören* (pp. 26–27). Boston: Heinle.

Altmayer, C. (2002). Kulturelle Deutungsmuster in Texten: Prinzipien und Verfahren einer kulturwissenschaftlichen Textanalyse im Fach Deutsch als Fremdsprache. *Zeitschrift für Interkulturellen Fremdsprachenunterricht, 6*(3). Retrieved from http://zif.spz.tu-darmstadt.de

Apter, E. (2006). *The translation zone: A new comparative literature.* Princeton, NJ: Princeton University Press.

Bakhtin, M. M. (1994). *The dialogic imagination* (C. Emerson & M. Holquist, Trans.). Austin: University of Texas Press.

Bernhardt, E. B. (1991). *Reading development in a second-language.* Norwood, NJ: Ablex.

Block, D., & Cameron, D. (Eds.). (2002). *Globalization and language teaching.* London: Routledge.

Bourdieu, P. (1977). *Outline of a theory of practice* (R. Nice, Trans.). Cambridge: Cambridge University Press.

Bourdieu, P. (1991). *Language and symbolic power* (G. Raymond & M. Adamson, Trans.). Cambridge, MA: Harvard University Press.

Bourdieu, P. (1993). *The field of cultural production* (R. Johnson, Ed.) New York: Columbia University Press.

Bourdieu, P., & Wacquant, L. (1999). On the cunning of imperialist reason. *Theory, Culture, and Society, 16*(1), 41–58.

Bretz, M. L. (1990). Reaction: literature and communicative competence: A springboard for the development of critical thinking and aesthetic appreciation. *Foreign Language Annals, 23*(4), 335–338.

Butler, J. (1997). *Excitable speech: A politics of the performative.* New York: Routledge.

Byram, K., & Kramsch, C. (2008). Why is it so difficult to teach language as culture? *German Quarterly, 81*(1), 20–34.

Carrell, P. L. (1984). The effects of rhetorical organization on ESL readers. *TESOL Quarterly, 18*(3), 441–469.

Carroli, P. (2008). *Literature in second language education: Enhancing the role of texts in learning.* London: Continuum.

Casanova. P. (1999). *Le republique mondiale des lettres.* Paris: Editions de Seuil.

Curriculum Project. (n.d.). Retrieved from http://www1.georgetown.edu/departments/german/faculty/byrnes/publications/manuscripts/39022.html

de Certeau, M. (1984). *The practice of everyday life* (S. F. Rendall, Trans.). Berkeley: University of California Press.

Goffman, I. (1964). The neglected situation. *American Anthropologist* (Pt. 2, Special Issue), *66*(6), 133–136.

Grice, H. P. (1975). Logic and conversation. In P. Cole & J. Morgan (Eds.), *Syntax and semantics 3: Speech acts* (pp. 41–58). San Diego, CA: Academic Press.

Hall, G. (2005). *Literature in language education.* New York: Palgrave Macmillan.

Kaplan, R. (1966). Cultural thought patterns in intercultural education. *Language Learning, 16*(1), 1–20.

Katz, S. (2001). Teaching literary texts in the language classroom: A structured input approach. In V. Scott & H. Tucker (Eds.), *SLA and the literature classroom: Fostering dialogues. Issues in language program direction: A series of annual volumes* (pp. 155–171). Boston: Heinle.

Kern, R. (2002). Reconciling the language-literature split through literacy. *ADFL Bulletin, 33*(3), 20–24.

Kramsch, C., Howell, T., Warner, C., & Wellmon, C. (2007). Framing foreign language education in the U.S.: The case of German. *Critical Inquiry in Language Studies, 2–3*, 151–178.

Krueger, Cheryl. (2001). Form, content and critical distance: The role of "creative personalization" in language and content courses. *Foreign Language Annals, 34*(1), 18–25.

Lantolf, J., & Thorne, S. L. (2006). *Sociocultural theory and the genesis of second language development.* Oxford: Oxford University Press.

Long, D. R. (1989). Second language listening comprehension: A schema-theoretic perspective. *Modern Language Journal, 73*(1), 32–40.

Magnan, S. (2004). Rediscovering text: Multiple stories for language departments. *Profession*, 95–106.

Maxim, H. (2006). Integrating textual thinking into the introductory college-level foreign language classroom. *Modern Language Journal, 90*(1), 19–32.

Modern Language Association. (2007). Foreign languages and higher education: New structures for a changed world. Retrieved from http://www.mla.org/flreport

Moretti, F. (2005). *Maps, graphs, trees: Abstract models for a literary history.* London: Verso.

Morewedge, R. T. (2004). *Mitlesen, Mitteilen: Literarische Texte zum Lesen, Sprechen, Schreiben und Hören*. Boston: Heinle.

Nostrand, H. L. (1989). Authentic texts and cultural authenticity: an editorial. *Modern Language Journal, 73*(1), 49–52.

Özdamar, E. S. (1998). *Mutterzunge*. Cologne: Kiepenheuer & Witsch.

Paran, A. (2008). The role of literature in instructed foreign language learning and teaching: An evidence-based survey. *Language Teaching, 41*(1), 465–596.

Schultz, J. M. (2002). The Gordian knot: Language, literature and critical thinking. In V. Scott & H. Tucker (Eds.), *SLA and the literature classroom: Fostering dialogues* (pp. 3–31). Boston: Heinle.

Scott, V. M. (2001). An applied linguist in the literature classroom. *The French Review, 74*, 538–549.

Swaffar, J., Arens, K., & Byrnes, H. (1991). *Reading for meaning: An integrated approach to language learning*. New York: Prentice Hall.

Thorne, S. L., & Reinhardt, J. (2008). "Bridging activities:" New media literacies and advanced foreign language proficiency. *CALICO Journal, 25*(3), 558–572.

Chapter 6

The Health Care Professional as Intercultural Speaker

Peih-ying Lu, Kaohsiung Medical University, Taiwan

John Corbett, University of Glasgow

Abstract

This chapter considers points of contact and departure between intercultural language education and cross-cultural competence training in medicine. Educators in the fields of language education and medical communication have developed frameworks of intercultural competence that characterize the knowledge, attitudes, and skills that learners can draw on. While competence-based frameworks can guide curricula and audit programs, we argue that a language pedagogy also requires a process-oriented approach, a method of teaching and learning that sees the learner as a situated individual and an increasingly skilled practitioner. Medical students have the opportunity to become active and reflective practitioners in two complementary contexts: problem-based learning and the medical humanities. Additionally, medical students studying in a second or other language have the opportunity to use a variety of resources to explore how language is used in a wide range of health care contexts. Exploration of "authentic" instances of intercultural language encounters as well as online corpora of general and specific English provide an evidence base for the use of language in professional contexts and convey the everyday experience of being a patient, a caregiver, or an advocate.

Introduction

The blossoming of English into a global lingua franca has impacted on numerous aspects of professional and everyday life for millions of people. One area where professional life and everyday life interact is health care provision. In today's world, doctors, caregivers, and patients migrate between countries, institutions, and cultures. Encounters in which health is the focus of communication take place in hospitals, clinics, and the home. These encounters may involve doctors and nurses talking with patients and their family members or friends and companions, professionals discussing health care with their peers, lecturers and students engaged in medical education through the medium of English as a second language, or call-center workers transcribing oral recordings of case histories sent from a distant land. Many of these health care encounters are intercultural in the broadest sense; that is, they involve people from different countries, ethnicities, and social and professional backgrounds. Communication in general combines *transactional* and *interactional* functions: the transactional function refers to the transfer of information, and the interactional function refers to the simultaneous construction of a personal identity and management of relationships. Health care encounters are transactional in that factual medical information is transferred from one interlocutor to another. These encounters are also interactional in that medical communication necessarily impinges on the patients' personal identity, often at its most fragile and vulnerable; medical talk constructs the hierarchical networks of doctors, nurses, auxiliary workers, caregivers, and patients; and medical advice has to negotiate the interlocutors' complex and often dissonant systems of value and belief. This chapter therefore focuses on health care providers as intercultural speakers. We focus on some of the ways in which evolving theoretical frameworks of intercultural language education might engage with the ways in which members of the medical profession have addressed cultural difference.

The Intercultural Speaker

It can be argued that any systematic approach to learning a language explicitly or implicitly constructs a theoretical speaker of that language and that these theoretical speakers differ according to the pedagogical values or curricular emphases of any given course of instruction. Thus, grammar-translation courses undertaken in the age before mass tourism implicitly theorize the learner as a reader rather than a speaker, a mute armchair traveler whose boundary crossing extends to the exploration of canonical literature in the target language. Language courses geared toward vacationers theorize the learner as a tourist, negotiating physical space and acquiring cultural capital in the form of experiences and souvenirs by way of phrasebook-assisted inquiries and remembered textbook formulae. More general communicative language courses envisage the learner as a walking thesaurus of notions and functions, differentiated according to a principle of appropriacy. Mastery of these linguistic exponents transforms the learner into an accomplisher of tasks in a manner indistinguishable from that other theoretical construct, the native speaker.

The communicative language learner is theorized as a set of linguistic and social competences; for example, he or she should be able to make requests, suggestions, or inquiries and to do so according to the conventions of politeness that are supposed to govern behavior in the target culture. Increasingly, though, the language learner has been posited as someone who understands and navigates cultures. The *Standards for Foreign Language Education: Preparing for the 21st Century* (American Council for the Teaching of Foreign Languages, 1996) proposed that learners should address the practices and products of different cultures as a way of apprehending unfamiliar cultural perspectives. Cross-cultural engagement is thus embedded into the language learning through a process of comparison and making connections between communities. The intercultural speaker in the more detailed formulations devised by Michael Byram and fellow educators such as Gerhard Neuner, Lynne Parmenter, Karen Risager, and Geneviève Zarate is a model explicitly constructing the theoretical learner as having linguistic, sociolinguistic, and discourse competence and adds to this the notion of intercultural knowledge and skills, defined as a set of *savoirs* (Byram, 1997, 2008; Corbett, 2003; Neuner & Byram, 2003):

- *Attitudes*—openness to otherness
- *Knowledge*—how social interaction occurs
- *Skills of interpreting and relating*—the ability to relate the linguistic outputs of the other to those of the self
- *Skills of discovery and interaction*—the ability to observe, understand, and operationalize knowledge of a new culture
- *Critical cultural awareness/political education*—critical evaluation of cultural practices of the self and other (cf. Byram, 2008)

The nature of the *savoirs* has been challenged and subjected to reformulation, for example, by Karen Risager (2007), who suggests that they are less a set of characteristics of intercultural speakers and more an instrument of assessment, especially given Byram's involvement in embedding the *savoirs* into the *Common European Framework of Reference for Languages: Learning, Teaching, Assessment* (Council of Europe, 2001). Risager reshapes Byram's inventory and offers a set of what she calls "resources" that theoretical intercultural speakers should be able to draw on and adds two further items: "linguistic identity" and "poetics."

Whether the learner is envisaged as someone whose skills and knowledge are gradually being enhanced or as someone who draws on linguistic and cultural resources with ever greater effectiveness, in many respects the intercultural speakers theorized by Byram and Risager are similar; he or she is a secondary school pupil, being exposed simultaneously to the complexities of a second language and the liberal precepts of citizenship education. While Byram and Risager may be concerned primarily with devising robust curricular frameworks to encourage intercultural language learning in malleable youth, it is part of the attraction of these frameworks that they can be adapted for other circumstances and other speakers, such as business and health care professionals. These learners can be theorized as "situated speakers" whose shared concerns and communicative demands have over the past four decades given rise to the educational industry of teaching English for "specific purposes." Addressing the demands of "situated speakers" gives educators an opportunity to refine our models of linguistic and intercultural competences and skills. They also give us an opportunity to reflect on the degree to which the education of intercultural speakers is served by inventories of knowledge, attitudes, and skills.

Cross-Cultural Competence

In the United States, there has been a growing concern to develop intercultural skills generally among the undergraduate population. For example, Bok (2006, p. 249) stresses the need for all students to develop the "open-mindedness, tolerance, and respect" required for living and working in a global society. Much of the literature relating to the intercultural speaker as health care professional is specifically concerned to address the disparities in medical provision that arise out of cross-cultural misunderstandings. Intercultural speakers are constructed as professionals in a complex "community of practice" (cf. Wenger, 1998) who need to be sensitized in order to reduce these disparities. Cross, Bazron, Dennis, and Isaacs (1989) extend the application of cross-cultural competence from the individual health care provider to the entire organization, "at every level of organization, including policy making, administration, the recruitment and training of labor, service delivery, family and communities." Their definition of intercultural competence is designed to enable each part of the organization and community to come together "to work effectively in the context of cultural differences." The need for understanding of culturally conditioned communication styles is accentuated by research that suggests that high incidences of failure among medical professionals from ethnic communities were not on the grounds of prejudice but on the grounds of candidates' nonadherence to privileged discursive strategies (e.g., Wass, Roberts, Hoogenboom, Jones, & Van der Vleuten, 2003).

The skills and attitudes that relate specifically to doctors have been extensively discussed, and medical education can be monitored to evaluate whether it addresses the sensitization of individual learners. For example, Mutha, Allen and Welch (2002) have devised a "tool kit" to determine the extent to which medical curricula include learning objectives pertinent to the development of culturally competent communication. Among the recommended learning objectives are the following:

Participants who successfully complete the curriculum will be able to

1. describe how cultural influences shape individual health behavior,
2. describe cultural differences that can influence patient–physician relationships,
3. discuss how explanations of disease etiology can differ among diverse patients,
4. identify and address cultural barriers that may affect communication in patient–physician relationships,
5. employ culturally appropriate questions that effectively elicit patient information in the clinical encounter,
6. work effectively with a medical interpreter, and
7. apply communication techniques to resolve conflicts in culturally sensitive ways.

These objectives can easily be related to the types of competence and resources formulated by Byram, Risager, and colleagues working in general intercultural language education. For example, general intercultural language education emphasizes the importance of the learner developing ethnographic skills, acting as a cultural mediator, and being aware of the differences in value and belief that affect the relationship between the self and others. Health care professionals who are intercultural speakers may draw on the anthropological literature and their ethnographic skills, for example, to observe how particular communities, such as working-class Scottish, American, or Taiwanese males or first-generation Chinese or Vietnamese immigrants to the United States, give information about their health problems and the extent to which they will be inclined to comply with medical advice given. As Strathern and Stewart (1999) observe,

> In addition to the mode of medical training received, the value systems of individual medical students and physicians vary greatly and influence how information is transmitted and obtained. Attempting to understand the whole patient and treat the whole person who exists within a complex social nexus is one of the more insightful ways of lessening communication problems. (p. 181)

As Strathern and Stewart suggest, issues relating to attitudes and belief are central for health care professionals. In the United States, attitudes and beliefs have been interrogated with respect to parity of care. For example, Churak (2005) explores the multifactorial causes of disparity in renal transplants among minority patients, noting that individual, interpersonal, and institutional forms of racism are part of the picture:

> For example, substantial evidence exists that physicians and other caregivers unconsciously and automatically use "stereotype application," whereby a patient's age, gender, diagnosis, sexual orientation, and race/ethnicity influence the health care provider's beliefs about and expectations for that patient. The patient may unintentionally be identified by the clinician as being less deserving of treatment. Epidemiological data from minorities may indeed be applied to individual patients by clinicians in a way that reinforces marginalization. (p. 153)

Various institutions have sought to address the attitudinal and factual bases for disparity and inefficiency in dealing with patients of different cultures. For example, the University of Washington Medical Center (2007) issues guidelines to guide health care professionals dealing with different cultural groups and offers the following tips:

> The Chinese culture emphasizes loyalty to family and devotion to traditions and puts less emphasis on individual feelings. Assess your patient's kinship relationships and determine which family members are most influential in decision making. When possible, engage the whole family in discussions that involve decisions and education about care. (p. 2)

Clearly, there are dangers as well as virtues in abstracting a set of supposedly common characteristics from such a general group as "the Chinese" and projecting them onto any individual patient.

Issues of stereotyping are well recognized in the literature on culturally competent health care; for example, Betancourt (2006) cautions against broadly applying stereotypes to individuals who seem to fall into categories such as "the Hispanic patient." Teal and Street (2009) also discuss specific strategies to counteract stereotyping that they acknowledge as a natural human process. They recommend a focus not primarily on the cultural group to which a patient nominally "belongs" but on "core cultural issues":

> Core cultural issues which physicians should be taught to recognize and assess include beliefs about gender roles, physician authority, physical space, family roles, beliefs or practices about death, religious beliefs, and explanations of disease (Davidhizar, Giger, & Hannenpluf, 2006; Rapp, 2006). Communication is also a core cultural issue with several aspects, including recognition of status (e.g., use of first names), non-verbal behaviors (e.g., the meaning and use of gestures), and communication styles (e.g., what is considered rude or overly direct speech). (p. 536)

In short, in the medical literature, we can see the extension and adaptation of debates about intercultural speakers and intercultural language education that are familiar to those in general language education. The Tool for Assessing Cultural Competence Training (TACCT, 2006), a questionnaire on knowledge, skills, and attitudes developed at the University of California, Irvine, as a tool for medical schools to assess their cultural competence training (American Association of Medical Colleges, 2006; Lie, Boker, & Cleveland, 2006), can be seen as an elaborate version of Byram's *savoirs*, Risager's "resources," or indeed a version of the *Common European Framework of Reference for Languages* devised for American medical educators. The TACCT balances the need to consider cultural predispositions against the risk of stereotyping. Users are encouraged to match the content of preclinical and clinical courses against "domains" that include the definition of cultural competence and its key aspects, the impact of stereotyping on decision making, awareness of health disparities, and cross-cultural skills, such as working with an interpreter. The extent to which any given medical course addresses intercultural competences should then be apparent.

Questioning Competence

However, even granting the utility of an extended and adapted list of intercultural knowledge, skills, and attitudes tailored to the specific needs of health care professionals, there is still a reductive element to the specification of competence as a set of inventories. Approaches to intercultural language education that are driven by inventories of resources, *savoirs*, or cross-cultural medical knowledge, skills, and attitudes may be in danger of reducing complex, situated, learned expertise to a more or less nuanced set of abstractions that are more of a metaphor for knowledge than knowledge itself. It is instructive to consider that any inventory of "competences" governing intercultural behavior is as much of an abstraction as the medieval notion of the "humors" that governed the Hippocratic model of the body. The humors were supposedly bodily fluids that had to be kept in balance for the health of the individual. Humoral theory was elaborated to explain, for example, "sexual and racial differences, character, disposition, psychological traits—in fact, every significant aspect of human life" (Porter, 2005, pp. 45–46). Porter observes that the four humors "proved wonderfully versatile as an explanatory system" because they afforded "a neat schema with unlimited explanatory scope" (p. 47). A striking feature of this system is that apparently cognitive or affective characteristics—melancholy, anger, and even-temperedness—were made to correspond to an individual's physical makeup, appearance and behavior. As Porter (2005) observes,

> A human being was thus represented in traditional biomedicine as a complex, differentiated but integrated whole. . . . The humors formed one facet, and their disposition was reflected in the "complexion" (or outward appearance) and the "temperament"—or, as we might say, the personality. Humors, complexion and temperament constituted an interactive system, equipped with feedback loops. (p. 49)

It may seem flippant to compare Byram's *savoirs*, Risager's "resources," or the domains that make up TACCT to humoral theory. We acknowledge the utility of inventories of skills in shaping curricula, guiding assessment, and auditing the quality of courses of instruction. Yet it is precisely *because* the humors were such a successful explanatory system for so long—while being so wrong—that they are a useful test case for any other model of human psychology and behavior. At the very least, they remind us that the process of language education must necessarily be distinguished from abstracted accounts of its outcomes.

Porter (2005) recalls that Samuel Johnson defined human beings as "incorporated minds," and a definition of intercultural speakers might well be "incorporated *savoirs*." Such a notion underlies Barnett's (1994) notion of "intercultural being" and Phipps and Gonzalez's (2004) construction of the learner as "languager," that is, a learner who uses language to engage "with the whole social world" and manifest an "embodied disposition for action" (p. 29). The shift in focus from advocating intercultural communicative competence to intercultural being has several consequences. One is a shift in pedagogical focus from the auditing of knowledge, skills, and attitude to the means whereby these qualities might be fostered. Another is the shift in perception of language learners as "people with skills" to the more integrated, active and developing perception of learners as "skilled practitioners" (Phipps & Gonzalez, 2004, p. 90).

To become "skilled practitioners," learners need to be exposed to situations where they can make decisions, commit errors, reflect on their performance, and try again. In medical education, two developing areas of action and reflection are found in problem-based learning and the increasingly burgeoning field of medical humanities.

Problem-Based Learning as a Site of Action

Problem-based learning (PBL) is a relatively recent and popular innovation in the delivery of medical education. Pioneered at McMaster University in Canada, by the end of the twentieth century it was used in about half of Canadian medical schools and a quarter of American ones (David, Patel, Burdett, & Rangachari, 1999). Today it is a cornerstone in the delivery of preclinical medical education in Europe and

Asia. There are different versions of PBL, but in essence a large part of the curriculum at the preclinical level is devoted to a cycle of case studies that offer problems
for the students to address in groups.

PBL is an attempt to engage students in "real-life" learning situations, and
in doing so it promises to engage the learner "with the whole social world" as it
relates to a medical case. A PBL cycle at Kaohsiung Medical University in Taiwan
typically lasts six hours—three two-hour sessions (Chen et al., 2008). In the first
session, the tutor presents the group of about 10 with a case study as a "trigger." The students make hypotheses and identify learning issues; for example, if
they suspect diabetes, they might consider the regulation of glucose and insulin
and complications such as hypertension. They then go off and research those topics, and, in the second session, they present and discuss their results in groups
and identify further learning issues. In the final session, they present their overall
findings, draw conclusions, and suggest courses of action.

The pedagogical literature on PBL exhibits similar debates to those found in
the literature on communicative and task-based learning, specifically about the
balance between range and depth of learning achieved, whether PBL in fact out-
performs lecture-based learning, and, crucially for us here, how "authentic" the
problems are (e.g., Antepohl & Herzig, 1999; Colliver, 2000). More recently, there
have been calls for a move away from "paper-based" PBL to "real-patient" PBL.
"Real-patient encounters," according to some research on students' perspectives
(Dammers, Spencer, & Thomas, 2001; Diemers et al., 2007; Stjernquist & Crang-
Svalenius, 2007), serve as "a powerful driving force for learning" and "enhance
integration of theory and practice." As a result, real-patient PBL is advocated as a
preparation for clinical training. Preclinical encounters with authentic case studies,
according to Dammers et al. (2001), help students to acquire transferable relevant
knowledge and critical appraisal skills when facing new sets of events. In addition,
they also foster in students the qualities of responsibility and empathy through
active engagement with real patients' problems.

The PBL approach to general preclinical education has been used to engage
learners with cross-cultural issues. Betancourt (2004) suggests that

> interactive, case-based sessions that highlight clinical applications
> are the ideal methods for teaching cultural competence. When used
> selectively as the clinical scenario dictates, the skills acquired from
> such situations can help illuminate the patient's values, beliefs and
> behavior. (p. 954)

Thus, cross-cultural concepts are embedded into PBL sessions as "case-based
triggers" that attempt to raise students' awareness of cross-cultural issues while
avoiding the stereotyping that may come from simplistic accounts of cultural
predisposition. Shields (2008) describes PBL sessions that present case studies
of patients presenting with gastrointestinal complaints: an obese woman unable
to pay for essential medication, an Asian woman who uses alternative therapies,
and a male American war veteran with hepatitis C and alcohol-related liver cir-
rhosis who is addicted to salty bar snacks. The students are encouraged to think
"creatively," not mechanically, around the topics of racial, socioeconomic, and

professional biases toward or against particular ethnic groups, social classes, and alternative practitioners; they are invited to consider, for example, whether questions about preferences for alternative medication might be relevant only for Asian patients. Students are invited to consider how they would work with patients who wish to combine alternative and "Western" medication, how they might influence patients whose destructive dietary regime is in some way part of their identity and socialization (e.g., as a relatively hard-drinking war veteran), and how they might involve nutritionists in patient care.

In short, the assumption underpinning PBL is that the intercultural speaker's key skills are acquired not from an exposure to a checklist of competence definitions or even from "thin," managed simulations with simple and predictable outcomes but rather from an exposure to rich, immersive educational experiences that are closely modeled on real-life case studies. The intercultural speaker is not just a "person with skills"; he or she is an increasingly skilled practitioner whose managed experiences encourage sensitivity to complexity, creativity in eliciting, and openness to possibility. PBL offers numerous challenges to students, particularly those for whom the activities that are set are culturally unfamiliar or conducted in a second or other language (e.g., Khoo, 2003; Mpofu et al., 1998). However, when conducted imaginatively, PBL offers one way of addressing intercultural issues in medicine and encouraging learners to engage in "intercultural being."

The Medical Humanities as a Site for Reflection

The degree to which a PBL session is sometimes "facilitated" or "managed" toward a predicted, socially sanctioned outcome leads us to an uncomfortable fact in intercultural communication, medical education, and, indeed, life. Some problems do not have solutions, or at least the solutions to the problems may not be easily open to generalization. Insights into the situated complexities of intercultural speaking can be gained from the growing literature by medical specialists whose memoirs offer glimpses into "their world." Gabriel Weston's (2009) *Direct Red* is a lightly fictionalized account by a female English literature graduate who crossed several borders into the competitive, male world of the medical student and trainee surgeon. One episode in her memoir can be reconfigured as a case study for PBL. As an inexperienced surgeon, she encountered profuse bleeding in an adult tonsillectomy patient. As the patient began to lose large quantities of blood, she panicked and called on a more experienced consultant for help. The experienced consultant's response—which turned out to be an abrupt and profane command to get on with the job—can be used as a "trigger" for classroom discussion. The consultant's attitude seems a far cry from the empathy earlier advocated by the very same person in a communications skills session. Indeed, Weston, angered by the consultant's response, pulled herself together and completed the operation. Later, having talked to the consultant, she reflects that, in this case, the profane refusal to give assistance was exactly the right response to have made. If the anecdote is true, it speaks to the consultant's confidence in Weston's ability and her knowledge of just how to make Weston angry enough to continue the operation alone. We can recognize and applaud the consultant's competences as an educator and mentor, but they are difficult ones to abstract, break down, and teach.

There is perhaps space, then, in a medical education program for what Karen Risager (2007) calls the "poetics" of intercultural communication. Aspiring intercultural speakers can use memoirs, fiction, poetry, art, and the other media to prompt reflection on aspects of professional life, such as what to do in moments of panic, how to deal with conflict, how to cope with an error of judgment, and so on. These problems are open ended and not easily soluble, yet the growing field of medical humanities testifies to the need felt by many medical practitioners to engage with such issues in a creative yet rigorous manner (e.g., Evans & Finlay, 2001; Evans, Ahlzén, Heath, & MacNaughton, 2008). In a broad definition of medical humanities, Evans and Finlay argue for its importance in terms that resonate with Phipps and Gonzalez's (2004) call for critically reflective "intercultural being." Evans and Finlay (2001) call for medical educators to

> refocus on the meaning of "the human," bringing the philosophical method of critical reflection—in effect, a responsible refusal to take unexamined assumptions for granted—to medicine. . . . This approach can be taken to all the scientific and humanities disciplines which together bear upon the human patient, so that they all focus appropriately on *human values* and they all employ an appropriate common method. This approach recaptures a tradition in which arts and sciences are intertwined and in which sciences, however powerful, remain oriented within a concern for human values. (p. 8)

In medical curricula, where time for "reflection and recursion" in Phipps and Gonzalez's (2004) terms is scarce, space for the medical humanities is strongly contested, but it can be found. In the United Kingdom, since the publication of *Tomorrow's Doctors: Recommendations on Undergraduate Medical Education* (General Medical Council, 2003), there has been an emphasis on education rather than training in medicine, and medical educators in Britain and elsewhere have sought to build bridges with colleagues in the humanities. At Kaohsiung Medical University in Taiwan, students undergo two years of general education before embarking on their preclinical training. This part of their course of study encompasses language development, including an element of literary and cultural exploration, as well as an ethical strand. At Glasgow University, undergraduate medical students can opt to take "special study modules" that, in the past, for example, have looked at a concept like the family through the lens of Plato's *Republic* (Downie, 2001). In addition, Glasgow University has a visual artist, Christine Borland, working with the Medical Humanities Unit. In one of her video installations, *Simulated Patient*, Borland (2004) turns medical communication training into art. She plays the role of a woman to whom "bad news" must be broken; real medical students are charged with revealing the diagnoses: HIV, terminal cancer, and infertility. Each conversation unfolds in turn on a separate screen while, on the other two, the student/doctor waits silently for the interview to begin. Written instructions outline the information to be imparted or assimilated. As each encounter is repeated with two students, the differences in the students' deliveries have the effect of prolonging or alleviating the patients' agony (see Borland, 2004; Lu, 2010).

Through curricular and extracurricular activities, then, health care professionals are being encouraged to think beyond the more or less managed strictures of PBL. These courses may be embedded in an undergraduate curriculum, or they may be options taken only by a minority of students; however, they represent potential spaces for intercultural exploration and the crossing of disciplinary borders.

Evidence-Based Health Communication

PBL and reflective activities based on art, literature, communications, philosophy, and history can contribute toward the development of intercultural speakers in the medical professions by engaging them in action through structured case studies and by inviting them to reflect on less easily soluble issues through an engagement with the humanities. However, as noted earlier, the load of intercultural language education in the medical field is clearly greater when students are learning and practicing in a second or other language. In the final section of this chapter, we wish to turn to the more practical aspects of learning medicine and practicing health care in a second language.

In a recent and wide-ranging discussion of health care communication, targeted primarily at first-language speakers, Brown, Crawford, and Carter (2006) discuss various aspects of experiential learning and what they term "evidence-based health communication." Among many provocative notions raised in this book is the idea that health care professionals might learn from other professions, such as the hospitality industries, whose kinship to medicine might not be immediately apparent. Brown et al. make the point that doctors are commonly engaged in examining, assessing, and recommending courses of action to patients in situations characterized by time constraints—consultations, in other words, lasting only a few minutes where empathic connection may be seen by the professional as having a low priority, while the patient desperately seeks reassurance. In this so-called "blip culture," doctors may learn from cabin crew staff on aircraft whose "emotional labor" and "sentimental work" are deployed strategically, primarily to control others. Lest their readers become too cynical about this manufactured sincerity, Brown et al. (2006) observe that

> emotion work in health care settings is not exclusively about an economically motivated process of exchange. As Bolton (2001) argues, as social beings, emotion management by health care practitioners is a way of "paying respect with feeling"; it is a personal gift given freely, sometimes unconsciously, and sometimes without the counting of costs, and as Mann and Cowburn (2005) add, many

practitioners felt that their emotional labour performance helped the clients cope with their own emotions. Indeed, Bolton (2001) described nurses as "accomplished social actors and multiskilled emotion managers." (p. 188)

In second-language situations, the linguistic demands on intercultural health care practitioners who are managing emotions while attempting diagnosis are even more acute. As discussed earlier, inventories of competences and useful functions are useful to teachers and curriculum designers. For example, Teal and Street (2009) offer a characterization of cross-culturally competent discourse features, including recognition of potential cultural differences:

Establishing relationship	Attend to patient discomfort
	Recognize negatively perceived behavior and assess cause
	Acknowledge others accompanying patient
Gathering information	Explore changes in the patient's life, especially for immigrants ("How is medical care different here than in your country?")
	Assess the patient's explanatory model for the disease and treatment
	Ask about tangible and community resources

The second-language learner can seize on the bland questions offered ("How is medical care different here than in your country?"), but there is little guidance here on how to accomplish "emotion work." Training in emotion work can take different guises, including explicit "textbook" training, language awareness activities, and the exploration of digitized language corpora. Conventional, textbook-based language training is increasingly supplemented by exploration of an evidence base of health care interactions and texts through reflections on recorded encounters between providers and patients (simulated or real) and analyses of language corpora.

In their standard textbook on medical communication, Lloyd and Bor (2009) give the following counsel to students faced with a distressed patient:

> Try to control your anxiety (it may be communicated to the patient), avoid rushing in with questions and give the patient an opportunity to express emotion. You can help the patient to do this through empathy, perhaps by touching the patient's hand, or using reflective comments:

> *"I understand that this must be very upsetting for you."*

> *"I can understand why you are so upset."*

> *"Perhaps you would like to tell me more about how you feel."*
> (pp. 47–48)

This potentially useful but still generic advice can be enriched by the use of resources that draw on actual intercultural encounters between health care providers and patients. Moss and Roberts (2003) and Roberts, Atwell, Swanwick, and Chana (2008) draw on video-recorded intercultural encounters in four London general practices to demonstrate different critical incidents and communicative strategies, many of which include emotion work, such as building trust through reassurance, persuasion, negotiating agreement, and dealing with a humorous response to a serious illness. The training materials are based on discourse analyses of consultations recorded as part of the PLEDGE project (Patients with Limited English and Doctors in General Practice: Education issues; see also Moss & Roberts, 2005). Health care providers are enjoined to focus on three issues in their intercultural encounters: the patients' identification of symptoms, context, and stance. Key to success is the health care provider's willingness to listen strategically. In the following extract, the doctor allows the patient space to describe her situation, which involves a marital breakdown. The booklet that accompanies the DVD notes that, rather than asking a formulaic question such as "How do you feel about that?," the doctor creates a caring space, hands out a tissue, and gently but persistently seeks clarification (Roberts et al., 2008). When the extract below begins, the patient has already been talking for about three minutes in response to the doctor's greeting of "good morning":

> P: just [.] being bullied for the last four months in the office and erm I'm going [starts crying] sorry I'm going through a marriage break-up with my husband [.] we gone through the first stage er which is the decree nisi that was on the er thirty-first of erm last month and since that day he he said he's gonna show me in the this country and he'll show me
>
> D: he'll show you what does that mean
>
> P: that he'll teach me a lesson
>
> D: what does that mean

In this case, the patient's physical symptoms seem related to emotional stress in the home and at work, so the doctor elicits the nature of the problems, establishing the context and the patient's perspective before beginning to negotiate preliminary action. By creating the space for the patient to explain her situation clearly, the doctor has begun to build up a relationship of trust. As Phipps and Gonzalez (2004) attest, intercultural listening is as important as intercultural speaking.

Reflection on the discourse analysis of intercultural encounters provides a strong and immediately relevant resource for reflection by health care practitioners. Other forms of linguistic analysis can supplement and extend this kind of activity. Brown et al. (2006) consider the use of online corpora as a further evidence base to raise health care professionals' awareness of aspects of medical communication. Brown and his colleagues use corpus tools, for example, to probe a Web site called *Teenage Healthfreak* for insights into young people's conceptions of and anxieties about "normality." They observe that teenagers are disproportionately likely to use the question "Is this normal?" contrastively in relation to symptoms about which they are worried. The frequency alerts health care professionals to the "positive valuations" that young people ascribe to "being normal" (Brown et al., 2006; Harvey, Brown, Crawford, Macfarlane, & McPherson, 2007).

As more and more oral and written records relating to health care and people's experience of it become available online in a searchable corpus format, students of medicine and language will be able to explore the language that professionals and nonprofessionals use to articulate their perspectives of health and illness from both a factual, transactional angle and the more interactional angle of emotion work. The use of online corpora to interrogate aspects of language is now well established in general language studies (see, e.g., Anderson & Corbett, 2009). The following is an example of the kind of activity that can be facilitated by evidence-based study:

1. Go to http://www.scottishcorpus.ac.uk/corpus/bnc/compair.php.
2. Type *sick* in the first box and *ill* in the second box.

The results of this corpus search indicate those words in British English that are most closely associated with *sick* and *ill*, according to mutual information scores drawn from an analysis of the 100 million words of the British National Corpus (see the following screen shot). The results suggest, for example, that British people are much more likely to say "chronically sick" than "chronically ill." The words in the middle of the table go equally well with *sick* and *ill*. The results are suggestive in other ways. Underneath the string of collocates lie idiomatic phrases like *worried sick, sick and tired, ill at ease, ill afford*, and even *not quite himself—* expressions that color the experience of proficient users of the language. Such expressions can be used to articulate the emotion work that accompanies discourse on health issues, as in the following exchange from the records of the Scottish Parliament, in which a backbench member questions the health minister on the issue of personal care for the elderly:

> Dennis Canavan (Falkirk West): Is the minister aware that some old people are literally *worried sick* about how they are going to meet the costs, if and when they are taken into residential care? Will the Scottish Executive therefore implement Professor Suther-land's recommendations in full, particularly the recommendation that personal care costs should be met from public funds? Will he do that and do it soon, rather than simply follow the shabby com-promise announced by the Government at Westminster? (Scottish Parliament, 2000)

The results of corpus searches have to be used with some caution. For example, the collocations suggested by the "ComPair" results include formulae such as *statutory sick leave* and *Royal Hospital for Sick Children*, which have a relatively high incidence of occurrence in the United Kingdom but may be used relatively infrequently elsewhere. The 400 million words of the Corpus of Contemporary American English, for example, show not a single instance of *statutory* preced-ing *sick*; the most frequent adjectives preceding *sick leave* in the American data are *unpaid, accumulated, extended*, and *accrued*, which again suggest the legal-istic registers to which the term contributes (http://www.americancorpus.org). It is generally true that the results of such corpus searches confirm the situated, cultural aspects of language. If they are going to develop as skilled practitioners of medical language, intercultural learners of English in health care contexts need to be exposed to rich, unpredictable, "natural" contexts of use and be given the space to reflect on this exposure critically and imaginatively.

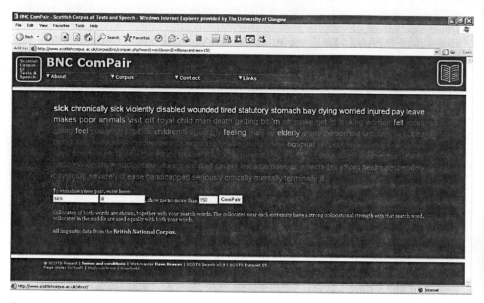

Screen shot of "BNC ComPair" comparing collocates of *sick* and *ill*.

Conclusions

The intercultural speaker can be conceived as an "incorporated" set of competences and skills. The inventories suggested by Byram's *savoirs* and Risager's resources provide a useful framework for the competences expected of intercultural speakers, and this kind of framework can be adapted and extended in the light of the demands made on intercultural speakers who are health care professionals. The TACCT inventory itemizes the kinds of cross-cultural competence that are expected of graduates of American medical schools. However, as Bou-Franch and Garcés-Conejos (2003) note, with respect to pragmatics, competence "is a delicate area and it is not immediately obvious how it can be 'taught'" (cited in Brown et al., 2006, p. 186). Other intercultural language theorists advocate a view of the intercultural speaker as *skilled practitioner* or *intercultural being*, a conceptualization that involves a more holistic engagement in formation of skills through "action, reflection, and recursion" (Phipps & Gonzalez, 2004, p. 29).

In the formation of skilled practitioners, intercultural language education, like medical education, privileges PBL based closely on real-life situations. And in medical education, as in general language education, PBL sessions may be more or less managed toward predetermined outcomes. In medical situations that involve intercultural encounters, PBL may be directed toward external clinical objectives, such as increased patient compliance with physician advice. PBL may also involve students in the simulation of *emotional labor* as appropriate to contexts such as a brief consultation or the more extensive delivery of bad news to a patient or a patient's relative. The direction of PBL toward predetermined goals, however, may suggest that certain values are beyond critical reflection. Since some problems are open ended and since values are negotiable, there is a vital place in the curriculum for the medical humanities—space where those involved in health care can reflect on their own attitudes and engage in what Teal and Street (2009) call "situational and self-awareness." The visual arts, drama, fiction, poetry, memoir, biography, and anecdotal narrative may all have a part to play in such reflective practices.

For intercultural speakers who are involved in utilizing English as a second language, an evidence base that allows access to the diverse genres used by health care professionals and their patients will increasingly act as a resource that they can draw on to enhance their linguistic repertoire. Such resources include the kind of videotaped data transcribed, analyzed, and presented by the PLEDGE project for reflection and discussion. They also, increasingly, include corpus data whose patterns of collocation and metaphor give additional insights into the ways in which different cultures address issues of health and well-being.

The professional development of health care professionals raises the stakes for theoreticians and practitioners of intercultural language education. Health care professionals work in messy and stressful environments; the demands on their time and expertise are often urgent, complex, and emotionally demanding. Educators from the fields of medicine, language, social sciences, and cultural studies variously theorize "interculturality" as a taxonomy of competences, a set of linguistic and cultural resources to draw on, a ritualized set of discourse practices to apply to predictable situations, and an all-encompassing "way of being," something akin to a fifth humor. In a crowded curriculum, the "well-rounded professional" needs to be exposed to several models of interculturality in order to compare and appraise their strengths and weaknesses.

References

American Association of Medical Colleges. (2006). TACCT resource guide. Retrieved from http://www.aamc.org/meded/tacct/tacctresourceguide.pdf

American Council for the Teaching of Foreign Languages. (1996). *Standards for foreign language education: Preparing for the 21st century*. Alexandria, VA: Author.

Anderson, W., & Corbett, J. (2009). *Exploring English with online corpora*. London: Palgrave Macmillan.

Antepohl, W., & Herzig, S. (1999). Problem-based learning versus lecture-based learning in a course of basic pharmacology: A controlled, randomized study. *Medical Education, 33*(2), 106–113.

Barnett, R. (1994). *The limits of competence: Knowledge, higher education and society*. Buckingham: Open University Press.

Betancourt, J. R. (2004). Cultural competence—Marginal or mainstream movement? *New England Journal of Medicine, 351*(10), 953–955.

Betancourt, J. R. (2006). Cultural competency: Providing quality care to diverse populations. *The Consultant Pharmacist, 21*(12), 988–995.

Bok, D. (2006). *Our underachieving colleges: A candid look at how much students learn and why they should be learning more.* Princeton, NJ: Princeton University Press.

Borland, C. (2004). *Simulated Patient.* Exhibited at the Lisson Gallery, London (see http://www.studio55.org.uk/researchers/christine/simulated.html#nogo).

Bou-Franch, P., & Garcés-Conejos, P. (2003). Teaching linguistic politeness: A methodological proposal. *International Review of Applied Linguistics in Language Teaching, 41*(1), 1–22.

Brown, B., Crawford, P., & Carter, R. (2006). *Evidence-based health communication.* Maidenhead: McGraw-Hill/Open University Press.

Byram, M. (1997). *Teaching and assessing intercultural communicative competence.* Clevedon: Multilingual Matters.

Byram, M. (2008). *From foreign language learning to learning for intercultural citizenship: Essays and reflections.* Clevedon: Multilingual Matters.

Chen, Cheng-Sheng, Chung-Sheng Lai, Peih-ying Lu, Jer-Chia Tsai, Hung-Che Chiang, In-Ting Huang, et al. (2008). Performance anxiety at English PBL groups among Taiwanese medical students: A preliminary study. *Kaohsiung Journal of Medical Sciences, 24*(3, Suppl. 1), S54–S58.

Churak, J. M. (2005). Racial and ethnic disparities in renal transplantation. *Journal of the National Medical Association, 97*(2), 153–160.

Colliver, J. A. (2000). Effectiveness of problem-based learning curricula: Research and theory. *Academic Medicine, 75*(3), 259–266.

Corbett, J. (2003). *An intercultural approach to English language teaching.* Clevedon: Multilingual Matters.

Council of Europe. (2001). *Common European framework of reference for languages: Learning, teaching, assessment.* Cambridge: Cambridge University Press.

Cross, T., Bazron, B., Dennis, K., & Isaacs, M. (1989). *Towards a culturally competent system of care* (Vol. 1). National Technical Assistance Center for Children's Mental Health, Georgetown University Child Development Center, Washington DC, and NWICWA (see http://gucchd.georgetown.edu/programs/ta_center/topics/cultural_linguistic_competence.html).

Dammers, J., Spencer, J., & Thomas, M. (2001). Using real patients in problem-based learning: Students' comments on the value of using real, as opposed to paper cases, in a problem-based learning module in general practice. *Medical Education, 35*(1), 27–34.

David, T., Patel, L., Burdett, K., & Rangachari, P. (1999). *Problem-based learning in medicine.* London: Royal Society of Medicine.

Davidhizar, R., Giger, J. N., & Hannenpluf, L. W. (2006). Using the Giger–Davidhizar Transcultural Assessment Model (GDTAM) in providing patient care. *Journal of Practical Nursing, 56*(1), 20–25.

Diemers, A. D., Dolmans, D. H., Van Santen, M., Van Luijk, S. J., Janssen-Noordman, A. M., & Scherpbier, A. J. (2007). Students' perceptions of early patient encounters in a PBL curriculum: A first evaluation of the Maastricht experience. *Medical Teacher, 29*(2–3), 135–142.

Downie, R. (2001). Medical humanities: Means, ends and evaluation. In M. Evans & I. Finlay (Eds.), *Medical humanities* (pp. 204–218). London: BMJ Books.

Evans, M., Ahlzén, R., Heath, I., & MacNaughton, J. (Eds.). (2008). *Medical humanities: Vol. 1. Symptom.* Oxford: Radcliffe Publishing.

Evans, M., & Finlay, I. (Eds.). (2001). *Medical humanities.* London: BMJ Books.

General Medical Council. (2003). *Tomorrow's doctors: Recommendations on undergraduate medical education.* London: General Medical Council.

Harvey, K. J., Brown, B., Crawford, P., Macfarlane, A., & McPherson, A. (2007). "Am I normal?" Teenagers, sexual health and the internet. *Social Science and Medicine, 65*(4), 771–781.

Khoo, H. E. (2003). Implementation of problem-based learning in Asian medical schools and students' perceptions of their experience. *Medical Education, 37*(5), 401–409.

Lie, D. A., Boker, J., & Cleveland, E. (2006). Using the Tool for Assessing Cultural Competence Training (TACCT) to measure faculty and medical student perceptions of cultural competence instruction in the first three years of the curriculum. *Academic Medicine, 81*(6), 557–564.

Lloyd, M., & Bor, R. (2009). *Communication skills for medicine* (3rd ed.). London: Elsevier.

Liu, P. (2010). Medicine as art: An interview with Christine Borland. *Language and Intercultural Communication, 10*(1), 90–99.

Moss, B., & Roberts, C. (2003). *Doing the Lambeth Talk: Real-life GP-patient encounters in the multi-lingual city* [DVD & booklet]. London: King's College/London Deanery.

Moss, B., & Roberts, C. (2005). Explanations, explanations, explanations: How do patients with limited English construct narrative accounts in multi-lingual, multi-ethnic settings and how can GPs interpret them? *Family Practice, 22*(4), 412–418.

Mpofu, D. J. S., Lanphear, J., Stewart, T., Das, M., Ridding, P., & Dunn, E. (1998). Facility with the English language and problem-based learning group interaction: Findings from an Arabic setting. *Medical Education, 32*(5), 479–485.

Mutha, S., Allen, C. and Welch, M. (2002). *Toward Culturally Competent Care*. San Francisco: University of California Center for the Health Professions.

Neuner, G., & Byram, M. (Eds.). (2003). *Intercultural competence* (Vol. 1). Strasbourg: Council of Europe.

Phipps, A., & Gonzalez, M. (2004). *Modern languages: Learning and teaching in an intercultural field*. London: Sage.

Porter, R. (2005). *Flesh in the age of reason*. London: Penguin.

Rapp, D. E. (2006). Integrating cultural competency into the undergraduate medical curriculum. *Medical Education, 40*(7), 704–710.

Risager, K. (2007). *Language and culture pedagogy*. Clevedon: Multilingual Matters.

Roberts C., Atwell, C., Swanwick, T., & Chana, N. (2008). *Words in action: Communication skills for doctors new to UK general practice* [DVD & booklet]. London: King's College/London Deanery.

Scottish Parliament. (2000, July 9). *Official report* (Vol. 8, No. 2). Available as Document 1239 of the SCOTS corpus at http://www.scottishcorpus.ac.uk

Shields, H. (2008, November 15). *Integrating cross-cultural care into a pre-clinical science course: A faculty development program for tutors*. Paper presented at the Conference on Cultural Competence in Medical Education, Kaohsiung Medical University, Taiwan.

Stjernquist, M., & Crang-Svalenius, E. (2007). Applying the case method for teaching within the health professions—Teaching the students. *Education for Health, 20*(1). Retrieved from http://www.educationforhealth.net

Strathern, A., & Stewart, P. J. (1999). *Curing and healing: Medical anthropology in global perspective*. Durham: North Carolina University Press.

TACCT: Tool for Assessing Cultural Competence Training (2006). Retrieved from http://www.aamc.org/meded/tacct/tacct.pdf

Teal, C. R., & Street, R. L. (2009). Critical elements of culturally competent communication in the medical encounter: A review and model. *Social Science and Medicine, 68*(3), 533–543.

University of Washington Medical Center. (2007). Communicating with your
    Chinese patient. Retrieved from http://depts.washington.edu/pfes/PDFs/
    ChineseCultureClue.pdf
Wass, V., Roberts, C., Hoogenboom, R., Jones, R., & Van der Vleuten, C. (2003). Ef-
    fect of ethnicity on performance in a final objective structured clinical examina-
    tion: Qualitative and quantitative study. *British Medical Journal, 326*, 800–803.
Wenger, E. (1998). *Communities of practice: Learning, meaning and identity.*
    Cambridge: Cambridge University Press.
Weston, G. (2009). *Direct red: A surgeon's story.* London: Jonathan Cape.

Chapter 7

Theorizations of Intercultural Communication

Maria Dasli, Edinburgh Napier University

Abstract

Within the fields of applied linguistics and modern language education, intercultural communication has experienced two significant developmental turns. The first I call *the traditional view of intercultural communication*, which refers to the ability of language learners to confront the cultural practices of the Other with flexibility and tolerance. The second I term *the critical view of intercultural communication*, which encourages language learners to actively demonstrate their concerns by means of reasoned debate and reflective thinking when entering the intercultural arena. While recent years have seen a shift of focus toward the critical view without, however, dismissing flexible attitudes toward otherness, some language instructors exclusively favor the first view to the detriment of the second. In a time of large-scale migrations mobilized by the recent financial crisis and terrorist threats stimulated by the absence of dialogue between the East and the West, I suggest that we closely focus on the critical view of intercultural communication. Drawing on the works of major intercultural theorists, I discuss how intercultural communication has been brought to a position of refinement while additionally introducing the theory of communicative action (Habermas, 1984, 1989) as a means of elaborating the critical view of intercultural communication.

Introduction

Over the past few decades, intercultural communication has experienced a remarkable growth within the fields of applied linguistics and modern language education. This has had powerful implications for pedagogic practice, for it has taken the study of language and culture far beyond the contestable notion of native speaker by which language learners were required to assimilate a static and monolithic target culture to new ethics that have the potential to improve our societies. Broadly speaking, this took place in two significant developmental turns within which intercultural communication has aimed to realize its original project—that of transforming intercultural human consciousness. The first I call *the traditional view of intercultural communication*, which emphasizes the ability of language learners to confront the cultural practices of the Other with flexibility and tolerance. The second, which derives from the field of critical pedagogy, I term *the critical view of intercultural communication*. This encourages students to demonstrate their concerns when entering the intercultural public sphere by means of reasoned debate and reflective thinking. The purpose, nature, and direction of both views have been considerably debated. However, they have eluded clear definition. While this correctly highlights their overlapping and emerging character rather than their linear progression, many intercultural theorists still favor the traditional view by disregarding the need for the second (Deardorff, 2006). Without misapprehending the benefits tolerance and flexibility bring to cross-cultural encounters, in a time of large-scale migrations mobilized by the recent financial crisis and terrorist threats stimulated by the absence of constructive dialogue between the East and the West, I propose that we redefine the goals of modern language education by closely focusing on the critical view of intercultural communication.

Against this background, the purpose of this chapter is to revisit the two significant developmental turns that intercultural communication has experienced. In doing so, the first part of this chapter concentrates on the traditional view of intercultural communication by briefly presenting the notion of intercultural speaker (Byram & Zarate, 1997). In describing the fundamental implications of this notion, my intention is to demonstrate how it contributed to the intercultural canon by informing pedagogic practices. Here, attention is paid to ethnography as one of the most beneficial methods aiming to facilitate intercultural speaker development. The second part of this chapter concerns the critical view of intercultural communication. In describing the agenda of the critical view, reference is made to critical pedagogies and critical literacies. I also suggest that the critical view be informed from the theory of communicative action (Habermas, 1984, 1989), as it provides a broader lifeworld understanding of conflict management through the articulation of problematic claims aiming to reinstate the possibilities of being and becoming for language learners.

The Traditional View of Intercultural Communication

Language and culture pedagogy seeks to familiarize language learners with the culture of a particular country or of a group of countries, depending on the language taught, in the belief that culture shock is likely to occur on crossing the political boundaries of nation-states (Byram, 1989; Kramsch, 1998). This was initially achieved through the introduction of a preestablished canon of texts that presented a fixed set of bipolar cultural dimensions (e.g., low versus high power distance and monochronic versus polychronic time) deemed to be shared by all the indigenous inhabitants of a country without acknowledging the shifting nature of culture. However, this method was soon questioned, as the application of general, timeless, and universal values to all encounters, regardless of their simplicity or complexity, did little to promote harmonious cross-cultural interactions (Dlaska, 2000; Phipps & Gonzalez, 2004). As a consequence, new approaches to the teaching of language and culture were developed that aimed to respond more successfully to the difficulties such encounters offer.

One of these approaches was proposed by Michael Byram and Genevieve Zarate (1997), who coined the term "intercultural speaker" in the course of writing a paper on the assessment of sociocultural competence as defined in the work of the Council of Europe. This term portrays someone who crosses frontiers while bringing two cultures into a relationship (Byram & Zarate, 1997). To achieve this, Byram (2003) argues that language learners need to act as mediators able to see how two different cultures relate to each other by comparing similarities and differences. Here, the act of mediation does not expect students to deny their own cultural backgrounds that formed them and created them as social beings. Instead, it encourages them to take an external perspective by which they will be able to analyze how underlying values, beliefs, and attitudes unconsciously direct the behaviors of the cultural Other. An understanding of these behaviors can then enable language learners to demonstrate flexible and tolerant reactions toward otherness by adapting the norms of the Other where desirable. For Guilherme (2004) and Shaules (2007), this adaption is likely to eliminate the notional distinction of "us" versus "them" while creating and maintaining a "community of shared meanings"—an ever-expanding cultural platform of shared knowledge on which both the Self and the Other coconstruct their diverse identities.

Ethnography and Intercultural Language Pedagogy

In British tertiary education, the development of intercultural speakership is realized through a variety of pedagogic methods that have recently seen a shift of focus from classroom-based practices to ethnographic approaches. These encourage language learners to become ethnographers during their year abroad in order to gain an integrated vision and a comparative understanding of different facets of culture (Kelly, 2005; Phipps & Gonzalez, 2004). This shift of focus has been stimulated largely by a longitudinal study, the Ealing Ethnography Project, which took place in the 1990s at Thames Valley University in London. According to Roberts (2003), the purpose of the project was to explore the ways by which students "learn ethnographically" in terms of the meanings and cultural practices they seek to interpret during their ethnographic encounters with otherness as well as the effects these meanings have on their personal development. The project was completed in three phases. The first phase concerned a taught module of 45 classroom hours delivered in the second year of a four-year undergraduate degree during which learners were introduced to ethnographic training. The second phase referred to extended periods of residence abroad where participants were required to undertake extensive fieldwork in order to investigate a topic of their choice. The third phase was associated with the production of an ethnographic description based on data the students gathered during their fieldwork experience.

As part of the first phase of the project, learners were encouraged to engage with home ethnography. For Southall (1973), home ethnography begins with an understanding of the ways by which a community selected for investigation by ethnographers is structured. Here, community does not refer to a large geographical territory, such as a nation-state or a region. Rather, it denotes any microsociety where individuals are perceived to identify with each other on the basis of shared norms and cultural practices. Communities can include a neighborhood, a classroom, or a local pub. Once the microsociety is selected, language learners are encouraged to identify those who inhabit the community. If we take a local pub as one example, inhabitants can include employees and customers. The first should be differentiated in terms of the tasks they are likely to undertake in the pub as a consequence of managerial requests. The second should be distinguished for age differences (i.e., young adults or middle-aged or retired persons), as these can denote diverse interests contributing to the community's heterogeneity. At this stage, learners may also wish to consider the purpose of habitation. For instance, some customers may be enjoying a quiet lunch break, whereas some others may be celebrating a companion's achievements or birthday. Cultural practices may also vary depending on the time of habitation. On weekdays, for example, individuals may choose to leave the pub earlier than they would on weekends because of commitments due to take place the next working day. Additionally, the roles inhabitants play in the community should be differentiated with reference to their vague or precise definition. Considering, for example, that musicians can play live music in a pub, their roles would be professionally defined if they were to entertain an audience as opposed to their friends in a relaxed setting.

The ways by which a community can be structured are by no means limited to the aforementioned ideas. However, as Agar (1986) proposes, they should be considered as a starting plan of action—"a stock of knowledge"—according to which further methodological steps should be undertaken. Usually, the first of these methodological steps is that of participant observation where ethnographers become involved in the activities of a specific community while observing collective cultural practices and individual patterns of behavior (Greenblatt, 1999; Inglis, 2002). Rosaldo (1999) argues that participant observation does not require special training, as we are all "born ethnographers" in that we unconsciously interpret the behaviors of others on a daily basis. To return to the preceding example of the local pub, I have asked my students to carry out a one-hour observation in a pub of their choice while following the instructions below (Box 1). At this stage, learners are encouraged only to practice note taking while completing what Geertz (1973) has termed "thin description"—a description that details what is observed without offering an interpretation. This task was also completed by participants of the Ealing Ethnography Project, with minor variations.

LOCAL PUB: AN ETHNOGRAPHIC OBSERVATION

As part of your ethnographic training, you are required to complete an ethnographic observation during which you will practice taking notes. You can complete the task in small groups or pairs.

Where

Your ethnographic observation should take place in a pub of your choice, a setting that provides relatively easy access for everyone.

When

To avoid practical difficulties (e.g., noise), conduct your observation in the afternoon, when pubs are not as busy as they are in the evening but are still full of activity to offer interesting data.

Why

In Britain, pubs are generally considered to be socially integrative environments with their own customs and values. These very often differ from those operating in the outside world, especially in terms of status distinctions. The lack of status distinctions makes pubs egalitarian environments facilitating social bonding.

How

1. Go to a pub of your choice. Spend <u>one hour</u> there depending on how much is happening. Once you feel that nothing more is happening, leave the pub.
2. While at the pub, make notes of <u>what you see and hear</u>. For now, you <u>don't have to interview anyone</u>.
3. Should you feel that events are taking place very quickly for you to note down, don't worry. You can document your observations once you have left the venue on the basis of what you remember. However, don't leave this for too late, as it is very unlikely that you will remember anything.
4. Draw a rough map of the venue (e.g., where the bar, sitting area, and pool table are).

What to Look For

Social Organization, Typical Routines, and Patterns of Interaction

1. Differences between the patrons who visit the venue.
2. Division of labor between employees.
3. Method by which patrons enter and leave the pub.
4. Standing at the bar.
5. Interaction patterns between employees, between patrons, between patrons and employees (e.g., forms of address, gender relations, ordering a drink, paying for a drink, joining a conversation, turn taking in conversation, striking up a conversation with a stranger, etc.).

Emerging Themes

1. Is there anything that strikes you as unusual? Why?
2. How do participants deal with it?

With acknowledgment to Fox (2004) and Roberts, Byram, Barro, Jordan, and Street (2001).

While some language learners return to the classroom empty-handed, the majority puts forward interesting findings. These usually include the invisible formation of a queue at the bar counter, the round-buying drink routine, and/or the escape from mainstream social hierarchies that are offered for classroom discussion. During classroom discussion, learners are encouraged to move away from the thin description to that of "thick description," where findings are interpreted in accordance with the context in which they took place (Geertz, 1973), that is, an account explaining how the cultural Other may think, feel, see, and imagine while demonstrating certain practices.

Although the interpretations students offer account to a degree for these practices, in some respects they are limited to the interpreters' cultural frames of reference. So, learners cannot be entirely certain that their interpretations accurately reflect the participants' thoughts and feelings. For this reason, Jackson (2006) as well as Monaghan and Just (2000) argue that the ethnographic method should not be reduced to observation. Rather, it should employ a variety of techniques to elicit information including that of interviewing. Interviews can range from highly structured exchanges of information where participants strictly respond to a prespecified set of questions to informal conversations or even unanticipated encounters during which informants offer their views without interruption. For modern language learners, however, who encounter the technique of interviewing for the first time, Corbett (2003) proposes that ethnographic interviews should synthesize a structured and an open-ended approach. A structured approach allows students to form questions depending on themes emerging out of observations. An open-ended approach provides respondents with the opportunity to take full control of the interview as the ethnographer enters the setting with no preplanned agenda. This synthesis results in what social researchers term "semistructured interviews" where interviewers obtain answers for all their questions while informants elaborate on their responses in their own pace (Cohen, Manion, & Morrison, 2000; Kvale, 1996; Wiersma, 1986).

Over the course of a semistructured ethnographic interview, interviewers are expected to understand "what respondents actually do," "what they say they do," "what they say they should do," and "what meanings they assign to their behaviours" (Wolcott, 1988). This is a tall order, one that student ethnographers do not always address immediately. However, if they are to reach anywhere near it, Corbett (2003) suggests that language learners be informed by, at least, three fundamental principles of interviewing: "avoid leading questions," "elicit responses with as little evaluation as possible," and "encourage interviewees to elaborate on topics." For Corbett (2003), a leading question would, for example, state, "How do you show you are proud to be Scottish?" Here, the interviewer assumes that the informant *is* proud to be Scottish when the questions "Are you Scottish?" and "What does this mean to you?" would offer unguided responses. To elicit information, interviewers can employ back-channeling, where an informant's answer is repeated, or follow-up questions, such as "What do you mean by . . . ?" to a response supplied already. While both techniques largely allow for elaboration, learners need to additionally remember not to hastily progress from one topic to another. They can achieve this by avoiding direct questions after topics that interviewees have only briefly discussed.

Roberts et al. (2001) state that students can best practice the technique of interviewing before entering the research setting. They argue that learners can engage with role-playing activities in the classroom during which they can interview each other first in their mother tongue and then in the target language. Although at this stage they could adopt the roles of the characters they encountered during their local pub observations, such an adoption would possibly yield responses emerging out of the students' own cultural frames rather than those of the patrons and employees. So, it may be wiser to recount their own experiences from meeting the cultural Other in the form of critical incident scenarios, which refer to narratives illustrating misunderstandings between two or more participants from different cultural backgrounds (Corbett, 2010; Jackson, 2002). This method has recently gained added currency within the Common European Framework for Languages, where Byram et al. (2009) encourage language learners to construct their own "autobiography of intercultural encounters" by describing one experience they have had with someone different from themselves. Following the written description of the encounter, learners can then exchange their autobiographies in order to form interview questions for each other. While reminding themselves of Corbett's (2003) three fundamental principles of interviewing, their questions can, as a starting point, include the following: "How did you feel at the time of the incident?," "How do you think the other person felt?," and "What do you think caused the misunderstanding?" Provided that the task is completed successfully, students can then enter their research settings with confidence. At this stage, they can revisit their local pub ethnographic observations. However, if they are to conduct interviews with the patrons and employees, they need to start from the very beginning, as new customers cannot account for the behaviors of participants whom students had previously encountered. Alternatively, learners can visit a new research setting such as a shopping mall or a supermarket in order to investigate the ways by which cultures of consumption are enacted in these two places.

Following the collection of the data, learners are encouraged to provide an ethnographic description—an "experience-distant observation" (Geertz, 1993)—referring to a written analysis of empirical evidence. Analysis can take various forms. It can include quotations where students directly report their findings from observations or interviews and paraphrasing where themes are discussed in the interpreter's own words. While forms of analysis play a role in the way by which data are explained, Roberts et al. (2001) argue that the most important aspect of interpretation is that of "reflexivity." Here, reflexivity implies a sensitive approach to data analysis digressing from oversimplified and stereotypical presentations of the Other to focus on ways by which informants perceive themselves. This is not to suggest that interpretation should be free from critical judgment. On the contrary, it proposes a departure from culturally determined presuppositions where behaviors are taken for granted as fixed rather than culturally relative. For example, although the anthropologist Edward T. Hall (1960) offered celebrated accounts of contrasting managerial styles between American and Arab managers, they are arguably problematic. The first are depicted as money minded ("U.S. managers are materialistic"), whereas the second are viewed as friendship seeking ("Arab managers look not for material possessions but for family and friendship relationships") throughout Hall's (1960) piece. Such ethnographic descriptions tend to be exaggerated caricatures that can be misleading if taken as the truth. Learners need to be thoughtful when analyzing their data since subjects may not necessarily wish to be presented as such.

Roberts et al. (2001) argue that the production of a sensitive ethnographic description of otherness involves primarily an understanding of the Self as a contextually situated subject instead of a static and monolithic object. To achieve such an understanding, they suggest that learners become aware of their own assumptions about cultural knowledge and the ways by which these are legitimized in their own societies before beginning their ethnographic investigations. Early in the ethnography class, learners are introduced to a series of incidents illustrating diverse cultural practices of individuals originating from the students' own cultural backgrounds. For instance, during the Ealing Ethnography Project, learners were shown a small incident in a restaurant during which a diner leaves money, presumably as a tip, on the table and one of his companions gathers the tip after the original diner is away. This incident, which raised issues regarding tipping, stealing, and friendship during classroom discussion, encouraged learners to question their predetermined and possibly positive assumptions about their own cultures while acknowledging that normality can be viewed differently by individuals inhabiting the same community. At this stage, students were not, of course, required to side with the companion but rather to reflect whether his reaction took place in response to preceding events. Perhaps this example is one of exaggeration, as it stretches the ability of learners to remain unconditionally tolerant to the Other. However, as the Ealing Ethnography Project reveals, it has facilitated the production of sensitive ethnographic descriptions, as in the case of one student who initially viewed the practice of bullfighting in Spain as brutal but now appreciates that it emerges from a long line of historical events without necessarily having to like it.

Modern language learners who participate in study-abroad programs usually attend debriefing sessions on their return during which they state how ethnographic study has helped them to retheorize their assumptions about the Self and the Other. The Ealing Ethnography Project demonstrates that most participants saw personal benefits, as they showed curiosity and openness to difference. For example, one student challenged her preconceived beliefs about Englishness as she gradually settled in France, while another learner managed to overcome his fears of homosexuality by observing and interviewing male transvestite prostitutes in Spain (Roberts et al., 2001). Other projects, however, show that some students cannot completely acclimatize in the host country and thus return home with increasingly ethnocentric attitudes toward otherness (Alred & Byram, 2006; Jackson, 2006; Papatsiba, 2006). While these may stem from linguistic barriers, homesickness, and sociocultural adjustment stress, Branscombe (1999) argues that this is likely to take place when the Other is not receptive to change and thus expects sojourners to fully adopt values, norms, and beliefs perceived to be shared by the indigenous inhabitants of the new environment. At this stage, sojourners should not distance themselves from the Other. Instead, they should engage in "dialectics of conflict" (Beck, 2006), the aim of which is not to overpower otherness but to help the Other see the world through the eyes of sojourners. Such a stance toward cultural knowledge has paved the way toward the construction of the critical view of intercultural communication that brings the politics of voice and difference center stage for language and culture pedagogy.

The Critical View of Intercultural Communication

Within the context of language and culture pedagogy, Byram (2003) translates the politics of voice and difference as *"savoir s'engager"* (critical cultural awareness/ political education). Critical cultural awareness invites language learners to speak out their concerns when entering the intercultural public sphere by means of reasoned debate and logical thinking. Although here tolerance and flexibility remain unaltered expressions of intercultural identities, the author questions the common core in civil society communication, which was based only on shared meanings. Thus, he is looking for radical alternatives. These aim, first, to challenge traditional approaches to the teaching of language and culture whose boundaries ethnography has greatly unsettled and, second, to refine the notion of intercultural speaker.

To explain this agenda, *Guilherme (2002)* defines a critical approach to language and culture as

> a reflective, exploratory, dialogical and active stance towards cultural knowledge and life that allows for dissonance, contradiction, and conflict as well as for consensus, concurrence, and transformation. It is a cognitive and emotional endeavour that aims at individual and collective emancipation, social justice and political commitment. (p. 219; original emphasis)

The core of this approach suggests that language learners should become critical when dealing with otherness. To achieve this, they need to reconceptualize their own self-identities as intercultural speakers. Here, intercultural speakers are no longer characterized by an unconditional being for the Other. Rather, they are marked by their abilities to raise their objections to hypostatized powers in order to enable political autonomy, choice, and a culture rooted in human rights. This is not to propose, however, that intercultural speakers should engage in continuous disagreements with otherness. Such a stance toward cultural knowledge would deprive them of the very act of knowing, during which individuals make problematic what was perceived as unproblematic in the process of self-discovery.

A number of academics agree with Guilherme's (2002) vision of critical intercultural language pedagogies. For example, Giroux (2003) persuasively declares that students are in need of new vocabularies and subject positions that will allow them to reform relationships of subordination and oppression. Luke, Luke, and Mayer (2000) share this perspective when arguing that the schooling system is only theoretically organized to improve life chances. While they invite instructors to question their teaching methods by engaging in open-ended and provisional reforms, they also acknowledge the difficulties teachers have to tackle to accomplish this. Here, the authors do not attribute difficulties to a presumably skeptical teaching position where students are perceived as naive inductees. Rather, they suggest that teacher education is designed in such a way so that it only reproduces universally practical models of teaching, including lesson planning, microteaching, classroom organization, and behavior management, without responding to students' diverse cultural needs. Although it is challenge for teachers to shake such educational foundations, Thurlow (2004) proposes, from a modern language perspective, that instructors should take radical initiatives that can be easily embedded in traditional curricula. These radical initiatives refer to the "autobiographical imperative," which is defined as the ability of the teachers to disclose the private into the public through a process of personal storytelling (see, e.g., Kramsch, 2009; Phipps, 2006). This process allows teachers to discuss their own agendas, needs, and frustrations by foregrounding the everyday in the classroom.

While this may be perceived as another method by which instructors transmit their cultural knowledge to passive observers, the intercultural narrative reveals that students equally engage in self-exposing dialogic practices in the classroom. These have been broadly captured in foreign language literature courses where the literary text is conceived as an object that stimulates deconstructive interpretation and self-discovery (Facke, 2003). For MacDonald, Dasli, and Ibrahim (2009), this occurs when the literary text produces signifiers to which learners respond by completing what is necessarily left unsaid. However, this process does not take place in isolation. It demands "significant others" (Mead, 1934), such as colleagues and teachers who contribute their own diverse interpretations of the literary text. These emerge out of their own experiences of pain, discomfort, and uneven memories or even pleasant encounters. Where literary texts are unavailable, Starkey (2002) argues that language instructors can take a critical discourse analysis approach where students can explore the ways by which dominance and inequality are enacted or resisted by a text located in a specific social and political context. To explain his argument, he draws on one example from an Irish university where students of Spanish studied a newspaper article on the theme of immigration. Having closely examined the article for linguistic and stylistic features, they saw how the discourse mechanisms of racism were reproduced by the text. Then they compared their findings to the Irish press while writing an account of their feelings about them.

In addition to print-based encounters with culture, Luke (2000) proposes that teachers should also focus on electronically mediated communication. Here, electronically mediated communication is not so much seen as an analysis of images. Rather, it is perceived as an understanding of the politics of location according to which readers and viewers position themselves in specific sociocultural contexts depending on the messages communicated. For Gee (2003, 2006), such an understanding can be accomplished when one attends to video games as an expanded form of critical literacy where players form "affinity groups." Affinity groups are not communities of practice with which individuals identify on the basis of affective ties. Rather, they are categories to which players denote their belongingness in order to accomplish a common endeavor. This common endeavor is not a decontextualized task but rather one that is organized around a whole process.

This process requires both extensive and intensive knowledge. Where extensive knowledge encourages players to continually reflect on their choices as means of seeing how they contribute to the completion of the broader activity, intensive knowledge brings the participants' outside experiences into play. The latter can include ethnic affiliations, which are demonstrated when players adopt the roles of specific characters featured by the video game. However, these are not seen as factors likely to detach players from each other. Instead, they are perceived as conditions that create and maintain learning experiences in ways that generate a greater sense of belongingness to the affinity group.

While belongingness to an affinity group can sensitize players to each other's needs, there is no guarantee that sensitivity will be demonstrated outside the domains of video games. For O'Regan and MacDonald (2007), a sensitive response to otherness becomes a complicated endeavor when interculturalists encounter dominant discourses such as "neoconservatives," "traditionalist religious groups," "female circumcisionists," and "antiabortionists," whose interests not only come into conflict with intercultural communication but also raise questions for intercultural praxis. These questions challenge the master template of tolerance and flexibility in that they assume that totalitarianism should be subordinated or even silenced by force if a presumably "intercultural truth" is to prevail. While subordination and silencing of others endanger the legitimacy of the discourse of intercultural communication by rendering it equally hegemonic, the authors argue that truth claims are significantly constrained by the absence of foundational guarantees characterizing postmodern societies. Absence of foundational guarantees is therefore conceived as another question as to which claims to support, respect, or condemn. In light of these questions, O'Regan and MacDonald (2007) ground intercultural communication to an ethics of responsibility where critical reason is exercised.

Responsibility, however, demands primarily an understanding of the construction of identity. For Hall (1996), the construction of identity requires more than one logic—the logic of the Other, which achieves its full dynamic potential only when it engages in discursive work with the Self. This can be best realized in societies that do not introduce entry standards according to which individuals are offered access to a specific community. Rather, they establish interdependent relationships of "solidarity and hosting" in the belief that the Self cannot exist without the Other. This conceptualization of solidarity and hosting derives from Freire's (1970) account of dialectics in *Pedagogy of the Oppressed*, which illustrates the tensions of unity and difference between the oppressed and their oppressors. Here, both the oppressed and the oppressors are, in the first instance, presented as manifestations of dehumanization. Dehumanization suggests a state by which the oppressors exploit the oppressed while the oppressed recognize oppressiveness without, however, taking action against it. The author thus invites both the oppressed and the oppressors to participate in a continuous pursuit of knowledge, invention, and reinvention in order to overcome the state of dehumanization. This can be achieved when they engage in a dialogic relationship.

Perhaps Freire's (1970) cultural vision sits in ambiguous metaphysical spaces. However, I do not wish to dismiss metaphysics out of hand. Rather, I wish to suggest that a further elaboration of metaphysical thinking can practically respond to the complexity of the Freirian argument. To address this, the following discussion focuses on the theory of communicative action (Habermas, 1984, 1989), which provides a broader understanding of conflict resolution where the unpredictability of face-to-face interaction meets a procedural pattern of communication.

In his *Theory of Communicative Action*, Habermas (1989) first draws our attention to the "lifeworld." The lifeworld is a transcendental site within which intersubjective consensus is to be attained. Here, human beings, as "epistemic," "practical," and "affective" subjects, satisfy a desire for a certain type of conversational fulfillment—that of providing each other with access to learning. For Habermas (1989), this is achieved through the use of language, a tool that is internal to the content of thought. This suggests that language offers linguistic structures that are objective so that interlocutors produce grammatically correct sentences. However, grammaticality does not limit them to certain conditions of possibility. Rather, it allows them to take a position toward criticizable validity claims by which they can verbalize their oppositions and correspondences with a view to gaining knowledge from each other. These validity claims are encapsulated in the idea of "a universal pragmatics," which attempts to create and maintain universal conditions of possible understanding (Habermas, 2002). For Habermas (1984), understanding is grounded on three presuppositions:

> That the statement is true (or that the existential presuppositions of the propositional content mentioned are in fact satisfied); That the speech act is right with respect to the existing normative context (or that the normative context it is supposed to satisfy is itself legitimate); That the manifest intention of the speaker is meant as it is expressed. (p. 99)

These three presuppositions suggest a background against which conversation satisfies its procedural nature. They can be glossed as follows. "Comprehensibility" refers to the speaker's ability to make intelligible statements that hearers will be able to understand. "Truth" proposes that the speaker tells the truth. "Truthfulness" is used to mean that the speaker intends to tell the truth. "Rightness" refers to the employment of the most appropriate utterance for a specific context.

Habermas (1995) argues that human beings are "variable," "accidental," and "supratemporal" in that they demonstrate self-referential characteristics, which are responsible for the apparent mismatches that exist in the world. Thus, they may not necessarily orient themselves toward a universal discourse ethics. However, the state of being necessitates some degree of cooperation by which chaos is avoided. In this respect, Habermas (2002) proposes that interlocutors should not terminate the conversation. Instead, they should continue on the level of argumentative speech. Argumentative speech suggests that speakers recognize that their claims are problematic—for if they were successfully addressed, interlocutors would have reached some sort of agreement. At this stage, the author states that interlocutors should not aim to satisfy the wider argument. Rather, they should narrow the discussion to the problematic claim by supporting it with further examples, experiences, and action consequences. Provided that the problematic claim is validated, it will be considered reliable. So, speakers and hearers will reach understanding and agreement on the basis of mutually shared subjectivity. However, their claims will again become open to critical discussion when speakers encounter other hearers with their own special domain of subjectivity.

The theory of communicative action that Habermas (1984, 1989) proposes is one that necessitates a process of discussion without which human beings would either distance themselves from each other or resort to violence to resolve their differences. As Freire (1970) argues, distancing suggests that individuals recognize that they are being oppressed but fear to speak and act while violence reverses the poles of the contradiction by situating the oppressed in the position of the oppressors. While both distancing and violence denote a posture of dehumanization, the Habermasian procedural pattern of communication offers human beings greater opportunities to achieve freedom by indicating a transformational response, one that aims to reconstruct the lifeworld through the articulation of problematic validity claims. To accomplish, however, such a transformational response, learners need to practice the theory of communicative action in the classroom in the belief that practice will facilitate some degree of confidence before students articulate their claims in the intercultural public sphere. Perhaps critical incident scenarios can be useful for this purpose. The following two examples, which my significant others have personally witnessed, can be presented as a starting point.

Critical Incident Scenarios

1. A woman works as a radio officer on a tanker ship. The ship stops in Saudi Arabia to load petroleum. When finishing her shift, the woman decides to take a walk up and down the harbor. It is 40 degrees Celsius. So, the woman wears a vest and shorts uncovering her shoulders and legs. Once she walks out of the ship, a local policeman thrusts a gun into her ribs. He forces the woman to cover her hair and the naked parts of her body; otherwise, she cannot walk up and down the harbor.

2. A Pakistani migrant in a Christian country, while on his way to work, takes a break to practice his religion. When a local policeman sees the man, he kicks him on the ground, hits him repeatedly, and tells him that he can worship only in a mosque.

The preceding scenarios illustrate two examples where local authorities abused their power in order to impose their religious beliefs on individuals originating from different religious backgrounds. When presenting these incidents in the classroom, some students side with the powerful in the belief that sojourners should always adhere to the seemingly determining norms and beliefs of the community visited. Thus, they invoke the proverbial saying "when in Rome, do as the Romans," which greatly departs from any progression toward liberation as it encourages individuals to adopt the stance of "going native" as a means of showing tolerance toward otherness. However, many others understand the negative consequences of religious fundamentalism. Without necessarily supporting any particular religious practices, they condemn violence by feeling the need to engage in a dialogue with the Other. At this stage, students are naturally divided into two groups. The first speaks in favor of local authorities, whereas the second stands for the voiceless and marginalized (i.e., the woman and the migrant). To follow the Habermasian procedural pattern of communication, each group is encouraged to make a list of claims supporting the individuals they represent. Once the groups decide their claims, they offer them for critical discussion, aiming to validate those underpinned by reliable arguments. Here, there is a danger of validating claims not always leading toward liberation, as some learners may be better discussants than others. For this reason, language instructors need to emphasize that discussion should not satisfy a desire of talking others into a specific point of view but rather focus on what is being unlearned in the course of this learning. For a theory of society, Habermas (2003) argues, "this possibility of unlearning has to be critical . . . to its own social setting, that is, it has to be open to self-criticism" (p. 242).

Conclusions

The aim of this chapter was to discuss the two developmental turns that intercultural communication has experienced. The first was termed the *traditional view of intercultural communication*, where language learners are encouraged to demonstrate tolerance and flexibility toward the cultural practices of the Other. The second was titled *the critical view of intercultural communication*, referring to the ability of students to actively manifest their concerns when confronting otherness as a means of enabling political autonomy and choice. Although these two views were presented as distinct, in many respects they overlap with each other in that the works cited present characteristics immediately recognizable in both views. For example, the notion of intercultural speaker (Byram & Zarate, 1997) is strengthened in the critical view with the addition of critical cultural awareness/political education. Equally, the introduction of ethnography, as a method likely to facilitate intercultural speaker development, does not simply move within comfortable learning spaces, indicating that any cross-cultural encounter will lead to a happy ending. Rather, it operates within the multiple sites of everyday discourse, as in the case of one language learner who observed the lives of male transvestite prostitutes in Spain (Roberts et al., 2001).

At this stage, one may question the reasons by which I decided to present the ideas of the aforementioned authors in my description of the traditional view when these neatly fit in the critical view of intercultural communication. One way to respond to skeptical readers is to remind them that these authors established language and culture pedagogy as an academic discipline almost two decades ago, when modern language education was facing very hard times. These were marked by the academy's refusal to acknowledge the marriage of language and culture or the assurance that the presentation of the fours Fs—foods, fairs, folklores, and (statistical) facts—would suffice to sustain understanding between cultures, a view that Kramsch (1991) problematizes. Any initial conceptualization of intercultural communication as a manifestation of tolerance and flexibility should be understood not only as a radical departure from familiar teaching establishments, then, but also as one questioning the defining approaches that characterized the time. Such initiatives brought intercultural communication to a position of refinement, a position, however, that remains a work in progress regardless of the fact that times have changed for the better thanks to these authors.

Although intercultural pedagogies reach beyond prescribed boundaries, some language instructors do not necessarily orient themselves toward the critical view of intercultural communication. While some of them believe that tolerance can reinstate the possibilities of being and becoming for language learners, others fear that any active manifestation of discomfort can endanger the students' security and well-being. Thus, they encourage them to reflect on unjust treatment without necessarily taking action against it under the assumption that reflection can mark a move toward freedom; perhaps it can when reflection denotes an oppositional stance toward human suffering, exploitation, and abuse of social power. However, it remains a partial response to public democratic culture when learners do not exhibit their differences in practice. It is therefore our responsibility to enable learners to progress from reflection to praxis. To achieve this, I proposed that the critical view of intercultural communication be informed from the theory of communicative action (Habermas, 1984, 1989), where conflict is managed through a procedural pattern of communication based on the transcendent power of language and an interminable questioning of truth, divorcing the Self and the often underappreciated Other from their unquestioned familiarity. Provided that the pattern is sufficiently practiced in the classroom, learners can gain a sense of confidence by which they will be able to tackle cacophonous dominant discourses and transform them into a language of possibility—a dialogic language out of which new experiences emerge for human beings.

References

Agar, M. (1986). *Speaking of ethnography*. London: Sage.

Alred, G., & Byram, M. (2006). British students in France: 10 years on. In M. Byram & A. Feng (Eds.), *Living and studying abroad* (pp. 210–231). Clevedon: Multilingual Matters.

Beck, U. (2006). *Cosmopolitan vision* (C. Cronin, Trans.). Cambridge: Polity Press.

Branscombe, N. R. (1999). The context and content of social identity threat. In N. Ellemers, R. Spears, & B. Doosje (Eds.), *Social identity* (pp. 35–58). Oxford: Blackwell.

Byram, M. (1989). *Cultural studies in foreign language education*. Clevedon: Multilingual Matters.

Byram, M. (2003). On being "bicultural" and "intercultural." In G. Alred, M. Byram, & M. Fleming (Eds.), *Intercultural experience and education* (pp. 50–66). Clevedon: Multilingual Matters.

Byram, M., Barrett, M., Ipgrave, J., Jackson, R., Garcia, M. C. M., Buchanan-Barrow, E., et al. (2009). *Autobiography of intercultural encounters*. Strasbourg: Council of Europe.

Byram, M., & Zarate, G. (Eds.). (1997). *The sociocultural and intercultural dimension of language learning and teaching*. Strasbourg: Council of Europe.

Cohen, L., Manion, L., & Morrison, K. (2000). *Research methods in education*. London: Routledge.

Corbett, J. (2003). *An intercultural approach to English language teaching*. Clevedon: Multilingual Matters.

Corbett, J. (2010). *Intercultural language activities*. Cambridge: Cambridge University Press.

Deardorff, D. K. (2006). Assessing intercultural competence in study abroad students. In M. Byram & A. Feng (Eds.), *Living and studying abroad: research and practice* (pp. 232–256). Clevedon: Multilingual Matters.

Dlaska, A. (2000). Integrating culture and language learning in institution-wide language programmes. *Language, Culture and Curriculum, 13*(3), 247–263.

Facke, C. (2003). Autobiographical contexts of mono-cultural and bi-cultural students and their significance in foreign language literature courses. In M. Byram & P. Grundy (Eds.), *Context and culture in language teaching and learning* (pp. 32–42). Clevedon: Multilingual Matters.

Fox, K. (2004). *Watching the English: The hidden rules of English behaviour*. London: Hodder.

Freire, P. (1970). *Pedagogy of the oppressed* (M. Bergman Ramos, Trans.). London: Penguin.

Gee, J. P. (2003). *What video games have to teach us about learning and literacy*. New York: Palgrave Macmillan.

Gee, J. P. (2006). Why game studies now? Video games: A new art form. *Games and Culture, 1*(1), 58–61.

Geertz, C. (1973). *The interpretation of cultures*. London: Fontana Press.

Geertz, C. (1993). *Local knowledge*. London: Fontana Press.

Giroux, H. (2003). Betraying the intellectual tradition. *Language and Intercultural Communication, 3*(3), 172–186.

Greenblatt, S. (1999). The touch of the real. In S. B. Ortner (Ed.), *The fate of "culture": Geertz and beyond* (pp. 14–29). Berkeley: University of California Press.

Guilherme, M. (2002). *Critical citizens for an intercultural world*. Clevedon: Multilingual Matters.

Guilherme, M. (2004). Intercultural competence. In M. Byram (Ed.), *Routledge encyclopaedia of language teaching and learning* (pp. 297–299). London: Routledge.

Habermas, J. (1984). *The theory of communicative action* (Vol. 1) (T. McCarthy, Trans.). London: Heinemann.

Habermas, J. (1989). *The theory of communicative action* (Vol. 2) (T. McCarthy, Trans.). Cambridge: Polity Press.

Habermas, J. (1995). *Postmetaphysical thinking* (W. Hohengarten, Trans.). Cambridge: Polity Press.

Habermas, J. (2002). What is universal pragmatics? In M. Cooke (Ed.), *On the pragmatics of communication* (pp. 21–102). Cambridge: Polity Press. (Original work published 1976)

Habermas, J. (2003). The tasks of a critical theory. In G. Delanty & P. Strydom (Eds.), *Philosophies of social science: The classic and contemporary readings*. Berkshire: Open University Press. (Original work published 1981)

Hall, E. T. (1960). The silent language in overseas business. *Harvard Business Review, 1*, 87–96.

Hall, S. (1996). Introduction: Who needs identity? In S. Hall & P. du Gay (Eds.), *Questions of cultural identity* (pp. 1–17). London: Sage.

Inglis, F. (2002). *Clifford Geertz: Culture, custom and ethics*. Cambridge: Polity Press.

Jackson, J. (2002). *Critical incidents across cultures*. Retrieved from http://www.llas.ac.uk/resources/gpg/1426

Jackson, J. (2006). Ethnographic pedagogy and evaluation in short-term study abroad. In M. Byram & A. Feng (Eds.), *Living and studying abroad: Research and practice* (pp. 134–156). Clevedon: Multilingual Matters.

Kelly, M. (2005). Cultural studies. In A. Coleman & J. Klapper (Eds.), *Effective learning and teaching in modern languages* (pp. 181–186). London: Routledge.

Kramsch, C. (1991). Culture in language learning: A view from the United States. In K. de Bot, R. B. Ginsberg, & C. Kramsch (Eds.), *Foreign language research in cross-cultural perspective* (pp. 217–240). Amsterdam: John Benjamins.

Kramsch, C. (1998). *Language and culture.* Oxford: Oxford University Press.

Kramsch, C. (2009). *The multilingual subject.* Oxford: Oxford University Press.

Kvale, S. (1996). *Interviews.* London: Sage.

Luke, C. (2000). New literacies in teacher education. *Journal of Adolescent and Adult Literacy, 43*(5), 424–435.

Luke, A., Luke, C., & Mayer, D. (2000). Redesigning teacher education. *Teaching Education, 11*(1), 5–11.

MacDonald, M. N., Dasli, M., & Ibrahim, H. (2009). Literature, culture and language learning. *Journal of Literary Theory, 3*(1), 103–127.

Mead, G. H. (1934). *Mind, self and society.* Chicago: University of Chicago Press.

Monaghan, J., & Just, P. (2000). *Social and cultural anthropology: A very short introduction.* Oxford: Oxford University Press.

O'Regan, J. P., & MacDonald, M. N. (2007). Cultural relativism and the discourse of intercultural communication: Aporias of praxis in the intercultural public sphere. *Language and Intercultural Communication, 7*(4), 267–278.

Papatsiba, V. (2006). Study abroad and experiences of cultural distance and proximity: French Erasmus students. In M. Byram & M. Fleming (Eds.), *Living and studying abroad: Research and practice* (pp. 108–133). Clevedon: Multilingual Matters.

Phipps, A. (2006). *Learning the arts of linguistic survival.* Clevedon: Channel View Publications.

Phipps, A., & Gonzalez, M. (2004). *Modern languages: Learning and teaching in an intercultural field.* London: Sage.

Roberts, C. (2003). Ethnography and cultural practice: Ways of learning during residence abroad. In G. Alred, M. Byram, & M. Fleming (Eds.), *Intercultural experience and education* (pp. 114–130). Clevedon: Multilingual Matters.

Roberts, C., Byram, M., Barro, A., Jordan, S., & Street, B. (2001). *Language learners as ethnographers.* Clevedon: Multilingual Matters.

Rosaldo, R. (1999). A note on Geertz as a cultural essayist. In S. B. Ortner (Ed.), *The fate of "culture": Geertz and beyond* (pp. 30–34). Berkeley: University of California Press.

Shaules, J. (2007). *Deep culture: The hidden challenges of global living.* Clevedon: Multilingual Matters.

Southall, A. (1973). The density of role-relationships as a universal index of urbanisation. In A. Southall (Ed.), *Urban anthropology: Cross-cultural studies of urbanisation* (pp. 71–106). Oxford: Oxford University Press.

Starkey, H. (2002). *Democratic citizenship, languages, diversity and human rights.* Strasbourg: Council of Europe.

Thurlow, C. (2004). Relating to our work, accounting for our selves: the autobiographical imperative in teaching about difference. *Language and Intercultural Communication, 4*(4), 209–228.

Wiersma, W. (1986). *Research methods in education: An introduction.* Boston: Allyn & Bacon.

Wolcott, H. F. (1988). A case study using an ethnographic approach. In M. Jaeger (Ed.), *Complementary methods for research in education* (pp. 187–206). Washington, DC: American Educational Research Association.

Chapter 8

Framing Ideas from Classical Language Teaching, Past and Future

Jan Parker, The Open University

Abstract

The Modern Language Association (MLA) Ad Hoc Committee report (MLA, 2007) raises large questions about the teaching not only of modern languages but of all cultural studies. What was striking were the many challenges that resonate with classical language teaching. In the study and teaching of classical languages, we have access only to vestigial and overtly alien and often alienating texts; the impossibility of mother-tongue competence or total immersion in the other's culture actually provides a relevantly comparative model of the effect on identity of various kinds of intercultural study and the claims that can be made for such study in a global, complex, and destabilizing world. This chapter thus endorses the call to rethink and disseminate the values of our two related disciplines; it is throughout argued that "theory" should bring all of us into "the MLA project": to reflect on models, lenses, and paradigms that enable real innovation.

Introduction

The MLA Report and its various responses (e.g., Pfeiffer, 2008; Wellmon, 2008), which in part frame the discussions in this volume, raise very large questions about the teaching not only of modern languages but of all cultural studies. What was striking were the many challenges that resonate with classical language teaching, my area: the concern with reversing falling numbers, the emphasis on the importance of languages as offering a lens on "self" by offering access to "others," the importance of an integrated curriculum bringing "language" and "content" teachers together in the planning process, and a call to rethink and disseminate the values of our discipline. In this chapter, I offer details of some of those resonances but also explore what seem to be differences in emphasis in classics pedagogy. It draws on a similarly alternative definition of "theory"—not in the European sense of conceptual framing such that, once adopted, it affects all writing and thinking but something more personal, one that language teaching is well placed to develop. It suggests that this latter sense of theory, to do with stance and looking, is one desired outcome of all language and intercultural programs.

    Of course there are fundamental differences between a program that can at least aim at mother-tongue competence and can be taught by mother-tongue teachers and that can send its students to communities where they can be immersed in the living languages and one where none of this is possible, as is the case with "dead" classical languages. Yet, wishing to defend my languages against the charge of being "dead," there seem from outside the modern languages professional communities to be potential pedagogical problems with the above model. And there are issues that classicists have to confront immediately that may, conversely, resonate with modern language professionals—about student motivation, intercultural competences or at least sensibility, ongoing skill claims, and student authority and autonomy. Finally, this chapter offers some possibly provocative conclusions about ways of meeting some of the MLA Report's aims for the discipline.

Language Pedagogy: What Theory Do We Need?

In *The Structure of Scientific Revolutions*, Thomas Kuhn (1962) distinguished between times of "normal" science, when work was carried out underneath a paradigm, comprising and defining theory, methodology, and objectives, from times of change. The MLA Report resonates with this notion in that it proposes that we move out from previous paradigms, move from "normal science," and start to build a new paradigm from shared objectives and what Howard Gardner, Csikszentmihaly, and Damon (2001) called "good work." The MLA Report points to the need to incorporate intercultural and identity theoretical framings; I propose that rather than importing wholesale any such framings, we should use thoughtful investigation of language teaching objectives and current student experiences to begin to formulate new theoretical framings that are language generated and inflected. Some will come from this very volume; I hope that my discussions of classics institutional and pedagogic framings will offer thoughts about alternative lenses, for good and bad.

Classics Language Pedagogy: Past Experience, Future Possibilities

When, in a seemingly similar climate to that surrounding at least some modern languages, the already declining number of well-qualified classics linguistic applicants began to drop alarmingly, many issues came to the fore. I conducted a case study of one cohort of students to try to illuminate some of these issues (Parker, 2001).

Different institutions devised different curricula to cope with an intake now largely comprising an ab initio cohort and a cohort who had taken one language for a few semesters at high school. (The author was the writer of the major overview report on the state of the classics discipline in England and Scotland, the result of a five-year government-funded investigation of teaching in all classics departments, and the brief outline below is drawn from that.) In many single-discipline classics degrees, a progression was devised over the three years for three strands—ab initio, those with some previous language, and those with good language qualifications. These went with "content" courses, with similar but separate progressions.

By contrast, some elite institutions invested in an intensive ab initio program, with an extra starter year devoted to language work. This was in order to get the lower stream up to the point where they could hang on to the more experienced groups in a text-based cultural curriculum relying on and inculcating expert linguistic and hermeneutic skills. So the aim was, as much as possible, to have common progression and potential outcomes for all.

Another successful solution was to rethink the traditional languages-and-content curriculum and develop new areas of the discipline. Genre and reception studies were and are extremely popular: many classics departments have been saved by enrollments in courses on the classics in film, and the crossover between classical and modern drama is popular and prestigious, especially when involving the theater department, which allowed students to act as well as study the text. When these courses started, there were doubts expressed as to whether these were "proper" classics courses not only because of their general popularity but also because language teaching was absent or voluntary: the courses were based on translation. Over the decades, however, a body of interdisciplinary theory has developed—reception, genre, film, comparative drama, and so forth—and now more such posts are advertised in classics departments than in the traditional subdiscipline areas of philosophy, literature, history, art history, and other such areas. High-quality publications have added to the prestige of the field; I will not say more here except that the move has been similar to the growth in the United States of non-language-based area studies from comparative literature, which is predicated on deep linguistic skills. There are also area studies in classics, such as the Mediterranean world, but here I am talking of separately theorized new disciplines, especially of reception, which are uncertainly positioned in the argument here because many maintain that no language is needed.

Without detracting from the potential excellence of these three answers to the lack of a large field of linguistically able entrants—differentiated outcomes, the deficit model with intensive language-only "catch-up" first-year modules, and the "language-free" disciplinary studies—I would like to explore some of the potential drawbacks to each, drawing on some extra considerations raised by students in the case study.

One potential problem with differentiated outcomes is, to what end? By keeping language groups separate but having common "content" with few language referents, the only connection is a vague sense that language is good for you, that an extra skill is being provided in the course—from the institution's point of view, that this is a proper classics course: there is immense cultural capital in classical languages, partly because historically so much of English elite education was built on and marked out by them and partly because their rarity now stems from the very low level or absence of *all* language teaching in state schools.

These seem good but not sufficient reasons to keep languages in the curriculum, though observing language teaching in many universities across England, I found students seemingly largely to be engaged by those language courses they chose to take. Student responses in the case study were illuminating: some said that they had come to college precisely to study the languages (I can empathize with this—I fell in love with Greek when a young teenager, and I still get a shot of excitement when opening a text), so differentiated curricula allow them to progress, to invest, in optimal conditions. For them, if not for me, a "pure" language course is satisfying; indeed, some complained at the demand that they should leave the language course book and do "content." For some, the case was exactly the opposite: deeply enthused by the classical world, which was the reason they had applied for university study, they resented what they saw as the hard and unrewarding work of language learning, where days of work on exercises or preparing set texts seemed "not to get anywhere." The courses that worked best were those that were best integrated: taught by faculty or language teachers involved in syllabus decisions and text choices that they could take back to the language classroom, which at least had a chance of inspiring the reluctant linguist and binding the enthusiast into the linguistic concerns of the discipline, of getting them—at least to some extent—to see language-in-use and reading practices as opening up new depths in the texts. But in this as in all, there has to be an explicit and thoughtful rationale for the language program, for the program within the course, and, I argue below, for the value and the values of the discipline itself.

Regarding the "language-intensive" based course, there are drawbacks to keeping a group separate, and any language-only program is a high-risk strategy: each year, there are people who leave not just the program but college altogether. That said, there were unexpected benefits: a strong work group and work ethic, explicit goals, and, for those who get through, a sense of identity achieved in the teeth of what at times had seemed impossible demands. (I am tempted to refer to the first-year language examinations as a *rite de passage*, a binding together of the group through pain!)

There are three cohorts in this program as they were in the last, above; the difference is that after that first year, they should move through a deeply language-based course together. I followed three of the earliest cohorts through to their final examinations and was somewhat surprised at what I found. I had presumed that those who arrived with excellent language abilities would be the most confident—that those given support for partial language expertise (measured by final school examinations and some initial needs tests) less so and the ab initio group the least. As has been suggested, though, this latter group was very strong, and the weakest was the "expert" group. The following are possible explanations, offered in the hopes that they might inform discussions in modern languages.

One element goes to identity: these expert linguists had formed their sense of self relatively young, in the early teenage years, around being such an expert. Now they were in an environment where they were expected to use their languages, not just "get them right." Possibly connected, there was a much-expressed sense of "imposterdom," of expecting to be found out. Some of this had to do with the linguistic environment: there was a hesitantly expressed confession that they could not just pick up a text and read it *as if it were English*, with the concurrent assumption that everyone else could do this. Inherent in such confessions was the denial of the text's challenging quality, where part of the process is to puzzle over the texts: they are multivocal and difficult, often alienating, as well as alien. Many learners appear to be unaware of the inter- or transcultural aspect that the MLA Report stresses as a vital reason for adults to learn a second language. This idea of imposterdom comes from the presumption that the reading should be easy, natural, immediate, and complete: conflating ease of translating with ease of meaning making.

Going with this is the trouble that this "top" group had engaging with texts: they had earned high marks in a school system that privileged a narrow correctness of largely one-to-one, word-for-word translation: set texts are taught for the examination rather than for language development or understanding. Lister (2009), in *Latin in Transition*, cites the outrageous advice *by the main high schools examination board* that learning the translation will enable weaker examinees to pick up marks. So their ab initio colleagues are frequently more adventurous, more questioning: generating meaning(s) is a very different exercise from showing an ability to parse or know the single word-for-word English translation.

Such language-intensive courses are provided only by colleges where the whole course is predicated on expert language use. This is something, however, that needs unpacking. Classicists cannot offer value-added courses in business languages, prepare summer visitors and expatriates with communication skills, or send our students to mother-tongue language communities. We do something more closed: rather than using language to communicate, we teach toward language expertise. We have a long-established pedagogy now enlivened by hypertext and Web-based exercises that should make us very aware of language and reading skills, and this gives to our understanding of language a different sense from some of those available to modern language scholars and teachers.

We would not embrace achievement of mother-tongue abilities as an objective—even if it were possible—for several reasons: sure all serious language learning is not about expertise but identity. It is neither possible nor desirable to "become" a native speaker or to acquire a mother tongue: that is why it is called a "mother tongue." We are keen to remain discrete and continually to reflect on the *distance* between what Attridge (2004) has called the "idioculture"—those layers of textual, cultural, and linguistic experiences and expectations that build up from birth—and the experiences and expectations that come from a "foreign" language. And some studies of study-abroad learning show that the effect can be the reinforcement of the home identity rather than the adoption of the native speakers' culture and identity or some blending of the two (Coleman, 1996, 2004). There is a wealth of anecdotal evidence of resistance to language and to rapid uptake of that very language when there is a change in the affordances—for good or ill—of life. As noted by Phipps (2009), speaking another language is a physical, visceral business, making all kinds of different demands and offering all kinds of permissions. It can act as the mask does in the theater: offering play with a different identity, a different way of being as well as communicating. My point is only that there is a multiplicity of needs and reasons to learn languages, many involving permissions precisely from the "foreign," that are vitiated if the aim is acculturation into an adopted nativeness. It is vital that students be allowed to play, to express, and to develop in that second, "other" language.

This is to say that we would not embrace a mother-tongue objective because it implies losing the continuous perception of difference that we prize as a major reason for studying our languages and our discipline. At the simplest, the lesson in difference and otherness is some version of the Sapir–Whorf hypothesis—languages construct *everything* differently: cultural, conceptual, ethical, emotional, medical, and cosmological frameworks. Texts in "other" languages enable and/or denude the possibilities for creative, performative, and textually multilevel and polyphonic questioning of those cultural frameworks. There are implications here for translation exercises, which, as explored below, in classics still tend to prize one to one "equivalence" and correctness rather than meaning making.

Another reason for not adopting native/mother-tongue competence as an aim is that there are questions of authority and ownership in language pedagogy. Any concept of mother-tongue/native-speaker status implies an unbridgeable gap between the authority of the teacher and the possible attainment of the student. If, as argued above, the student is seen as someone who is learning for complex reasons and involving complex identity development, he or she must be allowed to learn rather than be taught, to play and express as best he or she can without feeling that grammatical mistakes will shame or inhibit. Language learning is a much larger game.

And finally, we classicists know just how vestigial and partial is our corpus—a tiny selection, a selection usually made by later librarians and schoolteachers, of high literature; a few recorded speeches; and the very occasional graffito and later sayings but of course no oral corpus. So our grammars and dictionaries are or at least should be provisional, suggestive rather than pseudocomprehensive. Despite a nineteenth-century traditional hermeneutic that aimed at careful discrimination *between* meanings of a word, we can use translation classes to discuss the various potential valences. Corpus linguists bring ever new material into their corpora, showing how rapidly language changes. In classics, we have no access to anything like that, and no classics student could think otherwise. But that very vestigiality encourages and enforces attention to the particularity of the text, to the only partial embodiment and partial exemplarity of language and culture. Importantly, each text is both a product and a small transformation of the way a language inscribes meaning. Most ironically, in a living language with a massive number of texts created daily, the language teaching syllabus tends to reflect a univocality, an implication that the language the student is learning is *not* living but rather static, uniform, and controlled by "the authorities."

A second imperative in the MLA Report that resonated strongly with classics was the need to develop an integrated curriculum. The overview of British university classics curricula above set out various solutions to the problems of low numbers and low entrance language qualifications. But there is the larger question of the values and necessary content that distinguishes and defines our discipline. Some can be discerned in absence: when the "content" planning is divorced from language teaching, there can be an "emperor's-clothes" effect whereby the discipline is actually invisible. This affects faculty and students alike: language teaching goes on somewhere else, and students come to content modules presumed to be able to engage with texts or references as they come up. But language learning is extremely demanding, and progress is often slow, however motivated and able the student. It only takes one or two content classes where a student looks at the quotation and panics because he or she does not know where to start and is terrified that someone will ask him or her to translate, and damage is done. There is also a real problem with language-intensive starter courses: unless integrated with an imaginative cultural course, it risks draining the intellectual stimulus out of the start of college, which should feel as if it is a new kind of learning and experience. There is also some doubt about just how fast languages can be "acquired" if divorced from current users.

However, while nonlanguage modules are everywhere popular, few departments have worked at an integrated curriculum, partly because it means moving away from traditional curricula and pedagogy and partly because there has always been a difference in status between the professoriate and language instructors. Without of course claiming to be able to overcome the latter, an integrated content and language course we devised aims to redress both drawbacks.

We devised a multistrand, multilevel, multidisciplinary integrated course with a spine of core texts studied and taught by all faculty, focusing on the inscription of ideas, beliefs, and values on literary, dramatic, and dialogic form, textuality, linguistic web and hermeneutic issues, and the text as a material correlate of culture. Running alongside such teaching were language and reading classes on the texts through all four years for student groups with three levels of language attainment: those with little language, helped in lectures by key words and "glossed" translations; those with growing proficiency, helped to the independent use of parallel and hypertext texts; and those with "good" language skills.

The overall aim of the curriculum—a deep grounding in and cultural contextualization of the various seminal "classic" texts in each of the disciplines—is one of integration and coordination of both "content" and "language" teaching. Indeed, the whole point is to replace that divide with the reading, interpreting, and disciplinary understanding of texts. The overarching aim of classical language teaching—autonomous reading—would be common to all levels of language classes, but the route by which that would be achieved in four years would be different. For beginners, the aim would be to use glossed texts (translations with extensive notes on the source texts' linguistic structure) to stimulate and reinforce beginners' language courses. Rather than allowing students relievedly to give up the struggle at the upper levels, the aim would be that by the end of the four years the student had acquired a confident reading knowledge and, just as important, an ability to use and know when they were using translation and hypertext help in forming their interpretation (silent, unacknowledged use of translation I found to be pernicious, as it formed a dependency on that translation, whereas we proposed to teach the critical use of the products and understanding of the act of translation).

We proposed that the aims of the "middle" language strand (those able, with dogged use of dictionaries, annotated texts, and hypertexts, to be brought to translate and comment on a set text) should have a double function. Our recommendation was that the whole idea of the examination of a set text should be abandoned in favor of a reading examination where questions about translation should test understanding of the difficulty of translating a particular word in that text and context or the significance of, say, the dual form or optative mood at that point in the text. The larger focus would be on disciplinary textual criticism, on what it means to read a text in philosophy, in theater studies, in epic and lyric poetry studies, in history, and so forth and how they differed.

Classics and Modern Languages Future: Theory

Shona Whyte of the Université de Nice-Sophia Antipolis has analyzed the theoretical bases of language teaching in France over the past three decades (Whyte, in press), tracing the effect on the learner, the conception of language, the learning objectives, and the related hypotheses and methods that have come and gone. I copy below just one row: her analysis of the still dominant paradigm in France, socioconstructivism:

Learning Theories	Sources	Learner	Language	Learning	Hypotheses and Methods
Sociocon-structivism	Vygotsky	Learner	Process	Context	
	Lantolf; Firth and Wagner	Learners construct meaning together	Language competence develops during language activities with other learners	Collaboration is an end, not a means	Cooperative learning; project work

As a result of being part of an Agence Nationale de la Recherche–funded investigation of *La Didactique*, which I translate as the science of discipline-specific pedagogic delivery, I recognize here the French model of a disciplinary paradigm bringing together pedagogic and language theory and deducing methods. Whyte (in press) actually examines three systems: those for "modern languages," *Langues, Littératures, et Civilisation pour l'Enseignement*, which favors a strong cultural orientation (including literature, social and political history, and textual linguistics) and considers the development of language proficiency as a prerequisite and the students' responsibility; those for "foreign languages": *Langues pour spécialistes d'autres disciplines*, which "focuses on communicative language use (including comprehension and expression in the second language), with the culture of countries where the language is spoken a secondary concern"; and she compares the number of language teaching hours in U.S. systems to prepare French and other students for study in U.S. universities to acquire proficiency in academic English as a foreign language.

It is immediately clear that theory, pedagogy, language teaching methodology, objectives, and definitions of "proficiency" are all here constructed by the national disciplinary paradigm. However useful in times of a settled and stable paradigm, I read the MLA Report as an appeal for a new paradigm: one looking to draw its theories and objectives from intercultural and identity studies. I wish to suggest here that this should be a two-way process: that thoughtful, innovative, and integrated language curricula can provide new aspects to and new developments of such models and theories.

Theoria and Practice

It is sadly clear that much classics language pedagogy is still modeled largely on what Whyte (in press) calls the "standard" or default method:

> Language is viewed as a rule-based system including syntax, phonology and the lexicon; it is the task of the learner to learn these rules, by means left largely to his or her judgement. Success is then measured by the teacher in the form of tests of explicit knowledge of rules, and error-free production in planned tasks (written translations or essays, or prepared oral presentations).

This is the opposite of the theory-based principle for language pedagogy advocated here: theory not in the European sense of conceptual framing such that, once adopted, it affects all writing and thinking but something more personal, as used in queer and feminist studies, a sense that goes back to its Greek roots. For *theoria* is presenting oneself to be seen—as in "theater." So, theory can also be a liberating move: in order not to be constrained by the reviewing eye but instead claiming and reclaiming the place from which we need to be seen and indeed insist on being seen. The MLA Report makes it clear that we urgently need this latter version of theory, a common project that unites us all, ancient and modern language professionals alike.

The implications for language pedagogy include the necessity of allowing learners to explore and play with language, which perhaps tends against our wish to help them progress to expertise. In classics, the answer is through reading and writing rather than translation—reading that invites all to explore resonances, resistances, and alienations: anything that widens rather than reduces the gap between home and foreign languages that the "old" pedagogy of one-to-one translation enforced.

It may be particularly challenging in classics, but there are ways, even and perhaps especially with those with limited language who develop particularly quickly and position themselves as language learners. I have tried to realize this notion of *theoria* in pedagogical practice in various ways, such as by using disciplinary-response writing tasks. I take a particular genre, Greek tragedy, which was created and received by its contemporaries as troubling and disturbing. The writing task that students have before we meet for the first time is to make any two elements of a text their own. Parody, poetry, reflections, or any other kind of private writing is welcome, provided that it engages with the language and affect of the text. For pedagogic reasons, the two pieces of writing must address, first, some part of the text that the student "recognizes"—whatever that means to them—and, second, one that focuses on something the student finds alienating, offensive, or rebarbative. The reason is to start by tackling head-on two of the central points of the MLA Report: the importance of knowing who you are by "learn[ing] to comprehend speakers of the target language as members of foreign societies" and the importance of being "trained to reflect on the world and themselves through the lens of another language and culture" (MLA, 2007, p. 4). So, I begin by emphasizing the task as being one of engaging with another language, with another's text, one that must start by being personal and reflective. We start with recognition over millennia, without questioning what that means, and with alienation (given that these texts are full of dramatic and emotional alienations, it might seem strange that students choose just one). The aim of both writing exercises is that in the process students start to discriminate between what they see to be the result of the intercultural gap—the shock of contact with a skeptical, polytheistic society, a society that constructs ethics, philosophy, society, and the cosmos very differently—and alienating or sympathizing effects created in the text to which they respond.

Such writing takes students beyond the simple, incomprehensible alienation, which is not, I think, what is offered by the texts I teach. Crucially, it also signals that the aim is precisely *not* to translate these "other" texts into modern terms. The semester then continues, though I have them read aloud and act out scenes and choruses, even if they do not precisely understand the words. We also do a lot of work on modern versions and at the end of course go back to those initial questions: what and how are these texts and this culture alienating, how recognizable? The terms have usually changed: "alienating" has become "questioning" or "disturbing"; "recognizable" has become that which communicates sympathy and engagement across difference or that relies on theatrical and emotional dynamics recognizable from realist or modern works (e.g., metatheatricality, pathos, or disrupted closure), that is, features of the text rather than of the twenty-first-century reader, allowing a "naked" contact over time, which is one important aspect of identity-forming intercultural contact.[1] This account of a shocking encounter of reader with an "other" text is more violent than current reception theorists' model of losing oneself in the otherness of the text (Batstone, 2006) or even Gadamer's "fusion" of the horizons of reader and text. If for no other reason, current events seem to show that learning to deal with a violent reaction when being confronted by a pressurizing, impinging "other" is no unimportant outcome.

What Theory Do We Need?

There have been innovative language courses based on reading or on activities, with far-reaching effects on classics language pedagogy. But they have stayed within classical language pedagogy, whereas the MLA Report sets up values for the discipline and whole field of study. So, what theory "from outside" is needed to implement such a vision? Perhaps ideas of identity formation, foreignness, aligned curriculum, lenses of cognition, intercultural competences, psychology of otherness, familiarizing/defamiliarizing translation, New Literacy studies, or comparative and contrastive linguistics. I argued above that the MLA Report in some senses is a call to move out from a Kuhnian paradigm. If we are looking to build a new one, maybe we ought to be looking to draw ideas from any of the above and more, not as comprehensive theories but, to use a word from the report, as "lenses" that allow us to deepen our understanding of what we do and why we do it.

The curricula observed and hoped for above are described in terms of individual outcomes, but an important element in the MLA Report looks to the importance of a nation of citizens "trained to reflect on the world and themselves through the lens of another language and culture" who are "trained to comprehend speakers of the target language as members of foreign societies and to grasp themselves as Americans—that is, as members of a society that is foreign to others" (MLA, 2007, p. 4). But it is not just the MLA in the United States that is grappling with these issues. The European Commission recently identified as among the most damaging factors facing the enlarged Europe a fearfulness: fear of "others," fear of instability, and a climate of deep insecurity (Parker, 2008). The humanities panel convened by the European Commission responded with the features of humanities skills that were of vital importance in a newly globalized, complex, and fearful world: participation in a communication-based curriculum, learning to have a voice and be effective in various and swiftly changing conversations, skills of self-knowledge, and stability of identity in the face of the threatening or familiar foreign. We can claim "foreign" language and content courses as ideally equipped to "skill" our graduates to operate in such a world. Intercultural communication is—or should be—at the heart of all language courses; Intercultural communication is often unequal as it involves the effort of having to "comprehend speakers of the target language as members of foreign societies" (MLA, 2007, p. 4). The next clause is also important: stability of identity because they are then able "to grasp themselves as Americans" (p. 4).

Some Visions for the Future

Cultural awareness is one of the most important qualities needed in this ever more globalized world; it is also needed to negotiate the complexities and hostilities of communities coping with migrants, refugees, and immigrant families of every ethnic, linguistic, geographical, cultural, and religious/ethical background (a medium-sized town in England has just been reported as having 137 different languages in familial use daily). I share wholeheartedly the MLA Report's emphasis on the urgency as well as importance of "learn[ing] to comprehend speakers of the target language as members of foreign societies and to grasp themselves as Americans—that is, as members of a society that is foreign to others" (MLA, 2007, p. 4). Foreignness can come from the start of a language course, provided that it is embedded in an overarchingly intercultural curriculum, one that seek to develop the "home" identity while encouraging play with another. Traditional language pedagogy can conflate the two rather than encourage dialogue between them.

It also follows that the role of the teacher needs to be thought through: of course we want to bring students as speedily and as easily as possible into "our" culture. Language teaching may be the heart of giving students independent purchase on and autonomous access to culture, languages, and texts. It means stepping back at times, though, giving up some demonstrations of our own expertise.

In classics, translation is intimately involved: traditionally used as it has been as a test of language acquisition and so privileging demonstrations of correctness. Although I ask for all kinds of reading, I ask about a translation only when we have discussed a peculiarly difficult image or a word that runs through the text (as often happens in Greek tragedy). The point is to generate as many meaningful English translations as possible, partly as an exercise in comparative linguistics and partly to discuss the dramaturgy of certain, especially ethical, words—the hero can be brought down by a word. Just a few of those words, such as courage, guilt, a hero, innocence, blasphemy, fame, city, chance, or the people, can serve to open up different imaginative worlds. As observed by L. P. Hartley (2002), past cultures, just like contemporary cultures, are "a foreign country; they do things differently there" (p. 17).

The big challenge for us in classics is the integrated language-and-content curriculum because it involves radical rethinking about both the discipline's structure and epistemology. We must also devise sharp and innovative statements of what our disciplines offer our students and our stakeholders, employers, and so forth: autonomy, identity, gaining a voice, and intercultural skills and sensibilities, certainly, but also a sophisticated statement of communication skills—not just the ability to talk to others in their language, important though that undoubtedly is, but also the ability to operate in a multilingual world, to bring others into dialogue and a various discourse that may need to weave together dominant and hitherto almost silent partners and perhaps to be able to use and live with narratives that start from different points and have different concerns. It is an ever more complex world, and having meaningful intercultural skills seems to be ever more crucial.

Whatever the "lenses" modern languages can provide or remove, whatever the skills and competences we can claim, the claims have to be at the most inspiring and impressive. They then have to illuminate a rethought, integrated curriculum. Not all courses will be language based of course, but those that are have to deliver some of the values that emerge from the debates following the MLA Report. There is a fight to be fought for the values of our subject, values that can no longer be tacit or rely on traditional ideas of cultural capital.

Note

1. Attridge (2004) wrote of the effect of the singular text as fracturing and pressurizing the "idioculture," the reader's cultural carapace, formed of layers of expectation and cultural conditioning. The effect is for the singular text to open the reader to alterity, to otherness.

References

Attridge, D. (2004). *The singularity of literature*. London: Routledge.

Batstone, W. (2006). Provocation: The point of reception. In C. Martindale (Ed.), *Classics and the uses of reception* (pp. 1–18). Oxford: Oxford University Press.

Coleman, J. A. (1996). *Studying languages: A survey of British and European students. The proficiency, background, attitudes and motivations of students of foreign languages in the United Kingdom and Europe*. London: Centre for Information on Language Teaching and Research.

Coleman, J. A. (2004). *Residence abroad: Good practice guide*. Retrieved from http://www.llas.ac.uk/resources/gpg/2157

Gardner, H., Csikszentmihaly, M., & Damon, W. (2001). *Good work: When excellence and ethics meet*. New York: Basic Books.

Hartley, L. P. (2002). *The go-between*. Introduction by C. Tóibín. New York: New York Review of Books Classics. (Original work published 1953)

Kuhn, T. (1962). *The structure of scientific revolutions*. Chicago: University of Chicago Press.

Lister, B. (2009). Latin in transition. In D. Fitzpatrick & L. Hardwick (Eds.), *Arts and Humanities in Higher Education: An International Journal of Theory, Research and Practice* (Special Issue on Classics Teaching), *8*(2), 191–200.

Modern Language Association. (2007). *Foreign languages and higher education: New structures for a changed world*. Retrieved from http://www.mla.org/flreport

Parker, J. (2001). *Dialogic education and the problematics of translation in Homer and Greek tragedy*. New York: Edwin Mellen Press.

Parker, J. (2008). "What have the humanities to offer 21st-century Europe?" Reflections of a note-taker. *Arts and Humanities in Higher Education: An International Journal of Theory, Research and Practice, 7*(1), 83–96.

Pfeiffer, P. C. (2008). The discipline of foreign language studies and reforming foreign language education. *Modern Language Journal, 92*(2), 296–298.

Phipps, A. (2009, March 6). *"Space to language": Being intercultural in a breathless world*. Keynote address at the symposium Critical and Intercultural Theory and Language Pedagogy, Irvine, CA.

Wellmon, C. (2008). Languages, cultural studies, and the futures of foreign language education. *Modern Language Journal, 92*(2), 292–295.

Whyte, S. (in press). Learning theory and technology in university foreign language education: The case of French universities. *Arts and Humanities in Higher Education: An International Journal of Theory, Research and Practice, 9*(3).

Chapter 9

From Core Curricula to Core Identities: On Critical Pedagogy and Foreign Language/Culture Education

David Brenner, University of Houston

Abstract

This chapter argues that some form of critical pedagogy should be promoted and sustained in foreign language/culture education despite current ideological and social challenges to the paradigm. It is not readily apparent what form a twenty-first-century critical pedagogy, as a theoretically grounded praxis, should take. One option would be Gerald Graff's systematic, curriculum-centered approach, which advocates the teaching of academic controversies. A second would derive from a classroom-centered, "bottom-up" approach as represented by Ira Shor, which focuses on the needs and concerns of those we teach. A third model, and the one argued for in this chapter, would develop an identity-centered, psychologically informed approach to developing students' compassion in relation to others while examining the core causes of human behavior, based primarily on the work of Bracher (2006). At stake is whether foreign language/culture learners might respond to a "prosocial" pedagogy and revise their conventional "information-processing scripts" so as to approach or mediate other languages/cultures with communicative and also with ethical competence.

Introduction

The devaluation of foreign language/culture education in the United States continues despite renewed calls to improve it in the wake of the September 11, 2001, terrorist attacks. Whether its ongoing crisis is ultimately attributable to the anti-intellectual ideology of American society or to an American mythology of isolation from the rest of the world, one thing is clear: it is unjust to persist in blaming ourselves, that is, foreign language/culture educators. At the same time as our fields of practice continue to be in crisis, we are repeatedly called on to justify our efforts in an adversarial public sphere in which pundits insist that educators need to overcome their presumed "lack of accountability"—at least financially if not socially or ethically. In a context such as this, it is important to disentangle the present issues from the core structural problems in order to focus intellectual energy on the latter.

This chapter assumes that some form of critical pedagogy ought to be developed and sustained not only in education generally but also in foreign language/culture education in particular. My aim here, in the process of reviewing the options available, is to ascertain which form of critical pedagogy would be most effective and useful in the current climate. For even though critical pedagogy is a well-established body of theoretically informed practices, it is not readily apparent what version of it can or should be implemented in an environment that is set on ignoring or taming it. Should we adopt a curriculum-centered approach, as proposed by Gerald Graff, that requires the systematic teaching of academic controversies, on the assumption that these are "teachable moments"? Or should we engage in a classroom-centered, bottom-up model, following Ira Shor, that focuses principally on the needs and concerns of the (majority of) student-learners whom we educate? Or is perhaps a third way most appropriate, an identity-centered approach that seeks to link both curricular and classroom paradigms by focusing on students' social and psychological development? I argue here that this third approach, in part a synthesis of the first two, may be particularly effective in countering resistance to critical pedagogy in foreign language/culture education and elsewhere.

While I outline some of the methods available for enacting an effective critical pedagogy in this chapter, my approach assumes that critical inquiry—including the questioning of dearly held assumptions—is at least as important in the foreign language/culture classroom as are manageable solutions to discrete difficulties that might be addressed by "teaching tips." In alignment with ecological perspectives on language acquisition/socialization, a warrant of my approach is what Claire Kramsch (2002) has called the "poststructuralist realization that learning is a nonlinear relational human activity, co-constructed between humans and their environment, contingent upon their position in space and history, and a site of struggle for the control of social power and cultural memory" (p. 5).

Critical Pedagogies for "Translingual and Transcultural" Competence

The primary objective of critical pedagogy is "to critically appropriate forms of knowledge outside of [our] immediate experience, to envisage versions of a world which is 'not yet' in order to alter the grounds on which life is lived" (Simon, 1988, p. 2). Such knowledge must go "beneath surface meaning . . . dominant myths, official pronouncements, traditional clichés, received wisdom, and mere opinions, [in order] to understand the deep meaning, root causes, social context, ideology, and personal consequences of any action, event, object, process, organization, experience, text, subject matter, policy, mass media, or discourse" (Shor, 1992, p. 129). Kumaravadivelu (2006) points out that researchers in second-language interactional analysis, to take a related foreign languages example, "have shied away from any serious engagement with the ideological forces acting upon classroom discourse" (p. 73).

As a result, another warrant of the model of critical pedagogy proposed here is that the study of a foreign language/culture is uniquely capable of assisting students to increase their capacity for understanding others (for the purposes of this chapter, also designated as "the Other"). Put another way, in this chapter, I also assume that it is important for foreign language educators to be concerned with increasing students' awareness of the Other, including Others' suffering and/or their perceived lack of accountability for their problems, issues, or crises. In lieu of what he and others (e.g., Byram, 2008; Reagan & Osborne, 2002) view as the inadequately critical status quo in foreign language education, Kumaravadivelu (1999) proposes a "critical classroom discourse analysis," according to which

> negotiation of discourse meaning and its analysis should not be confined to the acquisitional aspects of input and interaction, or to the instructional imperatives of form/function focused language learning activities; instead, they should also take into account discourse participants' complex and competing expectations and beliefs, identities and voices, fears and anxieties. (p. 472)

The Modern Language Association (MLA) Ad Hoc Committee Report (MLA, 2007) specifically calls on students to learn "to *reflect* [emphasis added] on the world and themselves as members of foreign societies and to grasp themselves as Americans—that is, as members of a society that is *foreign* [emphasis added] to others" and not merely to function as "informed and capable interlocutors with educated native speakers in the target language" (pp. 4–5).

In the manner of ecological perspectives, all three of the models of critical pedagogy discussed here are both "relational" and reflective. Thus, in addition to helping students develop empathy with the suffering (or pleasures) of others, the study of a foreign language/culture should assist them in reflecting on what is conventionally held to be *knowledge*, *experience*, and *power* in various sectors of society.

Yet a reexamination of these issues is much older than Foucault's (1985, 1986) discussions of the knowledge/power nexus. Rather, such "relational" reflection intervenes in discussions dating back to John Dewey, Lev Vygotsky, and other major theorists of education. Again, such discussions go beyond the "merely theoretical," affirming a pragmatism to be found in both Dewey and Vygotsky. Consequently, the recent MLA/Association of Departments of Foreign Languages proposal of 2008 titled "Transforming College and University Foreign Language Departments" calls on language/culture curricula "to produce a specific outcome: educated users of a language in addition to English who have deep *translingual and transcultural competence* [emphasis added] in that language and English" (Pratt et al., 2008, p. 289).

Teaching (Academic) Conflicts and Controversies

Pratt and her coauthors urge that that their 2008 proposal be translated into action—and very soon. The idea of this chapter is that critical pedagogy provides one such paradigm for realizing such proposals, especially inasmuch as it is itself already a "translingual and transcultural" field of inquiry. To be sure, critical pedagogy may be seen as too "radical" or too "theoretical" for some. After all, when foreign language/culture educators are not engaged in humanistic inquiry with our students, we tend to fall back on instrumentalist rationales for our importance, such as the applied value of our offerings in improving globalized commerce or the equally globalized "War on Terror."

By contrast, critical pedagogy is by definition open to the notion that education is a culture of inquiry. Its aim is to reinvigorate education as a site for a learning praxis "committed to problematizing and not problem solving, to complicating and not resolving issues" (Slevin, 2002, p. 53). If we are truly involved in critical inquiry and critical pedagogy, then we need to apply those approaches that level the playing field "not just by bringing academic norms and expectations into the open but through classroom practices explicit in their interrogation and critique of those norms" (Slevin, 2002, p. 53).

Such approaches might be seen as immoderate or even dangerous. When translated into classroom practices, such a critical pedagogy

> focuses on an ethic of responsibility, on the valuing of difference, on negotiation and collaboration, on inclusion, on shared attempts at critical understanding. . . . [It] cannot easily occur in a 10- or 14-week parcel of time; nor can it develop easily in cramped and inhospitable and highly institutionalized, much less disembodied electronic "virtual," spaces. Even less can it develop where the system of rewards (grades) is linked thoroughly to traditional models of authority and to notions of institutional hierarchy and autonomous individualism. (Lunsford, 1996, p. 437)

Of course, many progressive or critical educators restrict themselves to discussions of "solo acts of teaching," as Gerald Graff (1996, p. 427) points out in a rebuttal to this and similar arguments. Graff, founder in 1991 of Teachers for a Democratic Society, is best known for his call to "teach the conflicts."[1] His approach has broad implications for classroom pedagogy and curricular design in universities. Its point of departure is that within and between disciplines, there are conflicts of many kinds—philosophical, epistemological, and so on. Unless we wish to shield students from these controversies, our curricula need to be restructured as conversations. If curricula do not become more dialogic, Graff (1996) reasons, students will continue to suffer from "severe cognitive dissonance" (p. 426). The dominant paradigm of "to each her own classroom" shelters us "from the criticisms of our assumptions to which we would risk exposing ourselves if our courses were in dialogue" (p. 429). In the interim, students get bounced back and forth between noncommunicating teachers or balkanized in separate (sub)disciplines. What Graff deems that a confusing, "à la carte" approach to curriculum does little to foster students' capacities for reflection or critical judgment.

Yet the insular notion of the classroom leaves teachers unexposed to the disagreements of their peers. "Although we professors are routinely accountable to peer criticism," writes Graff (1996), "when we publish articles and books or speak at conferences, this normal accountability is curiously assumed to cease once we enter 'the classroom'" (p. 429). Although he does not advocate a legislated form of accountability, Graff at times appears to presuppose an idealized speech community and/or Habermasian model of the public sphere. Graff's method has been critiqued as assuming a "fiction of liberal neutrality" (Nelson, 1997, p. 91). Similarly, the controversies Graff and others wish to teach are fundamentally confined to the university per se. The conflicts scholars tend to disavow are the broader, culturally embedded ones, for social inequalities reproduced in the professor–student relationship almost certainly interfere with pedagogy, rendering it—in foreign language/culture education and elsewhere—a less effective endeavor.

Teaching (the) Class

Ira Shor is frequently cited in discussions of pedagogies that are "democratic-critical" or "Freirean"—named for Paulo Freire, arguably the "founder" of critical pedagogy (Freire 2004; Freire & Shor, 1987). Shor has also debated Graff in public forums. In his 1996 book *When Students Have Power: Negotiating Authority in Critical Pedagogy*, Shor insists that

> before "teaching the conflicts" among scholars in any field, we first
> need to face the always already-existing conflicts between students
> and the teacher, between students and the institution, between
> students and the economic system (class, gender, racial inequi-
> ties), and between the students themselves (over issues of race,
> gender, sexual orientation, ethnicity, age, physical ability, appear-
> ance, choice of major, career competitiveness against each other
> for grades, etc.). (pp. 17–18)

Shor argues that if we begin our courses by introducing canonical subject matter or academic conflicts in a field, we have overlooked the destructive power of the conflicts that predetermine students' attitudes and perceptions. For "teaching any disciplinary material, including the academic conflicts among scholars, before negotiating the curriculum with students [in order] to share power, only front-loads the process with official authority" (p. 18). Teaching scholarly controversies renders students "silenced spectators in an education being done *to* them for their own good, not being done *by* them or *with* [emphasis added] them" (p. 18). While some foreign language/culture educators might claim that many of their class-rooms are truly student centered (for a critique of their claim, see Kumaravadivelu, 2006, chap. 4), there may be few classrooms where the students are so disem-powered or silent, especially when authority is implicitly granted to the native (or near-native) speaker. Further, as long as struggles for hegemony take place in a classroom or an institution, one ought to be teaching *to* and *through* these struggles, not merely *about* them. Such struggles may be exacerbated particularly in foreign language/culture education, in which students' "complex and compet-ing expectations and beliefs, identities and voices, fears and anxieties" come to the fore (Kumaravadivelu, 1999, p. 472). Critical approaches to curriculum such as Graff's otherwise appear to be condemned to irrelevance. While Shor's approach might be more successful in building a classroom community out of a diverse group of learners, he freely admits that "democratic practices in one classroom do not mean that school and society have been democratized" (Shor, 1996, p. 220). Rather, his method is to privilege dialogue that foregrounds student discourse in confronting "unilateral authority at every turn, in every course, in every social institution" (p. 221).

In directly addressing Shor's "student-centered" approach, Graff (in Graff, 2003) divulges that in his own teaching, "students would often still feel silenced or intimidated when disagreement broke out or when we criticized their work" (pp. 268–269). Yet Graff's response has been to diagnose the "shyness and passivity" of some students as a problem that is "cognitive" at its core instead of admitting that he had previously "not paid enough attention to the emotional and personal dimensions of academic conflict" (p. 269). Not until Graff had team taught in 2002 with Jane Tompkins (at the University of Illinois at Chicago) did it occur to him that "too often we were unable to make the [academic or scholarly] issues clear and compelling enough for those students to understand what the issues were and why they should give a damn about them" (p. 270). The same clarification would have to be made in the foreign language classroom, for it may be more difficult for students to understand what *those* issues are and just how they are relevant to them.

The practice of academic controversy proposed by Graff may leave students not only uninterested or unmotivated but also confined to the campus unless the disciplinary and systemic determinants of professor–student conflict are themselves dealt with. Although "core curricula" such as Graff's may have the potential to democratize or improve higher education, they may be ineffective if the social inequalities of the professor–student relationship are not addressed first. "The status quo presents opening obstacles to critical thought and democratic process," Shor (1996, p. 16) notes. He and other advocates of a similar type of critical pedagogy maintain that Graff's well-known proposal cannot be realized as long as classrooms reproduce the struggle for hegemony. Shor thus proposes a variation on realpolitik. We ought to "blame ourselves less for some of the restrictions or limits that we discover in experimenting and transforming, and understand that we're pushing against some powerful limits set by the climate. What we can do, we accomplish inside a specific setting in a real history" (Shor, 1997).

And I might add that what we can do, we accomplish inside a specific setting in a real history with real people.

Teaching (Prosocial) Identity: Psychological and Ethical Dimensions of Critical Pedagogy

The third model of critical pedagogy to be considered in this chapter strives to enhance students' social and psychological development. It is also an ethical approach inasmuch as it fosters students' compassion toward others in the process of examining the root causes of human behavior.[2] At stake in this third model of critical pedagogy is whether students are sociopsychologically capable of learning differently. Indeed, students of foreign language/culture, perhaps more than in other disciplines, are specifically asked to revise their conventional "information-processing scripts"[3] in order to identify causes of Others' behavior. Inasmuch as they are being asked to identify with the cultures and languages of these Others, they too are being asked to give up more control than usual, especially those taking (beginning-level) courses in a foreign language/culture.

In such a cognitive and emotional pedagogy of identity or identities, students are prompted to imagine what it is or would be like to *be* another person in his or her linguistically and culturally specific circumstances. If students and also *teacher*-learners work on establishing a metacognition of their information processing—keeping a journal, for instance, of their thoughts, emotions, and action orientations when encountering real and fictionalized others—they are in a better position to assess whether they have responded to these others with adequate information-processing scripts.

The ultimate objective of what I call an identity-centered, psychologically informed critical pedagogy is to help students develop *prosocial* metacognition in order to recognize and interrupt *antisocial* processing scripts whenever they have begun to activate them. Students are also assisted in recognizing when they have encountered those apparatuses that promote such antisocial processing scripts—the media, news formats and cycles, entertainment genres, and so on. In this third model of critical pedagogy, students learn to substitute more adequate, or prosocial, processing scripts for the flawed, or antisocial, ones. This aim is achieved by having student-learners keep *reflective* journals that document their own and others' uses of adequate and inadequate processing scripts. Such journaling is equally important, even for students just beginning to learn about a foreign language/culture.

The warrant of this third path to critical pedagogy is that an ethical and identity-informed approach grounds the critique of educational and other norms in a compelling theory of human development. According to its leading theorist, Mark Bracher (2006), improvements in teaching are illusory as long as we fail to examine identity issues faced by students and teachers. Bracher illustrates how the restructuring of students' identity components can alter the conditions under which learning takes place. This restructuring presumes that educators themselves begin to reflect systematically on the factors that motivate antisocial behaviors. As an identity-centered critical pedagogy, it focuses on revealing the emotional and cognitive capacities needed by students to learn, develop, and engage in "prosocial" behavior.

Now language itself, according to the MLA Report, "reveals us to others and to ourselves" (MLA, 2007, p. 5). In addition to synthesizing this constitutive view of language with psychology and cognitive science, Bracher's approach aims to explicate the root causes of crime, violence, substance abuse, racism, sexism, and homophobia. In the following, I would like to present some of Bracher's ideas that appear particularly relevant and useful for a critical-pedagogy perspective on foreign language/culture teaching and learning. His aim is to (re)integrate the study of literary and other texts not only into the fabric of our curriculum but also into students' subjective experiences of encountering the Other through language/culture study.

Bracher recalls at the outset of his *Radical Pedagogy: Identity, Generativity, and Social Transformation* the insight of psychologist James Gilligan that "people will sacrifice anything to prevent the death and disintegration of their individual or group identity" (Gilligan, 1996, p. 97, cited in Bracher, 2006, p. 3). In other words, humans are even more willing to risk biological than "ideological" death, that is, the demise of their sense of "self" in relation to implicit "others." Yet at the same time, our sense of self as humans is destabilized whenever we render "criminals," "addicts," and "terrorists" as externalized receptacles for our own antisocial or aggressive impulses. The senseless pursuit of "identity-protecting" scapegoats, according to Bracher, can lead us to seek the punishment of "not only violent offenders but also individuals and groups who are themselves the victims of misfortune and injustice, such as the poor, the homeless, the unemployed, the uninsured, and racial, ethnic, religious, and sexual minorities" (p. 6).

Whenever people belonging to such minorities are denied recognition, they have been denied a fundamental human need and hence a crucial motivation for personal learning and development. This need for recognition more than compensates for the identity support we lose if we relinquish our practices of "demonizing violent Others and externalizing our own disowned violent impulses onto them" (Bracher, 2006, p. 137). Consequently, in order to acquire secure, well-supported identities, students and, of course, their teachers must *integrate* rather than *exclude* those elements of the self that are harmful when enacted in different contexts. Among the types of recognition we must integrate, Bracher includes (1) the public self, that is, "those parts of oneself that one acknowledges and freely displays to others in hopes of their being recognized"; (2) the private self, that is, "elements that one . . . yearns to have others recognize and accept but that one hides from others"; and (3) the unconscious elements of oneself that "one is unaware of possessing because one has disowned them" (p. 164).

This third form of recognition (of the "unconscious" elements of the self) has particular consequences: while teachers also have a need for acknowledgment and affirmation, such a need can result in practices that undermine their efforts to facilitate student development. By owning up to some measure of narcissism or even rage, educators may achieve the prosocial recognition of what social psychologist Erik Erikson (1964) called our "need to be needed" (p. 130, cited in Bracher, 2006, p. 149). In his critique of "identity-undermining pedagogies," Bracher (2006, chaps. 6 and 7) effectively documents the failures of teachers to engage in various kinds of self-reflection. Following Erikson (1964), for whom "the teaching passion is not restricted to the teaching profession" (p. 131), Bracher posits a fundamental need to teach, itself subtended by a generative identity. But how might one specifically enact this generative desire to support the identity development of oneself *and* others, namely, the students?

While many who teach language/culture would agree that integrated, self-reflective identities are an ideal outcome of our curricula and teaching practices, at times (and unwittingly) we practice authoritarian pedagogies. To be sure, the fields of English and foreign languages/cultures have made significant antiauthoritarian strides since the 1960s. But even progressives and leftists have socialized students into desiring forms of disciplinary authority, going so far as to contend that young people should be consulting canonical or "core" works of literature when faced with (even practical) difficulties in their lives. In the case of Graff's "teaching the conflicts," discussed above, students are in effect asked to consult great works of scholarship rather than attending to their own experiences and capabilities. By the standards of such pedagogies, the students said to be the best are those who eschew naive or uncritical modes of interpretation. In that process, women, minorities, and other subaltern students are called on to reduce their incompatibility with their teachers. They therefore learn to integrate themselves into those larger institutional or cultural systems their teachers represent. In a criticism that bears reproducing in full here, Bracher (2006) maintains that

> the spectacle we offer our students of authoritative, knowledgeable, and enthusiastic subjects passionate about literature—that is, as subjects who appear to know how to become whole and recapture lost *jouissance* through literary study—functions in the same way as an advertisement of an attractive and satisfied individual enjoying a cigarette: both the teacher's performance and such advertisements elicit identification with the subject supposed to know, which promotes replication in the students or the advertisements' audience of this subject's identity. While our conscious pedagogical intentions might be more noble and the direct results less destructive than those of cigarette advertisements, the transferential effect and identity damage of such pedagogical practice are the same. (p. 94)[4]

It is therefore crucial to keep just as critical an eye on ourselves, the critical pedagogues, and underscore that not only authoritarian pedagogies but also unreflective pedagogies of resistance or "empowerment" can threaten the core identities of students. Here we may valuably contrast such pedagogies with the primary objective of psychologically informed education: to enable individuals to intervene in the formation of their own identities. For instance, when a patient in therapy demands to know "what his problem is," an identity-centered psychologist would not immediately attempt to provide him or her with answers. Rather, he or she would help the patient develop the capacity to form his or her own answers. Doing so thus requires the psychologist to abstain from the role of an ideal ego (or imaginary Other) despite the patient's efforts to address him or her as such. When the psychologist resists such expectations, the patient is compelled to recognize a difference between the "I" who speaks and the idealized ego projected onto the psychologist.

To clarify just the sort of "self" this third model of critical pedagogy proposes, consider a cautionary tale from the beginnings of critical pedagogy. The workers in Paulo Freire's literacy classes in 1980s Brazil were notably uncomfortable with his dialogic pedagogy, telling him, "'You're the one who should have been talking, sir. You know things, sir. We don't'" (Freire, 2004, p. 36). The deference shown toward Freire was a repetition of the authoritarian relations these workers experienced in their daily lives. These learners "transferred" onto the person of Freire the position of master. From this, he learned that if students were to become more aware of the forms of oppression in society, then he would have to allow for the repetition of those relations within the controlled space of the classroom:

> As these forms of oppression are rooted in authoritarian relations, repeating them in the classroom will inevitably involve transferring authoritarian positions—the Patriarch, the Bourgeois, the

Colonizer, the Bigot—onto the person of the teacher insofar as the teacher occupies the position of the "subject who is supposed to know." (Cho, 2009, p. 108)

Just as Freire had to control his responses and distance himself from authoritarian relations in the classroom, Jacques Lacan (2002) calls on fellow psychologists to refuse to reproduce such relations. This "refusal to reply," which he terms the "analyst's abstention" (p. 93), can be applied to the teacher/student relationship. This abstention, when redeployed by a teacher, is designed to undercut the student's tendency to identify with the teacher as the ideal form of subjectivity. While such imaginary relations may seem to be important in an effective teaching experience, teachers should hinder their development. By implication, some students will enact identities that thoroughly reproduce those of their teachers. Other students, when compelled to participate in a politically correct environment, might feel silenced even though the class was intended to "empower" them. Hence, whenever teachers practice an oppositional pedagogy, it can have the negative effect of confronting a student's identity at its most vulnerable.

In the worst-case scenario, when we do not grant "respectful recognition to those identities that are most responsible for institutional, structural, and cultural violence" (e.g., the identities of "angry white males"), we run the risk of "perpetuating the (evil) Other's traumatization, making him more rather than less likely to engage in cultural, structural, institutional, and even physical violence" (Bracher, 2006, p. 99). After all, few of us who practice critical pedagogies have managed to "express or engender sympathy for those individuals . . . who appear to be the most different from us" (p. 99) in our self-imagining as "humane, nonviolent" subjects. On the one hand, such "sympathy" may even require resources beyond the project of critical pedagogy, drawing on the literature of conflict transformation, a subject touched on in this volume but beyond the scope of this chapter. For learning to engage with individuals with whom we are in conflict is an important educational prospect and part of a translingual, transcultural pedagogy. On the other hand, Freirean models have also *staged* conflict as a way of enabling a pedagogical engagement with conflict, particularly in the "Theatre of the Oppressed" developed by Augusto Boal together with Freire and based on Freire's "Pedagogy of the Oppressed." Boal's method is akin to "active learning" but seeks, by way of the theatrical context, to transform audiences into active participants in a psychologically-informed theatrical experience.

Faced with evidence that the problems teachers wish to solve are at least partially of their own making or of unwitting neglect, it becomes their task in (self-) critical pedagogy to reflect more carefully on their own motivations and knowledge. One must apprehend how students attempt to manipulate educators into repeating the relationships they feel to have been the most supportive in their past. Similar efforts should be engaged in by teachers—to apprehend how *they* have attempted to manipulate students into repeating relationships that the *educators* feel to have been the most supportive in their past—if we are to depart from pedagogical practices that we unconsciously presume maintain our identities in accustomed ways.

A more complete and effective self-analysis of teaching would require time and energy, not to mention insight, commitment, and critical, yet compassionate work. It further assumes that we are willing to reassess our personal identity investments in specific teaching practices. As a result, Bracher suggests that teachers reflect in writing on the question of what being a teacher means. Having teased out and acknowledged the identity needs involved in our initial decisions to be educators, we might then ask whether these still have the same significance for us. Have other core identity needs come to replace them in the meantime? In particular, our desire for recognition entails a basic psychoanalytic point about desire, namely, "that it is always desire of the other" (Bracher, 2006, p. 150). As reformulated by Bracher, the fundamental question for the educator becomes "Have I acted in conformity with the desire for the other's well-being that is built into me?" (p. 151). Having then recognized such altruistic behavior as a core desire conveying a sense of gratification, "it tends to become a desire that we desire above others" (p. 151).

Toward Foreign Language Pedagogical Practice

Yet, how is all the preceding ultimately to be realized in practice? One of the warrants of Bracher's approach is that studying fiction is well suited to the development of complex identity structures. As a result, teachers of rhetoric/composition and foreign languages would be well served to consider texts that provide optimal degrees of identity support for particular students taught in a particular class. By dealing with texts that engage readers through empathetic identification with characters, students can experience or enact the specific stage of emotional and cognitive development most required at a given point in their lives.[5] As long as teachers offer students recognition, even conventional activities such as class discussions, group work, and journaling are capable of helping students cultivate more resilient selves.

Yet the precise forms which a psychologically informed pedagogy might take have to be decided on a case-by-case basis, in the situated contexts of the classroom. It is not that critical pedagogues are reluctant to give advice and tips on the bread and butter of conventional didactics. Rather, prescribing particular texts or assignments is a top-down tactic that may well backfire since an identity-centered pedagogy aims for students to find ways to recognize and integrate previously rejected parts of themselves. In moving beyond names, dates, and received interpretations, teachers of language/culture can take advantage of students' interest in and enjoyment of popular fiction, song, film, or other media. If, however, English/foreign language educators choose only those texts *we* find particularly gratifying, we may fail to engage *students*' core identities. As a result, students will fall short when attempting to own other excluded elements of their selves.

One way to avoid such pitfalls is to carefully record students' responses to their reading. Although English and foreign language/culture education conventionally privilege essay writing and standard elements of style, having students emulate canonical forms may not address their specific identity needs. It is instead more effective for students to discuss and reflect on their own responses to certain texts and aspects of those texts (such as plot, theme, character, and style) in order to "investigate the identity needs motivating their consumptions of and responses to these elements" (Bracher, 2006, p. 182). This means that rather than having students offer an interpretation or judgment articulating what they think the *author* (or text or character or teacher) means, we redirect their attention back to their own responses, thereby assisting them to become more aware of their own identity contents and sociopsychological issues. This is not an anything-goes pedagogy where the teacher abdicates all responsibility for learning or conveying his or her expertise, nor is it purely self-referential; rather, it is multiply intertextual, including the student's own "texts" (i.e., his or her own personal stories) as a foot in the door to connecting with texts as personal windows. These are windows on new cultures and new language, to be sure, but also windows on the student's own self. Through such strategies, students can begin to recognize and take responsibility for their own development as individuals and members of collectives.

What kind of strategies might achieve these objectives? Bracher (2006) recommends working with "narratives that are powerful elicitors of sympathy" (p. 176), those that help students recognize and accept such feelings, once activated. He recommends *Uncle Tom's Cabin, Invisible Man,* and especially *Native Son* as heuristic ideals of narratives that effectively combine "the evocation of strong feelings of pity, sympathy, and compassion with exhortations to readers to cultivate these emotions" (p. 176). In addition, Bracher provocatively suggests that students "cultivate guilt" in response to narrative literature, thus "remov[ing] a major motive for denying their own responsibility and blaming the victims" (p. 191). In a class on American culture, the strategy of cultivating guilt would diminish "the psychological need for arguments, such as, 'I don't own slaves, and none of my ancestors ever did, so why should I sacrifice financially or professionally for the benefit of black people?'" (p. 191). In the foreign language (or translingual) classroom, these strategies can also be deployed with a range of texts that confront issues of racism, sexism, colonialism, homophobia, or problematic historical events, such as the Holocaust and other genocides.

In my field of German studies, excellent materials and texts have become more "mainstream" in recent years. For example, the beginning German textbook *Deutsch zusammen* (Donahue & Watzinger-Tharp, 2000) now includes excerpts from *Schuldig geboren,* or *Born Guilty* (Sichrovsky, 1987, 1989), a well-known collection of first-person testimonies by the children of former Nazi leaders. Many teachers have adapted for instruction the novel *Der Vorleser,* or *The Reader* (Schlink, 1995, 1997), which addresses anti-Jewish racism in the Third Reich and the Holocaust as well as the guilt of "second-generation" non-Jews. The Jewish experience of the Holocaust is represented in a variety of texts, but a mainstream intermediate reader, *Mitlesen, Mitteilen* (Wells & Morewedge, 2004), has for some years included an excerpt from *Weiter leben,* or *Still Alive,* Ruth Klüger's (1992, 2001) important memoir of surviving Auschwitz-Birkenau. Teachers who find these options too difficult for their students may consider the pedagogical perennial *Damals war es Friedrich*, or *Friedrich* (Richter, 1961, 1987), the tragic story of two boys—one Jewish, the other non-Jewish—in the Nazi era. These are a few examples of how even very difficult subject matter can be brought into the classroom even at the introductory level, connecting students with new ways of seeing the new culture and themselves beyond the usual skills-based, communicative settings characteristic of many foreign language classes.

The failure of students (or teachers) to assume any form of "guilt" or to cultivate "sympathy" may threaten much more than individual identities. For Bracher, the continued existence of humanity depends on our acknowledging that our actions produce important consequences for other people. While critics will and should note the excesses of many psychoanalytic theorists and practitioners, from Lacan himself to Slavoj Žižek and others, numerous nonpsychoanalytic theorists of the self support Bracher's premise that there is a basic human desire for recognition.

Supporting this prosocial identity work in the language classroom is admittedly challenging in a society that seems to value such qualities less than ever. Instead, characteristics such as wealth, social status, athletic ability, physical appearance, or racial/ethnic affiliation appear to be desired or enacted by many students over characteristics such as intellect, self-reflection, compassion, or altruism. Perhaps for these reasons, a pedagogy of the sort described here has hardly been attempted.[6] But an identity-oriented critical pedagogy promoting prosocial identities for educators and learners aims to develop "a generativity in which our personal sense of self [as educators] is a function of our helping others to develop and flourish" (Bracher, 2006, p. 207). And the cognitive and emotional changes that this pedagogy aims to produce are a prerequisite for social and political changes.

Conclusion

In concluding, I would add that vigilance of an assertive kind is required as we continue to assess what is to be done about foreign language/culture education in the United States. For, as the MLA Report suggests, we who educate risk becoming too reasonable and diplomatic in the current environment. When faced, as of late, with accelerated reductions in state (and even private) support and expanded reliance on adjunct lecturers in the classroom, what would it mean especially for foreign language/culture educators to become less apologetic? Having already been compelled to compete for funding and recognition in an adversarial (and politicized) public sphere, we might consider the "added value" of challenging our critics more straightforwardly. Otherwise, we may never succeed in educating others to revise their information-processing scripts so that they might educate *themselves* about or at least respect and recognize the practice and theory of pedagogy. The models for such recognition proposed here do not just interrogate the idea of foreign language education as both "instrumentalist" and "constitutive" (MLA, 2007) but also challenge simplistic distinctions between theory and praxis. While remaining "realistic" and allowing for exigencies, foreign language/culture educators ought to strive to retain their capacity to "relate and reflect" at the same time despite the current circumstances that tend to render critical pedagogy more difficult—yet no less necessary—to practice.

Notes

1. Cf. Graff's (1992) classic statement of his position is in his *Beyond the Culture Wars* (1992): "Academic institutions are already teaching the conflicts every time a student goes from one course or department to another. . . . Students typically experience a great clash of values, philosophies, and pedagogical methods among their various professors, but they are denied a view of the interactions and interrelations that give each subject meaning. . . . This is what has passed for 'traditional' education, but a curriculum that screens students from the controversies between texts and ideas serves the traditional goals of education . . . poorly" (p. 12).

2. For the importance of ethical reflection generally in instructed second-language acquisition, see Ortega's (2005) relatively recent contribution.

3. For an early use of this term, see Huesmann (1988). Huesmann reasons that social behavior is controlled to a great extent by programs for behavior that are established during a person's early development. These programs can be described as cognitive scripts stored in a person's memory and are used as guides for behavior and social problem solving. Scripts persist in a child's repertoire as they are rehearsed and enacted.

4. By "transferential," Bracher is referring to the replication of another subject's identity or the projection of an idealized identity (or "ego") onto another person, such as a therapist or teacher. An example of such transference in teaching and learning is when students attempt to manipulate educators into repeating the relationships they feel to have been the most supportive in their past.

5. One anonymous reviewer of this chapter mentioned the Brechtian distancing effect (*Verfremdungseffekt*) in noting that the Germanophone writing I recommend here seems non-Brechtian. Although the issue of identification and distanciation in Brecht's dramaturgy is highly complicated and although my own approach to critical pedagogy is poststructuralist (in the manner of "ecological" perspectives), I do indeed favor texts in language/culture pedagogy that elicit empathetic identification and character development.

6. To take the example of German language/culture, progressive educators might be overestimating our effectiveness if we object, as one anonymous reviewer of this chapter did, "What about all the courses where the students are moved from whatever ideas they have about Nazi Germany to understanding better why such a thing can happen?" In my experience, getting students to "other" themselves and adopt an inherently complex, critical stance to the catastrophe of the Holocaust—one that would promote tolerance, compassion, and perhaps even social change—involves a potentially painful learning process. The psychologically informed, identity-centered approach to critical pedagogy offers a way to explain the (unfortunate) persistence of Holocaust denial—to take but one example of historical revisionism.

References

Bracher, M. (2006). *Radical pedagogy: Identity, generativity, and social transformation*. New York: Palgrave Macmillan.

Byram, M. (2008). *From foreign language education to education for intercultural citizenship: Essays and reflections*. Bristol: Multilingual Matters.

Cho, K. D. (2009). *Psychopedagogy: Freud, Lacan, and the psychoanalytic theory of education*. New York: Palgrave Macmillan.

Donahue, F. E., & Watzinger-Tharp, J. (2000). *Deutsch zusammen: A communicative course in German*. New York: Pearson.

Erikson, E. H. (1964). *Insight and responsibility*. New York: Norton.

Foucault, M. (1985). *The history of sexuality: Vol. 2. The use of pleasure* (R. Hurley, Trans.). New York: Pantheon.

Foucault, M. (1986). *The history of sexuality, Vol. 3. The care of the self* (R. Hurley, Trans.). New York: Pantheon.

Freire, P. (2004). *Pedagogy of hope: Reliving pedagogy of the oppressed* (R. Barr, Trans.). New York: Continuum.

Freire, P., & Shor, I. (1987). *A pedagogy for liberation: Dialogues on transforming education*. South Hadley, MA: Bergin and Garvey.

Gilligan, J. (1996). *Violence: Reflections on a national epidemic*. New York: Random House.

Graff, G. (1992). *Beyond the culture wars: How teaching the conflicts can revitalize American education*. New York: Norton.

Graff, G. (1996). Advocacy in the classroom—or in the curriculum? A response. In P. M. Spacks (Ed.), *Advocacy in the classroom: problems and possibilities* (pp. 425–431). New York: St. Martin's Press.

Graff, G. (2003). Conflict clarifies: A response (essay in the collection, Symposium: Teaching the conflicts at twenty years). *Pedagogy, 2*(3), 266–273.

Huesmann, L. R. (1988). An information processing model for the development of aggression. *Aggressive Behavior, 14*(1), 13–24.

Klüger, R. (1992). *Weiter leben: Eine Jugend*. Göttingen: Wallstein.

Kluger, R. (2001). *Still alive: A Holocaust girlhood remembered*. New York: Feminist Press.

Kramsch, C. (2002). How can we tell the dancer from the dance? In C. Kramsch (Ed.), *Language acquisition and language socialization: Ecological perspectives* (pp. 1–30). New York: Continuum.

Kumaravadivelu, B. (1999). Critical classroom discourse analysis. *TESOL Quarterly, 33*(3), 453–484.

Kumaravadivelu, B. (2006). *Understanding language teaching: From method to postmethod*. Mahwah, NJ: Lawrence Erlbaum Associates.

Lacan, J. (2002). *Écrits: A selection* (B. Fink, Trans.). New York: Norton.

Lunsford, A. (1996). Afterthoughts on the role of advocacy in the classroom. In P. Spacks (Ed.), *Advocacy in the classroom: Problems and possibilities* (pp. 432–438). New York: St. Martin's Press.

Modern Language Association. (2007). *Foreign languages and higher education: New structures for a changed world*. Retrieved from http://www.mla.org/flreport

Nelson, C. (1997). *Manifesto of a tenured radical*. New York: New York University Press.

Ortega, L. (2005). For what and for whom is our research? The ethical as transformative lens in instructed SLA. *Modern Language Journal, 89*(3), 427–443.

Pratt, M. L., Geisler, M., Kramsch, C., McGinnis, S., Patrikis, P., Ryding, K., et al. (2008). Transforming college and university foreign language departments. *Modern Language Journal, 92*(2), 287–292.

Reagan, T. G., & Osborne, T. A. (2002). *The foreign language educator in society: Toward a critical pedagogy*. Mahwah, NJ. Lawrence Erlbaum Associates.

Richter, H. P. (1961). *Damals war es Friedrich*. Munich: dtv.

Richter, H. P. (1987). *Friedrich* (E. Kroll, Trans.). New York: Puffin.

Schlink, B. (1995). *Der Vorleser: Roman*. Berlin: Diogenes.

Schlink, B. (1997). *The reader* (C. B. Janeway, Trans.). New York: Vintage.

Shor, I. (1992). *Empowering education: Critical teaching for social change*. Chicago: University of Chicago Press.

Shor, I. (1996). *When students have power: Negotiating authority in critical pedagogy*. Chicago: University of Chicago Press.

Shor, I. (1997). A conversation with Gerald Graff and Ira Shor. *JAC, 17*(1). Retrieved from http://www.jacweb.org

Sichrovsky, P. (1987). *Schuldig geboren—Kinder aus Nazifamilien*. Cologne: Kiepenheuer and Witsch.

Sichrovsky, P. (1989). *Born guilty: Children of Nazi families* (J. Steinberg, Trans.). New York: Basic Books.

Simon, R. (1988). For a pedagogy of possibility. In J. Smyth (Ed.), *The critical pedagogy networker, 1* (pp. 1–4). Victoria: Deakin University Press.

Slevin, J. (2002). Keeping the university occupied and out of trouble. *ADE Bulletin, 130*, 50–54.

Wells, L., & Morewedge, R. (2004). *Mitlesen, Mitteilen: Literarische Texte zum Lesen, Sprechen, Schreiben und Hören*. Boston: Heinle and Heinle.

Chapter 10

Postcolonial Complexities in Foreign Language Education and the Humanities

Robert W. Train, Sonoma State University

Abstract

This chapter develops a critical perspective on foreign language education by drawing on postcolonial theory and research in order to better conceptualize and address the complexity of language education in terms of ecologies of interconnected spaces of policy, curriculum, and classroom practice. Starting from the basic classroom issue of linguistic diversity and variability, this chapter offers a critical approach to language in education that strives to "situate language study in cultural, historical, geographic, and cross-cultural frames within the context of humanistic learning" (Modern Language Association [MLA], 2007, p. 4). This chapter advocates a critical, transcultural, and translinguistic humanism grounded in decolonial practices of foreign language education that are theoretically informed, educationally relevant, socially engaged, and ethically accountable. The chapter also attempts to bring increased historical and critical depth to how foreign language educators understand and perform the teaching of language in ways that connect to transdisciplinary research concerns in the humanities and beyond.

Postcolonial Complexities in Foreign Language Education and the Humanities

In this twenty-first century, it is difficult to imagine a foreign language department or program in which the study and theory of literature and culture does not include well-established courses offering students and faculty the space for explicit study, reflection, and debate surrounding multiple and complex postcolonial practices of language. In the case of French and Spanish, the two most commonly taught world languages at universities in the United States and also commonly taught in Europe, these courses are often conceptualized around convenient categories of francophone or Latin American studies. The same can be said of linguistics courses within those same departments and programs. The traditional "History of the Language" courses and the more recent sociolinguistically oriented classes on the linguistic diversity and variation of French or Spanish in the world must engage with the postcolonial and imperial contours of language in global contexts. And yet, can we language educators say that the critical vantage points afforded by explicit attention to postcolonial theories and practices figure prominently in the so-termed language courses and programs in those same departments where the object and subject of pedagogic knowledge known as "Spanish" or "French" can still seem disturbingly reductive with respect to the postcolonial complexities of language, culture, and identity?

Searching for a Postcolonial Space
in Lower-Division Language

In foreign language education, increased attention has been given to some of the surface phenomena of the postcolonial. For example, the canonical student representatives Jean-Jacques and Marie-France are now routinely accompanied by Ali and Fatou in first-year French textbooks. The cultural achievements and history of French communities of North America have become staple readings from the early settlements of the Acadians to the celebrity of the sports figure Tony Parker. Students are sometimes invited to sample the worldwide lexical diversity of French where the supposedly same referent can be named differently in Paris, Dakar, and Montreal. In Spanish class, Christopher Columbus unfailingly comes to America. In textbooks designed for lower-division Spanish courses (e.g., Spaine Long, Carreira, Madrigal Velasco, & Swanson, 2005), it is common to find chapters and cultural units that each feature their own nation beyond Spain. Learners of Spanish in universities—whether in foreign, native, or heritage language courses—are increasingly supplied with demographic information on Hispanics in the United States, often with considerable census data related to the various Spanish-speaking communities associated with immigration from Latin America. And the students are told that the supposed same things again can have different names in Havana, Madrid, and Mexico City.

The opening of foreign language education, however tentative, to the diversity and variability of language marks a significant change. In the traditional, overtly Eurocentric language curriculum and instruction, there was Paris or Madrid, beyond which everywhere and everyone else seemed like a day excursion into the quaintly local or a mortal combat with the barbarian Other. The expanded canon of Spanish and French as world languages opens new spaces for possible postcolonial understandings of language, culture, and speakership. These possibilities are all the more tantalizing for those learners who are also speakers of English, the most problematically and hegemonically global and, some would say, imperial of all world languages (see, e.g., Phillipson, 1992).

The worldliness of language and languages also begs for expanded and critical ways of reconceptualizing what we call "language" and "languages," along with the constellation of concepts surrounding language use and speakership (e.g., "competence" and "nonnative"). What is the place or multiple sites of language(s) within and beyond university foreign language programs? How can we address the recent calls for curricular reform to "situate language study in cultural, historical, geographic, and cross-cultural frames within the context of humanistic learning" (MLA, 2007, p. 4)? Questions arise about "the standard configuration of university foreign language curricula, in which a two- or three-year language sequence feeds into a set of core courses primarily focused on canonical literature" (p. 2). How can we begin or continue to break down this narrow and reductive "two-tiered model"? Moving toward a "constitutive" account of language as "a complex multifunctional phenomenon" will require foreign language education to focus on the translingual and transcultural (p. 2). Toward this end, how can we challenge the reductive and instrumentalist account of language and language use as "a skill to use for communicating thought and information" (p. 2)?

In keeping with the transcultural and translinguistic project, I suggest that an explicitly critical and postcolonial—even decolonial and decolonizing—perspective provides a necessary entry point into more constitutive—even *re*constitutive—accounts of language and language education in the humanities and beyond. As part of this perspective, I assert the foundational coloniality of language in education that has shaped what we do as foreign language educators. This move requires several accounts and recognitions to better conceptualize and address the complexity of foreign language education in terms of ecologies of interconnected spaces of policy, curriculum, and classroom practice. Drawing on interdisciplinary theory and research, I offer a brief, historically situated account of the ideological invention and reduction of language in and through pedagogy in imperial and colonial contexts. This account leads to the recognition of tensions surrounding the inclusion–exclusion attached to speakership and competence in the (re)production of inequalities in global and local contexts.

This perspective is not intended as a definitive statement or a manifesto but rather as a turn in an ongoing dialogue between language program directors, instructors, and researchers (not in fact mutually exclusive categories) who bring with us diverse fields of study, discussion, and debate that are critical to language, learning, and education.

Notes on Theory and Terminology: Imperialism, Colonialism, and Coloniality

One of the problems with bringing the postcolonial into foreign language education is the number of complex and contested concepts. Individual scholars have aligned their particular postcolonial approaches with or distinguished them from other scholars and approaches as a result of the ongoing practices and debates that may be discipline-specific but also cut across disciplinary boundaries. By way of example and for the benefit of the foreign language educator who may wish to further pursue postcolonial studies, I include a brief (but by no means exhaustive) list of some of the disciplinary diversity and interdisciplinary connectedness within the humanities that can be found among postcolonial approaches by historians (e.g., Prakash, 1995), literary scholars (Ashcroft, Griffiths, & Tiffin, 2007; Said, 1978; Young, 2001), philosophers (Spivak, 1999), applied linguists (Pennycook, 1998), educators (Willinsky, 1998), and anthropologists (Asad, 1991; Errington, 2007). As these scholars exemplify, a postcolonial perspective also requires a willingness to venture beyond one's primary academic discipline. For foreign language educators, understanding the postcolonial dimensions of what we do challenges us to go outside ourselves, beyond the borders constructed by or assigned to the teaching/learning of foreign languages in the university. However, the passage across and between boundaries to a broader view of foreign language education is fraught with transactions and negotiations involving the host of unruly debates, concepts, and terms that we encounter. Undoubtedly, this messiness is part of the complexity of theory in general and particularly the highly charged and contested areas such as postcolonial critique. Toward this end, I attempt to give a brief perspective on how some of these key terms and concepts (e.g., imperialism, colonialism, and coloniality) affect language pedagogy in practice. The ultimate goal is to work toward incorporating some of the large body of postcolonial inquiry into our own critiques, understandings, and practices of foreign language education.

Imperial(ism) and Colonial(ism)

Imperialism has been glossed as "the practice, theory, and the attitudes of a dominating metropolitan centre ruling a distant territory" while *colonialism*, which is "almost always a consequence of imperialism, is the implanting of settlements on a distant territory" (Said, 1993, p. 8, quoted in Ashcroft et al., 2007, pp. 40, 111). In spatial and causal terms, imperialism or neoimperialism has been described as "the phenomenon that originates in the metropolis, the process which leads to domination and control," while its "result, or what happens in the colonies as a consequence of imperial domination, is colonialism or neo-colonialism" (Loomba, 2005, p. 12). Without going into the terminological nuances and debates, the imperialism–colonialism dynamic helps us to understand foreign language education as situated within complex global and local relations of interwoven practices, policies, and ideologies involving, among other factors, distance, historicity, power, and control, as well as inequalities generated by hierarchical ordering and classification. In the case of French and Spanish imperialism and colonialism, a complex web of historically enacted ideologies, policies, and practices emanated from the metropolitan centers of power in the European capitals of empire in Paris and Madrid with the express design to rule over, for example, colonies in Quebec and Mexico. The metropole-centered imperialism(s) surrounding the French and Spanish languages supported the process of colonizing "their" distant territories in the Americas and across the globe (Ball, 1997; Mar-Molinero, 2000; Train, 2009b).

Coloniality

Increasingly, postcolonial strands of research have attempted to complexify the center-periphery/metropole-colony asymmetry and to look beyond imperialism and colonialism in narrow historical, economic, and territorial perspective. Most prominently, the term *coloniality* has emerged to engage the global dimensions of colonialism and imperialism as historically situated but dynamic world systems of relations, flows, ideologies, territorialities, and inequalities that have involved both domination and resistance as well as hegemony and agency. The notion of coloniality attempts to avoid any mechanistic view of imperialism–colonialism relationships by accounting for not only the control exerted by imperial power in colonial situations but also the agency, or the "socioculturally mediated capacity to act" (Ahearn, 2001, p. 112) by individuals and groups, among the colonizers and the colonized. The world languages of European imperial origin, like Spanish and French, have come to our classrooms as socioculturally mediated practices of language, culture, and identity that are charged with ongoing imperial and colonial histories. On the one hand, these practices constrain what we can do with language and who we can be as speakers according to a metropolitan model of native standard speaker. On the other hand, these world language practices also give rise to the often contested creation of new practices in the diverse local and global contexts beyond the distantly situated normative center in, for example, the idealized educated native speaker in Paris or Madrid.

This line of thinking offers us the insight that relations of coloniality are unequal but nevertheless mutually constitutive between the metropole/center and the colony/periphery. For example, the concept of coloniality has been linked to that of "Americanity" (Quijano & Wallerstein, 1992). The "geosocial construct" of the Americas that emerged beginning in the sixteenth century was "the constitutive act of the modern world-system" such that there could not have been a capitalist world-economy without the Americas (Quijano & Wallerstein, 1992, p. 549). Philosopher Enrique Dussel (1995) locates the "birthdate of modernity" in 1492, when Columbus arrived in the New World, thus highlighting the mutually constitutive role of the colonial/imperial project in shaping the societies, economies, cultures, discourses, and knowledge of Europe and the Americas.

From this perspective, the modern languages we teach and learn are somewhat disingenuously named after their supposed metropolitan centers of origin (e.g., Spanish, French, and English). In fact, the modernity of these languages is largely due to the complex linguistic, cultural, and material exchanges and appropriations generated through colonial/imperial encounters and exploitations. Would modern French still be modern French without, to cite a most ordinary example, *banane*—originally the Portuguese rendering of a Guinean word that today is used by French speakers to express a range of meanings beyond the primary tropical fruit referent to include, for instance, clothing apparel (*un sac banane*, fanny pack; *porter en banane*, wear around the waist; *un pull jaune banane*, a bright yellow sweater) and friendly insults (*espèce de banane!*)?

While recognizing that Europe would not have been modern without its colonies, postcolonial perspectives also point to the role that colonial and imperial enterprises have had in universalizing Eurocentric knowledge, perception, and classification in situations of local and global inequality. Coloniality can be seen as the creation of a set of states linked together within an interstate system in hierarchical layers, with the formal colonies at the very bottom. But far from disappearing with the end of formal colonial status, coloniality "continues in the form of a socio-cultural hierarchy of European and non-European" (Quijano & Wallerstein, 1992, p. 550). Pratt (2008) also notes the continuing coloniality in what she calls the "neocolony" of the Americas, particularly Latin America:

> The normative cultural referent is that of the metropole, which establishes the minor status of the local. This relation is sustained by the cultural and educational practices of the Creole elite, whom the metropole supplies with higher education for their young. Among

that elite, the neocolony tends to produce split subjectivities: one's lived reality lacks significance; the *"real" real* is elsewhere, and it owns you much more than you own it. The neocolony is seen as the receiving end of a diffusion of polished knowledge and processed goods. (p. 465)

In North America, "real Spanish" has been ideologically constructed and reconstructed in historical and current contexts both inside and outside the classroom as elsewhere in the United States despite the undeniable presence of generations of Spanish speakers within our national borders (Train, 2007b). Similarly, French language textbooks in the United States have typically assumed that the default value for unmarked "French" is France and the standard language associated with France (Wieczorek, 1994). The ongoing coloniality surrounding French in North America would seem to be present in the very limited presence of Canada in French teaching materials used in universities in the northern United States despite the obvious proximity to the continent's largest French-speaking community (Chapelle, 2009).

The notion of coloniality affords foreign language educators perspective on the spatial, temporal, sociocultural, educational, and political constructions of distance, domination, and hierarchy associated with imperialism and colonialism that have played out in a range of material, symbolic, affective, discursive, pedagogic, and institutional dimensions involving the supposed nativeness and foreignness of certain languages and their supposed speakers within an overarching common humanity. There is nothing simple about the language(s) that we have learned and come to teach as "native" and "foreign" or "first" and "second," and we are part of the multiple histories and contexts in which our languages and ourselves take shape.

The Critical Imperative of Post- and De-

Postcolonial theory involves critical analysis of the histories of colonialism and imperialism and investigates their contemporary effects. Postcolonialism's critical imperative of "making connections between that past and the politics of the present" (Young, 2001, p. 6) is "both contestatory and committed towards political ideals of a transnational social justice" (p. 58). The prefixes *post-* and *de-* articulate the need to supersede and undo colonialism and imperialism but also the postcolonial and decolonial stance that "signals an activist engagement with positive political positions and new forms of political identity" (Young, 2001, p. 58).

Basic to various formulations of postcolonial and decolonial critique, coloniality is at the heart of the transcultural, where the transformative practices—cultural, linguistic, and otherwise—from outside the imperial centers of power "reflect back on metropolitan discourses and such a perspective offers the possibility of dismantling previously maintained, hierarchized notions of centrality" (Thieme, 1996, p. 4). The contestation of centrality—geographical and metaphorical—is now increasingly difficult to dismiss as linguistically, culturally, and educationally irrelevant. Ongoing debates surrounding world Englishes and English as a lingua franca highlight the plurality and pluricentricity of world languages and the complexity of speaker identities beyond native and nonnative (Jenkins, 2007; Shin & Kubota, 2008). These postcolonial insights lead us to a fundamental conflict between the increasing recognition of the plurality of voices within what are usually conceived of as unitary language systems (such as "English," "Spanish," or "French") and the unfortunate fact that education in general—and language education in particular—deals very poorly with this plurality and diversity of language, culture, and speakership within and between human beings.

Coloniality affords us the insight that the imperial and colonial past is still present. Coloniality, then, implies historicity, a critical historical awareness that each supposed national history and the language attached to it are, in fact, inextricably intertwined with long-standing and shifting colonial and imperial webs of relation and power. For example, the (post)coloniality of Latinos in the United States has been delinked from the formal decolonization of Latin American nations because many people living in both once-colonized and once-colonizing countries are still subject to the oppressions put into place by colonialism (Klor de Alva, 1995; Loomba, 2005). Poststructuralist approaches recognize a "multiplicity of histories" in which the lives of oppressed peoples can be uncovered rather than a silencing single national history (Klor de Alva, 1995). In this sense, immigrant, minority, and heritage languages and learners are very much part of the voices that national histories on both sides of the Atlantic have largely silenced. Questioning whether we live in a postcolonial era, Pratt (2008) has offered a nuanced view:

> The *post* prefix is used here to call forth not a subject paralyzed between nostalgia and cynicism in a Fukiyaman "end of history," but a subject newly capacitated to read the present in light of a broadened more discerning reading of the past. This subject is oriented not toward a future frozen in a post-progress eternity but toward a renewed anti-imperial, decolonizing practice. The decolonization of knowledge is, I believe, one of the most important intellectual challenges of our time. (p. 460)

Taking up this challenge in explicitly critical terms, it is clear that decoloniality involves epistemological and ontological work to produce what Mignolo (2007) has called a "decolonial shift." This decolonization of knowledge and being "marks the Eurocentered limits of critical theory as we know it today," and "when critical theory becomes de-colonial critique it has of necessity to be critical border thinking" (p. 485).

From this perspective, crucial questions for foreign language educators emerge. How do we better understand the colonial/imperial complexities that are part and parcel of the languages we teach? From there, how do we use that understanding to move toward a decolonial shift by de-(Euro)centering traditional notions of what language and language learning are as well as their place in education? Working from constituted borders of knowledge, curriculum, and instruction, how can we critically reconfigure foreign language education in more inclusive ways?

Critically Rethinking the Borders in Foreign Language Education and the Humanities

In rethinking the foundational and ongoing coloniality of language in education, it is necessary to recall that the accounts of language and humanistic learning evoked in the MLA Report are situated with respect to long and complex histories surrounding the applied study of language. In the European tradition, those who wrote about and systematically reflected on language, its uses, and its users were typically doing so in the context of language teaching or more broadly in the context of language/culture-centered education. This tradition coalesced around the classical notion of the Greek *paideia* or the later Roman and European Renaissance *humanitas* built around a curriculum of *studia humanitatis* and *artes liberales*, from which we get our modern notions of the humanities and the liberal arts (Train, 2009b). Today, it is still in the liberal arts–based humanities that language and languages occupy a central curricular place in education.

From a postcolonial perspective, the contours of language education have been historically constructed in terms of shifting projects of humanistic learning (e.g., humanism, enlightenment, and modernity) grounded in reductive ideologies, policies, and practices. Traditionally, these projects of humanistic learning have relied on powerful, even hegemonic discourses of education, culture, and literacy based on standardizing ideologies of unity and purity of language that fuse with notions of speakership grounded in the dynamics of (not) belonging, inclusion, and exclusion. These discourses have a common goal of circumscribing the boundaries of languages, as well as the borders between their supposed speakers and learners.

The educational and cultural project of classical *studia humanitatis*, as Heidegger (1977) noted, has always been grounded in an opposition between the normative category of the civilized, humanized human (*Homo humanus*) characterized by *humanitas*, and its other, the *Homo barbarus*. Heidegger traced this opposition to what he called "the first humanism" of the republican Romans, which defined *humanitas* in terms of ideals of virtue embodied in the Greek notion of culture and education, *paideia*, acquired through scholarship and training in the valued skills or "arts" of good conduct (p. 200), which included correct linguistic comportment. This humanity acquired through education corresponded to the cultural and territorial category of Romanness (*romanitas*). *Humanitas* was both a justification and an explanation for the supposedly merit-based but transparently class-oriented inequalities between humans (Veyne, 1993). As a precursor to notions of meritocracy and distinction (Bourdieu, 1979) that have shaped modern education, desirable "humanity" was defined largely by educated language and its users in opposition to the "common people" and from "uneducated members of the propertied class who, by their lack of instruction, brought no honor to their class" (Veyne, 1993, p. 342). On another level, *humanitas* intersected with long-standing notions about the civilizing and humanizing mission of education within the larger political context of imperial conquest.

If the Romans produced the first humanism, they did so largely by constructing Latin, the first world language. As in the case of future world standard languages like Spanish, French, and English, the codification of languageness was part of a larger entextualization of ideologies and practices surrounding global hegemony and inequality. In terms of the humanities and liberal arts, languages in education were reduced to codified "arts" that were both texts, as in an *ars grammatica*, and a body of cultural-pedagogic knowledge and competence as one of the liberal arts, the first two being grammar and rhetoric, that were developed by the Romans and further institutionalized in medieval Europe. The goal and consequence of codifying Latin in grammars (*artes*) was to reduce and regulate speech by means of grammatical categories and also to separate, distinguish, and classify educated speakers from the unschooled masses. In a move that laid the foundation for standardizing linguistic and pedagogic practices up to our day, the language that the Latin grammarian taught was invented as simultaneously and paradoxically artificial and natural or, in other words, "a product of human skill that claimed objective validity and permanence" (Kaster, 1988, p. 19).

In ecological webs of practices, intertextualities, and ideologies, language in school and society was invented and reinvented for centuries in innumerable local contexts around these "arts" (*artes*), codified accounts of what educated speakers of world languages should be and how they should act. The *artes* concept was connected to the act of describing and governing language within regulated borders of use and speakership according to complex notions of nativeness and foreignness attached to supposed the unity and purity of language and identity. Language professionals constructed the "vices and virtues" of language with their lush taxonomies of error, which almost always included the "intolerable vices" of barbarism and solecism.

Describing syntactic error, the term *solecism* derives from the Greek concept of speaking incorrectly, as stated by ancient writers to refer to the supposed "corruption" of the Attic dialect among the Athenian colonists at Sóloi in Asia Minor. This traditional category of error was framed in terms of substandard or corrupted speech. In postcolonial terms, the supposed departure from linguistic and moral integrity evokes a context in which those who would claim Athens as the center of imperial power were able to marginalize the problematically native—that is, a colonial but not necessarily foreign— "other on the periphery." In conjunction with solecism, barbarism points to another modality of colonial and imperial marginalization, the "other as nonnative." "Barbarism" came to be used to describe word-level or morphological deviation or variation from a standard form used in either writing or speaking. Etymologically, it came into the European metadiscourse about language from the Greek term designating a "foreign mode of speech," derived from the verb "to behave or speak like a foreigner" (Barbarism, n.d.). However, as Calvet (1999) remarks, the notion of barbarism translated Greek linguistic racism into Western language ideologies. The original Greek word for "foreigners" (*bárbaros*) stems from a derisively onomatopoetic representation of someone who cannot speak coherently—as in the Latin word for "stammering," *balbus* (also Spanish *balbucear* and French *balbutier*)—or who only produces noises that could not be considered human, or at best deficiently so, from the standpoint of the Greeks (Calvet, 1999). The ideological, educational, and linguistic nexus of successive imperial regimes and European ethnocentrism involved complex reductions to binary relationships between the "civilized" center/metropole and the "barbarian other" on the supposed margins of empire or society. The grammarians, rhetoricians, schoolmasters, and other language professionals constructed these categories of error and identity in contrast to the standardizing categories of order, unity, and purity attached to the supposed Latinity (*latinitas*) or Greekness (*hellenismos*) on which the very notion of "the" language was seen to rest (see Versteegh, 1987).

Modern education grounded in imperial world languages (e.g., Spanish, French, and English) would appropriate the classical categories of language, error, and speakership to stake out the boundaries of language, identity, and empire between the natives and nonnatives, between "ourselves" and others (see Train, 2009a, 2009b; Willinsky, 1998). Alongside the classification of languages and speakers as native and nonnative, modern education reworked classical *humanitas* into a fundamental cosmopolitanism, recently characterized as "the Enlightenment's hope of the world citizen whose commitments transcended provincial and local concerns with ideal values about humanity" (Popkewitz, 2008, p. 1).

The current world languages of today's classrooms were invented according to this European model of language that has ideologically reduced the complexity and diversity constituted by variable language practices to a "language form" that can be named, represented, codified, policed, and studied as "the/a" language, whether native or nonnative, first or second language. Despite the long-standing assumption of "linguistic naturalism" (see critique in Joseph, 2000) that underpins modern linguistics and language education, languages are not "natural objects," but rather, as Makoni and Pennycook (2007) argue, they were, "in the most literal sense, invented, particularly as part of the Christian/colonial and nationalistic projects in different parts of the globe" (p. 1). In direct relation with the invention of languages through social, cultural, and political movements, a metadiscursive regime emerged based on "an ideology of languages as separate and enumerable categories" (p. 2). In postcolonial and poststructural terms, the enumerability of languages can be understood as part of a broader project of governmentality associated with a Eurocentric culture that relentlessly observed, classified, and codified all aspects about the non-European culture and language (Makoni & Pennycook, 2007). Critical anthropological perspectives have recently highlighted the "linguistic in the colonial" as local languages in imperial/colonial contexts of power and meaning have been reduced to writing according to the Eurocentric model of language (Errington, 2007). The very notion of bilingualism—the use of two languages—has been invented and reinvented by competing institutions, groups, and individuals as a social construct around contested colonial and postcolonial frames of citizenship, language, and the state in local contexts (Stroud, 2007).

Engagement with Decolonial Practice in Foreign Language Education: Toward a Critical Transcultural and Translinguistic Humanism

At the heart of the humanities and foreign language education in the United States is, to quote Said (1989), "the deep, the profoundly perturbed and perturbing question of our relationship to others—other cultures, other states, other histories, other experiences, traditions, peoples, and destinies" (p. 216). As the MLA Report implies, this relationship to others is also grounded in awareness of our own positions with respect to language, culture, identity, education, and so forth. Hence, the report offers the central theme of the transcultural, where "language is understood as an essential element of a human being's thought processes, perceptions, and self-expressions; and as such it is considered to be at the core of translingual and transcultural competence" (MLA, 2007, p. 2). However, there is also the inconvenient fact that the humanities and language education have been historically and ideologically grounded in a deeply contradictory and troubling invention of the human and humanity in ongoing ecologies of coloniality. Among the many aspects of coloniality, this chapter has touched on the complex reduction of the diverse and variable human language-culture practices to a conveniently coherent whole ("a language") that is seen to constitute legitimate or appropriate humanity. This reduction–invention of humans and our language(s) has been linked to the marginalization of those variable practices and speakers associated with them that are deemed to fall outside the discursively policed boundaries of the supposed linguistic, cultural, and pedagogic unity surrounding language and education. In short, the hope for participation in language and education has been extended to all human beings, yet language and education have also been constructed in ways that position some humans outside full participation.

For foreign language education, one can posit a double coloniality and a double decolonial challenge. On the one hand, learners in foreign language programs in the United States—arguably the current imperial hyperpower (Chua, 2007)—occupy a complex and asymmetrical position as speakers of English (whether native or nonnative) in regard to other peoples, languages, and cultures of the world. On the other hand, foreign language learners and educators participate in linguistic utopias of maximally homogeneous objects of study (Pratt, 1987). The learning and teaching of "French" or "Spanish" has traditionally privileged the notion of a minimally variable and maximally homogeneous (i.e., standard) language. This utopian, even delusional, stance toward linguistic homogeneity and variability comes attached to imagined communities of target language speakers, whose ideal colonial/imperial representation of monolingual, native speakership, and competence are distantly situated beyond the grasp of all but a few if any nonnatives as well as many native speakers of colonial and immigrant heritage languages, to use Fishman's (2001) terms. For example, the varied but often unsatisfactory experiences with schooling that many native or heritage language learners of Spanish encounter in the United States highlight the urgent need to rethink how we can do language education in more decolonial ways. The language diversity embodied in immigrant and minority speakers is at the center of the seemingly endless "crisis," the constant "state of emergency" (Agamben, 2005) surrounding language in ideologically monolingual nations. The devaluing of immigrant languages often involves a larger context of hostility toward languages other than English, notably Spanish (Valdés, Fishman, Chávez, & Pérez, 2006). This situation is especially acute in the Southwest, where the postcolonial and neoimperial histories of Spain, Mexico, and the United States have intersected in complex ways. The institutional neglect of Spanish language education and the focus on valuing practices of Spanish outside North America contribute to the positioning of many bilingual Spanish speakers in the United States as somehow "deficient" in their own language (Ortega, 1999; Train, 2007b; Valdés, González, López García, & Márquez, 2003).

To avoid any misunderstanding, the intent of this chapter is not to argue against the MLA Report, the humanities, and the importance of language(s) in a humanistic education. Quite the opposite: I am advocating, as Said (2004) and others have, a post-911 humanism that is connected or reconnected to critical practice as a foundational component of education, a humanism that informs what one does as a "scholar-teacher of the humanities in today's turbulent world" (p. 2). Taking into account the concerns of those engaged in education, a new transcultural humanism of the sort suggested in the MLA Report would strategically chart a course between a complete rupture with and a conventional entrenchment in traditional practices of language in education. Foreign language educators might consider that

> it is possible to be critical of humanism in the name of humanism and that, schooled in its abuses by the experience of Eurocentrism and empire, one could fashion a different kind of humanism that was cosmopolitan and text-and-language-bound in ways that absorbed the great lessons of the past . . . and still remain attuned to the emergent voices and currents of the present, many of them exiled, extraterritorial, and unhoused, as well as uniquely American. (Said, 2004, pp. 10–11)

In keeping with the historical perspective offered in this chapter, critical transcultural humanism is solidly grounded in a sense of historicity, or, in Said's (2004) terms, "human beings in history," where the "core of humanism" is "historical knowledge based on the human being's capacity to make knowledge, as opposed to absorbing it passively, reactively, and dully" (p. 11). This belief in human agency grounded in historical consciousness and purposeful activity is consistent with major sociocultural currents of research in language learning (see Lantolf & Thorne, 2006) as well as with more explicitly critical approaches aimed at transforming existing social relations in the interests of greater equity in schools and society (see Norton & Toohey, 2004).

In this concluding section, I offer some points of reflection and discussion for foreign language educators (i.e., program coordinators, instructors, professors, and teaching assistants) to consider regarding what a critical decolonial foreign language teaching and learning practice might look like within a frame of a transcultural humanities. I organize these points around four broad goals for rethinking and reshaping foreign language education in decolonial ways in terms of fostering approaches to the teaching and learning of language that are (1) theoretically informed, (2) educationally relevant, (3) socially engaged, and (4) ethically accountable.

Theoretically Informed Practice

In keeping with the overarching theme of this volume, I will reiterate the importance of framing language teaching and learning in terms of integrating theory into practice and practice into theory. Theory, then, must avoid, where possible, reducing the complexity of language(s), teaching, learning, theory, and practice to conveniently compartmentalized categories that can mask the interrelations between them within larger ecologies. A critically humanistic interdisciplinarity is basic to reconstituting language in education through poststructuralist, postcolonial, and decolonizing accounts of language, culture, and identity from a variety of broad fields in the humanities and social sciences, including sociolinguistics, applied linguistics, education, literature, history, philosophy, and anthropology. Without discounting the institutional requirements and advantages attached to specialization within constituted academic disciplines, language teaching and learning must cut across those boundaries by virtue of being truly foundational in doing the academic work of any given discipline in the humanities and social sciences. In this sense, a critical decolonial perspective always seeks to transcend the boundaries that are imposed on and constructed by foreign language education in a given historical moment and local context. Applied linguistic research continues to provide considerable theoretical support for expanded conceptions of teaching and learning of foreign language as sociocultural practice, historical practice, and social semiotic practice (see Kramsch, 2000). These perspectives open up possibilities for border-transgressive thinking capable of theorizing the displacement of traditional analytic and pedagogic categories as well as conventional representations of language and speakership beyond the limits of constituted boundaries. For example, as outlined in the preceding section, the conveniently reductive binaries of native/nonnative speaker, first language/second language, and error/correctness have been constructed in shifting colonial and imperial ecologies since the very earliest times of language education. An interdisciplinary, retheorized, and transcultural foreign language education would seek to go beyond the still-reigning binarism—the either/or of bounded languages and identities—toward decolonial third spaces (Bhabha, 1994; Kramsch, 1993; Pérez, 1999).

To this effect, the MLA Report skillfully appropriates the basic humanity or, rather, the fundamental necessity of communication between human beings as an argument in favor of legitimizing foreign languages in education. The pillar of this humanity-in-communication is translingual and transcultural competence, articulated in the report as a basic goal, outcome, and measure of foreign language education. The translingual and transcultural model of competence offers a powerful rejection of the structuralist/Chomskyan postulate of the educated native speaker—assumed to be a monolingual-like human being—as the locus of competence. The translingual and transcultural turn serves to reframe who speaker-learners are as potentially multilingual individuals in multicultural settings and what speakers can do, as seen from a more complex sociocultural and ecological view of language and competence (see van Lier, 2004). This line of research is complemented by the important concept of "symbolic competence" that brings together complexity theory and postmodern sociolinguistics to explore how an ecological approach to language data can illuminate aspects of language use in multilingual environments (Kramsch & Whiteside, 2008).

With respect to the notion of competence, we should proceed strategically, as in the MLA Report, but also cautiously given the long history of competence that has reproduced privilege for narrow groups of speakers. Perhaps competence might ultimately be a category too fraught to critically recover (Train, 2007a). Are there limits to the theoretical reworking of the reductive categories that have largely positioned nonnative, second-language, foreign language, heritage, and bilingual speakers as "deficient communicators" (Belz, 2002)? Already the notion of standard communication is emerging in global language teaching practices based on institutionalizing some people's preferred practices and competence as the standard norm for "effective communication" that, in turn, defines large numbers of other people as inadequate or substandard communicators (Cameron, 2002). National/colonial/imperial models of language and competence do not adequately account for the complexity of what bilingual, multilingual heritage language speakers do in performing multiple, complex identities (see Blackledge et al., 2008). Given the colonial baggage surrounding notions of native speaker competence, the question remains, how do we incorporate into foreign language education a more performative view of language use that has been basic to postmodern theorizing of discourse in recent years (see Butler, 1997)? The key theoretical issue involves rethinking what speakers and learners actually do with language in their lives inside and outside the classroom according to more performatively oriented views informed by poststructural and decolonial critique. Stressing the agency of speakers, the recent concept of symbolic competence significantly brings performativity or "the capacity to perform and create alternative realities" into focus (Kramsch & Whiteside, 2008, p. 666). The relationship of performance—that neglected twin of Chomskyan linguistics—and postmodern performativity to competence remains an area that will merit further investigation.

Educationally Relevant Practice

A critical, transcultural humanism would recognize that the constitution of the components of foreign language education as institutional, pedagogic, and academic entities is part of larger ecological webs. Foreign language education cannot or should not be reduced to a set of discrete courses, programs, departments, and debates disconnected from other areas of educational importance, including language in education policy. Learning Spanish, French, German, Chinese, and so forth is not separate from learning English or from science, history, and so on.

In terms of language teaching and learning in the university, we would do well to heed the advice of postcolonial scholars who call for "the humanities in dialogue with the social sciences":

> If the Kantian university was based on *reason*, the Humboldtian university was based on culture and the neoliberal university on excellence and expertise, a future [. . .] university shall be envisioned in which the humanities will be rearticulated on a critique of knowledge and cultural practices. (Mignolo, 2000, p. xii)

Language education should not be removed from the political questions of what gets taught, when, and to whom. Why, for example, is English the only mandatory subject taught to every student in California schools from kindergarten to at least freshman year in college, while other languages are currently considered a college prep or elective course that is not a requirement for high school graduation or in most cases for college graduation? In California—to use the example of the state with by far the most Spanish speakers—Spanish is not a significant part of most students' formal education, even that of bilingual Spanish-speaking students.

Socially Engaged Practice

In conjunction with the educational relevance of foreign language education, a transcultural and translinguistic humanism would connect in complex ways what goes on in the classroom to the lives of our students and ourselves outside the classroom as social actors in local, national, and global ecologies. Transcending a narrowly theoretical postcolonial frame in favor of what I have called decolonial practice, one may look to a range of possibilities for "post-postcolonial" language education that depends on "the demands, constraints and revolutionary possibilities of particular local material and cultural conditions" (Luke, 2005, xvii). As foreign language educators, we have to ask, what are those conditions for the languages and learners we teach, where we teach them? Rather than assume that whatever constitutes foreign language education can be uniformly applied to all local contexts, we must engage with the social contours of our different programs and diverse students. How would transcultural and translinguistic competence play out in some of the countless permutations in California, such as Spanish at an undergraduate public regional university in rural northern California? How would it play out in German at a large public research university in the greater Los Angeles area, French at a community college in the suburban Central Valley, and Chinese at a small private liberal arts in the urban Bay Area? In terms of the "big ideas" in education, a socially engaged foreign language education would recognize that "standards," "accountability," or pedagogical method all have very complex and differential effects on different students—to the contrary of the purported equality attributed to large-scale educational reform (it's good for everyone) and pedagogical method (it works for everyone). Rethinking foreign language education can take a page from postcolonial literary scholar John Thieme (1996), who wrote that one of the consequences of the popularity of "hybridization" theory has been "a tendency (at odds with the practice of a theorist such as Bhabha) to dehistoricize and dislocate writing from the temporal, geographical and linguistic factors which have produced it in favour of an abstract, globally conceived notion of hybridity which obscures the specificities of particular cultural situations" (p. 3). We foreign language educators might find ourselves someday saying the same of transcultural competence if it becomes plugged into the existing reductive discourses of reform. Again, an ecological view offers to keep the big ideas grounded in the local contexts of individual learner, classroom, program, institution, and setting in a complex and problematized relationship with larger standardizing and centralizing contexts.

Ethically Accountable Practice

In uttering the "A" word, accountability, I'm not arguing for a standards-based alignment of practice with current reductionist notions of accountability. Instead, a critical decolonizing perspective recognizes that the foundational coloniality of language education has produced tensions in the lives of speakers whose tensions live within us and beyond us. Any attempt to reconstruct education means coping with "intractable American dilemmas" (Cuban & Shipps, 2000) as well as "the pervasive tensions in postcolonial communities" (Canagarajah, 2005) that exist worldwide. Rather than uncritically embracing the latest iteration of educational reform or accountability, we should ask the basic ethical questions of who is included in our reinventions or reconstitutions of language. Who will be affected? And how? As language educators, we can benefit from a poststructuralist view along the lines of Judith Butler, who has pointed out the ethical dimensions of subjectivity, that is, the performance of myself in terms of who I am at a given moment. For Butler (2005), ethical reflection involves giving an account of myself that must reflect the social conditions under which I emerge, which requires a turn to social theory to understand these social conditions. Coming full circle, back to theoretically informed practice, part of our work in the humanities as foreign language educators and scholars is to interrogate the reductive simplicity in which language—and particularly foreign language in education—is so often portrayed. There is nothing simple about language, learning, and education, much less the interdiscursive complexity of so much of our work in the humanities. Our world as language educators has become all the more complicated as the United States has taken on an unparalleled imperial role in the world, reflected in the defense-related funding that has come to dominate public investment in foreign language education. In this context, foreign language educators may well appreciate the words of Loomba (2005), who ends her remarkable synthesis of colonialism and postcolonialism on an ethical note:

> If universities are to remain sites of dissent and free intellectual inquiry, if scholarship is not to be at the service of American or any other power, critiques of past and ongoing empires are going to be more necessary than ever. (p. 228)

Much work remains to be done in the principled practice of decolonial, translinguistic, and transcultural crossing and negotiating of the historically constituted borders of language, culture, and speakership. Framed in these terms, our professional activity as foreign language educators in the humanities must also include engagement in increasingly global discussions regarding history, political consciousness, ethical intercultural being, and criticality in language education (see a European perspective in Phipps & González, 2004). This ongoing work of education, engagement, and research may prove to have what Said (1989) called the "instigatory force" to be "of startling relevance to all the humanities and social sciences as they continue to struggle with the formidable difficulties of empire" (p. 225).

References

Agamben, G. (2005). *State of exception* (K. Attell, Trans.). Chicago: University of Chicago Press.

Ahearn, L. M. (2001). Language and agency. *Annual Review of Anthropology, 30,* 109–137.

Asad, T. (1991). Afterward: From the history of colonial anthropology to the anthropology of Western hegemony. In G. Stocking (Ed.), *Colonial situations: Essays on the contextualization of ethnographic knowledge* (pp. 314–324). Madison: University of Wisconsin Press.

Ashcroft, B., Griffiths, G., & Tiffin, H. (2007). *Post colonial studies: The key concepts* (2nd ed.). London: Routledge.

Ball, R. (1997). *The French speaking world: A practical introduction to sociolinguistic issues.* London: Routledge.

Barbarism. (n.d.). In *Oxford English dictionary.* Retrieved from http://dictionary.oed.com

Belz, J. A. (2002). The myth of the deficient communicator. *Language Teaching Research, 6*(1), 59–82.

Bhabha, H. K. (1994). *The location of culture.* London: Routledge.

Blackledge, A. et al. (2008). Contesting 'language' as 'heritage': Negotiation of identities in late modernity. *Applied Linguistics, 29*(4), 533–554.

Bourdieu, P. (1979). *La Distinction, Critique sociale du jugement.* Paris: Editions de Minuit.

Butler, J. (1997). *Excitable speech: A politics of the performative.* New York: Routledge.

Butler, J. (2005). *Giving an account of oneself.* New York: Fordham University Press.

Calvet, L.-J. (1999). *La Guerre des langues et les politiques linguistiques.* Paris: Hachette.

Cameron, D. (2002). Globalization and the teaching of "communication skills." In D. Block & D. Cameron (Eds.), *Globalization and language teaching* (pp. 67–82). London: Routledge.

Canagarajah, A. S. (2005). Accommodating tensions in language-in-education policies: An afterword. In A. M. Y. Lin & P. W. Martin (Eds.), *Decolonisation, globalisation: Language-in-education, policy and practice* (pp. 194–201). Clevedon: Multilingual Matters.

Chapelle, C. A. (2009). A hidden curriculum in language textbooks: Are beginning learners of French at U.S. universities taught about Canada? *Modern Language Journal, 93*(2), 139–152.

Chua, A. (2007). *Day of empire: How hyperpowers rise to global dominance—and why they fall.* New York: Doubleday.

Cuban, L., & Shipps, D. (2000). *Reconstructing the common good in education: Coping with intractable American dilemmas.* Stanford, CA: Stanford University Press.

Dussel, E. (1995). *The invention of the Americas: Eclipse of "the Other" and the myth of modernity* (M. Barber, Trans.). New York: Continuum.

Errington, J. J. (2007). *Linguistics in a colonial world: A story of language, meaning, and power*. Malden, MA: Blackwell.

Fishman, J. A. (2001). 300-plus years of heritage language education in the United States. In J. K. Peyton, D. A. Ranard, & S. McGinnis (Eds.), *Heritage languages in America: Preserving a national resource* (pp. 81–97). Washington, DC: Center for Applied Linguistics.

Heidegger, M. (1977). *Basic writings from* Being and time *(1927) to* The task of thinking *(1964)* (D. F. Krell, Ed.). New York: Harper and Row.

Jenkins, J. (2007). *English as a lingua franca: Attitude and identity*. Oxford: Oxford University Press.

Joseph, J. E. (2000). *Limiting the arbitrary: Linguistic naturalism and its opposites in Plato's Cratylus and modern theories of language*. Philadelphia: John Benjamins.

Kaster, R. A. (1988). *Guardians of language: The grammarian and society in late antiquity*. Berkeley: University of California Press.

Klor de Alva, J. J. (1995). The postcolonization of the (Latin) American experience: A reconsideration of "colonialism," "postcolonialism," and "Mestizaje." In G. Prakash (Ed.), *After colonialism: Imperial histories and postcolonial displacements* (pp. 241–275). Princeton, NJ: Princeton University Press.

Kramsch, C. (1993). *Context and culture in language teaching*. Oxford: Oxford University Press.

Kramsch, C. (2000). Second language acquisition, applied linguistics, and the teaching of foreign languages. *Modern Language Journal, 84*(3), 311–326.

Kramsch, C., & Whiteside, A. (2008). Language ecology in multilingual settings: Towards a theory of symbolic competence. *Applied Linguistics, 29*(4), 645–671.

Lantolf, J. P., & Thorne, S. L. (2006). *Sociocultural theory and the genesis of second language development*. Oxford: Oxford University Press.

Loomba, A. (2005). *Colonialism/postcolonialism* (2nd ed.). London: Routledge.

Luke, A. (2005). Foreword: On the possibilities of a post-postcolonial language education. In A. M. Y. Lin & P. W. Martin (Eds.), *Decolonisation, globalisation: Language-in-education, policy and practice* (pp. xiv–xix). Clevedon: Multilingual Matters.

Makoni, S., & Pennycook, A. (2007). Disinventing and reconstituting languages. In S. Makoni & A. Pennycook (Eds.), *Disinventing and reconstituting languages* (pp. 1–41). Clevedon: Multilingual Matters.

Mar-Molinero, C. (2000). *The politics of language in the Spanish-speaking world: From colonisation to globalisation*. London: Routledge.

Mignolo, W. D. (2000). *Local histories/global designs: coloniality, subaltern knowledges, and border thinking*. Princeton, NJ: Princeton University Press.

Mignolo, W. D. (2007). Delinking: The rhetoric of modernity, the logic of coloniality and the grammar of de-coloniality. *Cultural Studies, 21*(2–3), 449–514.

Modern Language Association. (2007). *Foreign languages and higher education: New structures for a changed world*. Retrieved from http://www.mla.org/flreport

Norton, B., & Toohey, K. (Eds.). (2004). *Critical pedagogies and language learning*. Cambridge: Cambridge University Press.

Ortega, L. (1999). Rethinking foreign language education: Political dimensions of the profession. In K. A. Davis (Ed.), *Foreign language teaching and language minority education* (pp. 21–39). Honolulu: University of Hawaii, Second Language Teaching and Curriculum Center.

Pennycook, A. (1998). *English and the discourses of colonialism*. London: Routledge.

Pérez, E. (1999). *The decolonial imaginary: Writing Chicanas into history*. Bloomington: Indiana University Press.

Phillipson, R. (1992). *Linguistic imperialism*. Oxford: Oxford University Press.

Phipps, A., & González, M. (2004). *Modern languages: Learning and teaching in an intercultural field.* London: Sage.

Popkewitz, T. (2008) *Cosmopolitanism and the age of school reform. Science, education and making society by making the child.* London: Routledge.

Prakash, G. (1995). *After colonialism: Imperial histories and postcolonial displacements.* Princeton, NJ: Princeton University Press.

Pratt, M. L. (1987). Linguistic utopias. In N. Fabb, D. Attridge, A. Durant, & C. McCabe (Eds.), *The linguistics of writing: Arguments between language and literature* (pp. 48–66). Manchester: Manchester University Press.

Pratt, M. L. (2008). In the neocolony: Destiny, destination, and the traffic in meaning. In M. Moraña, E. Dussel, & C. A. Jáuregui (Eds.), *Coloniality at large: Latin America and the postcolonial debate* (pp. 459–475). Durham, NC: Duke University Press.

Quijano, A., & Wallerstein, I. (1992). Americanity as a concept, or the Americas in the modern world-system. *International Social Science Journal, 44*(4), 549–557.

Said, E. W. (1978). *Orientalism.* New York: Pantheon Books.

Said, E. W. (1989). Representing the colonized: Anthropology's interlocutors. *Critical Inquiry, 15*(2), 205–225.

Said, E. W. (1993). *Culture and imperialism.* New York: Knopf.

Said, E. W. (2004). *Humanism and democratic criticism.* New York: Columbia University Press.

Shin, H., & Kubota, R. (2008). Post-colonialism and globalization in language education. In B. Spolsky & F. M. Hult (Eds.), *The handbook of educational linguistics* (pp. 206–219). Malden, MA: Blackwell.

Spaine Long, S., Carreira, M., Madrigal Velasco, S., & Swanson, K. (2005). *Nexos: Introductory Spanish.* Boston: Houghton Mifflin.

Spivak, G. C. (1999). *A critique of postcolonial reason: Toward a history of the vanishing present.* Cambridge, MA: Harvard University Press.

Stroud, C. (2007). Bilingualism: Colonialism and postcolonialism. In M. Heller (Ed.), *Bilingualism: A social approach* (pp. 25–49). London: Palgrave Macmillan.

Thieme, J. (1996). *The Arnold anthology of post-colonial literatures in English.* London: St. Martin's Press.

Train, R. W. (2007a). Language ideology and foreign language pedagogy. In D. Ayoun (Ed.), *French applied linguistics* (pp. 238–269). Amsterdam: John Benjamins.

Train, R. W. (2007b). "Real Spanish": Historical perspectives on the ideological construction of a (foreign) language. *Critical Inquiry in Language Studies, 4*(2–3), 207–235.

Train, R. W. (2009a). "Todos los peregrinos de nuestra lengua": Ideologies and accounts of Spanish-as-a-(foreign) language. In M. Lacorte & J. Leeman (Eds.), *Español en Estados Unidos y otros contextos de contacto: Sociolingüística, ideología y pedagógica/Spanish in the United States and other contact environments: Sociolinguistics, ideology and pedagogy* (pp. 191–207). Madrid: Vervuert/ Iberoamericana.

Train, R. W. (2009b). Toward a "natural" history of the native (standard) speaker. In N. M. Doerr (Ed.), *The native speaker concept: Ethnographic investigations of native speaker effects* (pp. 47–78). Berlin: Mouton de Gruyter.

Valdés, G., Fishman, J. A., Chávez, R., & Pérez, W. (2006). *Developing minority language resources: The case of Spanish in California.* Clevedon: Multilingual Matters.

Valdés, G., González, S. V., López García, D., & Márquez, P. (2003). Language ideology: The case of Spanish in departments of foreign languages. *Anthropology and Education Quarterly, 34*(1), 3–26.

van Lier, L. (2004). *The ecology and semiotics of language learning: A sociocultural perspective.* Boston: Kluwer Academic.

Versteegh, K. (1987). Latinitas, Hellenismos, 'Arabiyya. In D. J. Taylor (Ed.), *The history of linguistics in the classical period* (pp. 251–274). Amsterdam: John Benjamins.

Veyne, P. (1993). Humanitas: Romans and non-Romans [Humanitas: Les Romains et les autres]. In A. Giardina (Ed.), *The Romans* (pp. 342–369). Chicago: University of Chicago Press.

Wieczorek, J. A. (1994). The concept of "French" in foreign language texts. *Foreign Language Annals, 27*(4), 487–497.

Willinsky, J. (1998). *Learning to divide the world: Education at empire's end.* Minneapolis: University of Minnesota Press.

Young, R. (2001). *Postcolonialism: An historical introduction.* Oxford: Blackwell.

Chapter 11

Collaboration and Interaction: The Keys to Distance and Computer-Supported Language Learning

James A. Coleman, Regine Hampel, Mirjam Hauck, and Ursula Stickler,
The Open University

Abstract

This chapter describes the very practical approach to distance and online language learning that has allowed the United Kingdom's largest university, The Open University (OU), to deliver effective language learning to tens of thousands of students over the past 15 years. It starts from theoretical underpinnings: critical pedagogy, the specifics of adult learners, the achievements and shortcomings of the communicative approach, sociocultural understandings of language learning, and the central role of interaction and collaboration in achieving both linguistic and intercultural outcomes. An enumeration of the particular challenges of learning languages at a distance—facilitating interaction, managing affect, and effectively integrating technologies—is followed by a concise review of the evolution of distance language learning and of relevant research. Issues such as evolving technologies, task design, and student anxiety are also addressed. Distance language education at the OU is conceived not just as a technical challenge but also as an undertaking that engages actively in social issues and the promotion of universal values. The student body is exceptionally inclusive, with a high proportion of disabled and otherwise disadvantaged learners. This social mission adds to the complexity of curriculum design and delivery; neither the materials nor the actual teaching follows conventional models. Providing opportunities for learner interaction is a pedagogic challenge that can be addressed by integrating telecollaborative activities into the language learning experience.

Introduction

Each year, the OU welcomes some 230,000 students, all of whom are part-time and distance taught. Since adding foreign languages to the course portfolio in 1995, the OU has become, through its innovative teaching informed by cutting-edge research, one of the world leaders in distance and online language learning. In addition to addressing the theoretical and practical approaches which together deliver successful language learning on a very large scale, the authors here outline the ways in which distance language learning (DLL) at the OU makes it possible to integrate the following successfully:

- The principles of open and distance education
- Cognitive and sociocultural approaches to language teaching
- Learner autonomy
- Intercultural communicative competence
- Educational inclusivity

- New technologies
- Collaboration

We first locate our work theoretically within critical pedagogy, adult learning, the recent history of language teaching, and the particular challenges of DLL. After reviewing research findings and our own specific context, we consider experiences of telecollaborative learning and the lessons that have emerged.

Critical Pedagogy

The founding principles, the ongoing ethos, and indeed the very name of the OU represent a view of education as a social process and one that is inseparable from social change. Building on the work of Paolo Freire (e.g., 1973, 1998), critical pedagogy is an approach to education that seeks to help learners not merely to absorb the knowledge and wisdom of their teachers but rather to encourage learners to use their learning to challenge existing social and political structures and understandings. The goal of education is not to reinforce but to question the status quo. The educational establishment, in the shape of traditional schooling, is seen by critical pedagogy as a means of reinforcing society's norms rather than encouraging learning (e.g., Illich, 1971). A similar approach to learning—but focusing on the individual's capacity rather than societal responsibility—is taken by humanistic pedagogy (e.g., Rogers, 1983).

Within applied linguistics, critical pedagogy has been defined by Pennycook (1990) as an approach that "seeks to understand and critique the historical and sociopolitical context of schooling and to develop pedagogical practices that aim not only to change the nature of schooling, but also the wider society" (p. 24). The issues have been addressed, among others, by Crookes (e.g., Crookes & Lehner, 1998) and Canagarajah (2005) as well as Pennycook (e.g., 2001). Critical pedagogy, through dialogue and inquiry, engages the learner beyond the classroom. There is thus a link to Barnett's (1997) call for education to foster citizens who possess the skills of criticality and are hence capable of independent thought and action. It has been shown through a detailed longitudinal study (Brumfit, Myles, Mitchell, Johnston, & Ford, 2005) that university language courses can develop precisely the skills and attitudes embraced by the term "criticality."

Adult Learning

The great majority of language learners at the OU are adults who build on an already existing and confirmed knowledge base. Adult learning can be seen as a challenge to teaching, as established ways of perception and cognition need to be questioned to allow for new input to have an effect. On the other hand, adult learning can also be seen as an advantageous position from which meaningful reevaluation of a person's interpretation of the world can be achieved (Mezirow, 1997).

Based on the three categories of learning developed by the German philosopher Jürgen Habermas, Mezirow (1981) develops his theory of "perspective transformation" as a form of learning only adults can achieve. He defines perspective transformation as

> the emancipatory process of becoming critically aware of how and why the structure of psycho-cultural assumptions has come to constrain the way we see ourselves and our relationships, reconstituting this structure to permit a more inclusive and discriminating integration of experience and acting upon these new understandings. It is the process by which adults come to recognize their culturally induced dependency roles and relationships and the reasons for them to take action to overcome them. (pp. 6–7)

For adult language learners, this is evidenced quite clearly in the cultural aspect of language learning, which often leads to students' questioning their own cultural assumptions and which—if successful—will reintegrate their worldview with newly acquired perspectives (see, e.g., Baumann, 2010; Stickler & Emke, in press; Taylor, 1997). Cultural differences, in turn, can be seen as catalysts for perspective transformation (Ziegahn, 2005).

Beyond the Communicative Approach: Language for Interaction and Collaboration

Thanks to the elevated status of the classical languages Latin and Greek, when "modern" languages were added to school and university curricula in the early twentieth century, they were taught in the same way—as dead languages. Although this approach, with an emphasis on learning grammar paradigms and on translation as the key exercise, survives in traditional university departments, the 1960s and 1970s saw a move toward the communicative approach, so called because communication was both the method and the desired outcome. Language was described in terms of the functions and notions it conveyed (Wilkins, 1976) rather than as an abstract system. The components of communicative competence were set out (Canale, 1983; Canale & Swain, 1980).

According to Hymes (1976, p. 281), the following judgments in relation to language are crucial:

1. Whether (and to what degree) something is formally *possible*
2. Whether (and to what degree) something is *feasible* in virtue of the means of implementation available
3. Whether (and to what degree) something is *appropriate* (adequate, happy, successful) in relation to a context in which it is used and evaluated
4. Whether (and to what degree) something is in fact done, actually *performed*, and what its doing entails

The communicative approach introduced the use of the target language in the classroom, with a focus on appropriate language use and meaning rather than correct usage (Widdowson, 1978). Input, interaction, and output became central concepts in language acquisition. The use of authentic input materials became more central, as did the development of oral skills (fostered, e.g., by the use of the audio lingual method). As a result, certain task types, such as role plays or information gap activities, gained popularity to help develop students' functional communicative competence. Although there was more consideration of the learner and his or her needs, the focus remained on learning by teaching, and, in general, language learning was perceived as an act of individual cognition or a behaviorist process.

In contrast, socioconstructivist communicative concepts of learning do not follow the "transmission model" where knowledge is passed from an expert to a novice but rather describe learning as an attempt to reconcile the external world experienced through the senses and the internal world that the mind has created as a representation of reality (Glasersfeld, 2007). The sociocultural view of mental development is based on the psychology of Lev Vygotsky (Prawat & Floden, 1994; Vygotsky, 1978; Wertsch & Tulviste, 1992), who emphasized the role of tools that mediate our mental processes and our interaction with the environment. One of the most important tools is language (Vygotsky 1978; Wertsch, 2007); learning a new or second language (L2) makes the necessary mediation process more complex (Pavlenko & Lantolf, 2000).

Another tool that plays an increasingly important role in distance language education is the computer or, more specifically, computer-mediated communication (CMC). Planning a learning environment includes reflection on all the mediating elements that learners will have to cope with: a new and often unfamiliar language, learning materials, other learners to interact with, and—increasingly—new digital tools for communication and collaboration. It is today accepted that the Internet is by no means a "culturally neutral" environment where, as Kramsch and Thorne (2002) put it, language learners and native speakers can be in touch with each other "as linguistic entities on a screen, unfettered by historical, geographical, national or institutional identities" (p. 85). Thorne in particular has demonstrated in his work that the Internet itself is based on specific cultural principles and values and that its users are influenced by their own culturally specific communicative norms and modes of behavior that are sometimes not compatible with those of other online users. This learning environment provides the starting point for the language learner to make choices; engage with materials, tutors, and fellow learners; and create a learning event. "Scaffolding," a term based on further developments of Vygotskian thoughts, can be provided by various means: through the teacher, through the structure of the materials, and through support from peers.

Sociocultural theories have significantly informed research into language pedagogy. Instead of seeing language learning as an act of individual cognition or a mechanistic behaviorist process, sociocultural theories support a view of language as a vehicle to both convey information and situate people in a social system (Resnick, 1991). They oppose the idea of matching preset educational standards, for example, in terms of quantifiable linguistic skills, with the idea of the transformative power of learning (Kinginger, 2002; Phipps & González, 2004).

Sociocultural theories thus stress the pivotal role played by language and other tools in the meaning-making process and in the social construction of the mind and the self.

Knowledge, individual and social identity, the set of group-sanctioned conventional behaviors that we know as "culture"—all these are initially built and subsequently shaped by contact with others. So too are both the mother tongue(s) or first language(s) and new languages. In this view, although there is a role for individual study and private interaction with materials, linguistic input is not merely data for the individual mind to compute but also a vital, dynamic, collaborative process. Within a sociocultural approach, learner motivation is related to the idea of the L2 self and identity as a collaborative construction (Ushioda & Dörnyei, 2009).

Whereas in the cognitive paradigm interaction is seen as "the means by which input is made available to the black box [i.e., the human mind] or as an opportunity for producing output" (Ellis, 2003, p. 175), in sociocultural theories it is defined in social terms. Interaction can take different forms, one being collaboration, which allows learners to develop not only learners' linguistic skills but also their sense of community and their higher-order critical inquiry (Hopkins, Gibson, Ros i Solé, Sawides, & Starkey, 2008). Today, learners can collaborate beyond the walls of the traditional classroom, with new digital environments enabling interaction with other learners or speakers of the language.

Such collaboration can also promote intercultural competence, which is now widely considered as inseparable from language learning, and while there are many theoretical models of intercultural competence, the most influential in Europe, particularly through the collaborative work of the Council of Europe, has been the intercultural communicative competence (ICC) model of Byram (Byram, 1997, 2008; Byram, Zarate, & Neuner, 1997).

The Challenges of DLL

Learners and teachers of languages in a distance setting face the same issues as in a conventional classroom, plus some more. How far can the sociolinguistic, pragmatic, interactional, and sociocultural elements of communicative competence be integrated with the fundamental language skills? Are there other essential outcomes, such as cultural knowledge, intercultural competence, e-literacy skills, learning strategies, and the metacognitive competence that shapes a more reflective and effective learner? Paradoxically, distance learners have a need for increased autonomy but at the same time rely on the provision of carefully structured learning environments.

What practical skills and what theoretical understandings will distance teachers actually need? How can their initial training and ongoing support be best provided? What emotions will learners experience, and how can those involved optimize positive feelings and address the challenges of negative affect? How should feedback be provided to give learners an encouraging awareness of progress alongside the knowledge of areas of weakness to be addressed?

For distance learning providers, the three greatest supplementary challenges are facilitating interactions, managing affect, and integrating appropriate technologies. In both cognitive and sociocultural approaches, it is accepted that people learn a language by using it. Input and output are essential, but it is only in meaningful interaction with others that the mechanisms for acquiring, developing, and refining a new language system are fully activated. Additionally, physical isolation may be accompanied by emotional isolation—a feeling of loneliness that, if left unaddressed, can undermine motivation, self-efficacy, and success and heighten debilitating anxiety.

Which technologies maximize interaction while enhancing the distance learner's experience? From the rapidly evolving technical resources available, how do we select and integrate the many possibilities for CMC, both synchronous and asynchronous, and with a range of affordances from video to virtual whiteboards, which may be more or less suited to DLL?

Course design for distance learners needs to take account of such technological factors alongside human, institutional, logistical, and pedagogical concerns. In what follows, we attempt to address all these issues, reviewing how conventional challenges are addressed in distance contexts while giving more attention to the specific challenges of DLL.

Research into DLL

Simple presentation of subject matter at a distance is relatively straightforward. Complexity comes with the process whereby the interactions between materials, channels of communication, tutors, and students create effective learning. Holmberg's pioneering work (e.g., 1989) is complemented by four other major sources which together provide an overview of DLL: White's (2003) *Language Learning in Distance Education*; a special issue of the journal *Open Learning* (Shelley and White, 2003) that focuses on transferring good practices; the collection of chapters in *Distance Education and Languages* (Holmberg, Shelley, & White, 2005), which deals with the key issues of learner autonomy, learner perspectives and support, development of intercultural competence, methodology and course design, learning environments, and language teacher development; and White's (2006) state-of-the-art literature review.

White (2006) identifies four successive phases in technologies of bidirectional distance learning: print-based, broadcast, multiple-media, and Internet-based real-time interaction. She finds the whole domain undertheorized, arguing that "innovations in technology and practice have clearly outstripped theory development" (p. 250).

On both theory and practice, White (2003, 2005, 2006) eschews a focus on institutional concerns, program, and courseware development in order to foreground the real experiences of the distance learner. Her history of distance learning theories contrasts a socioeconomic analysis of DLL as an industrialized form of teaching with the humanistic views of Holmberg and others, who have emphasized the fostering through dialogue of learner independence and interdependence. The theory of collaborative control sees learner independence not as a matter of organizing self-instructional materials but, in a constructivist perspective that is now widely accepted within DLL, as an ongoing process within a learning community where control is negotiated through interaction. White's own learner-context interface theory takes into account the perspectives of all the different participants in the DLL process.

Garrido (2005) provides a full account of the development and delivery of a distance language course at the OU, embracing the target language culture(s), varieties of global Spanish, uses of information and communication technologies (ICT), individual learner needs and differences, the development of intercultural competence (cf. Álvarez & Garrido, 2001), promotion of oral skills, assessment, and feedback inter alia. Informing all the contextual factors and key questions is the central problem of overcoming physical separation to ensure the essential interactions between students, teachers, and native speakers, which emerge, as the sociocultural paradigm would predict, as far more significant than interactions with materials (Fleming, Hiple, & Du, 2002).

Since distance language learners working independently at home are responsible for the pace and direction of their learning to a far greater extent than conventional students, autonomy—and in particular self-management—is also a central concern in DLL research and practice. The extent of supporting structures varies widely, and whereas for some providers self-pacing is an essential characteristic of all open learning, others insist on rigid study timetables. Hurd (2005a, 2005b, 2007) situates the autonomy debate and links it to other influential factors in DLL, including affect (notably motivation), previous learning, learning styles, strategies, and beliefs. She also outlines the Vygotskyan approach to learning through social interaction and the research underpinning the adoption of text-based and voice-based CMC. Students' active involvement equally dictates feedback. Ros i Solé and Truman (2005) advocate a form of marking that fulfills the three functions of assessing, communicating knowledge, and facilitating learning but also encourages learner reflection and self-evaluation.

Murphy (2005, 2007, 2008) describes experimental work at the OU to develop learners' use of critical reflection and metacognitive strategies. She finds distance learners to be already capable strategy users and reflective learners (cf. White, 1995), but their functional control can be extended by appropriately integrated support material or constrained by assessments. Distance learners are also distinguished by exceptional precourse knowledge of the target language community, which is enhanced by study. Cultural attitudes may appear to remain unchanged (Baumann & Shelley, 2003; Shelley & Baumann, 2005), but a more sophisticated research design can evidence movement toward greater intercultural competence (Baumann, 2010).

If open learning is especially suited to accommodating individual differences, it can nonetheless also promote interaction and collaboration as well as community building. The development of online communication tools in particular has enabled the OU to move toward a sociocultural approach that sees knowledge as socially constructed through interaction.

As White has noted, technology has multiplied still further the many forms of distance learning. Hauck and Hampel (2005) provide a clear and well-theorized introduction to the OU's *online* foreign language teaching, which then used the original in-house audiographic tutorial environment known as Lyceum. Like many learning environments, Lyceum offered multiple synchronous audio channels and a synchronous text chat as well as three shared graphic interfaces: whiteboard, concept map, and document. The authors trace the intensive research that has explored successive technologies (telephone, e-mail, voice-over-Internet, and audiographic conferencing) in a desire to help students develop oral fluency and target language interactive skills (Hauck & Haezewindt, 1999; Kötter, Shield, & Stevens, 1999; Shield, Hauck, & Kötter, 2000; Shield, Hauck, & Hewer, 2001; Stevens & Hewer, 1998). Online meetings, together with forums and a dedicated Web site, build confidence and autonomy and encourage risk taking by providing shared image and text resources and authentic communicative settings for meaningful target language interactions. The synchronous conferencing tool currently used at the OU, Elluminate, has a single graphic interface but allows students to meet online at any time in the absence of a tutor.

Early exercises and role plays have given way to task-based approaches building on research into written (a)synchronous communication. Hauck and Hampel (2005) detail the features of task design for collaborative interaction, taking into account a typology of fluency-oriented online tasks (Shield & Hewer, 1999) grounded in the more generic task-based learning literature. Lamy and Hassan (2003), however, tested three different instructional designs with OU learners of French, concluding that psychological and sociocultural factors have a major impact on the degree of reflective interaction among learners. Their findings concerning the complexity of research in this domain are echoed in a later U.K.–German–Australian study (Hampel, Felix, Hauck, & Coleman, 2005). Experience to date underlines the cognitive and affective advantages of such an approach as well as the affective challenges of motivation and anxiety (Hauck & Hurd, 2005; Hurd, Beaven, & Ortega, 2001). De los Arcos, Coleman, and Hampel (2009) have looked beyond anxiety, using discursive psychology to show that other emotions, including regret and pride, play a role in language learning in online environments. DLL students demonstrate high autonomy (Vanijdee, 2003)—although this in turn has significant implications for the role of tutors, who require targeted training in the distinctive pedagogy of DLL (Hampel, 2003, 2009; Hampel & Hauck, 2006; Hampel & Stickler, 2005; Hauck & Stickler, 2006).

Studies from Sweden and Australia (Hansson & Wennö, 2005; Tudini, 2005) suggesting that DLL can attain similar learning objectives to face-to-face teaching, albeit through different mechanisms and structures, have been confirmed for beginner learners of Spanish at the OU (Coleman & Furnborough, 2010). Pedagogical designs must match the cultural educational context of the participants (Fay & Hill, 2003).

Teaching and Learning in the OU Context

The Department of Languages at the OU not only has been a unique leader in teaching languages to learners with a wide range of profiles but also has pioneered approaches to DLL, backed by pedagogical research. While we believe that many of the principles that guide our work can be successfully applied to other contexts, our own university, which celebrated its fortieth anniversary in 2009, is unique as a consequence of its founding mission (http://www.open.ac.uk/about/ou/p2.shtml):

The Open University is open to people, places, methods, and ideas.

It promotes educational opportunity and social justice by providing high-quality university education to all who wish to realise their ambitions and fulfil their potential.

Through academic research, pedagogic innovation and collaborative partnership it seeks to be a world leader in the design, content and delivery of supported open and distance learning.

Being "open to people" means that the OU has always attracted students who missed their first chance at higher education and those who are unable to attend conventional residential universities. Special provision is made each year for around 10,000 students with disabilities, while the student body also comprises the geographically remote or isolated, such as submariners, embassy staff, military personnel serving in Afghanistan, and some 2,500 prison inmates, alongside the majority whose professional or family commitments make a traditional, full-time university course unattractive or impossible. Being "open to people" also underlines that distance learning, unlike campus teaching, is infinitely scaleable: some of our language courses attract up to 2,000 students in a single year.

While openness of access may be considered a central concern of all distance education, the practicalities can prove extremely challenging, in particular for language teaching with its increased demand on interactivity. Provision is made at the OU for disabled students to access, for example, transcripts of audio materials, image descriptions, and alternative assessment materials. Students in prisons often have limited access to live online materials and are supplied with alternative formats such as offline DVDs or printouts of tasks. Such considerations, which routinely inform materials development and teaching and learning strategies at the OU Department of Languages, bring into focus still existing inequalities that might go unnoticed in a face-to-face context where some students are excluded from the start.

A further important consequence of inclusiveness is that there can be no admission criteria and no compulsory attendance at classes. However, studying at a distance does not mean studying without support, and students are offered extensive support to counteract the possible negative implications of distance learning. The OU, through its 13 regional offices, employs teams of selected tutors (around 700 in languages alone) whose task is to provide the necessary local support. This is fundamentally different from working in conventional teaching contexts, and the "change in mind-set" (Cheng & Myles, 2003, p. 36) required from tutors means that extensive initial and continuing training must be provided. But within the OU model of higher education, tutor–class contact is *limited*—typically to a short group tutorial each month, an occasional day school, and perhaps a one-week summer school—and *optional*. Individuals have e-mail and telephone contacts and receive individual, structured feedback on regularly submitted formative and summative course work assignments. But because not all students are able to attend classes, the teaching materials themselves, created centrally by a team of academics, must be self-sufficient and as nearly error free as possible. The "teacher's voice" (Rowntree, 1994)—in other words, all the functions that we as teachers perform in a conventional classroom, from presenting new structures through building a group dynamic to constructing a coherent curriculum—must be integrated from the start into the course materials, which typically take the form of printed books, DVD-ROMs containing audio, video or CALL (computer-assisted language learning) materials, and a Web site. The course Web site includes written and spoken materials as well as assessments and discussion forums and links to authentic online resources. All are integrated within the open-source platform Moodle.

The target language is taught not as a single fixed code but in its global sociolinguistic variety. World Spanishes, authentic Austrian speech, different notions of Chinese language, and a section on *québécois* writing all figure in the materials. In a further rejection of traditional models that separate language learning from "content" classes, language is intimately integrated with material providing insight into the cultures (rather than Culture, though literature is neither excluded nor privileged) where the language is spoken. Learning strategies are acquired alongside target linguistic structures and vocabulary and activities designed to build intercultural awareness. Sample language course materials are freely available via OpenLearn (http://openlearn.open.ac.uk) or iTunes U (http://www.open.ac.uk/itunes): the former site has already achieved 10 million hits and the latter 24 million hits, of which seven out of eight are from outside the United Kingdom. In August 2010, the top four OU downloads were Beginners' French Introduction, Beginners' Spanish Introduction, Beginners' Chinese Introduction, and Beginners' German Introduction, with two other language tracks also in the top 10 (http://projects.kmi.open.ac.uk/itunesu/impact).

OU language students cannot be easily characterized since they embrace all ages, abilities, interests, and backgrounds. We have learners with postgraduate qualifications learning a fourth or fifth language and young men and women with no formal qualifications following their first-ever university course. However, the majority of students are adults and not in their first stage of education. About 70 percent are in full-time employment while taking a course with the OU.

While openness to people means social and educational inclusiveness, openness to places means supported distance learning, openness to ideas is essential to the ethos of all true universities, and openness to methods dictates a close relationship between teaching and research. Our pedagogy builds on and feeds into intensive research (nationally, the OU ranks third for educational research), with a particular focus on integrating new technologies.

North American readers will recognize the challenges faced by language teachers in a country that, despite the more complex reality, perceives itself as a monolingual community sharing a single standard variety of English—a language that the rest of the world seems to be adopting. Despite the societal, political, and media factors that undermine language learning in the United Kingdom (Coleman, 2009), the OU continues to grow its language student numbers and with around 9,000 students a year is the largest provider of university language courses in the country.

Indeed, while our society is typically portrayed as a monolingual one, dominated by speakers of English, the reality is very different: multilingual communication and collaboration are crucial prerequisites for human coexistence and economic success in today's globalized world. Developing linguistic and (inter)cultural competence is central, and a growing number of institutions are becoming committed to a view of language pedagogy that goes beyond the dichotomy of literature and language and sees language learning as a transformative process that helps learners become active agents who are able not only to understand but also to shape their worlds.

Telecollaborative Encounters

One way of engaging language learners beyond the classroom and to promote the aforementioned critical skills—both in face-to-face and distance settings—is through telecollaborative models of learning. Telecollaboration is one form of computer-supported collaborative learning and has been defined as the use of "Internet communication tools such as e-mail, synchronous chat, threaded discussion, and MOOs . . . in order to support social interaction, dialogue, debate, and intercultural exchange" (Belz, 2003, p. 2) among language learners from different parts of the globe. Apart from the linguistic benefits (e.g., in terms of linguistic accuracy and fluency; Kinginger & Belz, 2005; O'Rourke, 2005; Ware & O'Dowd, 2008), the main attraction of telecollaborations tends to be seen as the potential increase in the participants' intercultural competence—comprising skills, attitudes, knowledge, and critical cultural awareness as established by Byram (1997)—and awareness (Müller-Hartmann, 2000; O'Dowd, 2006; Ware, 2005) as well as autonomy (O'Rourke, 2007; Schwienhorst, 2000) and e-literacy (Hauck 2007). Telecollaborative activities seem particularly well suited to help achieve one of the key aims of the Europe-wide Bologna process (http://www.ond.vlaanderen.be/hogeronderwijs/bologna/about), which perceives "academic mobility" (both virtual and physical) as the main contributing factor to the development of intercultural competence, respect for diversity, and linguistic pluralism.

Over the past decade, the scope of these online encounters has been extended to include exchanges based on the use of a lingua franca (e.g., Guth, 2008) between participants who are not all language learners (e.g., Belz & Müller-Hartmann, 2003; Hauck, 2010; Hauck & Lewis, 2007) and who might not even be far away from each other (e.g., Fratter, Helm, & Whigham, 2005). At the same time, the arrival of tools and applications associated with networked digital technologies and online social networking such as media-sharing sites (e.g., *Flickr* and *YouTube*), social bookmarking (e.g., *delicious* and *connotea*), blogs, wikis, and multiuser virtual environments (e.g., Second Life) has considerably expanded the potential of first-generation CMC technologies in relation to telecollaborative exchanges (Thorne, Black, & Sykes, 2009).

The result is a wider understanding of telecollaboration that is probably best captured by Guth and Helm's (2010) concept of "telecollaboration 2.0." Derived from O'Reilly's (2005) use of the term "Web 2.0" to describe changes in the way people use and interact via the Internet, telecollaboration 2.0 identifies the shift of focus to dialogue building and social networking. It encompasses the development of language proficiency, ICC, and new media literacy skills. Guth and Helm (2010) further conceptualize telecollaboration 2.0 based on what the aforementioned networked technologies allow learners to do, namely, generating, sharing, and jointly evaluating content and becoming part of online communities. This view is complemented by an understanding of knowledge as being collaborative—that is, the property of the social networks that created it—and of culture as participatory (Jenkins, Clinton, Purushotma, Robison, & Weigel, 2006; Pegrum, 2009).

While Web 2.0 technologies seem to be applicable to a range of disciplines in an educational context, they have been embraced by foreign language educators and researchers first and foremost (Thomas, 2009), particularly in distance learning contexts. This is not surprising given the reliance of online communities on asynchronous, near-synchronous, or even synchronous written and spoken communication. In the past, distance education used to be incompatible with collaboration, thus making it a rather solitary approach to learning languages. However, Web 2.0 and its gradual integration into formal language education contexts has changed this dramatically, taking "distance" out of distance language learning and teaching and making interaction with the tutor and with other students the rule rather than the exception.

Although telecollaborative activities are not necessarily unproblematic at the levels of learners, teachers, and institutions (O'Dowd & Ritter, 2006), the Department of Languages at the OU has been trying to integrate telecollaboration in various forms as supplement for distance language learners' notorious lack of direct contact. E-mail Tandem between German native speakers and OU learners was established in 2003 (Lewis & Stickler, 2007; Stickler, 2004; Stickler & Lewis, 2008). This small initiative was expanded to a multicultural European-funded project (LITERALIA 2006–08) that took place in multiple settings online and face-to-face. The project offered participants the opportunity to develop ICC and language competences in informal, nonformal, and formal learning (Stickler & Emke, in press).

Hampel et al. (2005) explored the benefits and pitfalls of using audiographic conferencing tools to facilitate collaborative language learning across time, geographical space, and individual difference. In the intensive exchange between learners from the United Kingdom, Australia, and Germany, critical success factors (see also Hauck, 2007) include participants' familiarity with the available tools and their ability to cope with the simultaneity of several forms of meaning-making processes as well as personality factors, such as tolerance of ambiguity and locus of control (White, 1999).

Further projects also broke away from the standard pattern of Tandem exchanges. With a wider range of participants, an attempt at a more dynamic, comparative approach to intercultural encounter was made (e.g., Hauck & Lewis, 2007; Hauck & Youngs, 2008). The *Tridem* pilot project, which linked three partner institutions, combined different tools for student collaboration, namely, blogs and audioconferencing, to enable students to socialize and interact together informally. The main findings showed that, although synchronous CMC tools enable students to establish direct real-time contact with native-speaker learning partners, asynchronous virtual spaces offer learners more time for reflective activities and give them freedom to work in their own time and at their own pace. The project was followed by further three- and four-way exchanges that built on and expanded Byram's (1997) understanding of ICC (Hauck, 2010) by drawing on Guth and Helm's (2010) conceptualization of telecollaboration 2.0. Acknowledging that Byram's model was developed before the dramatic rise of ICTs but continues to be an important reference point for ICC in language learning and telecollaborative contexts, the authors seek to integrate ICC into their new framework for "the multifarious goals of telecollaboration 2.0" (Guth & Helm, 2010).

The Role of the Teacher in Online Interaction and Collaboration

Unsurprisingly, the role of language professionals in computer-mediated intercultural foreign language education has become a focus of CALL research: "the importance (but not necessarily the prominence) of the teacher and, ultimately, teacher education programs . . . increases rather than diminishes" (Belz, 2003, p. 92). Barney (2005, p. 111), for example, talks about the need for "critical technological literacy" for teachers.

As many studies on collaborative learning report problems with teachers not having the necessary skills to support collaborative learning (e.g., Engstrom & Jewett, 2005; Hampel 2009; Mangenot & Nissen, 2006; O'Dowd, 2006), a study was carried out at the OU in 2008 in order to (1) find out more about distance teachers' experience of facilitating online group work, (2) identify development needs in this area, (3) try out the potential of particular asynchronous and synchronous tools to support collaborative learning, and (4) test possible development activities. The study identified a range of skills that teachers require for collaborative learning to be successful (Hampel, 2009). Teachers need to be technically literate, employ tools best suited for the task, moderate activities, provide careful scaffolding of tasks, and give detailed instructions. Other studies have also shown that they have to motivate learners to participate, regulate learner emotion and affect, help students create a sense of community, and find a balance between encouraging learner autonomy and learner control (Hampel, 2009). In addition, telecollaborations across different countries require teachers to regulate learners' intercultural experiences and to work with other teachers across institutions and curricula.

Conclusion

This chapter has used the context of the OU to link open learning and distance language learning and teaching with the use of new technologies both at a theoretical and at a practical level. It has shown how a theoretical framework based on sociocultural theories and concepts like learner autonomy, ICC, interaction, and collaboration can be brought together to inform new approaches to learning and teaching, approaches that include, for example, telecollaboration.

We want to round off this chapter with some dos and don'ts for collaboration and interaction at a distance and online (Table 11.1).

Table 11.1. Dos and Don'ts for Collaboration and Interaction

	Dos	**Don'ts**
Learner aspects	Ensure inclusiveness of access	
	Avoid assumptions about "the learner"	
	Allow for different learner types	
	Encourage the development of an individual learning style (constructivist learning, adaptive learning)	
	Encourage peer learning and peer support (online communities)	
Environmental aspects	Structure the environment in a clear and meaningful way ("scaffolding")	Focus on technology to the detriment of language
	Make materials relevant to the learner	Overestimate the relevance the course/ learning has for the learner ("overcrowd the curriculum")
	Make materials "talk" to the learner ("tutorial in print")	
	Ensure flexibility of learning pathways, learning preferences	
	Support the acquisition of ICT skills through engaging learners in meaningful language tasks	
Teacher aspects	Support the learner where and when needed ("guide on the side")	Set rigid structures and pathways
	Supplement the learning materials	Assume your learners will learn like you would
	Treat students as adults with relevant experiences and varied backgrounds	Assume your learners are a monolithic unit
	Maximize student contribution, not "teacher talk" (learner centeredness)	Rely on "on-the-fly" feedback or support
	Integrate ICT training but don't teach ICT instead of language	Overtechnologize
	Measure outcomes on set tasks, not learners (i.e., assess not the person but the performance)	
	Provide feedback in a clear and meaningful way	
	Encourage collaboration between peers ("facilitator")	

Provided that learners, teachers, and course designers are well aware of the distinct challenges and advantages of learning languages at a distance and combine the best-available technology with the best-suited pedagogy, this form of learning can offer, through collaboration and interaction, the same—if not better—chances of success for the adult learner.

References

Álvarez, I., & Garrido, C. (2001). Strategies for the development of multicultural competence in language learning. In J. A. Coleman, D. Ferney, D. Head, & R. Rix (Eds.), *Language learning futures* (pp. 150–163). London: Centre for Information on Language Teaching and Research.

Barnett, R. (1997). *Higher education: A critical business*. Buckingham: Open University Press.

Barney, D. (2005). The problem of education in technological society. *International Journal of Education Knowledge and Society, 1*(4), 107–113.

Baumann, U. (2010). *Exploring intercultural communicative competence in a distance learning environment*. Unpublished doctoral dissertation, The Open University.

Baumann, U., & Shelley, M. (2003). Adult learners of German at the Open University: Their knowledge of, and attitudes towards Germany. *Open Learning, 8*(1), 61–74.

Belz, J. A. (2003). Linguistic perspectives on the development of intercultural competence in telecollaboration. *Language Learning and Technology, 7*(2), 68–99.

Belz, J. A., & Müller-Hartmann, A. (2003). Teachers negotiating German-American telecollaboration: Between a rock and an institutional hard place. *Modern Language Journal, 87*(1), 71–89.

Brumfit, C., Myles, F., Mitchell, R., Johnston, B., & Ford, P. (2005). Language study in higher education and the development of criticality. *International Journal of Applied Linguistics, 15*(2), 145–168.

Byram, M. (1997). *Teaching and assessing intercultural communicative competence*. Clevedon: Multilingual Matters.

Byram, M. (2008). *From foreign language education to education for intercultural citizenship: Essays and reflections*. Clevedon: Multilingual Matters.

Byram, M., Zarate, G., & Neuner, G. (Eds.). (1997). *Sociocultural competence in language learning and teaching*. Strasbourg: Council of Europe.

Canagarajah, A. S. (2005). Critical pedagogy in L2 learning and teaching. In E. Hinkel (Ed.), *Handbook of research in second language teaching and research* (pp. 931–949). London: Lawrence Erlbaum Associates.

Canale, M. (1983). From communicative competence to communicative language pedagogy. In J. C. Richards & R. W. Schmidt (Eds.), *Language and communication* (pp. 2–27). New York: Longman.

Canale, M., & Swain, M. (1980). Theoretical bases of communicative approaches to second language teaching and testing. *Applied Linguistics, 1*, 1–47.

Cheng, L., & Myles, J. (2003). Managing the change from on-site to online: Transforming ESL courses for teachers. *Open Learning, 8*(1), 29–38.

Coleman, J. A. (2009). Why the British do not learn languages: Myths and motivation in the United Kingdom. *Language Learning Journal, 37*(1), 111–127.

Coleman, J. A., & Furnborough, C. (2010). Learner characteristics and learning outcomes on a distance Spanish course for beginners. *System, 38*(1), 14–29. doi:10.1016/j.system.2009.12.002.

Crookes, G., & Lehner, A. (1998). Aspects of process in an ESL critical pedagogy teacher education course. *TESOL Quarterly, 32*(2), 319–328.

De los Arcos, B., Coleman, J. A., & Hampel, R. (2009). Learners' anxiety in audio-graphic conferences: A discursive psychology approach to emotion talk. *ReCALL*, *29*(1), 3–17.

Ellis, R. (2003). *Task-based language learning and teaching*. Oxford: Oxford University Press.

Engstrom, M. E., & Jewett, D. (2005). Collaborative learning the wiki way. *TechTrends: Linking Research and Practice to Improve Learning*, *49*(6), 12–15.

Fay, R., & Hill, M. (2003). Educating language teachers through distance learning: The need for culturally-appropriate DL methodology. *Open Learning*, *8*(1), 9–27.

Fleming, S., Hiple, D., & Du, Y. (2002). Foreign language distance education at the University of Hawai'i. In C. A. Spreen (Ed.), *New technologies and language learning: Issues and options* (Technical Report No. 25) (pp. 13–54). Honolulu: University of Hawai'i, Second Language Teaching and Curriculum Center.

Fratter, I., Helm, F., & Whigham, C. (2005). Cross-cultural exchanges at the language centre of the University of Padua and the issue of language. In A. Moravìková, C. Taylor Torsello, & T. Vogel (Eds.), *University language centres: Broadening horizons, expanding networks. Proceedings of the 8th Cercles Conference. 9th–11th September, 2004*. Bratislava: Comenius University in Bratislava, Slovak Republic. (pp.177–195).

Freire, P. (1973). *Education for critical consciousness*. New York: Continuum.

Freire, P. (1998). *Pedagogy of freedom: Ethics, democracy, and civic courage*. Lanham, MD: Rowan & Littlefield.

Garrido, C. (2005). Course design for the distance learner of Spanish: More challenges than meet the eye. In B. Holmberg, M. Shelley, & C. White (Eds.), *Distance education and languages: Evolution and change* (pp. 178–194). Clevedon: Multilingual Matters.

Glasersfeld, E. V. (2007). Learning as a constructive activity. In M. Larochelle (Ed.), *Key works in radical constructivism* (pp. 3–19). Rotterdam: Sense Publications. (Original work published 1983)

Guth, S. (2008, November 14). *The multi-faceted focus of international collaboration*. Paper presented at the COIL Conference, Purchase, NY. Retrieved from http://www.slideshare.net/lamericaana/the-multifaceted-focus-of-international-collaborations-presentation

Guth, S., & Helm, F. (2010). *Telecollaboration 2.0—Language and intercultural learning in the 21st century*. Bern: Peter Lang.

Hampel, R. (2003). Theoretical perspectives and new practices in audio-graphic conferencing for language learning. *ReCALL*, *15*(1), 21–35.

Hampel, R. (2009). Teaching languages in online environments: Fostering interaction and collaboration. *Innovation in Language Learning and Teaching*, *3*(1), 35–50.

Hampel, R., Felix, U., Hauck, M., & Coleman, J. A. (2005). Complexities of learning and teaching languages in a real-time audiographic environment. *German as a Foreign Language*, *3*. Retrieved from http://www.gfl-journal.de

Hampel, R., & Hauck, M. (2006). Computer-mediated language learning: Making meaning in multimodal virtual learning spaces. *JALT CALL Journal*, *2*(2), 3–18. Retrieved from http://jaltcall.org/journal

Hampel, R., & Stickler, U. (2005). New skills for new classrooms: Training tutors to teach languages online. *CALL Journal*, *18*(2), 311–326.

Hansson, H., & Wennö, E. (2005). Closing the distance: compensatory strategies in distance language education. In B. Holmberg, M. Shelley, & C. White (Eds.), *Distance education and languages: Evolution and change* (pp. 278–294). Clevedon: Multilingual Matters.

Hauck, M. (2007). Critical success factors in a TRIDEM exchange. *ReCALL*, *19*(2), 202–223.

Hauck, M. (2010). The relevance of multimodal communicative competence in telecollaborative encounters. In S. Guth & F. Helm (Eds.), *Telecollaboration*

2.0—Language and intercultural learning in the 21st century (pp. 219–244). Bern: Peter Lang.

Hauck, M., & Haezewindt, B. (1999). Adding a new perspective to distance (language) learning and teaching: The tutor's perspective. *ReCALL, 11*(2), 39–46.

Hauck, M., & Hampel, R. (2005). The challenge of implementing online tuition in distance language courses: Task design and tutor role. In B. Holmberg, M. Shelley, & C. White (Eds.), *Distance education and languages: Evolution and change* (pp. 258–277). Clevedon: Multilingual Matters.

Hauck, M., & Hurd, S. (2005). Exploring the link between language anxiety and learner self-management in open language learning contexts. *European Journal of Open, Distance and E-Learning*. Available: http://www.eurodl.org/materials/contrib/2005/Mirjam_Hauck.htm

Hauck, M., & Lewis, T. (2007). The Tridem Project. In R. O'Dowd (Ed.), *Online intercultural exchange: An introduction for foreign language teachers* (pp. 250–258). Clevedon: Multilingual Matters.

Hauck, M., & Stickler, U. (2006). What does it take to teach online? Towards a pedagogy for online language teaching and learning. *CALICO Journal, 23*(3), 463–475.

Hauck, M., & Youngs, B. (2008). Telecollaboration in multimodal environments: The impact on task design and learner interaction. *Computer Assisted Language Learning, 21*(2), 87–124.

Holmberg, B. (1989). *Theory and practice of distance education*. London: Routledge.

Holmberg, B., Shelley, M., & White, C. (2005). *Distance education and languages: Evolution and change*. Clevedon: Multilingual Matters.

Hopkins, J., Gibson, W., Ros i Solé, C., Sawides, N., & Starkey, H. (2008). Interaction and critical inquiry in asynchronous computer-mediated conferencing: A research agenda. *Open Learning, 23*, 29–42.

Hurd, S. (2005a). Autonomy and the distance language learner. In B. Holmberg, M. Shelley, & C. White (Eds.), *Distance education and languages: Evolution and change* (pp. 1–19). Clevedon: Multilingual Matters.

Hurd, S. (2005b). Distance learning in modern languages. In J. A. Coleman & J. Klapper (Eds.), *Effective learning and teaching in modern languages* (pp. 142–147). London: Routledge.

Hurd, S. (2007). Anxiety and non-anxiety in a distance language learning environment: The distance factor as a modifying influence. *System, 35*(4), 487–508.

Hurd, S., Beaven, T., & Ortega, A. (2001). Developing autonomy in a distance language learning context: Issues and dilemmas for course writers. *System, 29*, 341–355.

Hymes, D. H. (1976). On communicative competence. In J. B. Pride & J. Holmes (Eds.), *Sociolinguistics: Selected readings* (pp. 269–293). Harmondsworth: Penguin. (Original work published 1971)

Illich, I. D. (1971). *Deschooling society*. London: Calder & Boyars.

Jenkins, H., Clinton, K., Purushotma, R., Robison, A. J., & Weigel, M. (2006). Confronting the challenges of participatory culture: Media education for the 21st century. Chicago: MacArthur Foundation. Retrieved from http://digitallearning.macfound.org/atf/cf/%7B7E45C7E0-A3E0-4B89-AC9C-807E1B0AE4E%7D/JENKINS_WHITE_PAPER.PDF

Kinginger, C. (2002). Defining the zone of proximal development in US foreign language education. *Applied Linguistics, 23*(2), 240–261. doi:10.1093/applin/23.2.240.

Kinginger, C., & Belz, J. A. (2005). Sociocultural perspectives on pragmatic development in foreign language learning: Case studies from telecollaboration and study abroad. *Intercultural Pragmatics, 2*(4), 369–421.

Kötter, M., Shield, L., & Stevens, A. (1999). Real-time audio and email for fluency: Promoting distance language learners' oral and aural skills via the Internet. *ReCALL, 11*(2), 47–54.

Kramsch, C., & Thorne, S. (2002). Foreign language learning as global communicative practice. In D. Block & D. Cameron (Eds.), *Language learning and teaching in the age of globalization* (pp. 83–100). London: Routledge.

Lamy, M. N., & Hassan, X. (2003). What influences reflective interaction in distance peer learning? Evidence from four long-term online learners of French. *Open Learning, 8*(1), 39–59.

Lewis, T., & Stickler, U. (2007). Les stratégies collaboratives d'apprentisssage lors d'un échange en tandem via Internet. *LIDIL, 36*(2), 163–188.

Mangenot, F., & Nissen, E. (2006). Collective activity and tutor involvement in e-learning environments for language teachers and learners. *CALICO Journal, 23*(3), 601–621.

Mezirow, J. (1981). A critical theory of adult learning and education. *Adult Learning, 32*(1), 3–24.

Mezirow, J. (1997). Transformative learning: Theory to practice. *New Directions for Adult and Continuing Education, 74*, 5–12.

Müller-Hartmann, A. (2000). The role of tasks in promoting intercultural learning in electronic learning networks. *Language Learning and Technology, 4*(2), 129–147.

Murphy, L. (2005). Critical reflection and autonomy: a study of distance learners of French, German and Spanish. In B. Holmberg, M. Shelley, & C. White (Eds.), *Distance education and languages: Evolution and change* (pp. 20–39). Clevedon: Multilingual Matters.

Murphy, L. (2007). Supporting learner autonomy: Theory and practice in a distance learning context. In D. Gardner (Ed.), *Learner autonomy 10: Integration and support* (pp. 72–92). Dublin: Authentik.

Murphy, L. (2008). Supporting learner autonomy: developing practice through the production of courses for distance learners of French, German and Spanish. *Language Teaching Research, 12*(1), 83–102.

O'Dowd, R. (2006). *Telecollaboration and the development of intercultural communicative competence*. Berlin: Langenscheidt.

O'Dowd, R., & Ritter, M. (2006). Understanding and working with "failed communication" in telecollaborative exchanges. *CALICO Journal, 23*(3), 623–642.

O'Reilly, T. (2005). *What is Web 2.0? Design patterns and business models for the next generation of software*. Retrieved from http://oreilly.com/web2/archive/what-is-web-20.html

O'Rourke, B. (2005). Form-focused interaction in online Tandem learning. *CALICO Journal, 22*(3), 433–466.

O'Rourke, B. (2007). Models of telecollaboration (1): eTandem. In R. O'Dowd (Ed.), *Online intercultural exchange: An introduction for foreign language teachers* (pp. 41–61). Clevedon: Multilingual Matters.

Pavlenko, A., & Lantolf, J. P. (2000). Second language learning as participation and the (re)construction of selves. In J. P. Lantolf (Ed.), *Sociocultural theory and second language learning* (pp. 155–178). Oxford: Oxford University Press.

Pegrum, M. (2009). *From blogs to bombs: The future of digital technologies in education*. Perth: University of Western Australia Press.

Pennycook, A. (1990). Towards a critical applied linguistics for the 1990s. *Issues in Applied Linguistics, 1*, 8–28.

Pennycook, A. (2001). *Critical applied linguistics: A critical introduction*. London: Lawrence Erlbaum Associates.

Phipps, A., & González, M. (2004). *Modern languages: Learning and teaching in an intercultural field*. London: Sage.

Prawat, R. S., & Floden, R. E. (1994). Philosophical perspectives on constructivist views of learning. *Educational Psychology, 29*(1), 37–48.

Resnick, L. B. (1991). Shared cognition: thinking as social practice. In L. B. Resnick, J. M. Levine, & S. D. Teasley (Eds.), *Perspectives on socially shared cognition* (pp. 1–20). Washington, DC: American Psychological Association.

Rogers, C. C. (1983). *Freedom to learn for the 80's.* New York: Macmillan.

Ros i Solé, C., & Truman, M. (2005). Feedback in distance language learning: current practices and new directions. In B. Holmberg, M. Shelley, & C. White (Eds.), *Distance education and languages: Evolution and change* (pp. 72–91). Clevedon: Multilingual Matters.

Rowntree, D. (1994). *Preparing materials for open, distance and flexible learning: An action guide for teachers and trainers.* London: Kogan Page in association with The Open University, Institute of Educational Technology.

Schwienhorst, K. (2000). *Virtual reality and learner autonomy in second language acquisition.* Unpublished doctoral dissertation, Trinity College, Dublin.

Shelley, M., & Baumann, U. (2005). Assessing intercultural competence gain in a German distance language course for adults. In B. Holmberg, M. Shelley, & C. White (Eds.), *Distance education and languages: Evolution and change* (pp. 119–139). Clevedon: Multilingual Matters.

Shelley, M., & White, C. (Eds.). (2003). Language in distance education [Special issue]. *Open Learning 18*(1).

Shield, L., Hauck, M., & Hewer, S. (2001). Talking to strangers—The role of the tutor in developing target language speaking skills at a distance. In Kazeroni, A. (Ed) *Proceedings of Untélé 2000* (Vol. 2, pp. 75–84), Compiegne: Technological University of Compiegne.

Shield, L., Hauck, M., & Kötter, M. (2000). Taking the distance out of distance learning. In P. Howarth & R. Herrington (Eds.), *EAP learning technologies* (pp. 16–27). Leeds: Leeds University Press.

Shield, L., & Hewer, S. (1999). A synchronous learning environment to support distance language learners. In K. Cameron (Ed.), *CALL and the learning community: Proceedings of Exeter CALL 99* (pp. 379–391). Exeter: Elm Bank Productions.

Stevens, A., & Hewer, S. (1998). From policy to practice and back. In *Proceedings of LEVERAGE Conference Cambridge 1998*. Retrieved from http://greco.dit.upm. es/~leverage/conf1/hewer.htm

Stickler, U. (2004) ". . . And furthermore I will correct your mistakes": Kulturelle Unterschiede bei der Fehlerkorrektur im Tandem. *Theorie und Praxis. Österreichische Beiträge zu Deutsch als Fremdsprache, 8,* 79–93.

Stickler, U., & Emke, M. (in press). LITERALIA: Towards developing intercultural maturity. *Language Learning and Technology.*

Stickler, U., & Lewis, T. (2008). Collaborative learning strategies. In T. Lewis & M. Hurd (Eds.), *Language learning strategies in independent settings* (pp. 237–261). Clevedon: Multilingual Matters.

Taylor, E. W. (1997). Building upon the theoretical debate: A critical review of the empirical studies of Mezirow's transformative learning theory. *Adult Education Quarterly, 48*(1), 34–59.

Thomas, M. (Ed.). (2009). *Handbook of research on Web 2.0 and second language learning.* Hershey, PA: IGI.

Thorne, S. L., Black, R. W., & Sykes, J. (2009). Second language use, socialization, and learning in internet interest communities and online games. *Modern Language Journal, 93*(Suppl. 1), 802–821.

Tudini, V. (2005). Chatlines for beginners: negotiating conversation at a distance. In B. Holmberg, M. Shelley, & C. White (Eds.), *Distance education and languages: Evolution and change* (pp. 212–229). Clevedon: Multilingual Matters.

Ushioda, E., & Dörnyei, Z. (Eds.). (2009). *Motivation, language identity and the L2 self.* Clevedon: Multilingual Matters.

Vanijdee, A. (2003). Thai distance English learners and learner autonomy. *Open Learning, 8*(1), 75–84.

Vygotsky, L. S. (1978). *Mind in society: The development of higher psychological processes.* Cambridge, MA: Harvard University Press.

Ware, P. (2005). "Missed" communication in online communication: Tensions in a German-American telecollaboration. *Language Learning and Technology, 9*(2), 64–89.

Ware, P., & O'Dowd, R. (2008). Peer feedback on language form in telecollaboration. *Language Learning and Technology, 12*(1), 43–63.

Wertsch, J. V. (2007). Mediation. In H. Daniels, M. Cole, & J. V. Wertsch (Eds.), *The Cambridge companion to Vygotsky* (pp. 178–192). Cambridge: Cambridge University Press.

Wertsch, J. V., & Tulviste, P. (1992). L. S. Vygotsky and contemporary developmental psychology. *Developmental Psychology, 28*(4), 548–557.

White, C. (1995). Autonomy and strategy use in distance foreign language learning: Research findings. *System, 23*(2), 207–221.

White, C. (1999). Expectations and emergent beliefs of self-instructed language learners. *System, 27*, 443–457.

White, C. (2003). *Language learning in distance education.* Cambridge: Cambridge University Press.

White, C. (2005). Towards a learner-based theory of distance language learning: The concept of the learner-context interface. In B. Holmberg, M. Shelley, & C. White (Eds.), *Distance education and languages: Evolution and change* (pp. 55–71). Clevedon: Multilingual Matters.

White, C. (2006). Distance learning of foreign languages. *Language Teaching: The International Research Resource for Language Professionals, 39*(4), 247–264.

Widdowson, H. G. (1978). *Teaching language as communication.* Oxford: Oxford University Press.

Wilkins, D. A. (1976). *Notional syllabuses.* Oxford: Oxford University Press.

Ziegahn, L. (2005). Critical reflection on cultural difference in the computer conference. *Adult Education Quarterly, 56*(1), 39–64.

Web Sites

OpenLearn (http://openlearn.open.ac.uk)

iTunes U (http://www.open.ac.uk/itunes)

http://www.ond.vlaanderen.be/hogeronderwijs/bologna/about

Open University Mission (http://www.open.ac.uk/about/ou/p2.shtml)

Chapter 12

A Social Constructivist Approach to Foreign Language Writing in Online Environments

Idoia Elola, Texas Tech University

Ana Oskoz, University of Maryland, Baltimore County

Abstract

While communicative approaches promote collaboration in the classroom, linguistic and cultural content knowledge is often regarded as information to be transferred most effectively from teachers to learners. Applying sociocultural and socioconstructivist perspectives and taking critical pedagogy into consideration, this chapter discusses the implementation of curricular changes into two hybrid Spanish courses: an advanced writing course and a beginning-level Spanish course. The use of social tools such as wikis, chats, and discussion boards not only emphasized collaboration among participants but also generated and developed content and linguistic knowledge in what is called the architecture of participation. The pedagogical shift possible through the use of social tools reshaped the foreign language context setting by expanding the physical classroom into a larger e-classroom and creating writing communities that used a language of their own. Learners actively participated in a community of writers in which, through dialogue, they created knowledge and achieved common goals both through the integration of the group and through their own voice.

Introduction

A collaborative approach to foreign language and culture learning expands learners' experiences and puts them in touch with social contexts different from their own. Guiding learners toward and through these practices of collective and critical learning implies, therefore, a need to modify the foreign language curriculum. Despite communicative approaches that promote collaboration in the classroom, linguistic and cultural content knowledge is often regarded as information to be transferred most effectively from teachers to learners. From this educational context, learners emerge with an amalgam of experiences that they have internalized with the help of the instructor or, less frequently, of their peers. This approach to learning reflects the traditional Cartesian view of knowledge in which the teaching–learning focus rests on the individual as a cognitive entity—a view that has hitherto been dominant in classroom pedagogy. However, it does not fit with the most current view of learning as a social endeavor or with the development of new technologies that allow the expansion of the physical classroom into "virtual" spaces that encompass independent online components. Within the social learning paradigm— an approach that focuses on the individual "as a person-in-the-world, as a member of a sociocultural community" (Lave & Wenger, 1991, p. 52)—learning is seen not as the product of one individual's efforts but rather as deeply connected to their surroundings, tools, and the entire context in which the learning takes place.

In line with second-language acquisition and learning theories, the foreign language curriculum frequently includes collaborative endeavors in which learners can actively participate in the foreign language community. On the one hand, these efforts take the form primarily of oral interactions in which the goal is to practice grammatical structures or vocabulary (Harklau, 2002), and, on the other hand, these interactions give learners little opportunity to engage in a critical dialogue that makes them active agents of their own learning. Considering that foreign language courses do not always provide a learning environment that emphasizes meaningful interactions (Ortega, 2007), we recognized the need to test new methodological approaches to support learners with their foreign language writing. This led us to experiment with the integration of social tools to allow learners to engage in multiple dialogues that would go beyond the classroom walls.

Applying sociocultural and socioconstructivist perspectives and taking critical pedagogy into consideration, we implemented curricular changes into two hybrid Spanish courses: an advanced writing course and a beginning-level Spanish course. In both courses, the aim was to foster the development of writing conventions through the use of the target language and learners' cultural knowledge. The hybrid courses were taught online for at least 25 percent of the class time and integrated the use of social technologies (i.e., wikis and chats). Collaborative tasks were set to provide learners with an environment where knowledge could be constructed through "ongoing, dynamic processes of discussion and negotiation that take full advantage of a collaborative approach to learning" (Hirvela, 1999, p. 8).

The pedagogical shift proposed in this chapter has reshaped the foreign language classroom setting in several ways: (1) it expanded the physical classroom setting into a larger e-classroom, and (2) it created writing communities that used a language of their own. Recognizing that learning is mediated by language, interaction, and artifacts (Ohta, 2000), the introduction of collaborative assignments, whether peer reviewed or coauthored, allowed learners to practice with writing conventions and to discover features of genres as they were generating content knowledge.

Constructing Knowledge

In a constructivist view of learning, how learners construct knowledge depends on what they already know, which in turn rests on the types of experiences they have previously had and how they came to organize those experiences into existing knowledge structures. Thus, the learner actively engages in the learning process, which moves beyond pure cognitive skills. This contrasts with a teacher-centered paradigm in that the teacher is no longer the authoritative figure and sole distributor of knowledge but is perceived rather as a facilitator of learning, guiding and supporting learners in the process of knowledge construction. The principles underlying constructivism are based on the following premises: (1) learning is not the result of development; learning is development; (2) disequilibrium facilitates learning; (3) reflective abstraction is the driving force of learning; (4) dialogue with a community engenders further thinking; and (5) learning proceeds toward the development of structures (Fosnot, 1996). In the socioconstructivist paradigm, founded primarily on the work of Vygotsky (1978, 1986), the learning process should not be seen as a solitary endeavor—on the contrary, it is highly collaborative. During their participation in collaborative activities, learners develop multiple perspectives and are exposed to disparate points of view, a process that in itself creates a rich bank of common knowledge.

Learning through Dialogue

Socioculturalism adds to social constructivism "by positing that reality is not only a matter of interpretative construction but that it is also radically collective and social, appropriated and transformed" (Ortega, 2009, p. 217). In this view, the individual participates and relates with others in an ongoing, social, and interactional process; that is, members interact, "do things together, negotiate new meanings, and learn from each other" in communities of practice (Wenger, 1998, p. 102). From a social-cultural point of view, "learning as increasing participation in communities of practice concerns the whole person acting in the world" (Lave & Wenger, 1991, p. 49). As van Lier (2000) suggests, from an ecological perspective, when observing learners' interactions, it is essential to avoid narrow interpretation of language as words that are transmitted from sender to receiver and of learning as something that happens only "inside a person's head" (p. 258). Cognitive processes need to be related to social processes; that is, language has to be contextualized into other semiotic systems and into the world as a whole (van Lier, 2000).

Because learning is mediated by language, interaction, and artifacts, there is a growing interest among second-language teachers and researchers in understanding how second-language development occurs through situated interactions in classrooms and other teaching–learning contexts (Ohta, 2000). The relevance of language or dialogue for learning has been widely discussed (Ohta, 2000; Swain, 2000; Wells, 1999, 2000). Wells (2000), citing Franklin (1996), states that "knowledge is created and re-created in the discourse between people doing things together" (p. 71). In the foreign language classroom, collaborative dialogue constructs both content and linguistic knowledge. As learners engage to complete a task, they are able to focus their attention on what they are saying and then produce alternative messages. As a result of this dialogue, "together [learners'] jointly constructed performance outstrips their individual competences" (Swain, 2000, p. 111). It has also been pointed out that the dialogue in question needs to be defined as both internal and external conversations that a learner has with a multitude of voices, not least of which is their own voice (Weisberg, 2008).

Adding a Critical Perspective

Critical pedagogy encourages learners to become active participants of their own learning, challenging existing social and political structures and understandings. In this view, educators themselves attempt to disrupt the classroom's traditional power relationships in search of a more equalitarian environment. The instructor is no longer seen as the only active agent of learning, the one who "deposits" knowledge in the learners, and the learners are not seen as the "depositories" of knowledge either (Freire, 1970), but the classroom per se is envisioned as a site where new knowledge, grounded in the experiences of learners and teacher alike, is produced through meaningful interactions.

Education in a second language is not understood just as the teaching and learning of an additional linguistic system; rather, it is about the social and cultural knowledge and, "perhaps even more, about helping students to develop critical approaches to examining and understanding such knowledge" (Reagan & Osborn, 2002, p. 30). As Brumfit, Myles, Mitchell, Johnston, and Ford (2005) suggest, foreign language programs, although expected to contribute to learners' ability to engage in the world as critical human beings, are primarily skill and knowledge based, especially in basic language courses. Yet Brumfit et al. note that programs that emphasize critical thinking include three traits: being able to use the language as a tool for critical reasoning, being able to provide critical reasoning within the language classroom, and being able to foster independent learning—all of which can be observed even from the early stages of language learning.

Dialogue in a Technology-Oriented World

In an era in which technology is "reconstituting how we communicate, making it possible to exchange information and to create new meaning collaboratively in new ways and at new rhythms" (Magnan, 2008, p. 1), the integration of constructivist and sociocultural perspectives with technology has proved to be a neat fit; it has led to pedagogical change and the transformation of learning environments. Technologies, particularly socially oriented technologies such as wikis (Web pages that anyone can edit from their own computer) and chats (voice or written synchronous computer-mediated communication), have had a profound impact "on the roles of teachers and learners by creating a more equal learning environment in which instructors and students collaborate in the construction of knowledge" (Van Deusen-Scholl, 2008, p. 193; see also Thorne & Payne, 2005), reconfiguring the traditional learner–instructor relationship. Socially oriented tools, then, not only emphasize collaboration among participants but also can generate and develop both content and knowledge in what is called the architecture of participation. Furthermore, the importance of communication tools such as wikis and chats in terms of their educational purposes stems from the *affordances*—actions that individuals can perform using a particular tool—of sharing, communicating, and information discovery (McLoughlin & Lee, 2007).

It is important to note here that while technology and social software tools offer potential enhancements to student learning, they do not automatically lead to positive learning results (Lindblom-Ylänne & Pihlajamäki, 2003). Therefore, in any educational context it is essential to consider the relationship between the properties of these technologies and how learners use them to acquire knowledge (Kirschner, 2002). Further, as McLoughlin and Lee (2007) suggest, there is a need to recognize that "technologies are intricately related to many other elements of the learning context" (p. 666), such as subject content, curriculum, communication, process, resources, scaffolding, and learning tasks. Thus, as classroom practitioners, it is crucial that we understand how the use of social tools supports the effective development of class content and how it enhances the role of each learner in their own learning.

Tools for Collaboration

In our approach, teachers can opt to work with diverse social tools to create more collaborative writing assignments. The first step is to choose an appropriate tool to suit the purpose of the planned activity. From the array of social tools available to educators, three tools—discussion boards, wikis, and chats—were chosen for consideration here.

Discussion Boards

Discussion boards are online forums that provide "a critical common space in which [to] share and verify hypotheses and points of view, to ask for help deciphering meanings of words and concepts, and to constantly negotiate meanings and interpretations" (Bauer, deBenedette, Furstenberg, Levet, & Waryn, 2006, p. 35). They have been instrumental in helping learners to elaborate course content (Weasenforth, Biesenbach-Lucas, & Meloni, 2002) and to promote cultural reflections (Bauer et al., 2006; Oskoz, 2009; Wildner-Bassett, 2005). We chose to use discussion boards because the time lag that occurs between reading and posting in an online discussion provides "time to recognize connections, understand other's ideas, and develop a detailed response or posting" (Meyer, 2003, p. 60). It also gives learners the opportunity to bring in outside material and experiences (Kol & Schcolnik, 2008) and to link ideas and make relevant connections (Arnold & Ducate, 2006; Kol & Schcolnik, 2008; Newman, Johnson, Cochrane, & Webb, 1996) more effectively than can face-to-face interactions (Sengupta, 2001).

Wikis

Wikis are collaborative Web-based environments that anyone can edit. As modeled in the well-known Wikipedia, wikis support collaborative writing in educational settings by providing learners with the opportunity to coauthor a document (Farabaugh, 2007; Jones, 2007; McLoughlin & Lee, 2007; Parker & Chao, 2007; Trentin, 2008). Because this software operates flexibly to facilitate the shaping and sharing of knowledge when learners work collaboratively, wikis have attracted the attention of educators in many settings (Augar, Raitman & Zhou, 2004;

Byron, 2005; Farabaugh, 2007; Honegger, 2005; Oskoz & Elola, 2010; Trentin, 2008; Tsinakos, 2006). An important feature of wikis when used for educational purposes is that learners hold authorial rights to create, transform, and erase their work. At the same time, the wiki allows instructors to follow the writers' collaborative actions by tracking who is making changes, what changes are being made, how often, and when.

Chats

Online chats, or "written synchronous communication," encourage learners to participate more in the class, create a sense of community among class members, and allow learners to think about and edit their messages before they send them (Beauvois, 1992). Chats allow learners to construct knowledge collaboratively by providing each other with implicit or explicit feedback (Lee, 2002, 2006; Morris, 2005; Pellettieri, 2000; Sotillo, 2005; Tudini, 2003). They also provide learners with a communicative setting that encourages exchanges of ideas and a focus on content (Beauvois, 1992; Chun, 1994; Kelm, 1992).

Implementing Social Learning in Foreign Language Writing

Our learners were attending a commuter university that has developed online components to compensate for reduced hours of face-to-face instruction. Learners at both beginning and advanced levels of Spanish participated in both computer-mediated communication and face-to-face interactions in the classroom. The integration of social tools allowed learners to engage in a coconstruction and meaning-making process in which they exchanged ideas on specific topics and created new knowledge collaboratively—either linguistic, cultural, or both. As suggested by McBride and Wildner-Bassett (2008), several ground rules were established for learners to allow their "sociability" to develop naturally. Outside the classroom, learners worked individually and collaboratively with the online tools according to the different requirements of each course. In the lower-level course, our emphasis was primarily on creating opportunities for developing writing with communicative purposes in mind, whereas in the advanced class, the main intent was to move beyond simple written communication linked to cultural topics to develop these students' skills in the genre of academic writing.

Advanced Writing Course

The advanced writing course is a regular course taught every other semester by the same instructor. There were 21 learners in this particular course. The main goal of the course is for learners to develop their second language, achieve academic writing skills in Spanish, and develop cultural knowledge by working on several writing activities that include the development of argumentative and expository texts. Based on previously mentioned sociocultural and socioconstructivist perspectives, collaborative writing assignments were introduced as an important component of the course. The objective was to create meaning-oriented situations in which learners could engage in a dialogue with each other about the linguistic features, writing conventions, and cultural topic of the assignment. Given the social implications of the topics selected, the instructor encouraged writers to research, critically discuss, and question their findings for learners to become critical producers of meanings and texts (Kellner, 2000). In order to expand the physical classroom into a virtual space that learners could access from different sites (necessary because of learners' commuting schedules), discussion boards, wikis, and chats were introduced into the intensive writing course.

The Procedure

During class, learners worked face-to-face on grammar exercises and the organization and structure of different writing genres and held in-class discussions about the cultural topics of the writing assignments. The topics of the writing varied each time: the role of men and women in Latino America, globalization, an iconic person in Latino America (see Example 1), and immigration. The instructor selected the first three topics based on the content of the textbook; echoing Canagarajah's (2002) suggestions, the final theme, immigration, was selected because of learners' expressed interest in the topic.

Example 1 Discussion board prompt (translated into English)

The person as symbol

There are people who acquire a symbolic or mythical stature in the consciousness of a people or in the consciousness of humanity. Think of a person that has played a significant role, preferably in the Hispanic world in general or in a specific Hispanic country.

Group Leader: Think of a person who has or may have had a great impact due to his or her political, social, environmental, or artistic work. As a group leader, describe the person that you chose and analyze why and how they became a symbolic figure.

Group Members: Respond to the group leader and to another group member by supporting the group leader's suggestion, explaining your reasons, and also adding more information. If you do not agree with the person proposed by the group leader, propose another person whose social, political, or environmental work you consider to be more important. Describe the person, the work he or she has done, and its value in society.

After an initial class discussion, grounded in the experiences of learners and instructor alike, learners further discussed the topics online via the discussion boards and worked on their writing assignments in the wikis with the assistance of the written or oral chats. Because learners had to work with four writing assignments (two argumentative and two expository essays), they worked with each genre both individually and collaboratively. In this way, learners could establish both external and internal conversations with multiple voices, including their own (Weisberg, 2008). The first time they encountered the new genre they worked collaboratively (essays 1 and 3), and the second time they worked individually (essays 2 and 4). To maintain the same approach to all the writing assignments, each of the four assignments followed the same instructional three-week-long schedule, which helped learners to organize themselves effectively. The first week, learners discussed the topic of the writing in the discussion boards. Following Arnold and Ducate's (2006) suggestions, each discussion board group had a leader, and this position rotated periodically. The leader was in charge of starting, maintaining, and wrapping up the content of the discussion, while the other three members answered the group members' postings. As Wanner (2008) also noticed, the strict thematic organization of the discussion boards encouraged an information-based style of communication in which learners provided snippets of information as well as discussing the pros and cons of a topic. The second week, after an initial discussion in class about content, structure, and form, learners completed the first draft of the writing in the wiki. When working on the assignments, learners were accessing the wikis from different locations, so they communicated via written or oral chats. Although learners were not obligated to communicate any specific number of times or to address any specific topics, they were encouraged to communicate with each other in Spanish. Learners used the chats to generate further ideas about the topic, discuss global issues such as structure and organization, and plan their work so each of them knew what they had to concentrate on while working separately. Then, in the following class (in week 3), the learners and the instructor commented on a few of the essays, reading for content, structure, and accuracy. Finally, learners had a week to complete their assignment in the wikis, using the chats when working collaboratively.

Learners' Use of Social Tools

Learners found that generating and sharing ideas with the group (in the discussion boards) allowed them to discuss multiple possible ideas and arguments for the essay. For example, when researching a person of mythical stature in the Hispanic world, one of the groups discussed the respective merits of Zapata, Pancho Villa, and Bolivar. In this discussion board, Lisa, who was acting as group leader, started the conversation by citing a political figure that she had researched: Emiliano Zapata. The group was composed of Lisa, Becky, Jennifer, and Rachel (pseudonyms). Lisa's initial posting led to the interactions that follow:

Excerpt 1:

Becky (Posted: October 26, 2007)
I agree with Lisa. Zapata was a very important person in Mexico, and he tried to do much for his own country. . . .
Becky (Posted: October 28, 2007)
Sorry for my additions [but] I have to add more. During and after his life Pancho Villa was a well-known revolutionary symbol for his fights during and in favor of the Mexican Revolution. But as a great symbol, Zapata, in my opinion and through my investigation seems to be a better symbol. When

I looked for information about Zapata I did not find anything bad as in the case of Pancho Villa. Villa made use of more violence. I found a lot of information on Zapata in relation to the true cause of the Revolution.

Jennifer (Posted: October 28, 2007)
. . . Because of these facts, I think that Bolivar is as important as Zapata. Yet, I think I agree more with Zapata's ideas. . . .

Lisa (Posted: October 29, 2007)
As mentioned by Jennifer and Becky, Pancho Villa was involved in one of the same movements in which Zapata participated. When I was reading about Zapata, it was interesting because some writers believed that Pancho Villa was more popular and that his image and photo were used more frequently. I don't know if that is true, but I think that Zapata's work is better known, and as Becky said, we can see his ideology more today in the fight of the called *zapatistas*.

Jennifer (Posted: October 30, 2007)
. . . Zapata was a man who influenced the history of Mexico, but Zapata did not make the same contribution as Bolivar. Bolivar liberated six nations in Latin America, and even today many countries honor him. However, I think it is important to mention both, because, in my opinion, Bolivar was not a role model because the wealth and the opportunity of getting an education did not help him to identify with other individuals around him . . .

(Translated by the authors as close to the Spanish version as possible)

Taking the postings by Jennifer as an example, she is voicing an internal dialogue in which she debates the relevance of Bolivar's role in Latin America. In her two different postings, Jennifer contributes information about Zapata. In her first posting, Jennifer tentatively introduces another choice of person, Bolivar. Although she is intrigued by Bolivar, who "liberated six nations in Latin America, and even today [is honored in] many countries," she then discards Bolivar and counts the merits of Zapata more highly. This reflects, as Weisberg (2008) noted, the importance of defining dialogue as both internal and external conversations. In Jennifer's case, it was this internal dialogue that helped her toward an understanding of the differences between the two men.

In this way, the discussion board became a forum in which learners, by listening to and debating each others' contributions, discussed the merits and weaknesses of their selected personas and finally achieved an understanding beyond their initial individual positions (Bauer et al., 2006). The internal and external conversations that took place in the discussion boards directed the group toward a possible consensus, confirming Hirvela's (1999) notion of knowledge construction through ongoing, dynamic processes of discussion and negotiation. When it was time for the essay writing, learners could draw on their new knowledge from the conversations, as Weisberg (2008) suggests, but they could also listen to their own voices and finally choose to write quite convincingly about the historical figures they believed were most significant or charismatic in the Spanish-speaking world— figures such as Zapata, Rigoberta Menchú, or Juanes, among others.

As noted in previous research (Beauvois, 1992; Chun, 1994; Kelm, 1992), chats can also be a useful tool to develop content, as they allow learners to challenge their coauthor's ideas, forcing each discussant to justify his or her ideas. Overall, the process of listening to each other and contributing additional ideas enabled learners to present stronger arguments in their essays.

Excerpt 2:

LAUREN: After thinking about it last night, I don't think it's possible to argue that sexism is caused by only one thing.

MONICA: But domestic violence isn't an argument, it's not a position/point of view . . . I don't want to argue about whether sexism exists at all.

LAUREN: This is my opinion: we can argue that sexism exists [by examining] its consequences, like abuse against women, or workplace inequality, or anything like that.

MONICA: But the problem . . . I have with that is this: if we select abuse, we only have one reason that demonstrates that sexism exists. We can only say that it exists because there is violence and there's nothing else to support the argument that sexism exists. I think that if we are going to argue that sexism exists we need a lot of facts to support our argument.

LAUREN: We'll have to make a list of reasons why we think it still exists; maybe that can help us select one topic, inequality in the workplace, the division of chores at home . . .

MONICA: OK, if you want to do domestic abuse we can add that sexism causes domestic abuse, because domestic abuse isn't enough to argue that sexism exists.

LAUREN: OK, I agree: domestic abuse is a consequence of sexism.

(Translated by the authors as close to the Spanish version as possible)

Echoing Wells (2000), this example shows how, in their attempt to achieve the common goal, Monica and Lauren directed their efforts to develop an appropriate argument for the basis of their essay. Through their collaborative dialogue, not only do Monica and Lauren complete the task, but, by the exchange of alternative theses, they also achieve a result beyond what they would have achieved by working on their own (Swain, 2000).

Beginning Course

Following the success of including wikis in the advanced writing course, a wiki component was added to a winter course (a three-week course) to observe if the new collaborative technology could also facilitate learners' writing in lower-level courses. Consistent with critical pedagogy tenets, the instructor attempted to create a learning environment in which learners would grow from being passive recipients of knowledge to active agents of their own learning. Whereas in the advanced course learners worked collaboratively to create the same text, in the beginning course the collaborative work entailed only peer-review work that addressed both global issues (i.e., content) and local issues (i.e., vocabulary and grammar).

Applying a social learning approach to writing in a lower-level language course, while still possible, requires recognition of the lower language proficiency and possibly lower cognitive abilities of learners at this level. Previous research has reported the use of learners' first language as the medium of expression to allow learners to achieve higher levels of cultural reflection and understanding (Antón, DiCamilla, & Lantolf, 2003; Bauer et al., 2006; Belz, 2003; Chavez, 2003; Elola & Oskoz, 2008). As such, learners were allowed to provide feedback to each other using English, their first language. At the content level, while cultural issues were raised and discussed in the classroom and via the discussion board, the instructor suggested a less culturally specific writing activity and one closer to learners' immediate reality, that is, their need to find a roommate for the upcoming semester in a Spanish-speaking country. To keep things simple, the wikis were the only tool used in this introductory exercise. As in the advanced class, these learners were also trained in the technology and were briefed about how social tools could support their learning processes at the individual and collaborative levels.

The integration of wikis into the beginning language class brought with it two major pedagogical changes. First, instead of completing one or two writing assignments in the course, which had been the traditional approach in the past, learners were asked to complete only one three-week-long writing activity. Because these learners were going to spend one semester in Spain, living with a Spanish roommate, an obvious topic for a writing assignment was the composition of a letter to this person to gauge their mutual compatibility. In the wikis, learners composed drafts of the letter at different stages of the course; this highlighted for them that the more relevant Spanish vocabulary and grammar they learned to elaborate their content, the more sophisticated their letter would be. Learners were able in this way to keep revising the letter and adding new information, individually and with the help of their peers. Integrating the knowledge learned in class into the writing assignments, learners wrote almost daily to their potential roommate. The second major pedagogical change came with the provision of feedback on content and form, which followed a four-step process. In order to support the letter writing process, the instructor created a schedule that included both learners' writing and also feedback from learners to their partners.

The Procedure

In each lesson, learners participated in related communicative activities, such as introducing themselves to another person. After class and with reference to the class content, learners were asked to incorporate what they had learned in class into the draft letter they were composing. During the following lesson, the instructor and learners then discussed the wiki writing. Given the public nature of the wiki, learners felt that they had become an audience to which the letter was directed. This new identity, as recipients of the letter, allowed learners to provide appropriate feedback to their classmates not only pinpointing linguistic inaccuracies but also by emphasizing content-related shortcomings. An example of this approach to content is seen in the way they want their partners to improve the meaning of the letter:

Excerpt 3

Two aspects for improvement: The small corrections to the eye and hair color descriptions as well as additional information, such as telephone number and maybe a short physical description. The physical description is not very important, but just to make sure your potential roommate isn't three feet tall and living in a house with 4 foot ceilings.

Excerpt 4

. . . but from what I can see you don't have what you and a friend like to do on a regular basis (probably to use *nosotros*) or what you do not like to do with them. I see classmate (*compañero*) but no friends and she is asking for what you like to do with friends.

As seen in these two extracts, the learners address, even humorously, content issues to help their classmates improve their letter. As readers *and* reviewers, they are looking at ways to develop a letter that might better meet their potential roommate's expectations.

Final Thoughts

Sociocultural and socioconstructivist approaches to learning attach importance to collaboration as a way for learners to construct and reconstruct their knowledge. Working within this framework, the use of social tools can enhance the act of collaboration between foreign language writers and allow them to transcend their individual competences (Swain, 2000). The use of social Web technology has led to an expansion of traditional classroom boundaries (Ortega, 2007), re-creating communities that engage creatively with material presented by the instructors. The instructors can also observe how their learners meet second-language writing challenges aided by innovative Web tools. Virtual collaboration between learners, associated with meaningful practices, is a method that Ortega (2007) suggests is a perfect vehicle for language development. As they worked on their collaborative second-language writing projects, learners found many ways to talk about the second-language cultural content and language system with a newfound degree of sophistication.

In this process, discussion boards, wikis, and chats became integral to the learning context—the curriculum and the learning tasks—and a community emerged in which knowledge was no longer transmitted primarily from instructor to student but was constructed collaboratively by all members of the class (Van Deusen-Scholl, 2008). As seen in previous studies (Donato, 1994; Swain, 2000; Swain, Brooks, & Tocalli-Beller, 2002; Swain & Lapkin, 2002), the collaborative dialogue during the writing tasks built knowledge that did not previously exist in the minds of the individual participants. It also offered learners the opportunity to become members of a particular community of writers where they could create knowledge and achieve common goals (Wells, 2000) through multiple and personal voices (Weisberg, 2008).

Despite our emphasis on a collaborative student-centered approach, we should not underestimate the role of the instructor in bringing together and guiding pedagogical choices that can build on learners' strengths and be targeted to their needs and abilities. Similar to Reagan (2005), we recognize that, while students have the ultimate responsibility for their learning, the instructor is pivotal to this model as the person responsible for deciding the instructional and learning objectives. The instructors in our studies shaped a learning context in which knowledge building took place at the individual as well as the collaborative level while at the same time introducing learners to the value of using social Web-based tools in an educational context. This approach enabled learners to transition from using such applications for strictly social purposes to using them as fully fledged learning tools, embedded in a collaborative, social context in which all class members collaborated in the construction of knowledge (Van Deusen-Scholl, 2008).

Adopting a collaborative and critical approach to the foreign language writing class entails a significant change in pedagogical thinking for both instructors and learners. After exploring curricular approaches in both courses, we decided to incorporate the use of Web-based social tools into the foreign language writing component of the courses; this project had the multiple goals of constructing knowledge, developing linguistic competences, and promoting collaborative learning as well as facilitating the use of new educational technologies. Below we list some considerations that have emerged from our study; these will be helpful for teachers or program directors who are considering the implementation of collaborative approaches to writing:

- The importance of social applications for educational purposes resides in their enhancement of sharing, communicating in a critical manner, and information discovery. Integrating social tools and collaborative work has an impact, as Van Deusen-Scholl (2008) suggests, on the roles of the teacher and learners because they create a more equal learning environment in which instructors and learners work together to construct knowledge, and they also create a particular community of practice (Wenger, 1998). In particular, instructors first need to accept that the use of these tools changes their role from an authority figure to one that guides learners in a discovery process. Second, they need to provide specific pedagogical guidelines for learners regarding the appropriate ways to use social technologies.
- Despite the focus of this chapter on the collaborative approach, instructors need to make learners aware of the value of the learners' own voice. By alternating both individual and collaborative work, instructors can guide learners toward self-confident expression in a social context and prepare them to become independent thinkers. Ultimately, these are

skills and competencies that will be highly valued when learners enter the world of work.

• Working collaboratively appears to ease learners' sense of frustration when working and writing with unfamiliar content. However, there is a danger that coconstruction of knowledge might produce a certain insecurity due to the dynamics of working in a group and having to depend on others to complete the task. To counteract this, the instructor should emphasize that participating in a developing dialogue within an established community of practice can foster critical thinking and help them reach their educational goals.

Working collaboratively with social tools, while supported by current research, requires a training period that allows learners to become comfortable with using the tools in a pedagogical context. In addition to providing specific guidelines—how, when, and why to use the tools—there needs to be a clear understanding of each tool's pedagogical purpose. The study reported here, while based on socio-constructivist and sociocultural approaches that emphasize critical dialogue for knowledge construction, does not propose that collaborative work is superior to individual work. As suggested by Weisberg (2008), there are multitudes of voices, the individual one being every bit as relevant as the communal one. Having said that, we do propose a new learning environment in which, through dialogue and reflection, learners create a unique community of practice that allows them to create and re-create knowledge that can often surpass what they can achieve individually. We would therefore like to encourage other foreign language instructors or those of other disciplines to design courses that give learners an opportunity to participate in their own learning: after all, these are critical skills for living and working in today's diverse communities.

References

Antón, M., DiCamilla, F. J., and Lantolf, J. P. (2003). Sociocultural theory and the acquisition of Spanish as a second language. In B. A. Lafford & R. Salaberry (Eds.), *Studies in Spanish second language acquisition: The state of the science* (pp. 262–284). Washington, D.C.: Georgetown University Press.

Arnold, N., & Ducate, L. (2006). Future language teachers' social and cognitive collaboration in an online environment. *Language Learning and Technology, 10*(1), 42–66.

Augar, N., Raitman, R., & Zhou, W. (2004, December 5–8). Teaching and learning online with wikis. In R. Atkinson, C. McBeath, D. Jonas-Dwyer, & R. Phillips (Eds.), *Beyond the comfort zone: Proceedings of the 21st ASCILITE Conference* (pp. 95–104). Retrieved from http://www.ascilite.org.au

Bauer, B., deBenedette, L., Furstenberg, G., Levet, S., & Waryn, S. (2006). The *Cultura* project. In J. A. Belz & S. L. Thorne (Eds.), *Internet-mediated intercultural foreign language education* (pp. 31–62). Boston: Heinle & Heinle.

Beauvois, M. (1992). Computer-assisted classroom discussion in the foreign language classroom: Conversation in slow motion. *Foreign Language Annals, 25*(5), 455–464.

Belz, J. A. (2003). Identity, deficiency, and first language use in foreign language education. In C. Blyth (Ed.), *The sociolinguistics of foreign language classrooms: Contributions of the native, the near-native, and the non-native speaker* (pp. 209–248). Boston: Heinle & Heinle.

Brumfit, C., Myles, F., Mitchell, R., Johnston, B., & Ford, P. (2005). Language study in higher education and the development of criticality. *International Journal of Applied Linguistics, 15*(2), 145–168.

Byron, M. (2005). Teaching with wiki. *Teaching Philosophy, 28*(2), 108–113.

Canagarajah, A. S. (2002). *Critical academic writing and multilingual students.* Ann Arbor: University of Michigan Press.

Chavez, M. (2003). The diglossic foreign-language classroom: Learners' views on L1 and L2 functions. In C. Blyth (Ed.), *The sociolinguistics of foreign language classrooms: Contributions of the native, the near-native, and the non-native speaker* (pp. 163–208). Boston: Heinle & Heinle.

Chun, D. (1994). Using computer networking to facilitate the acquisition of interactive competence. *System: An Interactive Journal of Educational Technology and Applied Linguistics, 22*(1), 17–31.

Donato, R. (1994). Collective scaffolding in second language learning. In J. P. Lantolf & G. Appel (Eds.), *Vygotskian approaches to second language research* (pp. 33–56). Norwood, NJ: Ablex.

Elola, I., & Oskoz, A. (2008). Blogging: Fostering intercultural competence development in foreign language and study abroad contexts. *Foreign Language Annals, 41*(3), 421–445.

Farabaugh, R. (2007). "The isle is full of noises": Using wiki software to establish a discourse community in a Shakespeare classroom. *Language Awareness, 16*(1), 41–56.

Franklin, U. (1996). Introduction to the symposium *Towards an Ecology of Knowledge.* Toronto: University of Toronto.

Freire, P. (1970). *Pedagogy of the oppressed.* New York: Seabury Press.

Fosnot, C. T. (1996). *Constructivism: Theory, perspectives, and practice.* New York: Teachers College Press.

Harklau, L. (2002). The role of writing in classroom second language acquisition. *Journal of Second Language Writing, 11*(4), 329–350.

Hirvela, A. (1999). Collaborative writing instruction and communities of readers and writers. *TESOL Journal, 8*(2), 7–12.

Honegger, B. D. (2005). Wikis: A rapidly growing phenomenon in the German-speaking school community. In *WikiSym '05: Proceedings of the 2005 International Symposium on Wikis* (pp. 113–116). Retrieved from http://www.wikisym.org/ws2005

Jones, P. (2007). When a wiki is the way: Exploring the use of a wiki in a constructively aligned learning design. In *ICT: Providing choices for learners and learning. Proceedings of ASCILITE Singapore 2007* (pp. 460–467). Retrieved from http://www.ascilite.org.au

Kellner, D. (2000). Multiple literacies and critical pedagogies. In P. P. Trifonas (Ed.), *Revolutionary pedagogies* (pp. 196–221). New York: Routledge.

Kelm, O. (1992). The use of synchronous computer networks in second language instruction: A preliminary report. *Foreign Language Annals, 25*(5), 441–445.

Kirschner, P. A. (2002). Can we support CSCL? Educational, social and technological affordances for learning. In P. A. Kirschner (Ed.), *Three worlds of CSCL: Can we support CSCL?* (pp. 7–47). Heerlen: Open University of the Netherlands.

Kol, S., & Schcolnik, M. (2008). Asynchronous forums in EAP: Assessment issues. *Language Learning and Technology, 12*(2), 49–70. Retrieved from http://llt.msu.edu

Lave, J., & Wenger, E. (1991). *Situated learning: Legitimate peripheral participation.* Cambridge: Cambridge University Press.

Lee, L. (2002). Synchronous online exchanges: A study of modification devices on non-native discourse. *System, 30*(3), 275–288.

Lee, L. (2006). A study of native and non-native speakers' feedback and responses in Spanish-American networked collaborative interaction. In J. A. Belz & S. L. Thorne (Eds.), *Internet-mediated intercultural foreign language education* (pp. 147–176). Boston: Heinle & Heinle.

Lindblom-Ylänne, S., & Pihlajamäki, H. (2003). Can a collaborative network environment enhance essay-writing processes? *British Journal of Educational Technology, 34*(1), 17–30.

Magnan, S. S. (2008). *Mediating discourse online.* Amsterdam: John Benjamins.

McBride, K., & Wildner-Bassett, M. (2008). Interpersonal and intercultural understanding in a blended second culture classroom. In S. S. Magnan (Ed.), *Mediating discourse online* (pp. 93–123). Amsterdam: John Benjamins.

McLoughlin, C., & Lee, M. J. W. (2007). Social software and participatory learning: Pedagogical choices with technology affordances in the Web 2.0 era. *Proceedings ASCILITE Singapore 2007* (pp. 664–675). Retrieved from http://www.ascilite.org.au

Meyer, K. A. (2003). Face-to-face versus threaded discussions: The role of time and higher-order thinking. *Journal of Asynchronous Learning Networks, 7*(3), 55–65.

Morris, F. (2005). Child-to-child interaction and corrective feedback in a computer mediated L2 class. *Language Learning and Technology, 9*(1), 29–45. Retrieved from http://llt.msu.edu

Newman, D. R., Johnson, C., Cochrane, C., & Webb, B. (1996). An experiment in group learning technology: Evaluating critical thinking in face-to-face and computer-supported seminars. *Interpersonal Computing and Technology, 4*(1), 57–74. Retrieved from http://www.helsinki.fi/science/optek/1996/n1/newman.txt

Ohta, A. S. (2000). Rethinking interaction in SLA: Developmentally appropriate assistance in the zone of proximal development and the acquisition of L2 grammar. In J. P. Lantolf (Ed.), *Sociocultural theory and second language learning* (pp. 51–78). Oxford: Oxford University Press.

Ortega, L. (2007). Meaningful L2 practice in foreign language classrooms: A cognitive-interactionist SLA perspective. In R. M. DeKeyser (Ed.), *Practice in second language: Perspectives from applied linguistics and cognitive psychology* (pp. 180–207). New York: Cambridge University Press.

Ortega, L. (2009). *Understanding second language acquisition.* London: Hodder Education.

Oskoz, A. (2009). The use of online forums to integrate the *standards* into the foreign language curriculum. In V. Scott (Ed.), *Principles and practices of the standards in college foreign language education* (pp. 106–125). Boston: Cengage Heinle.

Oskoz, A, & Elola, I. (2010). Meeting at the wiki: The new arena for collaborative writing in foreign language courses. In M. J. W. Lee & C. MacLoughlin (Eds.), *Web 2.0-based e-learning: Applying social informatics for tertiary teaching* (pp. 209-227). Hershey, PA: IGI Global.

Parker, K. R., & Chao, J. T. (2007). Wiki as a teaching tool. *Interdisciplinary Journal of Knowledge and Learning Objects, 3,* 57–72.

Pellettieri, J. (2000). Negotiation in cyberspace: The role of chatting in the development of grammatical competence. In M. Warschauer & R. Kern (Eds.), *Network-based language teaching: Concepts and practice* (pp. 59–86). New York: Cambridge University Press.

Reagan, T. G. (2005). *Critical questions, critical perspectives: Language and the second language educator.* Greenwich, CT: Information Age Publishing.

Reagan, T. G., & Osborn, T. A. (2002). *The foreign language educator in society: Toward a critical pedagogy.* Mahwah, NJ: Lawrence Erlbaum Associates.

Sengupta, S. (2001). Exchanging ideas with peers in network-based classrooms: An aid or a pain? *Language Learning and Technology, 5*(1), 103–134. Retrieved from http://llt.msu.edu

Sotillo, S. (2005). Corrective feedback via instant messenger learning activities in NS-NNS dyads. *CALICO Journal, 22*(3), 467–496.

Swain, M. (2000). The output hypothesis and beyond: Mediating acquisition through collaborative dialogue. In J. P. Lantolf (Ed.), *Sociocultural theory and second language learning* (pp. 97–114). Oxford: Oxford University Press.

Swain, M., Brooks, L., & Tocalli-Beller, A. (2002). Peer-peer dialogue as a means of second language learning. *Annual Review of Applied Linguistics, 22,* 171–185.

Swain, M., & Lapkin, S. (2002). Talking it through: Two French immersion learners' response to reformulation. *International Journal of Educational Research, 37*(3–4), 285–304.

Thorne, S. L., & Payne, J. S. (2005). Evolutionary trajectories, Internet-mediated expression, and language education. *CALICO Journal, 22*(3), 371–397.

Trentin, G. (2008). Using a wiki to evaluate individual contribution to a collaborative learning project. *Journal of Computer Assisted Learning, 25*(1), 43–55.

Tsinakos, A. A. (2006). Collaborative student modelling: A new perspective using wiki. *WSEAS Transactions on Advances in Engineering Education, 3*(6), 475–481.

Tudini, V. (2003). Using native speakers in chat. *Language Learning and Technology, 7*(3), 141–159. Retrieved from http://llt.msu.edu

van Lier, L. (2000). From input to affordance: Social-interactive learning from an ecological perspective. In J. P. Lantolf (Ed.), *Sociocultural theory and second language learning* (pp. 245–259). Oxford: Oxford University Press.

Van Deusen-Scholl, N. (2008). Online discourse strategies: A longitudinal study of computer-mediated foreign language learning. In S. S. Magnan (Ed.), *Mediating discourse online* (pp. 191–217). Amsterdam: John Benjamins.

Vygotsky, L. (1978). *Mind in society: The development of higher psychological processes.* Cambridge, MA: MIT Press.

Vygotsky, L. (1986). *Thought and language.* New York: Cambridge University Press.

Wanner, A. (2008). Creating comfort zones of orality in online discussion forums. In S. S. Magnan (Ed.), *Mediating discourse online* (pp. 125–149). Amsterdam: John Benjamins.

Weasenforth, D., Biesenbach-Lucas, S., & Meloni, C. (2002). Realizing constructivist objectives through collaborative technologies: Threaded discussions. *Language Learning and Technology, 6*(3), 58–86. Retrieved from http://llt.msu.edu

Weisberg, R. (2008). Critiquing the Vygotskian approach to L2 literacy. In D. Belcher & A. Hirvela (Eds.), *The oral-literate connection: Perspectives on L2 speaking, writing, and other media interactions* (pp. 10–25). Ann Arbor: University of Michigan Press.

Wells, G. (1999). Using L1 to master L2: A response to Antón and DiCamilla's "Socio-cognitive functions of L1 collaborative interaction in the L2 classroom." *Modern Language Journal, 83*(2), 243–254.

Wells, G. (2000). Dialogic inquiry in education: Building on the legacy of Vygotsky. In C. D. Lee & P. Smagorinsky (Eds.), *Vygotskian perspectives on literacy research: Constructing meaning through collaborative inquiry* (pp. 51–85). New York: Cambridge University Press.

Wenger, E. (1998). *Communities of practice: Learning, meaning, and identity.* New York: Cambridge University Press.

Wildner-Bassett, M. E. (2005). CMC as written conversation: A critical social-constructivist view of multiple identities and cultural positioning in the L2/C2 classroom. *CALICO Journal, 22*(3), 635–656.

Chapter 13

Cognitive Grammar and Its Applicability in the Foreign Language Classroom

Carlee Arnett, University of California, Davis

Harriett Jernigan, University of California, Davis

Abstract

The theory of Cognitive Grammar (CG), despite its compatibility with preferred theories of instruction and teaching methodologies, has yet to make its way into the foreign language classroom. This chapter introduces CG, outlining the basic principles that are most useful in the language classroom: cognitive domains, which function well as instructional tools in a communicative classroom, and the concept of schemas and prototypes, which help students examine the relationships between syntax and meaning. A lesson plan illustrates how one applies the principles of CG to explicit grammar instruction, supplementing students' grammatical metalanguage and establishing a cognitive domain the instructor can use for future grammar lessons. CG, because it encourages experimentation and interpretation, complements communicative language teaching and speaks to the goals of the report from the Modern Language Association (MLA) Ad Hoc Committee on Foreign Languages (MLA, 2007), which calls for teaching students translingual and transcultural competence at the secondary and postsecondary level.

Introduction

While Cognitive Grammar (CG) has existed as a theory since the 1970s, some foreign language instructors have yet to hear of it, while others are familiar with it but still find the core concepts somewhat obtuse.[1] This chapter serves to introduce the reader to CG, providing concrete examples to illustrate some of the key pillars of the theory. In addition, the chapter also explores how CG, though similar to prevailing theories of grammar, distinguishes itself from them, particularly in the area of transitivity, and how it can complement foreign language instruction, not only facilitating student comprehension of grammar but also promoting translingual and transcultural competence, a priority identified in the MLA Report (MLA, 2007).

In our brief review of the theory of CG, we focus primarily on two core concepts that can be applied to foreign language instruction: cognitive domains, or schemas, and semantic/syntactic prototypes, two elements that differ significantly from other approaches to grammar. An explanation then follows of how these two elements can be applied directly to the explicit grammar instruction that takes place in the language classroom. The last section of the chapter then presents a lesson plan that applies the principles of CG, activating a cognitive domain and then using that cognitive domain to introduce particular syntactic/semantic prototypes, anchoring the students in the CG metalanguage that will inform the explicit grammar instruction that will take place throughout the quarter or semester.

Our CG approach to teaching grammar is not a rejection of current teaching methodologies that enjoy success in the foreign language classroom, nor do we claim that CG is a panacea for all the challenges instructors and students face in language instruction. CG is a theory of grammar; as such, it cannot serve without modification as a pedagogical grammar. However, CG can provide instructors with a perspective and tool that is compatible with existing theories of instruction and teaching methodologies. As CG is a usage-based theory and can be applied at almost all levels of instruction, it can help both instructor and student.

Cognitive Grammar

CG is a usage-based theory[2] that emerged from the exploration of the relationship between language and cognitive principles, moving away from the tendency to regard linguistic patterns as finite structures internal to and specific to language. CG instead examines the relationship of language structure to elements outside language, such as principles of human categorization and pragmatic and interactional principles. CG distances itself from the various forms of generative grammar known under the blanket moniker of universal grammar, which presuppose that language is innate and will be acquired in its own time with adequate exposure to input and that the patterns and structures of language already exists in the learner and must be activated. By contrast, CG asserts that not language but the processes of learning are innate and that language learning is at its core no different from any other type of learning. Language acquisition requires not just input but experimentation and feedback as well. In this regard, CG is a fundamentally *social* perspective of learning and knowledge, with a focus on language in use; this is a point of overlap or intersection with the sociocultural and ecological frameworks presented in the other chapters in this volume.

CG, along with other functional theories of syntax (Foley & Van Valin, 1984), rejects the notion that language is an autonomous system. Rather, syntax and semantics are inextricably linked; meaning is so central to language that it must be a primary focus of study. The theory of CG, developed by Langacker (1982, 1986, 1987, 1991), posits that grammatical structure is almost entirely present at the level of the clause; there are no derivations of a clause, which is the fundamental claim of generative grammar (Chomsky 1965, 1988). For example, the German *Die Krankenschwester wurde von dem Physiker erwürgt*,[3] "The nurse was strangled by the physicist," is not a derivative of the sentence *Der Physiker hat die Krankenschwester erwürgt*, "The physicist strangled the nurse." The statements highlight different participants in the event, the former statement placing emphasis on the nurse and the latter statement on the physicist.

CG does not view syntactic and semantic structures as finite autonomous levels of language; rather, semantic structure is "conventionalized conceptual structure, and grammar is the conventional symbolization of semantic structure" (Langacker, 1982, p. 23). Semantic structure depends on the conceptual imagery established in a speech community. Speakers learn semantic and syntactic structures through exposure to the conventional patterns of their language, extracting the "rules" of the language from the patterns. Langacker (1982) claims that semantic and syntactic structure is language specific and as such can vary across languages and dialects. Moreover, semantic and syntactic structure can also vary within speech communities, within speakers, and within learners.

According to CG, conventional patterns acquired as part of membership in a speech community are stored in the mind as schemas. Speakers extract schemas from specific expressions that actually occur, and these are used to construct and understand new expressions (Tomasello, 2000). For example, a schema in German is *haben*, "to have," + "physical or mental condition," represented by a noun. The schema expresses a number of conditions: *Hunger haben*, "to be hungry"; *Durst haben*, "to be thirsty"; *Bauchschmerzen haben*, "to have a stomachache"; *Kopfschmerzen haben*, "to have a headache"; and *Lust auf etwas haben*, "to feel like doing something." All these expressions are products of the same schema, as they all are composed of the verb *haben* and a noun.

An expression derives its meaning from the conception it activates in the speaker's mind (cf. Chafe, 1970; Jackendoff, 1983; Lakoff, 1987). Processing an expression involves a speaker activating knowledge structures, or cognitive domains (Langacker, 1987). Any concept of experience can be the cognitive domain for an expression. For example, the concept *das Internet*, "Internet," would be the cognitive domain for *der Computer*, "computer"; *die Email-Addresse*, "e-mail address"; *die Webseite*, "Web site"; *surfen*, "to surf"; and so forth. In order for a speaker to understand the expression *ich surfe im Internet*, "I'm surfing the Internet," the speaker must activate the cognitive domain *das Internet* first.

In addition, an expression's meaning contains both content and construal, content being the activated cognitive domain and construal the way content is represented in language. Content can be expressed in a variety of ways, such as "The physicist murdered the nurse" or "the physicist's murder of the nurse." What is relevant is the degree of prominence assigned to the elements that make up the content. Thus, semantics is conceptual rather than truth conditional. Langacker (1991, p. 37) refers to the expression "The road winds through the mountains" as an example of this phenomenon. He points out that the road does not literally wind its way through the mountains but is presented conceptually, or metaphorically.[4] Let's look again at the statement *Ich surfe im Internet*. The speaker is not literally surfing the Internet. There is no truth to the literal statement. Instead, the act of looking at different Web pages is presented metaphorically.

The schemas or conventional conceptual patterns that are activated can be characterized as semantic prototypes. Since syntax in CG has meaning, this model of semantic prototypes can be extended to include syntactic structures. For the purposes of this chapter, we refer from now on to syntactic/semantic prototypes. Prototypes are a key component of the theory of CG (Lakoff, 1987; Rosche, 1973, 1974, 1975a, 1975b; Taylor, 1989). Syntactic/semantic prototypes associate a syntactic structure with a prelinguistic concept or image.[5] Speakers are able to judge the degree to which a syntactic structure matches the prototype. Membership in the category or schema is determined by approximation to the best member, or prototype, rather than a set of discrete and necessary features

(Fillmore, 1975; Lakoff, 1972, 1987). The schema *haben* + "condition" is a prototype associated with a prelinguistic concept—a state of being—and the examples above fit the prototype well.

Additionally, the members of the category have some of the characteristic features of the prototype, but they do not need to have all of its features (van Oosten, 1986). In the context of our example prototype, consider the following exchange between an elderly husband and wife returning home after an afternoon walk. The husband says, *Ich habe Hunger*, "I am hungry," and sits down, with the intention that his wife make him something to eat. The wife replies, *Ich habe müde*, "I am tired," and also sits down in a chair. This exchange demonstrates two principles of CG. First, the husband's expression is an example of an association of a syntactic structure with a nonverbal cue (his statement in concert with his sitting down instead of going into the kitchen). This is a perfect instance of the prototype *haben* + "condition." Second, although the wife's condition, *müde*, is an adjective instead of a noun, which is typical of the prototype, the husband understands the wife's meaning because her utterance meets one important criterion: being tired is a condition. Her sentence is an extension of the prototype inasmuch as we subscribe to the notion that the best instance of the prototype is *haben* + "condition," represented by a noun. The wife's use of a nonverbal cue—sitting down—to convey her meaning also reflects the constant relationship between language and contextual information.

To condense this discussion of prototype schema into a short list of criteria, the prototype schema can be defined as follows (Coleman & Kay, 1981):

It contains a finite list of properties.

Individual properties are scalar or gradient.

Membership in the category is a gradient phenomenon.

Membership in the category is a matter of degree because the satisfaction of each individual property does not contribute equally to overall membership in the category. One must keep in mind that the prototype is the *best* instance of a category. Categorization takes place by comparison with the prototype or schema, and varying degrees of deviance are tolerated. Instances that deviate from the prototype are extensions of the prototype. In the case of *Ich habe müde*, the statement deviates from the prototype because the speaker employs an adjective instead of a noun. However, because it shares a number of the properties of the prototype, it remains a member of that category; it is an extension.

A famous example from German pop culture, soccer coach Giovanni Trapattoni's famous expression *Ich habe fertig!*, further illustrates the notion of extensions of prototype. Trapattoni's expression—literally translated as "I have ready/finished" and understood as "I'm through!"—made an indelible mark on the German imaginary. When working as the FC Bayern soccer coach in 1998, Trapattoni held a press conference in which he grammatically incorrectly—but incredibly emotionally—declared his dissatisfaction and frustration with the efforts of some of the players on the team. Among other expressions that, bizarre and incorrect as they were, communicated his displeasure was *Ich habe fertig!*

He obviously learned the prototype *haben* + "condition," as he uses it, and he explicitly understands that he is expressing a condition, but the expression is not at all considered a common one. However, because his expression is an extension of the prototype (*haben* + adjective to express a state of being or condition), he was understood. Although metaphorical snickers did initially fill the media, the expression has since become widely recognized, understood, and *used*,[6] particularly within the context of extreme frustration. It helps that Trapattoni, as a soccer coach in Germany, has cultural capital that enables him not only to introduce this expression into the language but also to ensure its endurance, another aspect of the relationship between elements outside language.

Additionally, the example of transitivity can be used to show how CG distinguishes itself from other syntactic theories in significant ways. In the CG view, transitivity is a property of a clause and not of a verb. According to Langacker (1991), "transitivity is not definable just in terms of nominals occurring in a particular structural configuration. It is instead a matter of degree and depends on the meaning of the clause as a whole" (p. 302). Lakoff (1987), Hopper and Thompson (1980), and Rice (1987) have shown that various factors determine the transitivity of a certain clause: (1) a transitive clause must have two participants expressed by overt nominals, which function as subject and object; (2) the clause describes an event (not a situation); (3) the event is energetic and relatively brief and has a clearly defined ending point; (4) the subject and object represent discrete, highly individuated physical entities; (5) these entities already exist when the event takes place, and they are not products of the event; (6) the subject and object are fully distinct and participate in a strongly asymmetrical relationship; (7) the subject participates volitionally, while the object's participation is nonvolitional; (8) the subject is the energy source, and the object is its target; and (9) the object is absolutely affected by the action of the subject. Any transitive clause can have some— but need not have all—of these factors in order to be transitive. Furthermore, these factors do not contribute equally to the transitivity of the clause.

Consider again the example *Der Physiker hat die Krankenschwester erwürgt*. This is an example of prototypical transitivity. The first participant, or agent, is volitional and causes change in the second participant, or patient. The two participants are distinct from each other and are in an asymmetrical relationship. The event and the speaker's construal of it determine which of the nine factors are relevant. These parameters affect all aspects of the German grammar that are characterized by transitivity, such as auxiliary selection (Shannon, 1990, 1992, 1996), passivization (Arnett, 2004; Shannon, 1988), and the ability to form participial adjectives. In the CG view, these structures are not analyzed as separate, discrete structures but rather are described as part of the semantic network of transitivity.

Transitivity in view of CG is not binary but rather a matter of gradation (Sorace, 2000). It is the degree to which the subject/agent affects the direct object/patient[7] by means of its action. We can then speak of "high" or "low" transitivity. Auxiliary selection, passivization, and participial adjectives are best motivated by the transitivity parameters, most specifically one versus two participants, volitionality, and affectedness of the second participant (if present).

CG and Explicit Grammar Instruction

In this section, we turn to the use of explicit grammar instruction in postsecondary or secondary language classrooms and how CG can enhance it. As CG focuses on the symbiosis of syntax and semantics, it can complement the theories of instruction and teaching methodologies that have enjoyed success in the language classroom, namely, focus on form, structured input, and communicative methodologies. Because of its compatibility, CG can enhance the explicit grammar instruction that already takes place in the classroom. Many first-year textbooks follow a grammar-driven syllabus that "seeks to isolate linguistic forms in order to teach and test them one at a time" (R. Ellis, 1997, p. 639). A grammar-driven syllabus in the first year is not necessarily undesirable, but it has the result of presenting each grammar point in isolation, and it is left to the instructor to show the students the coherence in the grammar. CG provides a tool for the instructor to reveal the network of form and function that underlies the grammar. For the purposes of this chapter, we define explicit grammar instruction as both providing students with a metalanguage to talk about grammatical structure as well as focusing student attention on grammatical form and function. In particular, this definition of explicit instruction is compatible with the teaching methodologies of focus on form (Doughty, 2003; Doughty & Williams, 1998; Long, 1991) and structured input (VanPatten, 1996).

There is still debate over how one defines implicit and explicit instruction and their effectiveness. R. Ellis's (1994) definition of implicit instruction is the most widely accepted one; he defines implicit instruction as asking students to induce rules by looking at examples. Explicit instruction is defined as presenting a specific rule and then having the students practice it. Ellis then reviews the research on which form of instruction is most beneficial and when. However, the results are inconclusive. He states that,

> on balance, the available evidence indicates that an explicit presentation of the rules supported by examples is the most effective way of presenting difficult new material. However, the effectiveness of an implicit or explicit instructional treatment may depend on the type of linguistic material being learnt and the characteristics of the individual learner. (p. 643)

Ellis concludes that both explicit and implicit instruction have their place in foreign language instruction but that it has yet to be determined what form of instruction is most useful, at what point in the process of learning, or why. But it is clear that learners can benefit from both types of instruction. Since CG is not a teaching methodology or a theory of second-language acquisition, there is nothing in CG's view of grammar or its application in the classroom that prohibits the instructor from using both explicit and implicit instruction, though CG itself is not an implicit approach. CG can be used to explain a grammatical structure either before or after students have worked with examples.

With regard to the benefits or effectiveness of explicit instruction alone, research has yielded mixed results. Lightbown (1991), Pienemann (1984, 1989), and White (1991) highlight the difficulty of pinpointing when explicit instruction has long-term benefits, or which structures can be taught and retained by students for an extended period of time. In short, it is hard to determine which structures the students will acquire and which ones they will learn only for brief manipulation in structured environments. The experienced classroom teacher often develops a keen sense of which structures these are and is aware that forms can be memorized and structures learned for short-term manipulation, but it does not mean that the structure has been acquired.

Further research is needed to know which grammatical structures are more easily understood at the metalinguistic level based on explicit or implicit instruction. Beyond the answer to that research question, studies are needed to show which approach yields the best results with respect to learning/acquisition for each particular grammatical structure. The research agenda is twofold. First, instructors should provide the students with a rubric for understanding grammar as a coherent whole that fosters their metalinguistic knowledge and that is an essential component of their translingual and transcultural competence and then test the rubric for its effectiveness. A second and parallel strand of research would be to study which structures are best taught explicitly and which are best taught implicitly and, as a corollary, when in the learning process the instructor should teach the structure. However, it is our assertion that CG presentations of the grammar will aid both types of research.

We are making the assumption in this chapter that structure can be taught at some point in the learning process. Pienemann (1989) proposes that language is teachable if the structure is taught close to the time when the student is ready to acquire it in the natural order of acquisition. The teachability hypothesis suggests that instruction does not impede the natural order of acquisition and that it may aid a learner's acquisition of certain structures. The challenge lies in teaching those grammatical structures that a student is ready to learn. Krashen (1985) has a similar hypothesis about how and when to direct student learning. Krashen has the notion of comprehensible input, which means that students receive and understand messages. They move ahead from i by being exposed to $i + 1$, which is the next level in the natural order of acquisition. This implies that the provider of comprehensible input or $i + 1$ will have to know what is next in the natural order of acquisition for the learner.

VanPatten (1996) focuses on another concept: structured input. Structured input requires that the input should contain the target structure and that the students should notice it. The materials that are given to the students to practice the structure should also foster awareness and facilitate noticing. The students should work from recognizing the structure to more unrestricted production, that is, free speech or writing, as the lesson progresses. VanPatten (1996) shows that carefully selected input can prompt students to notice a syntactic structure, recognize it, and reproduce it in controlled environments. Properly designed materials taught at the appropriate time for students can lead to long-term and continued acquisition (R. Ellis, 1997). As mentioned above, research can show what types of structures are amenable to explicit or implicit modes of teaching and whether students acquire a metaknowledge, the ability to manipulate forms in restricted environments (i.e., cloze tests and drills), or the ability to manipulate forms in unrestricted environments, such as free writing or speech.

The preceding discussion focused on whether students can learn and/or acquire structures the instructor teaches or exposes them to. We know that students cannot acquire all the rules of the grammar that they are exposed to, either implicitly or explicitly, in one year of instruction. It is possible, though, that teaching learners one structure will trigger or aid in the acquisition of others. Teaching a marked structure (i.e., one that differs from the more normative structures in a language such as the dative case in German) aids in the acquisition of the accusative and nominative functions (R. Ellis, 1997). This is why, in German at least, we should not stop teaching structures that we know students will not acquire until later in the process. We know that students will not acquire the dative case in the early stages of language learning, but the teaching of the dative case will aid in the acquisition of the accusative and nominative case functions.

Considering the multiple factors that influence acquisition, one may benefit from using a combined approach to grammar instruction, engaging in both implicit and explicit instruction (N. C. Ellis, 2005). In this respect, CG can be useful because it can be used to focus on specific linguistic forms in explicit instruction as well as facilitate induction in implicit instruction. Recently, articles have addressed the applicability of CG to the language classroom and its effectiveness for teaching grammar in the second-language and foreign language classroom (Archard, 2004; Cadierno, 2004; de Knop & de Rycker, 2008; Janda & Clancy, 2002; Lam, 2009; Lysinger, 2009; Masuda, 2005; Zyzik, 2006). Lysinger (2009) showed that a CG approach to case in first-year German and Russian produced statistically higher rates of accuracy on three measures (metaknowledge, cloze test of forms, and a free-written response to a prompt) than a control group who received no CG instruction. Both treatment and control groups received the same amount of instruction, but the control group's instruction was based solely on the textbook. To date, Lysinger (2009) and Lam (2005) are among the few studies that test the effectiveness of CG in a classroom environment.

Following Doughty and Williams (1998), R. Ellis (2001), Robinson (2001), and many others, we argue that a metalinguistic explanation of grammar has its place in classrooms teaching second-language acquisition, although not at the expense of language use. In the case of German, a metalinguistic explanation of grammar serves many purposes. It draws students' attention to the functions of the grammatical structures, which allows them to activate the internal cognitive processes involved in second-language acquisition (Anderson, 1983, 1985). Metalinguistic explanations show that the structure under consideration is important. In addition, it has been shown that novice learners benefit from explicit, metalinguistic explanations of errors (R. Ellis, Loewen, & Erlam, 2006). Given that students will be novices with respect to most aspects of German grammar until the advanced levels of instruction, a metalinguistic explanation is suited to the elementary, the intermediate, as well as the advanced classroom. CG can supplement these metalinguistic explanations.

An Example of a CG Lesson Plan

We emphasize in this chapter that explicit grammar instruction is beneficial in the foreign language classroom and that foreign language programs generally favor communicative language teaching, as manifested in the many textbooks based on communicative methodologies. Many textbooks and syllabi strive for what Doughty and Varela (1998) call "communicative focus on form," seeking a balance between explicit and implicit grammar instruction that centers on communicative tasks. CG, because it centers on prototypes rather than structures and the notion that meaning cannot be separated from form, creates an extra space in which students can experiment with concepts rather than words, relaxing the perceived division between language and meaning. This means that the instructor, when using a communicative focus on form syllabus, can use the metalanguage of CG to refine students' perceptions of the explicit grammar explanations in their textbooks.

The following four-part lesson plan illustrates how CG's metalanguage can complement explicit grammar instruction that may take place in the foreign language classroom. The lesson plan has two goals. First, it introduces students to the grammatical metalanguage they will use in class during explicit instruction, and, second, it provides a cognitive domain to which the instructor can return throughout the semester or quarter when explicitly presenting new grammatical structures or concepts. Because it is used during the first few days of instruction in an introductory language class, the lesson takes place in English. This will change as students become more proficient in the target language. It is also important to note that the lesson plan represents only part of what happens during the class hour; it is assumed that the instructor has other activities in addition to this focus on grammar.

The lesson plan uses a specific cognitive domain to which the instructor regularly returns when introducing new schemas and prototypes. The instructor chose an internationally famous pop singer, known here as Singer X, whose name, face, and voice have appeared in print media; on television, radio, and the Internet; and in many languages. Despite its ostensible simplicity and superficiality, this particular cognitive domain, as reflecting a pervasive cross-cultural discourse, is ideal for a number of reasons. First, Singer X's international fame makes for an accessible cognitive domain that many students share or could at least relate to. In other words, aspects of Singer X's music, career, and personal and public life are subject to ongoing, multiple, and differing interpretations in different cultures. In addition, this cognitive domain can easily be reactivated later to teach new structures. Finally, because of the figure's celebrity status, the instructor can choose from a wide range of images, recordings, and videos to present various prototypes, from simple to complex. In short, far from being a superficial cognitive domain, Singer X is a rich resource for CG and other sorts of instruction and experimentation on a number of levels.

Typically, the instructor devotes the last 10 minutes of class of the first three to four class sessions to explicit grammar instruction. This lesson plan is divided into four segments. At the beginning of the first segment, the instructor tells the students that she is going to introduce them to a new way of thinking about grammar. The instructor then projects on a screen an image of Singer X carrying her toddler son in her left arm and holding a baby bottle in her right hand. The image activates the cognitive domain before any discussion about grammar takes place.

After the instructor projects the image on the screen, she writes a series of questions on the board:

1. Who is that?   **2. What does she do?**   **3. Who is that with her?**

The instructor then asks the students the questions. As the students answer, the instructor records the answers, adjusting slightly to suit instructional needs. The answers appear as follows:

1. That's [Singer X].   **2. She's a singer.**   **3. That's her son.**

Once the instructor has recorded the responses, she returns to each statement and writes the corresponding CG symbols underneath each statement:

1. That's [Singer X].   **2. She's a singer/pop star. 3. That's her son.**

1. ○   **2.** ○   **3.** ○

Because CG asserts that grammar is present at the clausal level, the instructor does not treat "That's [Singer X]" as a derivative of "That is [Singer X]." Instead, the expression, because it is a product of different properties and functions outside language, stands on its own; the diagram illustrates the prototype. This prototype, though it needs to be explicitly presented, does not necessarily need a label; students can induce this structure.

The instructor then writes a fourth question on the board: "What is [Singer X] holding?" and asks the students. The instructor then records the answer underneath:

[Singer X] is holding a bottle.

The instructor then writes the prototype diagram next to the statement:

[Singer X] is holding a bottle.

At this point, the instructor typically ends the lesson, as this suffices to introduce the prelinguistic concepts that the instructor will continue to use.

At the end of the next class session,[8] the instructor projects the same picture on the screen and writes the four corresponding sentences on the board again. The instructor then underlines "[Singer X]" and asks the students what part of speech the word is. Someone will identify it as the subject of the sentence. The instructor writes an S below "[Singer X]" and below the clear circle. Then the instructor underlines "is holding" and asks the students what part of speech that is. Someone will reply that it is a verb, and the instructor writes V under "is holding" and under the arrow. Then the instructor underlines "bottle" and asks the class what part of speech that is. Typically, at least one student will call this a direct object. The instructor writes O under "bottle" and under the opaque circle:

[Singer X] is holding a bottle.

S.   V.   O.   S.   V.   O.

Here, the instructor raises two points. First, we agree that the elements in the sentence can be classified independently as things such as subject, verb, and object. However, the aim is that we begin to see expressions as more than the sum of grammatical elements; that is, students should start thinking in terms of prototypes or particular constellations of elements that express particular meanings. The prototype, as demonstrated by the diagram, shows us that there is a distinct relationship between the subject, verb, and object.

Now that the instructor has introduced the concept of semantic/syntactic prototypes, she can present the new terms that she will use to inform the students' grammatical metalanguage: agent, action, and patient. Underneath the CG diagram, the instructor writes these terms:

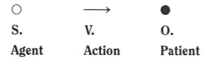

○	⟶	●
S.	V.	O.
Agent	**Action**	**Patient**

The instructor explains that the concepts of agent, action, and patient imply relationships between the elements in the sentence "An agent performs an action on a patient." This differs from "A subject is the part of the sentence or clause about which something is being said" or "A verb is the part of speech that expresses existence, action, or occurrence," which are explanations the students have likely heard before. The former statement about action, agent, and patient implies interdependence, whereas the latter statements about subject and verb imply that parts of speech are autonomous and arbitrarily linked together. The instructor may field questions and provide other sentences as examples if she so chooses but can also end the lesson for the day.

Some might object to the introduction of the terms "agent," "action," and "patient," arguing that this addition will ultimately create confusion rather than mitigate it. However, the CG metalanguage serves to provide students with a conceptual method of approaching the grammar, which may appeal to students with visual or spatial learning styles. As stated earlier, since it is difficult to determine what influences acquisition, a combined approach may benefit the instructor and student.

At the end of the third class session, the instructor projects the original image of Singer X on the screen, writes the four corresponding sentences on the board, and then projects a new image of Singer X next to the original, this time of her in a grocery store with her son. Her son sits in the child's seat of a shopping cart, and Singer X holds a box of cereal. The instructor then poses questions similar to the ones asked during the first lesson:

1. Who is that?   2. What is she looking at?   3. Who is the other person?[9]

As the students answer, the instructor records the answers for the students to see and then asks them to work in pairs and draw the correct diagrams for each sentence. They should also determine what each statement has: agent, action, patient, and what those are in each sentence. Once the students are done working together, the instructor can assign different pairs to put their diagrams on the board next to the corresponding sentences. The sentences should look something like the following:

1. That's [Singer X].   ○
                                          Agent

2. She's looking at some cereal.   ○   ⟶   ●
                                          Agent   **Action**   **Patient**

3. That's her son.   ○
                                          Agent

At this point, the students recognize and identify the syntactic/semantic proto-types. Once they have done this, the instructor asks them to find the same proto-types in a text.[10] The instructor assumes that the students will make some errors in recognizing the prototypes, as they do in other exercises in their textbooks, and she can intervene and correct the students.

At the end of the fourth class session, the instructor briefly reviews the proto-types with the students and then projects a third picture on the screen. The picture features Singer X, her husband, and her two sons. Singer X is pushing a stroller, and her husband is carrying one of his sons. The instructor then writes the two prototype diagrams on the board that the students are now familiar with and has them use the picture to construct as many sentences that match the prototype diagrams as possible. Possible sentences include "That's [Singer X]," "That's [Singer X]'s husband," "He's holding his son," and "[Singer X] has/is pushing a stroller." After reviewing the sentences, answering questions, and making any corrections that might be necessary, the instructor can end the lesson for the day.

Over the four class days, the instructor has managed to accomplish a number of things with this lesson plan. She has engaged in using a new metalanguage with the students that is both lingual and visual. She has encouraged the students to associate syntactic structures with prelinguistic concepts or images. She has asked students to recognize a structure, identify it, and then reproduce it. Finally, she has instructed the students in both implicit and explicit ways about grammar.

This extended lesson plan establishes the foundation on which further dis-cussions of grammar can take place. The students were introduced to a new way of conceiving of and talking about grammar (i.e., the syntactic/semantic proto-types of "agent," "action," and "patient"). These concepts and terms, which will be expanded on as instruction progresses, will later complement the grammatical explanations that the students will hear from the instructor and see in their text-books. Since the association has already been drawn between subject–verb–object and agent–action–patient, the instructor can provide a more refined explanation of grammar, one that focuses on meaning and thus is compatible with communi-cative language teaching.

Summary

CG considers meaning central to language, focusing on the relationship between syntax and elements outside language, which we have called "prelinguistic" here. Unlike universal grammar, CG asserts that an expression is more than the sum of the syntactic elements that represent it, that semantics is conceptual rather than truth conditional. CG also argues that not language but rather the processes of learning are innate. Exposure to language does not activate it within the learner; rather, the learner acquires language through exposure, extracting the "rules" and patterns from examples received.

According to CG, learners store these patterns in the mind as schemas, such as *haben* + "condition." These schemas have prototypes, a syntactic structure associated with a prelinguistic image or concept. *Ich habe Hunger*, for example, is a prototype of the schema *haben* + "condition." Speakers can judge the degree to which an expression matches the prototype, which depends on a number of factors, including what cognitive domain has been activated in the speaker's mind. Because an expression need not possess all the characteristics of a prototype in order to belong to a schema, deviations from the prototype are tolerated and are considered extensions of the prototype. The concept of prototype extensions, as well as CG's view of transitivity, distinguishes it from other theories of grammar.

Because CG asserts the importance of the relationship between syntax and meaning, it complements foreign language instruction, specifically focus on form, structured input, and communicative teaching approaches, which emphasize communication over a structural approach. The lesson plan demonstrates how CG can be introduced into the foreign language classroom and used to inform students' metaknowledge about grammar. Using a cognitive domain to activate schemas, the instructor explicitly presents a new grammatical concept, that of the prototype, and integrates the terms ("agent," "action," and "patient") into the students' grammatical metalanguage. More CG terms can be introduced to students as time progresses, but these three suffice as a beginning. The metalanguage of CG serves as a foundation on which other concepts can be placed, such as notions of transitivity, which complement explicit grammar instruction—of German case, for example.

Equally important, students might begin taking more risks in the classroom as well as outside it. For example, since the cognitive domain Singer X exists outside the textbook, it gives the instructor and the students the opportunity to experiment with the rules they learn in class and practice with exercises from the textbook. Unlike the topics that typically serve as the basis for the grammatical lessons in textbooks that employ a communicative approach, such as "Shopping," "Family," "Holidays," "Leisure Time," and so on, using the cognitive domain Singer X or other cognitive domains associated with pervasive cultural discourses, such as sports figures or other celebrities, significant historical events, or aspects of target-culture socialization, allows students to experiment with the language outside the scripted exercises that the students will first use. Once the students have become comfortable with the syntactic/semantic prototypes and have exhausted the exercises in the textbook, they can start experimenting with the prototypes, using the cognitive domain Singer X—or any cognitive domain the instructor chooses—to engage with the target language and regard it as more than the sum of its individual parts of speech and in the process improve their proficiency.

In a larger context, CG offers another benefit, namely, the promotion of translingual and transcultural competence, goals identified by the MLA Report as essential to combating the crisis in foreign language education. The committee defines translingual and transcultural competence as

> the ability to operate between languages. Students are educated to function as informed and capable interlocutors with educated native speakers in the target language. They are also trained to reflect on the world and themselves through the lens of another language and culture. They learn to comprehend speakers of the target language as members of foreign societies and to grasp themselves as Americans—that is, as members of a society that is foreign to others. They also learn to relate to fellow members of their own society who speak languages other than English. (MLA, 2007, p. 4)

In short, students should be able to comprehend and express themselves not only in the target language but also in the target *culture* and use that knowledge of the language and culture to deepen their understanding of their own language and culture, which then refines the manners in which they interact with members of other societies as well as their own. CG firsts assists this agenda by helping foreign language instructors conceive of transcultural elements that can be used in the classroom, particularly in the form of cognitive domains. On a material level, the instructor has the opportunity to seek and employ cognitive domains that reach across and exist between and among multiple cultures and languages. In this case, the instructor chose the cognitive domain Singer X because, though she is from the United States and part of U.S. mainstream pop culture, she is also a fixture in multiple communities and cultures around the world; almost everything about Singer X, from her music to her appearance to her behavior in public and private, is interpreted through various linguistic and cultural lenses. As the students become more proficient in the target language, the instructor can start investigating interpretations of the cognitive domain through the lens of the target culture and language. The instructor, if she so chooses, can use this cognitive domain to open a space for discourses of ethnicity, gender, socioeconomics, and cultural values.

On a linguistic level, CG provides another mode of analysis that prompts the kind of critical thinking that helps students become "capable and competent interlocutors," fleshing out grammar instruction and prompting students to engage actively with the language. In CG-informed grammar instruction, students are asked to "extract the rules," especially when working with the diagrams. Extracting the rules of a language implies many things. First, a pattern must be discerned and then repeatedly recognized. Second, the learner must induce, experiment, or inquire in order to extract the rules. "Extract" implies action, whereas prolonged exposure, a principle of universal grammar, implies passivity. Finally, if the discourse centers on "rules," then it is also a discourse of plasticity, the notion that rules can be amended, expanded, or eliminated when no longer current; new rules can also be added. This leads to the implication that CG deals not only with what is but also with what is possible.

Notes

1. The theory of CG focuses on phonology, syntax, semantics, pragmatics, and discourse in their relation to teaching and learning. Although the word "cognitive" is in the name, CG is not solely a theory of first- or second-language acquisition. Its closest relative in theories of second-language acquisition would be the connectionist approach (cf. N. Ellis, 2003; Pienemann, 1998). CG is not the best rubric for discussions of noticing, awareness (cf. Bialystok, 1982, 1992; Golanka, 2006), and learner strategies, topics that commonly come to mind with the word "cognitive."

2. Langacker (1991) defines the usage-based model as a nonreductive approach that views rules as schematizations of expressions. That means that the language that is analyzed is present at the level of the clause. CG does not seek to predict all and only the possible clauses that a language could produce. It seeks to analyze the structures that are produced.

3. These sentences, which draw on Friedrich Dürrenmatt's drama *Die Physiker* (1961), are very typical and fitting examples of transitivity. The play is a satire, and as it opens, a nurse in a mental institution has been strangled, and the police are investigating. Three patients believe themselves to be famous physicists, and this is the second nurse who has been killed. This play is commonly read in second-year German or upper-division German courses. It serves the dual purpose of being prototypically transitive and amusing the teacher.

4. For more information on metaphors in everyday life, see Lakoff and Turner (1980, 1989).

5. "Prelinguistic" is used to refer to imagery or concepts that are cognitively possible without language (Call, 1980; Suffridge, 1973).

6. Postcards, greeting cards, posters, and T-shirts are available with the infamous expression. In addition, the SPD used *Ich habe fertig!* as a slogan in their unsuccessful campaign against Helmut Kohl and the CDU/CSU soon after.

7. The term "patient" is used to describe a semantic role of the recipient of an action. In some languages, the patient is encoded in the accusative case. "Patient" is used to describe a participant who is in an asymmetrical relationship to another participant in a clause (Fillmore, 1968).

8. The instructor is served best by continuing the CG lesson plan at the end of class rather than the beginning in order to minimize the amount of explicit grammar instruction that will take place at any time and thereby not privilege grammatical accuracy over communicative proficiency.

9. One should note here that not only the order of the questions but also the verb used in the subject–verb–object sentence has changed,. The change in verb, though, does not exclude the statement from the category.

10. The text is as follows: "Singer X is an American pop singer. She was born in 1981 in Mississippi. She is the first female artist whose first four albums all made the number one slot on the pop charts. In less than 10 years, she sold

87 million albums. The RIAA places her among singers with the most sold albums in American history. She is the middle of three siblings and is the daughter of [mother's name] and [father's name]. She has a brother, whose name is [brother's name], and she has a sister, [sister's name]. As a child, she acted in commercials and was a Mouseketeer on the *New Mickey Mouse Club* show. She has two sons, [first son's name] and [second son's name]." Most students will identify the most basic structures: the first, third, and fourth sentences. Some students might identify more. Students will most likely make mistakes as well.

References

Achard, M. (2004). Grammatical instruction in the natural approach: A cognitive grammar view. In M. Achard & S. Niemeier (Eds.), *Cognitive linguistics, second language acquisition, and foreign language teaching* (pp. 165–194). Berlin: Mouton de Gruyter.

Anderson, J. (1983). *The architecture of cognition.* Cambridge, MA: Harvard University Press.

Anderson, J. (1985). *Cognitive psychology and its implications.* New York: Freeman.

Arnett, C. (2004) *A cognitive approach to the semantics of the German passive.* New York: Edwin Mellen Press.

Bialystok, E. (1982). On the relationship between knowing and using linguistic forms. *Applied Linguistics, 3*(3), 181–206.

Bialystok, E. (1992). Metalinguistic dimensions of bilingual language proficiency. In E. Bialystok (Ed.), *Language processing in bilingual children* (pp. 113–140). Cambridge: Cambridge University Press.

Cadierno, T. (2004). Expressing motion events in a second language: A cognitive typological approach. In M. Achard & S. Niemeier (Eds.), *Cognitive linguistics, second language acquisition, and foreign language teaching* (pp. 13–50). Berlin: Mouton de Gruyter.

Call, J. D. (1980). Some prelinguistic aspects of language development. *Journal of the American Psychoanalytic Association, 28*(2), 259–289.

Chafe, W. (1970). *Meaning and the structure of language.* Chicago: University of Chicago Press.

Chomsky, N. (1965). *Aspects of the theory of syntax.* Cambridge, MA: MIT Press.

Chomsky, N. (1988). *Language and problems of knowledge: The Managua lectures.* Cambridge, MA: MIT Press.

Coleman, L., & Kay, P. (1981). Prototype semantics: The English word lie. *Language, 57*(1), 26–44.

De Knop, S., & de Rycker, T. (2008). *Cognitive approaches to pedagogical grammar.* New York: Mouton de Gruyter.

Doughty, C. (2003). Instructed SLA: Constraints, compensation, and enhancement. In C. Doughty & M. H. Long (Eds.), *Handbook of second language acquisition* (pp. 256–310). Oxford: Blackwell.

Doughty, C., & Varela, E. (1998). Communicative focus on form. In C. Doughty & J. Williams (Eds.), *Focus on form in classroom second language acquisition* (pp. 114–138). Cambridge: Cambridge University Press.

Doughty, C., & Williams, J. (Eds.). (1998). *Focus on form in classroom second language acquisition.* Cambridge: Cambridge University Press.

Ellis, N. C. (2003). Constructions, chunking, and connectionism: The emergence of second language structure. In C. Doughty & M. Long (Eds.), *The handbook of second language acquisition* (pp. 63–103). Oxford: Blackwell.

Ellis, N. C. (2005). At the interface: Dynamic interactions of explicit and implicit language knowledge. *Studies in Second Language Acquisition, 27*(2), 305–352.

Ellis, R. (1994). *The study of second language acquisition*. Oxford: Oxford University Press.

Ellis, R. (1997). *SLA research and language teaching*. Oxford: Oxford University Press.

Ellis, R. (2001). *Instructed second language acquisition*. Oxford: Blackwell.

Ellis, R., Loewen, S., & Erlam, R. (2006). Implicit and explicit corrective feedback and the acquisition of L2 grammar. *Studies in Second Language Acquisition, 28*(2), 339–368.

Fillmore, Charles. (1968). The case for case. In E. Bach & R. T. Harms (Eds.), *Universals in linguistic theory* (pp. 1–88). New York: Holt, Rinehart & Winston.

Fillmore, C. (1975). An alternative to checklist theories of meaning. *Berkeley Linguistics Society, 1*, 123–131.

Fillmore, C. (1986). The case for case. In E. Bach & R. Harms (Eds.), *Universals in linguistic theory* (pp. 1–88). New York: Holt, Rinehart and Winston.

Foley, W. A., & Van Valin, R. D. (1984). *Functional syntax and universal grammar*. Cambridge: Cambridge University Press.

Golonka, E. M. (2006). Predictors revised: Linguistic knowledge and metalinguistic awareness in second language gain in Russian. *Modern Language Journal, 90*(4), 496–505.

Hopper, P., & Thompson, S. (1980). Transitivity in grammar and discourse. *Language, 56*(2), 251–299.

Jackendoff, R. (1983). *Semantics and cognition*. Cambridge, MA: MIT Press.

Janda, L., & Clancy, S. J. (2002). *The case book for Russian*. Columbus, OH: Slavica.

Krashen, S. D. (1985). *The input hypothesis: Issues and implications*. London: Longman.

Lakoff, G. (1972). Hedges: A study in meaning criteria and the logic of fuzzy concepts. *Chicago Linguistics Society, 8*, 183–228.

Lakoff, G. (1987). *Women, fire and dangerous things: What categories reveal about the mind*. Chicago: University of Chicago Press.

Lakoff, G., & Turner, M. (1980). *Metaphors we live by*. Chicago: University of Chicago Press.

Lakoff, G., & Turner, M. (1989). *More than cool reason. A field guide to poetic metaphor*. Chicago: Chicago University Press.

Lam, Y. (2009). Applying cognitive linguistics to teaching the Spanish prepositions "por" and "para." *Language Awareness, 18*(1), 2–18.

Langacker, R. W. (1982). Space grammar, analysability, and the English passive. *Language, 58*(1), 22–80.

Langacker, R. W. (1986). Settings, participants and grammatical relations. In S. DeLancy & R. S. Tomlin (Eds.), *Proceedings of the Second Annual Meeting of the Pacific Linguistics Conference* (pp. 1–32). Eugene, OR: Department of Linguistics.

Langacker, R. W. (1987). *Foundations of cognitive grammar: Theoretical prerequisites*. Stanford, CA: Stanford University Press.

Langacker, R. W. (1991). *Foundations of cognitive grammar*. Stanford, CA: Stanford University Press.

Lightbown, P. (1991). Input, instruction and feedback in SLA. *Second Language Research, 7*(2), ii–iv.

Long, M. H. (1991). Focus on form: A design feature in language teaching methodology. In K. de Bot, D. Coste, R. Ginsberg, & C. Kramsch (Eds.), *Foreign language research in cross-cultural perspectives* (pp. 39–52). Amsterdam: John Benjamins.

Lysinger, D. (2009). *Teaching case to L2 students of German and Russian*. Unpublished doctoral dissertation, University of California, Davis.

Masuda, K. (2005). *Learners' conceptualization of semantically complex particles in Japanese: A cognitive approach to Japanese locative postpositions*. Paper presented at the Ninth International Cognitive Linguistics Conference, Seoul, Korea, July 2005.

Modern Language Association. (2007). *Foreign languages and higher education: New structures for a changed world.* Retrieved April 20, 2010, from http://www.mla.org/flreport

Pienemann, M. (1984). Psychological constraints on the teachability of languages. *Studies in Second Language Acquisition, 6(2)*, 186–214.

Pienemann, M. (1989). Is language teachable? Psycholinguistic experiments and hypotheses. *Applied Linguistics, 10*(1), 52–79.

Rice, S. A. 1987. *Towards a cognitive model of transitivity.* Unpublished doctoral dissertation, University of California, San Diego.

Robinson, P. (2001). *Cognition and second language instruction.* Cambridge: Cambridge University Press.

Rosch, E. (1973). On the internal structure of perceptual and semantic categories. In T. E. Moore (Ed.), *Cognitive development and the acquisition of language* (pp. 111–144). New York: Academic Press.

Rosch, E. (1974). Linguistic relativity. In A. Silverstein (Ed.), *Human communication: Theoretical explorations* (pp. 95–121). New York: Halsted.

Rosch, E. (1975a). Cognitive representations of semantic categories. *Journal of Experimental Psychology, General 104*(3), 192–233.

Rosch, E. (1975b). Universals and cultural specifics in human categorization. In R. W. Brislin, S. Bochner, & W. J. Lonner (Eds.), *Cross-cultural perspectives on learning* (pp. 117–206). New York: Halsted.

Shannon, T. F. (1988). Relational grammar, passives and dummies in Dutch. In T. Broos (Ed.), *Papers from the Third Interdisciplinary Conference on Netherlandic Studies* (pp. 237–268). Lanham, MD: University Press of America.

Shannon, T. F. (1990). The unaccusative hypothesis and the history of the perfect auxiliary in Germanic and Romance. In H. Anderson & K. Koerner (Eds.), *Historical linguistics 1987: Papers from the 8th International Conference on Historical Linguistics* (pp. 461–499). Amsterdam: John Benjamins.

Shannon, T. F. (1992). Split intransitivity in German and Dutch: Semantic and pragmatic parameters. In R. Lippi-Green (Ed.), *Recent developments in Germanic linguistics* (pp. 97–114). Amsterdam: John Benjamins.

Shannon, T. F. (1996). Explaining perfect auxiliary variation: Some modal and aspectual effects on the history of Germanic. *American Journal of Germanic Linguistics and Literatures 7*(2), 129–163.

Sorace, A. (2000). Gradients in auxiliary selection with intransitive verbs. *Language, 76*(4), 859–890.

Suffridge, K. H. (1973). Prelinguistic imagery cognition: An individual experience. *The Volta Review, 75*(2), 82–87.

Taylor, J. (1989). *Linguistic categorization: Prototypes in linguistic theory.* New York: Oxford University Press.

Tomasello, M. (2000). First steps toward a usage-based theory of language acquisition. *Cognitive Linguistics, 11*(1–2), 61–82.

van Oosten, J. (1986). *The nature of subjects, topics and agents: A cognitive explanation.* Bloomington: Indiana University Linguistics Club.

VanPatten, B. (1996). *Input processing and grammar instruction.* New York: Ablex.

White, L. (1991). Adverb placement in SLA: Some effects of positive and negative evidence in the classroom. *Second Language Research, 7*(2), 133–161.

Zyzik, E. (2006). Learners' overgeneralization of dative clitics to accusative contexts: Evidence for prototype effects in SLA. In C. Klee & T. Face (Eds.), *Selected proceedings of the 7th Conference on the Acquisition of Spanish and Portuguese as First and Second Languages* (pp. 122–134). Somerville, MA: Cascadilla Press.

Chapter 14

After the MLA Report: Rethinking the Links Between Literature and Literacy, Research, and Teaching in Foreign Language Departments

Katherine Arens, University of Texas at Austin

Abstract

This chapter takes up today's literary and cultural theory as lacking attention to research and classroom implementation. The *National Standards for Foreign Language Learning*, I argue, can be used as a heuristic to develop these missing strategies, as they clarify what is at stake in learning culture. This chapter calls for a more responsible approach to curriculum, at all levels from beginner to graduate/professional, by focusing on appropriate stages of cognitive development and by insisting that the theory project be integrated into concrete and defensible pedagogical goals—an urgent necessity in a moment when institutional demands on humanities departments are forcing the encounter between theory and praxis.

Introduction

My topic is an endgame: language, literature, and culture departments at the "end of theory" and what to do with these core humanities departments after the 30-plus years of innovation in several branches of work loosely amalgamated under the rubric of "the theory project."[1] The thread I follow is a claim: that this legacy, seen in terms of disciplines and institutions, is a tragically unfinished project that may have sown the seeds of its own destruction in an era of tightening resources and a growing willingness to question traditional curricular assumptions about what constitutes a necessary element of undergraduate education.

"The end of theory" has been widely bruited about, as literature departments have made distinct turns toward cultural studies, especially studies of memory and identity in historical context. What I mean by that, however, is more explicit: that theory has come to its end because in terms of neither institutional mandates (departments, professional organizations, and other types of infrastructure) nor disciplinary structure ("knowledge projection" and "expertise") has the theory project moved past its first bloom of ideological relevance and into an identity that sets it apart from other disciplines. Instead, it has become largely a set of compulsory reference points and a limited set of terms that are in wide use within the humanities and social sciences.

To make the case for this assertion, I adapt to the U.S. configurations of the theory project the issues brought up in the 2007 Report issued by the Modern Language Association (MLA) Ad Hoc Committee (MLA, 2007). As a conclusion,

I move on to its institutional faces in order to suggest how very high the stakes are for the theory project if it does not adapt itself to the current context of needs.

My justification in taking on this project is threefold. First and foremost, my scholarly work has circled around the question of historical epistemology and its institutional ramifications. In addition, my own research and teaching have been dedicated to the idea of applying theory to them. Finally, this discussion seems to me to be critical because of current U.S. budgetary situations, which render the indecisive status of the relation between research, teaching, and theory a critical threat to the whole enterprise that falls under the large umbrella of the MLA.

After the MLA Report

The MLA Report suggested "translingual and transcultural competence" as the goal for a new generation of foreign language majors (MLA, 2007, p. 3). As this report was read by U.S. foreign language teachers, this goal translated first and foremost into a call to alleviate the familiar gap between lower- and upper-division curricula. In these contexts, the MLA's call often found a circumlocution: "culture from the first day, language until the last day" of the curriculum.

For the present purposes, it is just as important to note that the MLA Report has also recast traditional humanistic education to reflect many of the desiderata of the theory project. By asking for "competence," it highlights the agency of the learner—that the individual *learn* how to negotiate across cultural lines and across lines of language use and especially across languages that exclude each other because they fall on opposite sides of borders. The language teachers will immediately think in terms of a "native language" (L1, the learner's first language) and a "target language" (L2, the language being acquired), but there is nothing in the MLA's formulation to prevent a broader reading of the phrase to include borders between sociolects and other linguistic means that potentially block an individual speaker from participation in a language community other than his or her own, a border that can marginalize an individual and lessen his or her ability to function as an active social agent for their own purposes. And thus "transcultural" can include contact not only with the culture of one or more of the nation-states associated with a learner's L2 but also with a culture (a C2) outside the learner's home culture (a C1). That C1/C2 boundary to be crossed may well be defined sociopolitically as well as culturally, in terms of gender and socionormativity as well as language, or in any of the terms that current theory has identified as part of the mechanisms through which a society defines its "others."

Parsed this way, however, the MLA Report's demands, tacitly or overtly, also cast doubt on the theory project and the institutions through which it has been exercised. It does so by pointing to profound lacks in our newest traditions of humanistic research and teaching, on all levels of the postsecondary curriculum, including graduate curricula. The demands may sound familiar, but in fact there are virtually no institutional correlatives within curricula, institutions, and professional organizations for what teachers are supposed to teach and how learners are supposed to learn to achieve these ends of sociopolitical consciousness raising. Moreover, these demands also raise questions about the graduate curriculum, as we are supposed to train the future teachers who will be forced to reconstruct undergraduate curriculum without models.

This demand is not unprecedented. Older theories of literature and culture may well have been driven by hegemonic ideologies that purportedly marginalized alternate tastes and "others" of various definition (women, members of classes and ethnic groups not representative of the hegemony, and so on). Yet at the same time, the theorists of that generation were at pains to offer models for teaching as they issued very clear claims for the pedagogical goals that their models and theories were fulfilling. These claims were never empirically verified (Did contact with "the great poets" actually improve any individual's spirit? How would one verify that?). Still, they were carefully laid out and thus created literature classrooms at virtually all levels in which students were trained in a relatively common set of expectations, guided by teachers who had been immersed in works like Richards's *Practical Criticism* (1929), Wellek and Warren's *A Theory of Literature* (1949), or Ingarden's *The Literary Work of Art* (translated 1973 into English).

Since the advent of the theory project's contemporary version, with the appearance of Foucault and poststructuralism in California and Derrida and deconstruction in the Ivy League and their subsequent spread, we have seen an enormous number of new theories about the ideological content of literature and its impacts on readers, with a particular focus on identity politics. Yet these innovations do not have correlated models for pedagogy or classroom practice. This is not a historical necessity: Freire's *Pedagogy of the Oppressed* (1968, translated 1970) has been on reading lists since the start of the theory boom, and the second wave of feminism incubated not only new theories of gender and new campus units dedicated to the study of women and gender but also a distinct set of classroom pedagogies directed at consciousness raising.

The closer one looks at today's theory innovations, in fact, the larger such lacunae become. Not only are such classroom-centered innovations absent, but also are any claims at a consistent research methodology. Most practicing theorists have retreated into the realm of philosophy in order to practice critique structured along the lines of classical rhetoric—but without that discipline's attention to situation, audience, and appropriateness. We thus have theory-driven analysis, enacted by theorists who are performers rather than scientists—they are guided by ideological commitments rather than by a model of research and replicable results.

In addition, prior decades' appeals to the study of language and literature as claiming the status of science are widely decried. By "science," I mean not the lab-based natural science of today's big science but rather the *systematics* of any discipline, a definition reflected in locutions like the "human sciences" (*sciences humaines* or *Geisteswissenschaften*) that have never been favored in Anglo-American spheres. Thus, there is no call for validity, reliability, and reproducibility in today's study of culture; at best, a limited set of ideologies are reproduced that supposedly enact the liberation of subjects from the limiting norms of any hegemonic group or region, science included.

This attention to performance, instead of science, brings with it severe deficits in method and in analytic alternatives. We no longer believe that affect is more than individual, despite theories like those of Jacques Lacan and Julia Kristeva, who outline how subjects are in fact socially interpolated, including so-called personal structures of subjectivity, which are in form and content heavily determined by the symbolic order. We critique artifacts of culture without accounting for their manufacture and circulation, we study the purported effects of oppression and marginalization without attention to its instruments, and we critique hegemonies without accounting for the effects that units, groups, communities, infrastructure, and the like will have on individual behavior.

From the point of view of disciplines, this means that work on textuality, its cognition, its social constructedness, and its specific information value—the stuff of two postwar generations' work in literary studies—has as good as vanished from the stage. That generation of work on the linguistic nature of the literary work of art, on semiotics, and on critical discourse analysis has been shunted aside, no matter that this was among the crowning achievements of that generation. Despite the vaunted turn toward cultural studies in literature departments, moreover, several generations of work on sociology, social anthropology, and government, much with its own claim to acting as a critical analysis of the hegemony, have been overlooked, despite literary scholars' sporadic reference to individual theorists—leaving out examples like the social analyses of the Birmingham School, Pierre Bourdieu, or even the later Frankfurt School and Niklas Luhmann. Lacanian psychology was broadly popular in the 1980s and 1990s, but there are few if any follow-ups to the kinds of cultural analysis that Kristeva offers us—cultural-historical analyses of subject positions and their ideological deformations. Such a project reflects French historiography since Marc Bloch, Lucien Febvre, and the *Annales* School, to say nothing of the theoretical contributions of theorists like Hayden White or Michel de Certeau.

To be sure, the ideological turn in cultural analysis has its own validity as a political challenge to dominant disciplines. Deconstruction is, after all, premised on a kind of negative dialectics. Ideological critique understands that any claims for meaning and power within groups reifies that group and directs its power to objectify individuals, and so it claims that the subject is the proper object of study and that these other disciplines merely perpetuate the problems of ideology.

There is a paradox here in the institutional configuration of theory: analytic strategies like deconstruction claim the ability to raise consciousness, yet they have not been integrated into the pedagogy or research frameworks of the academy. These analysts generally reside within the academy yet merely as an internal challenge, not as a force to reinscribe individuals into new kinds of institutions, as theorists like Freire would demand. Theorists and cultural critics have not fostered new research projects (they have generated much analysis in the philosophical or essayistic mode) but have instead taken over whatever fragments of older research methods they choose, in their eagerness to counter, invalidate, or silence other ways of reading because of their purported origins. To be clear: today's theorists do not have a paradigm for reproducible results, only for performative analyses with validity only in local contexts and guided by ideological presets, and they eschew claims for lasting value, even as their cult of celebrity critics asserts such by example.

In today's climate of academic cutbacks, this approach— this new role for the academic critic—has the potential to be catastrophic.[2] The cult of celebrity is vulnerable at times of economic downturn, and as generations change, many of these celebrity critics are aging out of their own claimed sociopolitical relevance. They are not the 1950s and 1960s generations of critics of academia who went outside the academy and became public intellectuals—self-supported and committed to retaining relevance to current political conditions. The current generation of theorists, in contrast, stays resolutely within the academy, with ever-increasing salaries and a growing disparity between their own rates and those of the temporary faculty whose ranks are growing as literary and cultural studies seem ever more paraprofessional to university hierarchies.

Yet undeniably, professionals and the professions to which they belong will today be judged and funded by their ability to advocate for what they do in terms that are intelligible to other disciplines and to back up their commitment to performance and advocacy with hard data on how these activities can be taught to students, on how they serve professionally necessary goals, and on what this teaching achieves in terms of measurable outcomes for the hours of instruction and tuition dollars invested in them. Faculty may decry this as a sign of the increasing corporatization of the university, but most such demands would allow the individuals being questioned to set their own benchmarks, to define their own professional viability.

To be considered viable as elements within accountable postsecondary education (within the institutions that sponsor and host those "teaching machines" that Spivak (1993) identifies as *outside*), to be considered as a set of viable research disciplines in publishing and funding entities rather than simply as exercises in journalistic critique, a new generation of theory-driven research needs to be designed and conducted in ways that can be assessed and evaluated to address concerns about the generation, utility, control, and validity of the knowledge they produce. Any other approach is a kind of demagoguery or a reification of one generation's politics as normative for subsequent ones. If outcomes are not specified as I described earlier, we will have failed to teach subsequent generations to fish and instead given them fish without allowing them choice—a betrayal of the very notion of the liberation of the subject that is the purported object of theory and its critique.

To maintain institutional viability and not just a self-declared social-political relevance, in consequence, theory and theorists must now undertake efforts to uphold its professional viability. Theory needs to evolve a set of research practices beyond the confessional or beyond the more or less cookie-cutter imposition of ideologies onto data sets—these are the domains of philosophy and essays, perhaps even of literature. Beyond that, this research needs to be reformulated into new teaching practices at all levels of the curriculum, into new forms of assessment, and into textbooks and anthologies formulated on new premises (not just adding texts by *others* into existing frameworks or as parallel and alternate universes of reading). Empowerment of the individual learner in the face of hegemonic ideologies is indeed a viable goal for learning, but it cannot be considered sufficient grounds for teaching or research. Learners need to develop specific skills; these skills have to be developed hierarchically, in terms of learning hierarchies.

In line with such recent national recommendations, it would also behoove theory to design major sequences that model skills in both self-expression and research—to redefine the relation of major courses in the humanities to professional outcomes. How *do* we teach students to become effective critics of ideology rather than simply to replicate now time-worn critiques of the hegemonies of the bourgeoisie and neoliberalism? And, in turn, how do we teach graduate students to remain professionally viable over a career, possessing the skills they will need to negotiate their careers against shifting waters? —That their consciousness has been raised about hegemonic power is simply not enough preparation for a career that can extend over four decades or more.

A Way Out: The *Standards for Foreign Language Learning* as Ground for New Frameworks

The situation may not be as dire as painted, especially if theory professionals begin to pay attention to the teaching professions—to their peer scholars who work within institutional frameworks.

In 1993, a new heuristic for curriculum design was created that might help bridge this gap and show theory professionals the way into a new generation: the *National Standards for Foreign Language Learning*, a collaborative project of the American Council for the Teaching of Foreign Languages (ACTFL); the American Associations of Teachers of French, German, Italian, Russian, Spanish, and Portuguese; the American Classics League; the Chinese Language Association of Secondary-Elementary Schools; the Association of Teachers of Japanese; and the National Council of Japanese Language Teachers (National Standards in Foreign Language Education Project [NSFLEP], 2006).

The *Standards* were formulated by a group of educators and language acquisition researchers as a new way of representing what it means to learn a foreign language and specifically to move beyond the *ACTFL Proficiency Guidelines* in capturing more than normative language competence as an outcome for learning. The *Standards* are informed by theories of domains of culture and signification, community, and the effects of normative communication use. They do not *prescribe* what norms for language use might be but rather *describe* the domains of knowledge that individuals need to learn to negotiate as they learn a second language (L2) and its attendant culture (C2). They refer to a C2 in an L2, but they may also deal with C2s that do not necessarily lay across lines into a foreign language but perhaps do so only into a different community's sense of language use (one that might marginalize the speaker in relation to hegemonic norms).

The ACTFL's executive summary of the *Standards* project is sufficient for the present purposes, as it identifies the central challenge to learners in each of five domains:

- *Communication* is at the heart of second language study, whether the communication takes place face-to-face, in writing, or across centuries through the reading of literature. . . .

- Through the study of other languages, students gain a knowledge and understanding of the *cultures* that use that language and, in fact, cannot truly master the language until they have also mastered the cultural contexts in which the language occurs. . . .
- Learning languages provides *connections* to additional bodies of knowledge that may be unavailable to the monolingual English speaker. . . .
- Through *comparisons* and contrasts with the language being studied, students develop insight into the nature of language and the concept of culture and realize that there are multiple ways of viewing the world. . . .
- Together, these elements enable the student of languages to participate in multilingual *communities* at home and around the world in a variety of contexts and in culturally appropriate ways. (NSFLEP, 2010, p. 3)

Critical to note here is that the familiar *Standards* graphic represents cognitive dimensions of language and culture split into domains by social and information functions, not just linguistic form—that graphic maps and models the various forces at play in the phenomenon of language, defined broadly, not just in terms of formal linguistics.

It is thus possible to use this graphic as a cognitive map, as a way to rewrite research and teaching objectives to encompass the broad panoply of culture domains, beyond linguistic descriptions of language and into the realm of sociolinguistics pragmatics and beyond into the realm of society. Each of the domains helps map several concerns central to the post–World War II theory projects.

The first two domains are domains of knowledge within the C2, one that concerns signification and the other the elements of culture. *Communication* is the domain of communicative competence (according to language acquisition terminology), or signification, as theory would have it. Thus, it is the site of language-based social behaviors of the sort that are the subjects of interest of semiotics, speech act theory, and critical discourse analysis, not just formal linguistics or sociolinguistics. *Culture* maps out the domain of the knowledge deemed appropriate to members of a dominant or target culture, and thus it locates the site of hegemonic knowledge, practices, and traditions in relation to language. Here, investigations like Foucault's archaeologies (poststructural analyses of social power and ideology), deconstruction, postcolonial theory, and Lacanianism (its symbolic order) find their archive of traces of past cultural logics and the infrastructure that re-creates those logics for the next generation—often at the cost of individuals' freedoms and agency.

The domain of *connections* is central to the question of agency for the individual subject of knowledge, but it is a domain defined cognitively (and in terms that Lacan would recognize, wherein cultural logics are the fundament for individual affects). This standard points to a skill set, not a knowledge area: the ability of individual subjects to retrieve information from a target culture and the consequences of that retrieval. On the one hand, it may be the domain where the individual interacts more or less unconsciously within the culture, more or less uncritically enacting individual interests. On the other, it locates the individual's motivation in the way specified by Lacanianism, Pierre Bourdieu's notion of a field, or again Foucault.

The final two standards, *comparisons* and *communities*, are cognitively the most difficult of the five. *Comparisons* outlines the ability of the individual subject to negotiate *two* positions, one in the target culture and the other in one's own sphere—and hence it opens up the site of critique, the comparison of the self in relation to others, as targeted by notions like Deleuze's nomadology or in explicitly political criticism like feminist theory and postcolonial criticism. The *communities* standard highlights the groups within the field of culture with discernible cultural identities and hence the various sites at which identities are performed. Its domain comprises the various sites on which individuals are marginalized or exert their identity politics.

Together, these five standard domains also correlate with base patterns of research. *Communications* points to research in linguistics and semiotics, stressing sociocultural norms—contemporaneous media and forms of affiliation that facilitate communication. *Cultures* targets research on cultural forms and genres, domains of culture, institutions, or the like, including the histories of these various entities. *Connections* requires work based on other disciplinary domains, research that is situated within the C1 but that draws on the resources of a C2. *Comparisons* requires comparative work on culture; *communities* take into account the sociology of performance.

These options require research on specific data sets, drawing on particular methods to realize particular goals and specific ideologies of research. To this, a translation of theory imperatives into curricular sequences is needed that also includes criteria for presentation of work within professional fora, the acknowledgment of various genres of professional communication, and an awareness of the implications of Kant's categorical imperative (the differentiation between the public and private uses of reason, between what one contracts to do within a culture, with particular costs, and what one does as an individual, obligated as an agent of culture). That is, a curriculum fulfilling the kinds of ethical imperatives familiar from the theory project requires its designer to place what is taught within overt sites within the institution and its professional environment so that the learner not only acquires bits of knowledge but also becomes aware of what professional communities trade on through that knowledge and what social costs and benefits those professional communities seek.

This set of thumbnails about how research might be structured to conform with such theoretical bases resembles classical scientific hermeneutics, in which analysis and understanding precedes critique.[3] To translate such research imperatives into teaching strategies, however, requires attention to the learner as well as to the epistemological structures of the field of knowledge. That requires a research paradigm to be broken down into a hierarchy of teaching tasks, progressing from simple cognitive patterns *up through* critique, not starting with it. Only in this way can a learning pattern be considered explicitly student centered and constructivist rather than teacher or analyst centered.

What is meant by this can be encapsulated by reference to a long-favored tool in educational theory: Bloom's taxonomy, which breaks down learning sequences into a series of tasks, sequenced in terms of the cognitive complexity of the mental acts they require.[4] As such, it is a description not of the learners' cognitive structures but rather of a hierarchy of tasks, differentiated in terms of cognitive difficulty. This taxonomy (Bloom et al., 1956) is usually represented in a triangle articulated into six levels, working up from a broad base to a narrow apex.

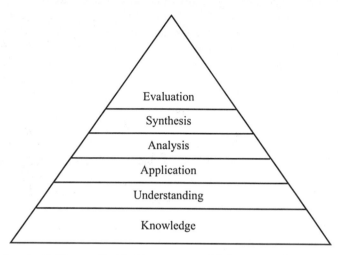

From Benjamin S Bloom Et Al. *Taxonomy of Educational Objectives* Book 1 Cognitive Domain Published by Allyn and Bacon, Boston, MA. Copyright (c) 1956, 1984 by Pearson Education. Reprinted by permission of the publisher.

Bloom's stages rest on the broad base of *knowledge*, which is acquired by a learner through a process of repetition, through reenactments that embed a culture's commonly held labels into mind and memory. It is associated with tasks that are cued by verbs like the following: arrange, define, duplicate, label, list, memorize, name, order, recognize, relate, recall, repeat, reproduce, or state. This corresponds with what in language acquisition is called comprehension, linked to the most minimum of production. It is analogous to what is required in the domain of the *culture* standard as well, reflecting what a learner must do as she is being trained explicitly in the vocabulary and data of a particular cultural site—the primary socialization into a basic C2 or into disciplinary speech conventions, into the cognitive hierarchies of a particular research paradigm, and into the communication norms for particular expert communities. Concomitantly, it circumscribes what learners need to practice at the basic levels of any curriculum—the lower-division courses, building the fundament for upper divisions.

Bloom's second stage, *comprehension*, does work that overlaps with the *communication* standard in that it comprises not the data of culture but rather the cognitive patterning and logics of specific cultural sites, including professional groups and disciplines. Here, the comprehension involved becomes more active and relational, with appeals to tasks represented by verbs like the following: classify, describe, discuss, explain, express, identify, indicate, locate, recognize, report, restate, review, select, or translate—all verbs that require discrimination and acts of choice and establishment of patterns, not just labeling. These tasks constitute explicit training in the logic and explanatory tools inherent in a culture or in a discipline and its expert communities (any C2, once specified). These logics are critical within major sequences because they are cognitive and social acts that are prerequisites to functioning as a member of that professional community. They represent the logics that are automatized in basic upper-division courses, the prerequisites to any more original production and thus to seminars.

Bloom's third and fourth levels are *application* and *analysis*, which circumscribe what in second-language acquisition is known as the transition between comprehension and production. The tasks involved in *application* are formulated with verbs like the following: apply, choose, demonstrate, dramatize, employ, illustrate, interpret, operate, practice, schedule, sketch, solve, use, or write. In *analysis*, commands move upward in cognitive complexity, moving from replication of patterns within different expressive domains and then toward patterns of assessment of what is absent, present, a member of the class/case, or not: analyze, appraise, calculate, categorize, compare, contrast, criticize, differentiate, discriminate, distinguish, examine, experiment, question, and test. These two stages need to be the purview of senior seminars, honors courses, and any curriculum presumed preprofessional (undergraduate or graduate).

The top of Bloom's hierarchy of tasks, the most cognitively complex ones, includes *synthesis* and *evaluation* (and some modern versions of the taxonomy reverse these two in what I believe is a shift in English usage). *Synthesis* points to tasks that draw together resources in more complicated patterns, often beyond replication into acts of production that also begin to exert agency on the part of the learner: arrange, assemble, collect, compose, construct, create, design, develop, formulate, manage, organize, plan, prepare, propose, set up, and write. *Evaluation* speaks explicitly to empowerment and to the performance of individual points of view—to the exercise of social power in original performances of and judgments about cultural logics, often in new terms: appraise, argue, assess, attach, choose, compare, defend, estimate, judge, predict, rate, core, select, support, value, and evaluate. Such acts need to be solidly in the purview of graduate and professional education because they describe performances of logic from within a site of culture or a discipline, where the performer acts as a potential part of a community of "native informants" or experts, a full equal in the production of knowledge (the fifth level) and only then exercising critique (the sixth or highest level).

I have shown elsewhere what this implies for the development of specific curricula.[5] What I emphasize here is that classes and curricula constructed along the lines of research and analysis set by various kinds of theory need to proceed through these levels if the learners targeted are to learn to fish. A poststructuralist in the vein of Foucault, for example, must be taught to identify elements that participate in an archaeology or genealogy—to "read" artifacts as evidence of cultural logics—and then to make arguments about how practices correspond to social power—the essence of Foucault's great texts, such as *Care of the Self* (1988).[6] A feminist needs to be taught to identify historically situated markers for what it means to be a woman within a culture, then to replicate standard analyses of female marginalization, and finally to construct new analyses of women's positions in examples that are self-chosen. This may include extensions of that standard paradigm that create analogies between the position of women and other minority others of hegemonic cultures. Roland Barthes's *Mythologies* (1970) speaks of the semiotics of hegemonic cultures, how they replicate their power for subjects; Pierre Bourdieu's analyses of the field of cultural production points toward the social-psychological costs that are incurred when an individual exercises that power.[7] These are but a few of the theory perspectives that could potentially be operationalized into learning hierarchies that teach novices to fish.

Such implementations of theory into research programs and teaching sequences have not been provided. Notable Anglo-American contributions on teaching, like Gayatri Spivak's (1993) *Outside in the Teaching Machine*, do not do this job—this text instead analyzes the position of the teacher rather than providing a curricular planning mechanism. And the typical seminar for senior majors or graduate students leaps over the nuts and bolts of constructing an analysis according to a theory being used and toward the ideology realized in the theory. In a real sense, such classes are simply applications, not representations of synthesis and evaluation, since they replicate the ideologies of a specific theory rather than encourage new visions of data.

Outlooks for Future Teaching and Research Agenda

This sketch of a relation between theory, research, and the classroom may well seem utopian, but it is mission critical for the survival of the humanities in an era when the theory project has never achieved a permanent home in the institutions of research and higher education—when grant agencies find many theory projects lacking in research finesse and when curricula have not been rebuilt from the ground up, remaining instead a profound disjunction between early and late phases of student education and ignoring what learning hierarchies like Bloom's taxonomy tell us about effective teaching and learning.

The credibility and survival of departments whose budgets are protected by general education requirements will, I believe, be conditioned by our responses to that lack. The ideologies behind the theory project no longer suffice to justify the humanities' place in general education environments just as their research funding drops (except when attached to precisely situated historical research). Departments are being reconfigured, majors eliminated or redefined fundamentally, and advanced degree programs cut. But the theory project has no particular claim to solutions except for continued insistence on the necessity of identity politics as a political corrective for learners. Without teaching and research paradigms, without an awareness of what kinds of knowledge that the theory project constructs, the next generation of humanists will be completely marginalized within the academy—through an act of self-immolation caused to no small degree by a lack of acknowledgment of theorists' own dependence on the academy.

Notes

1. A version of this chapter was presented as an invited Laila and Dudley Frank Distinguished Lecture on Language Teaching and Learning in the Humanities Language Learning Program at the University of California, Irvine, May 3, 2010.

2. I am here ignoring external threats to foreign language and culture teaching, such as the ideological problems associated with globalization, the almost arbitrary dedication of government funding to "critical" languages determined by the security community, and the ideological demands for cultural preservation. These are less relevant to my argument because I want to underscore those aspects of teaching and research that are in the control of the language and culture scholar, not those politics from without.

3. For an overview of classical hermeneutics, see the introduction to Mueller-Vollmer (1985).

4. See Bloom (1956). This work was the start of a scientific approach to teaching in general. See also Anderson and Lauren (1994) for an overview of the project's impact. The taxonomy has been multiply revised. A useful standard presentation of how the older version iterates with newer ones can be found at http://www.odu.edu/educ/roverbau/Bloom/blooms_taxonomy.htm.

5. See Arens (2005, 2008, 2009).

6. *Care of the Self* (*Souci de soi*, 1984) is the third volume of Michel Foucault's *Histoire de la sexualité*, which was published between 1976 and 1984.

7. The most famous of Bourdieu's works in English is *Distinction: A Social Critique of the Judgment of Taste* (1984), followed by *The Field of Cultural Production: Essays on Art and Literature* (1993).

References

Anderson, L. W., & Sosniak, L. A. (Eds.). (1994). *Bloom's taxonomy: A forty-year retrospective*. Chicago: NSSE/University of Chicago Press.

Arens, K. (2005). When comparative literature becomes cultural studies: Teaching cultures through genre. *Comparatist: Journal of the Southern Comparative Literature Association, 29*, 123–147.

Arens, K. (2008). Genres and the standards: Teaching the 5 C's through texts. *German Quarterly, 81*(1), 35–48.

Arens, K. (2009). Teaching culture: The *Standards* as an optic on curriculum development. In V. M. Scott (Ed.), *Principles and practices of the* Standards *in college foreign language instruction* (pp. 160–181). Boston: Cengage Heinle.

Barthes, R. (1970). *Mythologies*. Paris: Éditions du Seuil. (Original work published 1957)

Bloom, B. S. (Ed.). (1956). *Taxonomy of educational objectives, handbook I: The cognitive domain*. New York: Longman.

Bourdieu, P. (1984). *Distinction: A social critique of the judgment of taste* (R. Nice, Trans.). Cambridge, MA: Harvard University Press. (Original work published 1979)

Bourdeiu, P. (1993). *The field of cultural production: Essays on art and literature* (R. Johnson, Ed.). New York: Columbia University Press.

Foucault, M. (1988). *The care of the self* (R. Hurley, Trans.). New York: Vintage Books.

Modern Language Association. (2007). *Foreign languages and higher education: New structures for a changed world*. Retrieved from http://www.mla.org/flreport

Mueller-Vollmer, K. (Ed.). (1985). *The hermeneutics reader: Texts of the German tradition from the Enlightenment to the present*. New York: Continuum.

National Standards in Foreign Language Education Project. (2006). *Standards for foreign language learning in the 21st century: Including Arabic, Chinese, Classical Languages, French, German, Italian, Japanese, Portuguese, Russian, and Spanish* (3rd rev. ed.). Yonkers, NY: Author.

National Standards in Foreign Language Education Project. (2010). *National standards for foreign language learning: Executive summary*. Retrieved from http://www.actfl.org

Spivak, G. C. (1993). *Outside in the teaching machine*. New York: Routledge.

Epilogue
Paradigms in Transition

Alison Phipps, University of Glasgow

Glenn S. Levine, University of California, Irvine

Many of the preceding chapters take the space of relative autonomy of the classroom as a laboratory for pedagogies, which may align with critical and intercultural theory in language teaching. However, these are potentially doomed to wither on the vine when they are in the hothouse environment of skills and grades and functional performance. This is true of van Lier's vision and proposals, true of the Modern Language Association's (MLA's) thinking at a mesolevel, and true of the neat approaches to technology and language learning that come with social constructivism and e-learning or literature study or post-coloniality. At the end of the day, these new reflective embodiments of theories in practice (or praxis, as Freire defined it) are fragile things unless nourished structurally. So in classes such as those of Elola and Oskoz, Gramling and Warner, Train, Arnett and Jernigan, Parker, or Brenner, the practice proposed and theorized is not one that is sustained by the present dominant order. Theirs, ours, in this volume, is a hegemonic practice, we may even say struggle, to find strong and nourishing enough ecological conditions for these kinds of theories to be able to survive in practice.

For this to occur, there needs to be structural change as well as trial and error in individual classrooms. This is where Arens is so perceptive in her state-ment that in the humanities theory has existed in discreet enclaves and around the cult of personality, challenging the ideas but not the structures that can enable the embodiment of other ways of being and other ways of doing language learning, or languaging (Phipps & González, 2004). Indeed, the idea of languag-ing, as embodied language-as-social-practice, itself reflects the frustration of lan-guage pedagogies unable to find sustaining conditions for the kinds of practice that are needed within the academy.

Taking the example of assessment, we see that the kinds of proposals emerging in this volume for intercultural critical being and for language pedagogy are not now served by the dominant assessment forms of functional language pedagogy. Testing discreet skills does not "test" the complexity, the connectivity, the context and contingency, the capacity for compassion or conflict transformation. The state of the world suggests that these are capacities that are necessary in a time of austerity, of supercomplexity (Barnett, 2000), of deep ideological trouble and ecological scarcity. Thinkers in all ages have been needed to think about the big questions of every age and the big questions that endure; questions of life and death, good and ill, politics and morality. Those practiced at acting on those thoughts have been sustained by strong disciplines and structures in the past.

These have largely been elites, but in what is proposed here we see a democratization of the Socratic idea that "an unconsidered life is not worth living."

So at the end of this volume, we have set up the problem for future language pedagogy under the framework of theoretical ideas that a diversity of approaches to assessment, evaluation, and curriculum design will be required. In our view, summative tests do indeed have an important disciplining function in terms of breadth and depth of vocabulary and grammatical knowledge and even declarative knowledge about aspects of history and cultures, but to assess in valid and reliable ways the embodied capacities will require other forms.

These can include the following:

- Performative-based evaluative techniques (Mumford & Phipps, 2002)
- Process-based assessment (Littlewood, 2009), including of conflict transformation (see Lederach, 1995, 2003, 2005; Schirch, 2004; Zehr, 2002)
- Scripts of behavior that embody compassion and empathy (Lu & Corbett, this volume)
- Evidence of analysis and understanding of complexity and dynamic structures (Callon, 1981; Larsen-Freeman & Cameron, 2008; Latour, 2004; Sercu, 2004; van Lier, 2004)

In addition, there is the important work undertaken in Europe, under the academic leadership of Michael Byram and his colleagues, that has carefully considered a range of forms of assessment for intercultural communicative competence, following on from his now seminal work of 1997 and especially in the development of ethnographic assessments (Roberts, Byram, Barro, Jordan, & Street, 2001). This work also involves consideration of the potential for drama (Byram & Fleming, 1998) and critical intercultural frameworks for language learning (Guilherme, 2002).

There is a small but growing body of work to guide the reader in this, which not only focuses on assessing learning in a formative way (e.g., Bachman & Palmer, 2008) but also does so in ways that accommodate a dynamic, complex, sociocultural pedagogy. These include Poehner and Lantolf's (2005) model of dynamic assessment, Lee's (2007) assessment for learning approach, and Smith, Teemant, and Pinnegar's (2004) sociocultural approach to assessment. Smith, Teemant, and Pinnegar (2004) point out that "unless assessment practices are consistent with what we believe about knowing and learning, the inferences we make from student performances and the feedback we provide will not match the goals and outcomes we value most" (p. 40). "All too often," they write, "we see examples where the learning of students who have actively engaged in interesting and authentic group activities is assessed with traditional tests of narrowly defined fact knowledge that provide evidence of only a small part of the learning that has occurred" (p. 40). If assessment is to capture as much of the learning as possible, then it must also avoid the trap identified by Littlewood (2009), who advocates for process-oriented assessment but warns that if desirable outcomes are determined not by those involved in the pedagogical processes, then process-oriented assessment becomes a new means of control rather than empowerment and liberation. In a word, the assessment measures we develop out of the theoretical frameworks, problems, and proposals contained in these chapters must be as rigorous as the analytical methodologies that are the norm in research in the humanities and social sciences.

Not to do this, not to take seriously the need for the symbols of evaluation and assessment to be congruent with the theories and tentative practices taking place, means condemning these ideas to a lifetime of creating a space–time continuum in the classroom alone where they can be tried as alternatives but never mainstreamed. It leaves the teacher with such theoretical underpinnings to act as a lone ranger defending the lack of congruence with the dominant forms of assessment but never able to shift his or her knowledge and theory into the structures that ultimately make more possible than the individual, peripheral practice of alternatives. And not to do this, not to open a space, structurally, for other forms of assessment to become valid and reliable, according to the needs of the day, would be a fundamental abdication of responsibility toward language pedagogy and the role formal educational structures may play in enabling linguistic diversity to thrive and to be democratized.

Such change brings affect center stage as we begin to notice and fear that much is changing around us and that this needs new understandings and new ways of approaching language pedagogy. So, theory as practice really means that theory is felt, sometimes as fear, sometimes as potential, sometimes as excitement, opportunity, or even irritant. This "feeling" of being structured according to a different set of principles indexes the changes in a series of different ways of talking about language pedagogy in practice. The way different words describe the emergent practices is often moving, sometimes annoying, and often it surprises a bit with its difference. We know we are theorizing when our affective lives are in play. What the contributors to this volume offer is a fresh and much-needed language for twenty-first-century language work and classrooms. These are some of the words we found in use: "positionality," "language ecology," "criticality," "compassion," "translingual," "transcultural," "postcolonial," "care," "conflict," "disposition," and "languaging." These are not obvious words and are not words that we have found in the dominant theories of our functional practice. They are words that show that the world is indeed changing. They feel a bit awkward and difficult. Theory has to feel difficult, has to push us up toward the apex of Bloom's taxonomies (Arens, this volume) and challenge our ingrained habits and understandings if we are to really respond and break some—not all, obviously—of the habits of our twentieth-century consumer-technocracy–based pedagogies of skills and competence production to align ourselves with what is emerging and with the moments described so appositely in the MLA Report. The "grit" of the words brings theory to the level of our conscious attention and moves us into a critical frame, to question what we hear and read, and to question ourselves. The words grate on us and don't fit with our normal ways of describing the world; they bring us into conflict with our own ingrained practices or offer us a sense of solidarity with others in the new things we are trying out and which have thrilled us, too. Such is theory's gift to practice. "Critiques of power," says Eagleton (2003), "are of no use unless they develop a clear political engagement and ethical efficacy, unless it leads to embodiment in action" (p. 220). What better action can there be than really successful language teaching based on exciting, compelling theoretical foundations?

Which means that this book ultimately ends not in the classroom and its smaller-scale narratives of theory in practice and alternative theory struggling to practice or in some grand narrative of overarching theory that can solve all the problems either. Rather, it ends, when all these smaller-scale narratives and larger-scale theories are gathered together, in the grander narrative of politics and strategic political action, in conflict transformation and in the kinds of larger-scale actions that Freire (1970) was proposing for change, beyond the classroom or group-based training that has been so popular for practitioners of alternatives. Such work will require courage, creativity, collectivity, community—more Cs. The change is already on us.

The writers in this volume are trying to be the change they want to see. They already have a great set of theoretical resources and smaller-scale experiments in their bags. We may need more examples of this, but we would hesitate to suggest that more is necessarily better and instead suggest that what is needed for these theories to survive is a continued commitment to deep reflection and analysis, a continued critique of the status quo, and a willingness to work carefully and with compassion so that language teaching and learning may flourish within the academy and in ways that will not, in 20 years, be like any of those with which we are presently familiar.

References

Bachman, L. F., & Palmer, A. S. (2008). *Language assessment in practice.* Oxford: Oxford University Press.

Barnett, R. (2000). *Realizing the university in an age of supercomplexity.* Buckingham: Society for Research into Higher Education and Open University Press.

Byram, M. (1997). *Teaching and assessing intercultural communicative competence.* Clevedon: Multilingual Matters.

Top of Form

Bottom of Form

Byram, M., & Fleming, M. (1998). *Language learning in intercultural perspective: Approaches through drama and ethnography.* Cambridge: Cambridge University Press.

Callon, M. (1981). Struggles and negotiations to decide what is problematic and what is not: The sociologies of translation. In K. D. Knorr, R. Krohn, & R. Whitley (Eds.), *The social process of scientific investigation* (pp. 197–220). Dordrecht: Reidel.

Eagleton, T. (2003). *After theory.* New York: Basic Books.

Freire, P. (1970). *Pedagogy of the oppressed* (M. Bergman Ramos, Trans.). London: Penguin.

Guilherme, M. (2002). *Critical citizens for an intercultural world.* Clevedon: Multilingual Matters.

Larsen-Freeman, D., & Cameron, D. (2008). *Complex systems and applied linguistics.* Oxford: Oxford University Press.

Latour, B. (2004). *Politics of nature: How to bring the sciences into democracy.* Cambridge, MA: Harvard University Press.

Lederach, J. P. (1995). *Preparing for peace: Conflict across cultures.* Syracuse, NY: Syracuse University Press.

Lederach, J. P. (2003). *Conflict transformation.* Intercourse, PA: Good Books.

Lederach, J. P. (2005). *The moral imagination: The art and soul of peace building.* Oxford: Oxford University Press.

Lee, I. (2007). Assessment for learning: Integrating assessment, teaching, and learning in the ESL/EFL writing classroom. *Canadian Modern Language Review/La Revue canadienne des langues vivantes, 64*(1), 199–214.

Littlewood, J. (2009). Process-oriented pedagogy: Facilitation, empowerment, or control? *ELT Journal, 63*(3), 246–254.

Mumford M., & Phipps, A. (2002). Translating the strange, performing the peculiar: Marieluise Fleißer's *Fegefeuer/Purgatory in Ingolstadt. Studies in Theatre and Performance, 22*(2), 69–81.

Phipps, A., & González, M. (2004). *Modern languages: Learning and teaching in an intercultural field.* London: Sage.

Poehner, M. E., & Lantolf, J. P. (2005). Dynamic assessment in the language classroom. *Language Teaching Research 9*(3), 233–265.

Roberts, C., Byram, M., Barro, A., Jordan, S., & Street, B. (2001). *Language learners as ethnographers.* Clevedon: Multilingual Matters.

Schirch, L. (2004). *Strategic peacebuilding.* Intercourse, PA: Good Books.

Sercu, L. (2004). Assessing intercultural competence: A framework for systematic test development in foreign language education and beyond. *Intercultural Education, 15*(1), 73–89.

Smith, M. E., Teemant, A., & Pinnegar, S. (2004). Principles and practices of sociocultural assessment: Foundations for effective strategies for linguistically diverse classrooms. *Multicultural Perspectives, 6*(2), 38–46.

van Lier, L. (2004). *The ecology and semiotics of language learning: A sociocultural perspective.* Boston: Kluwer.

Zehr, H. (2002). *Restorative justice.* Intercourse, PA: Good Books.

Contributors

Katherine Arens (PhD, Stanford University) is professor of Germanic Studies, comparative literature, and women's and gender studies at the University of Texas at Austin. She is also affiliated with the UT Center for European Studies and the Center for Russian and Eastern European Studies. Her major concentration is intellectual history (*Geistesgeschichte*), with work on both sides of a line separating traditional literary-historical studies (Enlightenment through impressionism and Austria through the twentieth century) and more theoretical and philosophical work (German idealism, philosophy of language, literary and cultural theory, Lacanian theory and identity politics, WGS theory, and the history and theory of the humanities). This combination of theory and cultural studies has also led her to do work on reading theory and applied linguistics, modeling how culture, identity, and the politics of cultural identity can be researched and taught.

Carlee Arnett (PhD, University of Michigan) is associate professor of German at the University of California, Davis. She is director of the Basic Language Program for German and Russian and supervises Arabic, Hindi, and Hebrew. She is also the coeditor, together with Glenn Levine, of the journal *Die Unterrichtspraxis/Teaching German*. Professor Arnett's research interests include SLA, historical Germanic linguistics, and cognitive grammar. She is the author of *A Cognitive Approach to the Semantics of the German Passive* (2004) and numerous scholarly publications on cognitive grammar, Germanic linguistics, language pedagogy, and language program direction. She is currently researching dative verbs in Gothic and Old Saxon.

David Brenner (PhD, University of Texas at Austin) is the director of the Houston Teachers Institute at the University of Houston, where he also serves as an adjunct assistant professor of German Studies and comparative literature in the Honors College. He is the author of two books, *Marketing Identities: The Invention of Jewish Ethnicity* (1998) and *German-Jewish Popular Culture before the Holocaust: Kafka's Kitsch* (2008). His translation of Niklas Luhmann's *Religion as a Social System* will appear in 2011. In addition, he has published numerous articles and chapters on German and Jewish literary and cultural history. Presently, he is writing a memoir on teaching in both schools and universities.

James A. Coleman (PhD, University of Portsmouth) is professor of language learning and teaching at the Open University (UK), having also worked at Glasgow and Portsmouth universities. Author, editor, or coeditor of fourteen books and nearly 100 articles/book chapters, he has delivered over 140 lectures and papers, including invited keynote plenaries, in twenty-one countries. His work with professional associations has included the Chartered Institute of Linguists, University Council of Modern Languages, and Association for French Language Studies. Although he has published on the media in France and on French

Renaissance literature, including critical editions of poet Jean de La Péruse, his main work is in language learning and teaching, encompassing policy and practice, institutional contexts, pedagogy, applications of technology, e-learning, skills and employability, language testing, intercultural competence, and especially study abroad. He is currently investigating the long-term impact of study abroad in French West Africa on students from the United Kingdom. He was made *Chevalier dans l'Ordre des Palmes Académiques* in 1992.

John Corbett is professor of applied language studies at the University of Glasgow. He has published books and articles on intercultural language education, corpus-based language study, and literary linguistics. He is the director of the Scottish Corpus of Texts and Speech (http://www.scottishcorpus.ac.uk), a project funded by the Arts and Humanities Research Council of the United Kingdom.

Maria Dasli (PhD, University of Exeter) is lecturer in languages and intercultural communication at Edinburgh Napier University, Scotland, where she directs post-graduate programs in intercultural studies. She is also a graduate of Stirling and Essex universities. She is treasurer and membership secretary of the International Association for Languages and Intercultural Communication and a member of the executive Linguistics Research Committee at the Centre for Global Non-Killing.

Idoia Elola (PhD, University of Iowa) is assistant professor of Spanish and applied linguistics and second-language studies at Texas Tech University. She teaches a range of courses at the undergraduate and graduate levels from Spanish grammar to applied linguistics and second-language acquisition/instruction. Her research, quantitative and qualitative in nature, focuses predominantly on second-language writing with an emphasis on revision, collaborative writing through the use of social web technologies, and issues of writing fluency and grammar among Spanish-heritage speakers. She has published articles on the topics of foreign language writing, collaborative writing, and the use of technology in the language classroom.

David Gramling (PhD, University of California, Berkeley) is ACLS New Faculty Fellow in German Studies and an affiliated faculty member in the Program in Second Language Acquisition and Teaching at the University of Arizona in Tucson. His recent articles on multilingualism in the German cultural context have appeared in *German Quarterly* and *Die Unterrichtspraxis/Teaching German*, and his coedited volume *Germany in Transit: Nation and Migration 1955–2005* (with Deniz Göktürk and Anton Kaes, 2007) will be published in German in 2010 and in Turkish in 2011. Before coming to Arizona, David was teaching at Bilkent University in Ankara, Turkey, while continuing to develop his research on German Turkish axes in literature and film. Currently, he is completing a theoretical monograph titled *The Invention of Monolingualism* while developing a second book-length project on "translingual modernities" between Turkish and German literature in the early and mid-twentieth century.

Regine Hampel (PhD, Eberhard Karls Universität, Tübingen) is a senior lecturer in modern languages (German) at the Open University (UK). She is involved in open and distance language learning and has been playing a leading role in designing innovative approaches to language learning and the use of ICT. This is reflected in the courses that she has contributed to, courses that blend more traditional approaches to distance learning with interactive online elements. She heads the Open Languages Research Group in the Open University's Department of Languages. Her own research explores theoretical and practical issues around the use of digital technologies in language learning and teaching, and she is particularly interested in the impact of mediation on learning in new multimodal environments. She has given conference presentations and invited talks around the world, written numerous articles and book chapters, and is coauthor with Marie-Noelle Lamy of the book *Online Communication in Language Learning and Teaching* (2007). International projects include DOTS (ECML) and Medienpass (European Commission), which focus on online teaching skills, and a project on audiographic conferencing (Australian Research Council, British Academy). She has been involved in organizing conferences and seminars, including a two-day seminar on Spoken Online Learning Events and the IATEFL/SWON Conference on Autonomy in a Connected World.

Mirjam Hauck (MA, Ruprecht Karls Universität, Heidelberg) is senior lecturer and associate head of the Department of Languages (Faculty of Education and Language Studies) at the Open University (UK). She has written numerous articles and book chapters on the use of technologies for the learning and teaching of languages and cultures covering aspects such as task design, tutor role and training, the affordances of new media, and e-literacy skills. Apart from regular presentations and invited contributions to conferences, seminars, and workshops in Europe and the United States, she serves on the American Computer Assisted Language Instruction Consortium's executive board and on the executive committee of the European Association of Computer Assisted Language Learning (EUROCALL). She also chairs the EUROCALL Teacher Education SIG. She is the coeditor of the *European Journal of Open, Distance and E-Learning* and a member of the editorial board of the *CALL* journal. Her current research and publications explore the impact of mediation and the relevance of multimodal communicative competence for the development of intercultural communicative competence in online environments, particularly in the context of telecollaborative exchanges.

Harriett Jernigan (PhD, Stanford University) is a lecturer in German at the University of California, Davis. After leading the group that created Stanford's language placement tests in German, French, Spanish, Italian, and Chinese, she began developing interdisciplinary approaches to language teaching, focusing in particular on using English composition teaching methodologies to improve L2 writing proficiency. She has taught English as a foreign language and been a guest lecturer at the RWTH University Clinic in Aachen, Germany.

Claire Kramsch (Agrégation, Sorbonne University, Paris) is professor of German at the University of California, Berkeley, where she teaches German and applied linguistics at both the undergraduate and the graduate levels and directs doctoral dissertations in the Department of German and in the Graduate School of Education. Her areas of interest are the teaching and learning of foreign languages, second-language acquisition, multilingualism, and a discourse approach to language and culture. She is the past president of the American Association for Applied Linguistics and the past North American editor of *Applied Linguistics*. Her main publications are *Context and Culture in Language Teaching* (1993), *Redefining the Boundaries of Language Study* (1995), *Language and Culture* (1998), *Language Acquisition and Language Socialization: Ecological Perspectives* (2002), and *The Multilingual Subject* (2009).

Glenn S. Levine (PhD, University of Texas at Austin) is associate professor of German and German language program director at the University of California, Irvine (UCI). He is also director of the Humanities Language Learning Program. His areas of research include second-language acquisition and socialization and curriculum design and teaching. Professor Levine's publications address code choice in second-language learning; constructivist, ecological, and critical approaches to curriculum design and teaching; and issues of language program direction. He is the author of *Incomplete L1 Acquisition in the Immigrant Situation: Yiddish in the United States* (2000) and the forthcoming *Code Choice in the Language Classroom*. Together with Carlee Arnett, Professor Levine is coeditor of the journal *Die Unterrichtspraxis/Teaching German*. Currently, he is president of the American Association of University Supervisors and Coordinators, and on his home campus he also serves as faculty director of the UCI Center for International Education.

Peih-ying Lu (PhD, University of Glasgow) is associate professor in the Center for General Education, Kaohsiung Medical University, Taiwan. She has researched university-level intercultural language education in Taiwan and published articles in the areas of language education, problem-based learning, and the use of art and literature in the development of medical students. Her current research involves the integration of intercultural language education and the medical humanities with preclinical and clinical medical training. Recently, she has begun integrating experiential learning into the classroom. She has received funding from the Taiwan Ministry of Education to enhance intercultural English courses and task-based learning.

Ana Oskoz (PhD, University of Iowa) is associate professor of Spanish in the Department of Modern Languages, Linguistics, and Intercultural Communication at the University of Maryland Baltimore County. Her research focuses on the use of technology for second-language learning and second-language acquisition. She has examined the use of synchronous and asynchronous communication tools, such as online chats, discussion boards, blogs, and wikis, for second-language learning to promote cultural discussions, enhance second-language writing, and foster intercultural competence development. She has published articles on the topics of error correction, classroom-based assessment, and the use of technology in the language classroom.

Jan Parker (PhD, Clare College, Cambridge University) is chair of the Humanities Higher Education Research Group in the Institute of Educational Technology at the Open University (UK), researching higher-education pedagogy, disciplinary writing, and digital scholarship. She continues to work in her "home" discipline of classics and teaches Greek and comparative literature at Cambridge; her *Tradition, Translation, Trauma: The Classic and the Modern* (edited with Tim Mathews) is in press. She is founder and editor in chief of *Arts and Humanities in Higher Education: An International Journal of Theory, Research and Practice.*

Alison Phipps (PhD, University of Sheffield) is professor of languages and intercultural studies at the University of Glasgow, where she teaches modern languages, comparative literature, anthropology, and intercultural education. Her books include *Acting Identities* (2000), *Contemporary German Cultural Studies* (editor, 2002), *Modern Languages: Learning and Teaching in an Intercultural Field* (with Mike Gonzalez, 2004), *Critical Pedagogy: Political Approaches to Languages and Intercultural Communication* (edited with Manuela Guilherme, 2004), *Tourism and Intercultural Exchange* (with Gavin Jack, 2005), and *Learning the Arts of Linguistic Survival: Tourism, Languaging, Life* (2007). Her first collection of poetry, *Through Wood*, was published in 2009. She is a senior policy adviser to the British Council and a member of the Iona Community, and she is coconvener of the University of Glasgow's Refugee, Asylum and Migration Research Network.

Ursula Stickler (PhD, Karl-Franzens University, Graz) is a lecturer in German in the Department of Languages at the Open University (UK). She has contributed to the Open University's German language courses for all skills levels, integrating online and autonomous learning elements into more traditional distance teaching materials. She is currently head of the department's Virtual Learning Environment (VLE) group, responsible for supporting colleagues in the use of VLE tools and synchronous online conferencing. Her research interests are in the areas of independent language learning, including technology-enhanced language learning, and Tandem learning. She is involved in projects researching interaction in online language tutorials, the use of VLE tools for language learning, collaborative learning online, and tutor training. She has published book chapters and articles in all the above areas. International projects include LITERALIA (an EU-Socrates–funded multilateral Tandem project) and DOTS (an ECML–funded project focusing on teacher training). She has also been involved in organizing a two-day seminar on Spoken Online Learning Events at the Open University that combined synchronous online contributions with face-to-face presentations.

Robert W. Train (PhD, University of California, Berkeley) is an associate professor of Spanish at Sonoma State University, where he is also director of the Language and Culture Learning Center. Formerly a public high school teacher of Spanish and French, he has taught the full range of Spanish and French language courses at the university and secondary levels, from beginning classes to advanced composition. He also teaches courses on linguistics, language learning, and the history of the language designed for future language teachers. He has published and lectured on the intersection of ideologies of language and language teaching as well as language learning technologies. His research is interdisciplinary and socially engaged in bringing together insights from applied linguistics, anthropology, sociolinguistics, philology, historiography of language, education, and postmodern theory to consider the contours and consequences of ideologies, practices, and policies in the lives of speakers within and beyond the classroom. A philologist by training, he is currently investigating the foundational texts of Spanish language education in the United States from a postcolonial perspective. Professor Train is also actively involved in international education, serving since 2006 on the California State University Academic Council on International Programs.

Per Urlaub (PhD, Stanford University) is assistant professor of Germanic Studies at the University of Texas at Austin, where he also directs the German language program. He teaches at all levels of the undergraduate program as well as graduate seminars on foreign language teaching methods and second-language literacy. His research activities focus on the reading process in the second language, in particular the development of literary and critical reading skills. He currently serves as the president of the South Texas chapter of the AATG.

Leo van Lier (PhD, Lancaster University) was born in the Netherlands and has worked and taught in several countries in Europe, Latin America, and Asia as well as in the United States. His most recent books are *The Ecology and Semiotics of Language Learning* (2004) and *Scaffolding the Success of Adolescent English Language Learners* (with Aída Walqui, 2010). He is professor in the Graduate School of Translation, Interpretation, and Language Education at the Monterey Institute of International Studies, where he teaches courses in second-language acquisition, pedagogical grammar, classroom observation, and computer-assisted language learning, among other topics in educational linguistics. He is also the editor of the *Modern Language Journal* and of the Springer book series Educational Linguistics.

Chantelle Warner (PhD, University of California, Berkeley) is assistant professor of German Studies and an affiliated faculty member in the Program in Second Language Acquisition and Teaching at the University of Arizona. She has recently published an article on deixis, narrative, and the stylistic effect of authenticity in the journal *Language and Literature* and a piece on the application of literary pragmatics in the language classroom in *Die Unterrichtspraxis/ Teaching German*. Her current book project, *Legitimizing Lives: Authenticity Effects in German Social Autobiography*, examines the abundance of literary testimonies written in German during the second half of the twentieth century and the pragmatic-stylistic effects that have driven their reception. She has also begun a new research project on the use of hypermedia literature in the promotion of foreign language literacy and transcultural competence at the intermediate and advanced levels of language study.

AAUSC
The American Association of University Supervisors, Coordinators, and Directors of Foreign Language Programs

Purpose

Since its inception in 1980, the AAUSC has worked to:

- Promote and improve foreign and second language education in the United States
- Strengthen and improve foreign language curricula and instruction at the postsecondary level
- Strengthen development programs for teaching assistants, teaching fellows, associate instructors, or their equivalents
- Promote research in second language learning and development and on the preparation and supervision of teaching assistants
- Establish a forum for exchanging ideas, experiences, and materials among those concerned with language program direction

Who Can Join the AAUSC?

Membership in the AAUSC is open to anyone who is interested in strengthening foreign and second language instruction, especially, but not exclusively, those involved with multi-section programs. The membership comprises teachers, supervisors, coordinators, program directors, faculty, and administrators in colleges and universities that employ teaching assistants. Many members are faculty and administrators at undergraduate institutions.

How Do I Join the AAUSC?

Please fill out the following application for membership, and send it with annual dues to Robert Davis, or join online at *www.aausc.org*.

Dues (including yearly volume)

Regular .... $25.00/year, $40.00/two years
Student .... $15.00/year, $25.00/two years

Please make checks payable to:
Robert L. Davis, Secretary/Treasurer, AAUSC
Department of Romance Languages
University of Oregon
Eugene, OR 97403 USA
(541) 346-0956 phone
(541) 346-4030 fax
rldavis@oregon.uoregon.edu
www.aausc.org

AAUSC Application for Membership

New ☐   Renewal ☐

Name _____

School Address _____

_____

City _____ State _____ Zip _____

Telephone (work) _____   _____

Fax _____

E-mail _____

Home address _____

City _____ State _____ Zip _____

Telephone (home) _____

Languages taught: Arabic ☐   Chinese ☐   ESL ☐

   French ☐   Italian ☐   Japanese ☐   Portuguese ☐

   Russian ☐   German ☐   Spanish ☐   Other ☐

Are you a: Teacher ☐   Program Director ☐

     Dept. Chair ☐   Graduate Student ☐   Other ☐